LATIN AMERICA

ISSUE 248 JANUARY 2023

BRAZIL UNDE

MW01077742

Issue Editors: James N. Green and Tulio Ferreira

Contents

Cover photograph: Campaign materials depicting Brazil's former president, Luiz Inácio Lula da Silva, and President Jair Bolsonaro, Brasília, September 23, 2022 (Reuters/Alamy Stock Photo). Photo © Adriano Machado

Latin American Perspectives (LAP) is a theoretical and scholarly journal for the discussion and debate on the political economy of capitalism, imperialism, and socialism in the Americas. The authors, however—not **LAP** or **SAGE Publishing**—are responsible for their own views, sources of information, writing style, and so on. Our objective is to encourage class analysis of sociocultural realities and political strategies to transform Latin American sociopolitical structures. We make a conscious effort to publish a diversity of political viewpoints, both Marxist and non-Marxist perspectives, that have influenced progressive debates in Latin America. Top priority will be given to articles that strike directly at the most important theoretical issues, particularly subjects that have received inadequate discussion or that are in sharp dispute. We also attempt to encourage the work of relatively "unknown" students and scholars and to bring the work of Latin American scholars to the English-speaking world. **LAP** welcomes strong views as long as they are backed by cogent arguments, are grounded in Latin American reality, and are written to be comprehensible to a wide audience. **LAP** seeks writing that is clear and concise. Authors should keep in mind that the journal is interdisciplinary and avoid jargon and obscure language understood only by a narrow group of readers. Concepts with which readers may not be familiar and specialized terminology should be kept to a minimum and when used, should be clearly explained for non-specialist readers. Readers' criticism, comments, and proposals are welcomed.

Manuscript Submission and Review Process: Manuscripts of up to 8,000 words can be submitted in English, Spanish or Portuguese and should be sent as Word documents to lap@ucr.edu. Upon submissions, please include an abstract of 150 words, 5 keywords, and current biographical and contact information. LAP also publishes book review essays, film reviews, and occasional photo essays. The LAP website (http://latinamericanperspectives.com/publish-in-lap-overview/) provides complete information on manuscript submission and review, including current Calls for Manuscripts, manuscript specifications, LAP Style Guidelines, book review, artwork, and photo guidelines, and description of the review and copy editing processes. LAP policy discourages manuscripts from authors who have a manuscript accepted by the journal on a similar topic within the past three years. LAP will consider manuscripts that have been published in another language, usually with updating.

LAP is on Social Media!
Facebook: http://www.facebook.com/LAPerspectives
Twitter: http://twitter.com/LAPerspectives
Pinterest: http://pinterest.com/LAPerspectives
Linkedin: http://www.linkedin.com/in/LAPerspectives
Blog: http://laperspectives.blogspot.com/
Website: www.latinamericanperspectives.com
Instagram: https://www.instagram.com/latinamericanperspectives/

Latin American Perspectives (ISSN 0094-582X) (J273) is published bimonthly—in January, March, May, July, September, and November—by SAGE Publishing, 2455 Teller Rd., Thousand Oaks, CA 91320 on behalf of the *Latin American Perspectives* Editorial Collective, P.O. Box 5703, Riverside, CA 92517-5703. Periodicals postage paid at Thousand Oaks, California, and at additional mailing offices. POSTMASTER: Send address changes to *Latin American Perspectives*, c/o SAGE Publishing, 2455 Teller Road, Thousand Oaks, CA 91320.

Subscription Information: All subscription inquiries, orders, back issues, claims, and renewals should be addressed to SAGE Publishing, 2455 Teller Road, Thousand Oaks, CA 91320; telephone: (800) 818-SAGE (7243) and (805) 499-0721; fax: (805) 375-1700; e-mail: journals@sagepub.com; website: journals.sagepub.com. Subscription Price: Institutions: $926; Individuals: $74. For all customers outside the Americas, please visit http://www.sagepub.co.uk/customerCare.nav for information. Claims: Claims for undelivered copies must be made no later than six months following month of publication. The publisher will supply replacement issues when losses have been sustained in transit and when the reserve stock will permit.

Copyright Permission: To request permission for republishing, reproducing, or distributing material from this journal, please visit the desired article on the SAGE Journals website (journals.sagepub.com) and click "Permissions." For additional information, please see www.sagepub.com/journals-permissions.

Advertising and Reprints: Current advertising rates and specifications may be obtained by contacting the advertising coordinator in the Thousand Oaks office at (805) 410-7772 or by sending an e-mail to advertising@sagepub.com. To order reprints, please e-mail reprint@sagepub.com. Acceptance of advertising in this journal in no way implies endorsement of the advertised product or service by SAGE, the journal's affiliated society(ies), or the journal editor(s). No endorsement is intended or implied. SAGE reserves the right to reject any advertising it deems as inappropriate for this journal.

Change of Address: Six weeks' advance notice must be given when notifying of change of address. Please visit us at addressupdates.sagepub.com/support/tickets/new to complete the SAGE Journals Address Update form.

Printed on acid-free paper

Introduction

Brazil under Bolsonaro

by
Tulio Ferreira and James N. Green

Luiz Inácio Lula da Silva's triumph in the October 30, 2022, election for an unprecedented third term as president of Brazil has been considered an emblematic victory for democracy and progressive change by academic observers and the international press. Even though da Silva won by a narrow margin (1.8 percent of the vote), it was an important defeat for the antidemocratic extremist Jair Messias Bolsonaro, an "insignificant, low-level" (*baixo clero*) politician who represented the far-right in Brazilian politics for more than two decades before being elected the thirty-eighth Brazilian president in 2018. That year, Bolsonaro's election win also captured international attention but for different reasons. Newspapers and magazines worldwide, from a broad range of ideological perspectives, reacted to Bolsonaro's election mostly with apprehension. The British magazine *The Economist* wrote immediately prior to the elections that "the probable president [Bolsonaro] is reviving Latin America's unholy marriage between market economics and political authoritarianism."[1] The headline of the *New York Times* article on the presidential inauguration read: "Jair Bolsonaro Sworn in as Brazil's President, Cementing Rightward Shift."[2] Observers across the globe immediately appeared deeply concerned about Brazilian democracy and the effects Bolsonaro's election would have on the country's domestic and foreign policies.

Inside Brazil it was no different. Journalists, politicians, artists, and academics expressed concerns about the effects of Bolsonaro's election on economics, politics, social and human rights, the environment, indigenous people, Afro-Brazilians, the LGBTI+ community, and the poor and working classes. Former President Fernando Henrique Cardoso, who had been reluctant to openly criticize the candidate prior to the 2018 elections, has since declared that Bolsonaro could jeopardize Brazil's image abroad. Rubens Ricupero, one of Brazil's most experienced diplomats, said that the proposals of Jair Bolsonaro "could leave Brazil poorer, isolated, and despised."[3]

At the time of Bolsonaro's election, the far-right was on the rise worldwide. Political leaders around the globe have been elected as part of this trend. Erdoğan in 2014 in Turkey, Trump in 2016 in the United States, Duterte in 2016 in the Philippines, and Bolsonaro in 2018 in Brazil are prominent examples. Nationalism, antiglobalism, and populism are some of the terms that academics, the media, and ordinary people use to explain the phenomenon. Are we observing a new

Tulio Ferreira is an associate professor of international relations at the Universidade Federal da Paraíba. James N. Green is Carlos Manuel de Céspedes Professor of Modern Latin American History at Brown University and president of the board of the Washington Brazil Office.

LATIN AMERICAN PERSPECTIVES, Issue 248, Vol. 50 No. 1, January 2023, 3–13
DOI: 10.1177/0094582X231157700

wave of fascism? Why are human rights, socially marginalized groups, and social and political activists under attack? Is democracy in danger?

In *How Democracies Die*, Steven Levitsky and Daniel Ziblatt (2018: 4) argue that the current political situation contributes to the ways in which democracies may collapse. Different from military coups d'état, nowadays "democracies may die at the hands not of generals but of elected leaders—presidents or prime ministers who subvert the very process that brought them to power." Nevertheless, in the Brazilian case, the participation of the military in Brazilian politics dates to the founding of the republic in 1889 if not earlier, and this fact should be taken into account. The election of Bolsonaro calls for debate on the role of the military in national politics and its impacts on the quality of Brazilian democracy. Discussing the process of redemocratization in Brazil after military rule, the political scientist Alfred Stepan (1986: 108) considered that "for any contemporary democratic *polis* to increase its effective control of the military and intelligence system requires an effort by civil society to strengthen itself by improving its capacity for control." This debate becomes urgent in light of the persistence of military power in Brazilian politics. In a study from the 1970s, the Brazilian sociologist Edmundo Coelho (2000: 19) warned that the pursuit of identity of the Brazilian military had led to a double orphanhood of part of this social segment—a functional one reflecting the military's belief that society and its political elite had no regard for it and an institutional one reflecting its conviction that no one was listening to it or interested in the issues that concerned it. In Coelho's view, this pursuit of political protagonism was bound to lead to a desire to define as autonomous the objectives and strategies regarding national defense (or security) doctrine that it might eventually impose on the nation (20).

Observing the motto of the Bolsonaro government, "Brazil above everything, God above everyone," one recalls the argument of the Brazilian historian Alcir Lenharo (1986) that the business discourse of the 1940s sought to promote the physical and moral well-being of the working class as a way of strengthening the ties between employers and employees. To do so, the authoritarian Estado Novo (1937–1945) of Getúlio Vargas used precepts of the Catholic Church as the principal foundations for ordering Brazilian society, invoking the symbolism of the cross as the primordial representation of order. "Anyone who has obeyed an order retains resistance, like the prick of a thorn, inside him as a crystallized form of resentment and will be able to get rid of it only when a similar order is issued" (Lenharo, 1986: 189). Here the figure of the soldier appears as a "satisfied prisoner," who, as he rises in his career, will create new orders to goad his inferiors. Thus, totalitarianism is naturalized through the state, with fascism being a faith, a moral order. By defending the "New Man," the Brazilian manifestation of fascism in the form of Integralism,[4] conservative forces appropriated the religious discourse of God, Fatherland, and Catholic values. This process, layering religious values over politics, that Lenharo detailed in describing the authoritarian regime of Vargas in the late 1930s and the early 1940s can be helpful for us in understanding the Bolsonaro government.

Although Bolsonaro was elected in part because of a wave of anticorruption and anti–Partido dos Trabalhadores (Workers' Party—PT) sentiment, the concerns about Brazil's young democracy and its image worldwide should not be neglected. After more than three decades of the reconstruction of democratic institutions in Brazil, a former captain with a history of antidemocratic, homophobic, misogynist, and racist declarations and attitudes was elected president of the largest and richest country in South America. Two of Bolsonaro's declarations while a congressman (from a 1999 television interview) sum up his politics: "Elections won't change anything in this country. Things will only change on the day that we break out into civil war here and do the job that the military regime didn't do: kill 30,000. If some innocent people die, that's fine. In every war, innocent people die." More recently, his declaration of support for the impeachment of President Dilma Rousseff in 2016 extolled the military regime that came to power in 1964 and praised Col. Carlos Brilhante Ustra, who oversaw the torture of Rousseff in 1970 while she was a political prisoner.

In *How Fascism Works*, the U.S. philosopher Jason Staley (2018: 188) says that "the mechanisms of fascist politics all build on and support one another. They weave together a myth of a distinction between us and them, based on a romanticized fictional past featuring us and not them, and supported by a resentment of a corrupt elite, who takes our hard-earned money and threatens our tradition." In *From Fascism to Populism in History*, the Argentine historian Federico Fichelstein (2017: xii) argues that old and new populism and fascist experiences cannot be reduced to their national or regional conditions. "We now have no excuse to allow geopolitical narcissism to stand against historical interpretation, especially when analyzing ideologies that cross borders and oceans and even influence each other." In this sense, populism and fascism are not located solely in Europe, the United States, or Latin America but a transnational and global phenomenon.

Moreover, we cannot neglect certain aspects of Brazilian history and its authoritarian roots. In the words of the Brazilian anthropologist and historian Lilia M. Schwartz (2019: 37),

> Despite the fact that since 1988, and with the promulgation of the Citizens' Constitution, we have experienced the longest period of a rule of law and democracy in republican Brazil, we have not managed to reduce our inequality, combat institutional and structural racism against black and indigenous peoples, [and] eradicate practices of gender violence. Our present is indeed full of the past, and history does not serve as a consolation prize. However, it is important to face the present, especially because it is not the first time that we return to the past with questions that are related to the present.

Since achieving its independence from Portugal in 1822, Brazil has been navigating in troubled waters as an autonomous country. From 1822 to the fall of the monarchy in 1889, it struggled to be recognized as an independent actor in the international system, create a centralized state, reinsert itself into the international economic system as an agrarian country, and maintain slavery as its main labor force. These were all political decisions that the Brazilian elite considered necessary to create and maintain a consolidated nation with territorial integrity.

From the proclamation of the republic in 1889 to the so-called Liberal Revolution of 1930 (which was more a conservative pact among sectors of the economic and political elites than a revolution), successive Brazil governments defended the interests of agrarian exporters, sought international prestige, and pragmatically changed the diplomatic axis from Europe to the United States. In the context of World War I, there was a certain acceleration of industrialization, and from 1930 to the end of the Cold War in the early 1990s government policy used industrialization to pursue economic and social development. This plan was relatively successful, since the country did manage to industrialize, but it failed to distribute wealth and build a more egalitarian society. From the 1990s on Brazilian governments have been adjusting their strategies while still trying to be a fully developed country.

This historical journey has been embedded in a nationalism that might be considered an important variable in explaining Brazilian social and political characteristics and, more recently, an essential component in explaining Bolsonaro's government. The historian Bradford E. Burns (1967: 202) suggested that "the working and middle classes in the burgeoning metropolis were increasingly exposed to the nationalistic ideas of the intellectuals through the expanding networks of press and radio. Vargas saw the advantages of combining and using the political potential of its increasing working class and the growing popularity of nationalist doctrines." The dissemination of nationalist ideas found an audience interested in expanding the country's sovereignty and retaining a certain suspicion of foreigners. In a nutshell, nationalists pragmatically sought economic and social development and greater diplomatic independence, seeking to break free of the bipolar Cold War and its demand for ideological alignments.

Nationalism as an important component of Bolsonaro's rhetoric joins God and country in a single powerful image. In the arguments of Ernesto Araújo, the first minister of foreign affairs in the Bolsonaro government, nationalism is a means of restoring Brazil to the Western developed world. For him the West has economic and military superiority but suffers from a "mysterious evil," a loss of faith in values. In this connection, Araújo claims to understand and defend the "real" values of the West, as expressed in a speech President Donald Trump made in Poland in 2017 in which he argued that the nation was a spiritual stronghold necessary for the defense of the West, which had been experiencing serious challenges due to globalism. In Araújo's analysis of Trump's worldview, some of the biggest obstacles in the West are radical Islamic terrorism, bureaucracy, and the loss of identity. According to this reasoning, there are internal and external enemies that aggravate this loss of identity. For Trump, according to Araújo, the West is a community of nations with historical particularities that share cultural ties, tradition, and faith.

Citing Trump, Araújo (2017: 328) concurs with his analysis: "The West is certainly a group, but not a misshapen mass, much less a group of states based on a treaty, but a group of nations—entities defined each in its deep historical and cultural identity and not as legal entities [that are] abstract—conceived from unique experiences and not from cold principles or values. " Therefore, any arrangement that seeks to eradicate borders, promote supranationalism, and share values will be at variance with the basic principle of the West. The characteristics of this community, which is made up of nationalities, include works of art that inspire a belief in God; the celebration of heroes, traditions, and customs; the rule of law; freedom of expression; empowerment of women; the centrality of the family; the habit of debating and the desire to know; and the dignity of all lives that coexist in freedom.

The former minister of foreign relations under Bolsonaro has observed that postmodern Europe contributes to removing the past and the history of the

Western experiment, a movement that stems from the Enlightenment that created a liberal and revolutionary tradition without a past, without a soul, family, or God. For him, "postmodern man killed God a long time ago and doesn't like to be reminded of his crime." Thus, according to Araújo, to save the West Trump highlights the heroic figure so as to rediscover the collective unconscious that was abandoned by technocratic liberalism and political correctness. However, for him Western values should not be diluted in an "amorphous mass" of universal values. Furthermore, because global governance is impossible given the difficulties of multilateralism, the decisions of independent countries should be respected. "For Trump, countries in the international arena are governed by duties, not values" (334). Pan-nationalism is defended; cosmopolitanism is rejected. Thus, there is no international community, and there are no universal values because a community built on abstract values is not a community. The homeland is founded on the nation. Araújo, in criticizing the project of modernity/reason, wishes to see a Brazilian nation refounded on the Western principles to which it is linked by history: "Brazil, the supreme fruit of this mystery, has a deep and sacred origin, linked to the depths of the Western soul as manifested in the Portuguese race" (343).

Rationality in Brazilian society is another important element in understanding Bolsonaro's ideology and appeal. The Brazilian diplomat and philosopher Sérgio Paulo Rouanet (1987: 126) wrote that the country was undergoing a new wave of irrationalism: "On all fronts, reason is on the defensive." For him this wave had two complementary aspects, one external and the other internal. The first was the influence of the counterculture movement of the 1970s, which was theoretically poststructuralist and saw reason as a mere manifestation of power. Regarding the second he argued (125) that

> undoubtedly, Brazilian irrationalism is not an "out of place idea." Perhaps the authoritarian regime's educational policy is the most important of these internal factors. For 20 years, [the military dictatorship] methodically weeded out of the curriculum everything that had to do with general ideas and humanistic values. In this sense, what is at the origin of the "counterculture" is "unculture"—a politically engendered unculture. Young people do not challenge reason in the name of Nietzsche or Bergson, as the European irrationalists of the interwar period did, for the excellent reason that no one has taught them that these authors exist. The graduates of this deficient educational system simply transform their nonknowledge into a norm of life and a model for a new form of organization of human relations.

In short, the practical and theoretical consequences of such positions would be felt through the application of the logic of antireason to antiauthoritarian, anticolonialist. and antielitist tendencies (Rouanet, 1987: 144):

> In this irrationalist appropriation of three tendencies so fundamental to the work of reason, we feel the latency of an old theme that has accompanied Western thought as its shadow side, its curse, perhaps its hidden truth: that of reason as the enemy of life. It is the topos of the Counter-Enlightenment, the same that inspired the feudal fantasies of German Romanticism, Nietzsche's will to power, or the Aryan myth of the great Caucasian race. The theme is now being revived in Brazil, without people's generally realizing its origins, and, as in European conservative thought, it takes the form of a split between the pole of life and that of theory.

This process, which had previously led to fascism, could impose its opposite. Thus antiauthoritarianism could deprive the oppressed of the means to think about their own liberation, anticolonialism could reinforce dependency structures, and antielitism could strengthen the cultural monopoly of the upper class (145). In Rouanet's opinion, reflection on these consequences was urgent given the importance of the struggle against critical aspects of irrationalism.

Conservative thinking was already circulating and attacking what it called "cultural populism," which allegedly threatened the privileges of the "upper class." However, to leave critical thinking unchanged would grant victory to the conservatives and reactionaries. The resumption of reason could put it at the service of social transformation, making antiauthoritarianism a denunciation of a social system of domination based on the ignorance of those dominated. In the same vein, anticolonialism criticizes foreign mass culture, and antielitism rejects the "oligarchic cultural policy that reserves art, literature, and philosophy for the enjoyment of a minority but does not reject art, literature, and philosophy outright" (145–146). In this regard, the conservative and reactionary ideas expressed in the Bolsonaro government's arguments allow us to identify the traces of the debate regarding the condemnation of Enlightenment reason that was under way in the 1980s and indicate that the trenches in the defense of that reason had been abandoned and neglected for a long time.

All that said, after four years of Bolsonaro's government its characteristics and consequences should be analyzed. The need to understand the reasons for and implications of Bolsonaro's election and the nature and policies of his government is urgent and necessary. It also helps us understand his electoral defeat in 2022, as well as Lula's victory, including the fact that the contest was so close. This is the main aim of this issue. The editors have taken to heart the enlightened opinion of Fernand Braudel that researchers of the present may understand the "fine weaving" of structures, rejecting the real as it is perceived. In that spirit, we present a set of articles that reject simplistic perceptions in favor of recognition of the complexity of reality and the "fine weaving" of history. In order to make sense of contemporary Brazil, we have selected 16 articles written during the Bolsonaro years that should clarify the complexity of his rule.

"The Rise of Fascism in Brazil" by Armando Boito analyzes the Bolsonaro government, its most active social base of support, and the political crisis that gave rise to it and criticizes the classical and current bibliography on fascism. Operating with a concept of fascism embedded in the Marxist tradition, it characterizes the government and its social base as neofascist. It also argues for the development of a typology of political crises in capitalist societies, showing that the nature and dynamics of the 2015–2018 Brazilian political crisis are typical of the kind of crisis that gives rise to fascism.

In "The Social Base of Bolsonarism: An Analysis of Authoritarianism in Politics," Mariana Miggiolaro Chaguri and Oswaldo E. do Amaral show that the cohesion and resilience of the social base supporting Bolsonaro are grounded in an authoritarian perception of politics and society. Their article also demonstrates the existence of transversality in support of the president in terms of social stratification, arguing that Bolsonarism is a social and political phenomenon that responds to a varied set of demands present in contemporary Brazilian society. The authors articulate a statistical analysis of data from a national survey with a sociological approach to the construction of an authoritarian vision of politics and society in Brazil to suggest that the authoritarian right as a political and electoral force will persist in the country and that it has some characteristics that distinguish it from conservative movements in the Global North.

"Bolsonaro, the Last Colonizer," by Manuel Domingos Neto and Luís Gustavo Guerreiro Moreira, describes the indigenous policy of Bolsonaro's ultraconservative government, seeking to identify the foundations of its policies, its main actors, and its behavior. Employing the concepts of nationalism, colonialism, and the coloniality of power, the authors argue that the foundation of the relationship between the Brazilian state and native peoples is one of "guardianship" by the state. In their view, the ultraconservatism of this policy is facilitated by the capture of the state by agrarian and extractive capital elites that seek to exploit the Amazon rain forest at any cost, considering the indigenous peoples of the region an obstacle. The military has a prominent position in this offensive, which violates elementary notions of human rights. Given this fact, the legislative and judiciary powers deal ambiguously with national and international laws, statutes, and conventions. The authors also contend that the reelection of the Bolsonaro government will accelerate the extinction of the surviving indigenous ethnic groups.

In "Between Markets and Barracks: The Economic Policy Narrative of Brazilian Authoritarianism," Niels Søndergaard analyzes the economic policy narrative of Bolsonaro's electoral campaign in 2018 through the theoretical lens of authoritarian neoliberalism. He uses a conceptual perspective that facilitates an understanding of how Bolsonaro's economic policy narrative has worked by essentially relegating economic matters to technocratic management outside the sphere of democratic debate and instrumentalizing antagonisms of social groups and institutions with a redistributive objective.

"Development Projects, Models of Capitalism, and Political Regimes in Brazil, 1988–2021," by Carlos Eduardo Santos Pinho, considers the context of the promulgation of the 1988 Constitution and the promarket reforms generated by the circuits of financial globalization, investigates the new democratic developmentism as a strategy of economic growth with inclusion, and examines the specificity of the 2016 democratic breakdown and its culmination in the Bolsonaro administration, pointing to a model of unregulated capitalism combined with authoritarianism. It concludes that, in addition to the deepening of neoliberal reforms in the 1990s and the regression of the inclusive policies of the 2000s, there is a causal relationship between the content of neoliberal public policies, the reduction in the level of political participation in their implementation, and the degeneration of democratic institutions.

Joaze Bernardino-Costa, in "Opening Pandora's Box: The Extreme Right and the Resurgence of Racism in Brazil," argues that Bolsonarism emerged through the articulation of various groups that mobilized on social networks around key ideas such as a common enemy, moral conservatism, economic liberalism, patriotism, and public security. Based on research on social networks and journalism, his work aims to understand this phenomenon and its relationship with racism and antiracism. He argues that Bolsonarism has opened a Pandora's box, releasing a combination of racist antiracialism and racist racialism that aims to dismantle the recent achievements of the black population, especially the antiracist policies adopted during the PT administrations.

"Radical Reorganization of Environmental Policy: Contemporaneous Evidence from Brazil," by Mauro Guilherme Maidana Capelari, Ana Karine Pereira, Nathaly M. Rivera, and Suely Mara Vaz Guimarães de Araújo, offers an overview of the reorganization of environmental policy since Bolsonaro took office in January 2019. Employing an analysis of publications on the subject, it argues that the rise to power of a new political elite led to a radical change in Brazil's trajectory of climate change initiatives and environmental protection. It documents an association between the new political elite in power and the disruption of two factors historically relevant for the design of environmental policy: the participation of civil society in the governance of public policy and multilateralism in environmental policy.

In "The Far-Right Takeover in Brazil: Effects on the Health Agenda," Maíra S. Fedatto examines the impacts of the new government on public health by analyzing the Mais Médicos (More Doctors) Program, the new drug policy, and the restructuring of the HIV/AIDS Department. Among its conclusions is that the Neo-Pentecostal approach of Bolsonaro's government has effectively militarized its supporters on the basis of moral values and this orientation will challenge the future of the secular state and its substantial gains and leading role in human rights, environmental protection, and international cooperation for health.

In "The Fight against Hunger in Brazil: From Politicization to Indifference," Lourrene Maffra discusses how administrations have dealt with the problem of hunger in Brazil from Lula da Silva's government (2003–2010) until Bolsonaro's term. After offering an extensive literature review with an analysis of public policies and statistical data from reports of national research agencies and international organizations, she argues that the fight against hunger in Brazil reached the highest priority during the Lula da Silva government, with institutional structuring and an international model of public policy. From then on, a downward curve began in relation to the prioritization of the agenda to combat hunger in the country with subsequent governments, resulting in a complete neglect of the issue under Bolsonaro.

"Protests for Women's Rights and against the Bolsonaro Administration," by Olivia Cristina Perez, Joana Tereza Vaz de Moura, and Caroline Bandeira de Brito Melo, draws on news items and documents produced mainly by feminist social movements to examine the agendas of three protests: the one known as #EleNao, the one that took place on International Women's Day, and the Marcha das Margaridas. In general, these protests defended women's rights and criticized the Bolsonaro government. The article demonstrates changes in the relationship between social movements and the government, as well as changes in the strategies of social movements that are taking to the streets in defense of democracy and in favor of expanding their rights.

Andre Pagliarini, in "Tongues of Fire: Silas Malafaia and the Historical Roots of Neo-Pentecostal Power in Bolsonaro's Brazil," examines a prominent Brazilian Pentecostal pastor as a way of understanding the intersection of politics and religious power under Bolsonaro. In admittedly schematic and preliminary terms, he discusses the historical process by which Brazilian evangelicals in general went from accepting a position as junior partners in a broad governing coalition led by the PT in the past decade and a half to asserting themselves as an indispensable pillar of the Bolsonaro administration.

"Brazil's Cultural Battleground: Public Universities and the New Right," by Juliano Fiori and Pedro Fiori Arantes, proposes that public universities, sites of cultivation of a new moral radicalism of the left in recent decades, have become a primary cultural battleground. It contends that since assuming the presidency Bolsonaro has used the machinery of government to wage culture warfare. It explores the attacks on public universities (demonization of professors and curriculum content, unconstitutional government interference, budget cuts, and political persecution) through which Bolsonaro's government nurtured the reactionary imagination of Brazil's new right and challenged the cultural hegemony of the left. It argues that in so doing Bolsonaro was breaking with a biopolitical pact that tied public universities to the defense of a right to life.

Thiago Pezzuto, in "Blowtorching Freirean Thought Out of Bolsonaro's Brazil: Alagoas's Escola Livre Law," draws on punctuated-equilibrium theory to analyze a state law that prevents teachers from sharing opinions with their students that are political, partisan, religious, or philosophical in nature. Pezzuto argues that the return of the right in Latin America, the rise of evangelicals in Brazil, and the School Without Party (Escola Sem Partido) movement changed the shape of educational policy. He insists that the impeachment of Dilma Rousseff in 2016 offered a more favorable climate for the consideration of the Escola Livre law. He places special emphasis on the role of Bolsonaro, who vowed to "blowtorch" the educator Paulo Freire's thought out of Brazil's Ministry of Education because of its ideological content.

In "The Movimento Brasil Livre and the Brazilian New Right in the Election of Jair Bolsonaro," Marcelo Burgos Pimentel dos Santos, Claudio Luis de Camargo Penteado, and Rafael de Paula Aguiar Araújo analyze the uses of information and communication technologies by one of the exponents of the new Brazilian right that emerged after the June 2013 protests, supported the impeachment of Dilma Rousseff, and helped elect Jair Bolsonaro. They argue that through the strategic use of social networks, the MBL helped to expand a conservative agenda in line with what is happening in various parts of the world. The research evaluates the movement's mobilization strategies in recent years, assessing its communicative power, its capacity to produce engagement, and its mobilization power. The results indicate that its use of information and communication techologies has led to the emergence of new political actors on the Brazilian right.

Laís Forti Thomaz and Tullo Vigevani analyze the relationship between Brazil and the United States under Bolsonaro in "Bolsonaro's Subservience to Trump, 2019 and 2020: A Demanding Agenda and Limited Reciprocity." They hypothesize that Brazilian demands found little reciprocity on the part of the United States, frustrating any strategic gains. Examining current views of Brazilian foreign policy through six case studies, they conclude that decision makers have compromised their bargaining power in order to consolidate their internal power, profoundly altering the historical principles linked to the interests of the Brazilian state.

Last but not least, Feliciano de Sá Guimarães, Davi Cordeiro Moreira, Irma Dutra de Oliveira e Silva, and Anna Carolina Rapaso de Mello, in "Conspiracy Theories and Foreign Policy Narratives: Globalism in Jair Bolsonaro's Foreign Policy," analyze more than 2,041 speeches and social media posts on foreign policy issues by four cabinet members of Bolsonaro's government from January 2019 to December 2020 to understand whether Brazil's foreign policy narrative has adopted a conspiracy theory called "globalism" and, if so, under what circumstances. Conspiracy theorists explain current events in terms of a set of intrigues and stratagems carried out by fictitious enemies to undermine the national order. Thus, "globalism" assumes that international agencies and leftist China are trying to impose "cultural Marxism" on the "true people," seen as nationalist, anticommunist, and Christian. The findings suggest that this conspiracy theory not only has taken root in Brazil's foreign policy narrative but has been used consistently over time by the cabinet members responsible for Bolsonaro's foreign policy. The article also indicates that the use of "globalism" is not just a political strategy to convince voters but a worldview embedded in Bolsonaro's far-right cabinet.

We hope that this ensemble of diverse and insightful works will help us to make better sense of the complexity of contemporary Brazilian history.

NOTES

1. https://www.economist.com/the-americas/2018/10/27/jair-bolsonaro-and-the-perversion-of-liberalism.html.

2. https://www.nytimes.com/2019/01/01/world/americas/brazil-bolsonaro-inauguration.html.

3. https://revistaforum.com.br/politica/2018/10/25/ricupero-anuncia-voto-em-haddad-propostas-de-bolsonaro-podem-deixar-brasil-desprezado-35560.html.

4. Integralism was a right-wing political movement founded in Brazil in 1932 that adopted many ideas of Italian fascism.

REFERENCES

Araújo, Ernesto
    2007 "Trump e o Ocidente." *Cadernos de Política Externa*, no. 6, 323–357.
Burns, E. Bradford
    1967 "Tradition and variation in Brazilian foreign policy." *Journal of Inter-American Studies* 9 (2): 195–212.
Coelho, Edmundo Campos
    2000 *Em busca de identidade: O exército e a política na sociedade brasileira*. Rio de Janeiro: Record.
Finchelstein, Frederico
    2017 *From Fascism to Populism in History*. Berkeley: University of California Press.
Lenharo, Alcir
    1986 *A sacralização da política*. 2d edition. São Paulo: Papirus.
Levitsky, Steven and Daniel Ziblatt
    2018 *How Democracies Die*. New York: Crown Publishing Group.
Ricupero, Ricardo
    2017 *A diplomacia na construção do Brasil, 1750–2016*. Rio de Janeiro: Versal.
Rouanet, Sérgio Paulo
    1987 "O novo irracionalismo Brasileiro," pp. 125–146 in *As razões do iluminismo*. São Paulo: Companhia das Letras.

Schwarcz, Lilia Moritz
  2019 *Sobre o autoritarismo brasileiro*. São Paulo: Companhia das Letras.
Stanley, Jason
  2018 *How Fascism Works: The Politics of Us and Them*. New York: Random House Trade Paperbacks.
Stepan, Alfred
  1986 *Os militares: Da abertura à nova república*. Rio de Janeiro: Paz e Terra.

HONORARY DECEASED EDITORS
In recognition of their substantive work with the journal and Latin America.

The Rise of Fascism in Brazil

by

Armando Boito

Translated by
Heather Hayes

Analysis of Brazil's Bolsonaro administration, its most active social support base, and the political crisis that gave rise to it shows that, operating with a concept of fascism embedded in the Marxist tradition, it can be characterized as (neo)fascist. The political crisis of 2015–2018 that led to it involved a crisis of hegemony of the bloc in power, the crisis of party representation of the dominant classes, political activism by the state bureaucracy, the political defensiveness of the workers' and lower-class movement, and the formation of a reactionary middle-class movement. The option for fascism was not without risks, as is reflected today by the demonstrations of dissatisfaction with its administration.

Uma análise do governo Bolsonaro no Brasil, a sua base social a mais ativa e a crise política que lhe deve origem, mostra que, baseado num conceito de fascismo enquadrado na tradição marxista, este governo pode ser denominado como (neo)fascista. O governo (neo)fascista de Bolsonaro era decorrente de uma crise política nos anos 2015-2018 que implicou uma crise de hegemonia no bloco de poder, uma crise de representação partidária das classes dominantes, um ativismo político na burocrácia estatal, uma atitude defensiva política do movimento dos trabalhadores e classes pobres e a formação de um movimento reacionário da classe média. A opçao fascista não é isento de riscos vis-à-vis a burguesia como se reflete hoje nas manifestações de insatisfação com a administração burguesa.

Keywords: Brazilian politics, Bolsonaro government, Neofascism, Political crisis

The political crisis in Brazil that began with the movement to impeach Dilma Rousseff created conditions that typically prepare the ground for a fascist government, and this is what ended up happening. The first question that this statement raises is why Bolsonarism can be characterized as a version of fascism. The second is whether there is any relationship between the political crisis that began in 2014 and the emergence of Bolsonaro as a viable candidate and his eventual electoral victory. Marxist political theory provides several theories that can aid us in answering these questions. This is controversial subject matter. Why use the concept of fascism to characterize a political phenomenon that is taking place a century after Mussolini's rise to power? Is it possible to conceive of a classification of political crises and then use it to identify a specific type of crisis that would favor the rise to power of fascist movements?

Armando Boito is a professor of political science at the Universidade de Campinas and editor of the journal *Crítica Marxista* and a participating editor of *Latin American Perspectives*. His most recent book is *Reform and Political Crisis in Brazil* (2021). Heather Hayes is a translator living in Quito, Ecuador.

LATIN AMERICAN PERSPECTIVES, Issue 248, Vol. 50 No. 1, January 2023, 14–31
DOI: 10.1177/0094582X221140419
© 2022 Latin American Perspectives

ORIGINAL FASCISM AND NEOFASCISM

THE THEORETICAL CONCEPT OF FASCISM

The ideas proposed by writers such as Palmiro Togliatti (2010 [1970]), Daniel Guérin (1965 [1936]), and Nicos Poulantzas (1970) support the theoretical legitimacy of a general concept of fascism—one that transcends the particularities of the original Italian or German fascism. Much of the literature, both Marxist and non-Marxist, rejects this idea, identifying fascism as the movement led by Mussolini and Hitler and the dictatorships that were put in place in Italy and in Germany in the interwar period. Several writers even refuse to use the same concept when talking about the movements and dictatorships in Italy and in Germany. They treat this phenomenon very differently from others when it comes to the way in which political power is organized. While they discuss the concepts of democracy, dictatorship, monarchy, republic, and others in terms of their general characteristics, they do not accept that Jair Bolsonaro closely resembles Benito Mussolini.[1]

Meanwhile, Togliatti (2010: 8) defines fascism as a reactionary political regime based on mass mobilization, and Poulantzas (1970: 12) defines it as one of the political regimes that may be reflected in a capitalist state of exception, including options such as military dictatorship and Bonapartism. As we will see, Togliatti's and Poulantzas's definitions can be combined. They are at once theoretical and synthetic as opposed to the empiricist and descriptive definitions proposed by others. In fact, in the study of fascism it is common for historians and intellectuals aiming at a general characterization of the phenomenon to enumerate the various attributes that characterize it. Umberto Eco (2017) lists 14 attributes, including the cult of tradition, rejection of modernity, irrationalism, action for action's sake, fear of difference, appeal to the middle sectors, nationalism, and elitism. In his book *Anatomy of Fascism*, Robert O. Paxton (2004) defines fascism as political behavior marked by a set of some 20 attributes. In such definitions the theoretical criteria for selecting one or another attribute are not entirely clear. There is no clear explanation why there are 5, 10, or 20 attributes attached to the concept, and no mention is made of which of them are central and which secondary. In the end, the concept thus obtained is not especially useful as an analytical tool. Each historical phenomenon considered ends up presenting only some of the concept's attributes.

In both Togliatti's and Poulantzas's definitions, as opposed to the empiricist and descriptive definitions mentioned above, the Marxist theory of the state as the organizing force behind class domination, democracy, and dictatorship is consciously mobilized to characterize fascism, along with the empirical information available on political phenomena that, by some indicators provided by the aforementioned theory, can at least initially be grouped under a single concept. The resulting theoretical and synthetic definition highlights the essential aspects of the phenomenon and therefore is a much more dependable and enlightening guide for analysis than a detailed characterization of the phenomenon. The same thing happens when it comes to definitions of all the concepts of historical materialism: "the state" is the institution that organizes class domination, "capital" is the most valued, a "social class" is a group whose members occupy the same position in the production process, etc. Each of these definitions is theoretically informed—it depends on other concepts such as "class domination," "value," "accumulation," "production relations," etc.—and synthetic, and in order to produce knowledge about the phenomenon to which it refers it is necessary to examine that phenomenon.

The two definitions converge on a single point: *fascism is a dictatorship whose political regime is a reactionary mass regime*. For both of them, it is a military dictatorship and as such lacks a mobilized and minimally organized mass base. It is not—and Togliatti emphasizes this point—a fascist-type dictatorship, despite this kind of dictatorship's possibly having been instituted to fight the labor movement. Here it is important to add that if fascism is this political regime, the social movement that fights to establish it and the ideology that mobilizes it and legitimizes the fascist dictatorship must also be called fascist. In Brazil at the time of writing (October 2021), we do not have a fascist dictatorship; however, we do have a fascist movement, ideology, and government that, within the limits given by the existing correlation of political forces, is attacking bourgeois democracy and may, depending on the dynamics of the developing situation, result in the establishment of a fascist-type dictatorship.

THE CLASS NATURE OF ORIGINAL FASCISM AND NEOFASCISM

The "mass" of the "reactionary mass political regime" is not an amorphous agglomeration of random social composition. It is not a "mass" in the socially indeterminate sense in which it is conceived by members of the Frankfurt School such as Adorno (2006) but a predominantly petty-bourgeois mass as seen in the original fascism and one that in Brazilian neofascism is predominantly middle-class. The classic Marxist studies of original fascism highlighted the petty-bourgeois class character of the movement.[2] It is true that fascism greatly expanded its original base, but the main base was then and continued to be this group. For example, it was this niche that provided the most recruits for the fascist and Nazi party. One element that is mentioned but not sufficiently emphasized by the classic Marxist studies is that the fascist movement and party were defined by the presence of a social segment that, decades later, would, practically by consensus, end up being called the middle class. Barrington Moore Jr. (1987) is one of the writers who underscores the presence of the middle class as the grassroots force behind the Nazi movement and party. He provides detailed statistics on the party's socio-professional makeup, comparing the presence of socio-professional groups in the party with the proportions of each in the economically active population. In conclusion, he rejects attempts to deny the petty-bourgeois character of the movement and the party, highlighting the participation of middle-class professionals and the strictly working-class segment and the underrepresentation of manual workers. According to Moore, the National Socialist German Workers' Party had a special appeal for white-collar workers, who occupied an insecure social position in that they were dependent on management and performed nonmanual office functions. "This cause[d] them to look down on workers though they [did] not cease to fear them" (Moore Jr., 1987: 547–548).

Therefore, the fascist movement could be defined as *a reactionary mass movement rooted in the middle classes of capitalist social formations*. In the original fascism, the social base was mostly made up of small proprietors, the petty bourgeoisie; in the Brazilian neofascism of the twenty-first century, this social base is composed mainly of the middle class and, particularly, the upper middle class. The neofascist movement and its organizations were born out of demonstrations by the upper middle class supporting impeachment of former president Dilma Rousseff in 2015–2016 (Cavalcante and Arias, 2019; Galvão, 2016). Bolsonaro's first presidential electorate in 2017, as reflected in polls carried out throughout that year tracking voting intentions for presidential candidates, represented about 12 percent of the population intending to vote and tended to have a high level of formal education and high income. More recently, opinion poll analysts have found that the same social segment contained the most convinced Bolsonarists (Prandi, 2019).

The petty-bourgeois or middle-class fascist ideology is a critical ideology but stems from a conservative perspective. Poulantzas mentions "status quo anticapitalism" and Togliatti (2010) and Dimitroff (1935) propose, sometimes inappropriately, "fascist demagoguery." The fact of the matter is that the original fascism criticized big capital, speculators, and financiers from a conservative smallholder perspective while Brazilian neofascism criticizes corruption and the "old politics," the former from a conservative, idealistic, and moralistic perspective and the latter from an authoritarian perspective that praises the concentration of power in the executive branch and points to the end of parliamentary politics—in other words, the end of bourgeois democracy. Here it is worth adding that Brazilian neofascism is not lacking in criticism of the "economic elites" and the "political elites" who apparently aligned themselves with the communist left. The minister of education of the Bolsonaro administration, Abraham Weintraub, gave numerous lectures spreading these ideas and presented the middle class as the redeeming force that could defeat the alliance between the "wealthy" and the left.[3]

The critical aspect of fascist and neofascist discourse can and does, in different ways, achieve a popular impact that transcends its class origin. On this matter, there are two mistakes to be avoided. The first is imagining that fascism indistinctly and equally penetrates all the popular and dominant classes, which if true would allow us to disregard the division into classes when it comes to analyzing the fascist phenomenon. This is an error seen in many texts that turn to Freud to analyze fascism, mobilizing the idea of the lack of a protective and authoritarian father to explain the political success of the movement. An enlightening text by Poulantzas (1976) demonstrates that the popular impact of fascism followed a clear division by class, gender, and age. The other mistake is ignoring this popular impact. Communists made this mistake in fighting the original fascism.[4] In Brazil in 2018, the neofascism that arose out of the upper middle class managed to gain the support, though late and apparently volatile, of the working class. Approval ratings for the Bolsonaro administration indicate that it is in these working-class segments that the president has lost the most in terms of his approval rating (Prandi, 2019), but this support was sufficient for him to win the presidential election in 2018. That said, it is worth emphasizing that Bolsonaro was defeated, albeit by a rather small margin, by the Partido dos Trabalhadores (Workers' Party—PT) candidate, Fernando Haddad, among the low-income population; it was the huge vote that Bolsonaro garnered among the middle- and upper-income strata that handed him the victory.

The superficially critical though profoundly conservative discourse of fascism can even confuse democratic and popular organizations. In Brazil, a large number of the leaders of the PT and members of Dilma Rousseff's administration, at least initially, showed signs of believing that Operation Car Wash was, in fact, an operation to fight corruption and not an operation that politically instrumentalized the fight against corruption to lash out against national companies and the PT itself, satisfying the political interests and expectations of foreign capital and the upper middle class.[5] On the extreme left, illusions also flourished in the face of the neofascist discourse emerging at the time of Operation Car Wash. The Partido Socialista dos Trabalhadores Unificado (Unified Socialist Workers Party—PSTU) and at least one of the arms of the Partido Socialismo e Liberdade (Socialism and Liberty Party—PSOL), which was the party of the presidential candidate in 2014, supported Operation Car Wash, attracted by the apparently critical discourse against corruption mobilized by neofascism.

This is a mass movement of the middle class and the petty bourgeoisie that must be described as reactionary because *its main political objective is the elimination of leftist thought and movements*. In the original fascism, the left was made up of the mass workers' parties—the Socialist Party and the Communist Party—with their programs pointing to the transition to socialism. In this context of intense political polarization, fascism consciously mimicked communists and socialists and organized as a party of the masses, without which, Hitler claimed, it could not be victorious. In neofascism, the enemy is the democratic and popular movement, guided by superficial reformism and devoid of mass party organization. In this new context, one that reflects moderate political polarization compared with its previous iteration, at least thus far neofascism manifests itself through intense agitation on social networks with the support of Pentecostal and Neo-Pentecostal churches, which are organized alongside low-income groups and favor frequent street protests. This support was especially apparent in May and June 2020 and September 2021, when they called for closing down the Supreme Court and Congress.

In most countries where fascist movements came to fruition, they were unable to take over government power. In those places where they did so, they were not always able to establish a fascist-type dictatorship. However, in the countries where these movements came to power, they did so not as representatives of the interests of the middle class and petty bourgeoisie that gave rise to them but, having been politically confiscated by the bourgeoisie or one of its factions, ended up implementing an antidemocratic and antiworker government that went against the interests of the general population. The petty bourgeoisie and the middle class remain politically active under fascist governments and regimes but only as a supporting class. According to Poulantzas (1968), this class serves as the basis for a political regime established for ideological reasons without necessarily having its economic interests covered by the government. In fact, what studies of the original fascism show is that the petty bourgeoisie was the first victim of fascist economic policy, which is actually most favorable to big capital (Guérin, 1965 [1936]; Poulantzas, 1970). Those who co-opt fascism to take advantage of its political hegemony are factions within fascism and neofascism. After all, fascism is defined in terms of the form of state (dictatorship) and the political regime (mobilized mass base) and not in terms of the hegemonic bourgeois faction. Here I differ from the writers cited, who suggest or even claim that the hegemony of big imperialist capital is an integral part of the theoretical concept of fascism. On this subject, the only thing we can incorporate into the theoretical concept of fascism is the hypothesis that fascist governments are bourgeois.

In the original fascism, big and imperialist capital and monopolies co-opted the predominantly petty-bourgeois fascist movement to end the political hegemony of middle-sized capital. Despite the fact that monopoly capital predominated in the prefascist Italian and German economy, it had not yet managed to place its interests at the center of the state's economic, foreign, and social policy decisions. It was able to do so only when the fascist dictatorship was effectively implemented. This is different from the patterns reflected in central countries such as the United States and England. In Brazilian neofascism, big international capital ended up co-opting the predominantly middle-class neofascist movement alongside the Brazilian bourgeoisie faction that had become integrated into it. It was on the basis of this movement that these two bourgeois sectors regained the hegemony they had lost under the PT-led governments. The dynamics of birth from below and co-opting from above prevailed both in original fascism and in Brazilian neofascism. The legacy of this dynamic is ambiguous: it provides a mass base for the president in question (Mussolini, Hitler, Bolsonaro) but tends to create difficulties when it comes to the implementation of bourgeois policy. Frictions between original fascist governments and their petty-bourgeois bases are well known. Similarly, a salient fact in the current Brazilian political process is the relationship of (ideological) unity and (economic) conflict between the Bolsonaro administration and the truck drivers' movement, which is made up of active, radicalized supporters and pioneers of Bolsonarism. While the truck drivers have been fighting for lower fuel prices, the Bolsonaro administration has implemented a pricing policy for gasoline, diesel, and gas that is intimately tied to international oil prices and would result in paying of large dividends to national and international shareholders of the giant Brazilian oil company Petrobras, which is made up of mixed capital (public and private). In September 2021, the price of fuel increased six times more than inflation, causing anger and motivating protests among truck drivers.

THE CONVERGENCE OF POLITICAL CRISES IN THE RISE OF THE ORIGINAL FASCISM AND NEOFASCISM

A THEORETICAL PROPOSAL FOR CLASSIFYING POLITICAL CRISES

Fascism does not spring only from a cyclical crisis. Scholars of the original fascism have highlighted the late unification of Germany and Italy, the intermediate position of these countries in the imperialist chain, the significance of the surviving feudal institutions and ideology (Prussia, the Mezzogiorno), and the types of associative and party systems of these countries (Riley, 2010) as favoring the emergence of fascism in Europe. In Brazil, with its long and recent history of slavery, political changes implemented from above as seen in 1930 and 1985, the instability of its democratic regime, the tradition of authoritarian thinking, and the significant presence of segments of the middle class as an active social force (sometimes progressive but sometimes conservative) contributed, in different ways, to the formation of the historical framework that favored the emergence of neofascism. Gramsci (1973b) highlights a long-standing social element in explaining the emergence of fascism in Italy: the violence embedded in Italian society. As a hypothesis, we can assume that it is easier for a movement to emerge and grow in a society that worships violence and regularly practices it. This is precisely the case in Brazil.[6] Our analysis, however, will be limited to the environment and situation in which neofascism originated and that led to its rise to power.

The model that Poulantzas (1970) presents of the political crisis that generated the original fascism can be applied to the political crisis from which neofascism in Brazil originated despite the particularities of the Brazilian case. In both Italy and Germany, the political crisis led to the establishment of governments controlled by the fascist party, which was made up of bourgeois parties and then developed into the establishment of a fascist dictatorship. This transition took place gradually in Italy and abruptly in Germany. In Brazil, what we have thus far is a neofascist government that threatens democracy. It is arguable that there are underlying similarities between the political crisis that gave rise to original fascism and the political crisis that led to neofascism in Brazil. In the second decade of the twentieth century, despite the existence of financial and internationalized capitalism, this system and the international imperialist system were in different stages, and the working class was organized into socialist and communist parties while bourgeois Europe was facing the threat posed by the Russian Revolution of 1917. The political crises of the 1920s and the 2010s occurred in the context of the same type of state (capitalist) and came about within a political process articulating the conflicts between the ruling and the working classes in a way that was unprecedented in the history of class societies. These crises permeated institutions and mobilized political instruments originating within the same type of society such as the mass party and the frequent and legally permitted mobilization of the working classes. Here I am hypothesizing and assuming that political crises in capitalist societies have certain features that are different from those seen in slave and feudal societies and that these crises differ only within certain limits.

Nicos Poulantzas is not the first Marxist writer to have conceived the idea that fascism is born of a particular type of political crisis. However, he is, if I am not mistaken, the first to have tried to extract all its consequences from this idea. He maintains that the different political regimes of the capitalist form of a state of exception—fascism, military dictatorship, and Bonapartism—stem from different types of political crises. By doing so, he breaks with the economism and historicism that mark several Marxist traditions—the idea that it is only the economy that imposes itself on agents' intentions and the related idea that in politics everything can be explained by the specific circumstances of each situation and these circumstances, with their wide variations, are intractable when it comes to building explanatory models. This raises a possibility of classifying the political processes of capitalist societies in order to explain and, to a certain extent, predict the transition from a democratic state to a dictatorial state and, moreover, to a type of dictatorship, whether fascist, military, or Bonapartist (Poulantzas, 1970: 60).

In *Fascism and Dictatorship*, Poulantzas does not manage, in our view, to deliver all that he has promised on this issue. He provides a very rich characterization of the political crises that opened the way for the rise of fascism to power in Italy in 1922 and in Germany in 1933, showing that, despite their specificities, the model behind the crises is, in fact, the same. This is an important theoretical advance. However, he does not sufficiently clarify why the type of crisis he presents could not have opened the way for a military dictatorship, for example, which is a possibility that was present both in Italy and in the Weimar Republic. This omission originates in the fact that Poulantzas's work appears to lack a specific analysis of the *dynamics* of the political crisis that led to fascism. How do the different elements that Poulantzas uses to characterize the political crisis that gave rise to fascism act on each other? How does this action affect the evolution of the crisis? How does this evolution produce changes in the positions of the forces present? I believe that if such questions could be answered, we could move forward along the path that Poulantzas proposed.

Poulantzas points to 13 elements that he says are characteristic of the crisis that propitiates the rise of fascism to power: (1) intensification of conflicts within the bloc in power; (2) the crisis of party representation of the dominant classes; (3) the political instability and hegemonic incapacity of the dominant classes and factions; (4) the resistance to fascism of the traditional political parties of the bourgeoisie; (5) the political activism and strengthening of the civil and military bureaucracy of the state to the detriment of political parties; (6) conflict between branches and institutions of the state linked to class conflict and institutional crisis; (7) the characteristic difference between "formal power" and "real power"; (8) the impossibility of any ruling-class faction's establishing or maintaining its hegemony within the framework of the democratic regime; (9) the multiplication of attacks on political parties and parliamentary politics; (10) a series of defeats and a defensive political situation within the labor movement; (11) an offensive by the bourgeoisie and particularly by big business against the workers' movement; (12) the development of the petty bourgeoisie as a distinct social force; and (13) a generalized ideological crisis.

This list bears a striking resemblance to the Brazilian situation that gave rise to the Bolsonaro administration. The various points referring to the ruling class, its parties, and the state contain elements of circumstance and development that can be set aside as a general characterization of the political crisis characteristic of the birth of fascism, and therefore I focus on the following: intensification of conflict within the bloc in power, the crisis of party representation of the ruling classes, the political activism and strengthening of the civil bureaucracy (including the judiciary), the defensive situation of the labor movement, the development of the petty bourgeoisie as a distinct social force, and the generalized ideological crisis.

As for the dynamics of the political crisis, it is important to identify certain interactions and links between these elements and the political evolution they provide. It is the intensification of conflict within the bloc in power that triggers the political crisis: the labor movement is organized and active but defeated and on the defensive. The crisis of party representation of the bourgeoisie aggravates and prolongs the crisis. Bourgeois parties lose electoral support, and the bourgeoisie and its factions no longer recognize themselves in their proposals and programs. They are unable to demobilize the labor movement and make themselves available to adopt solutions that include breaking with the democratic game—something that, until then, would have been rejected as an adventurous ploy. The labor movement, although unable to present its own way out of the political crisis because of its defeats and defensive situation, remains sufficiently organized and active in its attempts to resist the deeper and more profound exploitation demanded by big business. In fact, both Poulantzas and Guérin point out something that is curiously similar to Mussolini's own assessment: that neither in Italy nor in Germany was fascism a direct response to a supposed threat of revolution, since the revolutionary crisis had already been overcome there. In the case of Brazil, there was no revolutionary crisis in the situation we are analyzing. According to the two writers, the issue was efforts to take away the gains that workers had made in the preceding period. Big capital no longer accepted the policy of conciliation that the governments of middle-sized capital, Giolitti (1920–1921) in Italy and Brüning (1930–1932) in Germany, proposed to Social Democracy (Poulantzas, 1970; Guérin, 1965 [1936]). The petty bourgeoisie, organizing through the movement and the fascist party as a distinct social force, assumed big capital's fight against the labor movement but revealed a remarkable incapacity for hegemony; it did not present its own coherent platform of economic, foreign, and social policy. This movement unleashed violent action against workers' organizations and a pronounced ideologization of political action that was a response to the social and economic rise of the workers in a situation still marked by the victory of the Russian Revolution. The absence of political parties representing the bourgeoisie made it necessary and the incapacity of the petty bourgeoisie made it possible for the tactics of monopoly capital to appropriate the petty-bourgeois fascist movement to establish its own political hegemony.

With the necessary modifications, this kind of political crisis and dynamic are similar to what we have seen in Brazilian politics in recent years (Table 1).

THE BRAZILIAN POLITICAL CRISIS AND THE RISE OF NEOFASCISM

The main conflict, albeit not the only one, within the Brazilian bourgeoisie has been the conflict between the large national companies that are the basis of what I have called the great internal bourgeoisie and foreign capital and the bourgeoisie associated with it (Boito, 2021). Foreign capital is heterogeneous and maintains various relationships with the Brazilian economy (Farias, 2018). There is foreign capital external to the country, which has a merely commercial or financial relationship with the Brazilian economy, and foreign capital that has been internalized, each relating to a different sector of the economy. Analyzing the political action of these bourgeois segments is a complex task.

TABLE 1
Brazil: 1995–2021 Administrations

Administration	General Characteristics	Policy
Fernando Henrique Cardoso (PSDB), 1995–2002 Sociologist. Opposed the military dictatorship (1964–1985). Party in the vanguard of neoliberalism in Brazil.	Dismantled the developmentalist state and implemented the neoliberal capitalist model.	Neoliberalism: small state apparatus, privatization, denationalization, reduction of social rights, foreign policy reflecting passive subordination to the United States. Moderately antiracist political measures.
Lula da Silva (PT), 2003–2010 Worker and former union leader. Party created by labor unions and progressive sectors of the middle class, today a center-left party whose voters mainly represent workers from the marginal mass, the progressive class, and the working class.	Maintained basic elements of the neoliberal capitalist model but changed economic, social, foreign, and citizenship policy to benefit national companies and the working classes.	Neovelopmentalism: state intervention to stimulate economic growth and poverty reduction and a more independent foreign policy with regard to the United States. Political recognition of black, feminist, indigenous, and LGBT movements. Concluded term with approval rating of 82 percent.
Dilma Rousseff (PT), 2011–2016 Economist in the developmentalist wing of the ECLAC, first woman to be president. Fought in the armed struggle against the Brazilian military dictatorship.	Second term interrupted by impeachment. Neo-developmentalist crisis.	Neodevelopmentalism with concessions to neoliberal fiscal policy. Active and outstanding participation in the creation of the BRICS Bank. Included domestic workers in the labor law, adopted measures in favor of black, feminist, indigenous, and LGBT movements, created Truth Commission to investigate the crimes of the military dictatorship.
Michel Temer (PMDB), 2016–2018 Formerly Rousseff's vice president. Party tends to support the administration in power..	Resumed and radicalized the neoliberal policy of the 1990s.	Resumption of privatization and denationalization. Radical neoliberal reform of the labor law. Approved a constitutional amendment that prevents the expansion of state social spending. Policy favorable to international oil companies in the exploration of Brazilian oil.
Jair Bolsonaro (no party affiliation), 2019–2022 Far-right politician, retired from the military. Defends the military dictatorship, torture, and the use of weapons by large landowners against peasants and indigenous people.	Unprecedented radicalization of neoliberalism; governs with the leadership of the armed forces and extreme-right politicians. Relies on Neo-Pentecostal churches, mobilizes his base among the middle class, and threatens democracy. Opposes protective measures against COVID-19.	Radicalization of neoliberalism: Neoliberal social security reform. New measures to reduce labor rights. Passive and explicit subordination to the United States. Ultraliberalism in the economy and fascism in politics. Anticommunist ideology with criticism and threats to liberal democracy. Hostility to black, feminist, indigenous, and LGBT movements.

Source: Data from Boito (2021).
Note: Brazil is a presidential democracy. The presidential term is four years. Power is concentrated in the Presidency of the Republic (authoritarian presidentialism), Congress has limited participation in government decisions. It is controlled by conservative parties, and the party system is very fragmented. During their presidential terms, Lula da Silva and Dilma Rousseff had to make agreements with conservative parties to guarantee support in Congress.

They do not openly proclaim their interests and prefer to act in the corridors of the state bureaucracy rather than on the political scene (Guilmo, 2019). One example of this is the Instituto Brasileiro do Petróleo, whose board has always included members representing large foreign oil companies and has put up resistance to the oil policy proposed by PT governments. Once the Temer administration took power, this group had a strong presence in the presidential palace and an important voice in changing sector-related policy (Narciso, 2019).

Insurance companies and foreign banks in Brazil were given the opportunity to express their opinions on the matters of pension reform and the constitutional changes the Temer administration promoted. It became public knowledge that the U.S. Department of Justice had offered several courses, provided information for training human resources, and participated in actions taken as part of Operation Car Wash that ended up liquidating the monopoly of the large national construction companies in the domestic public works market.

The associations and national states linked to foreign capital generally press for the implementation of extreme neoliberal policies: trade liberalization, financial deregulation, privatizations, primary surplus, reduction of labor, and social rights. Until Bolsonaro's election, it was the PSDB that voiced this platform on the political scene. The internal bourgeoisie selectively opposed aspects of it and in doing so came into conflict with international capital.[7] This conflict does not mean that there is no unity. The internal big bourgeoisie is not a national bourgeoisie. It neither takes action to break with imperialism nor has any interest in such a break. However, within the limits of this general unity, there are various conflicts between the different segments of the domestic bourgeoisie that are present in banks, industry, and agriculture and foreign capital, internalized or not, in the different branches of the economy. The Fernando Henrique Cardoso (PSDB) administrations of the 1990s primarily represented the interests of foreign capital and the associated bourgeoisie, while the governments of the PT between 2003 and 2016 represented the hegemony of the domestic big bourgeoisie. This shift in hegemony appears in the change in the state's economic, social, and foreign policy. This is the contrast between the neoliberalism of the PSDB and the associated bourgeoisie (trade liberalization, privatization, financial deregulation, passive subordination to U.S. foreign policy) and the neodevelopmentalism of the PT and the domestic big bourgeoisie (state intervention in the economy to stimulate growth and reduce poverty, with a foreign policy giving greater importance to relations with the countries of the Southern Hemisphere) (Boito, 2021).

The conflict between these bourgeois factions worsened in the political crisis of 2014–2018. This, as we have seen, is the first characteristic of a political crisis that can lead to fascism in any of its variants. The crisis began because of a restorative political offensive by international capital and the associated bourgeoisie against Dilma Rousseff's administration. The hegemony of the domestic big bourgeoisie had been achieved thanks to the PT administrations' strategy of forming a broad political front—what I have called a neodevelopmentalist front that incorporated a large part of the lower middle class (workers, peasants, and marginal-mass workers) into social policy measures. As I have suggested, the Cardoso administrations represented the hegemony of international capital and the faction of the bourgeoisie associated with it, with the upper middle class as their preferential base of support. However, working-class sectors were also present, as was reflected in the support these administrations and their neoliberal policies received from the Força Sindical. Cardoso radicalized trade liberalization, halving customs tariffs that had already been reduced by the Collor government. Together with Pedro Malan, he initiated an accelerated internationalization of the banking market while drastically reducing subsidized agricultural credit and freezing the public works market. One by one, these measures hurt the interests of different segments of the domestic big bourgeoisie to serve the interests of foreign industry, international banks, and financial capital. There was, however, one area that reflected clear unity between these bourgeois factions: the antiworking-class and antipopular dimension of neoliberalism, which focused on a reduction of labor and social rights. That said, for the most part, conflict increased throughout the 1990s (Boito, 1999: 23–77), eventually making possible a political rapprochement between the internal big bourgeoisie and Lula da Silva's candidacy for the presidency in 2002.

While there was economic growth during the PT-led governments, international capital and the associated bourgeoisie, represented on the party scene by the PSDB, remained on the political defensive. The situation began to change as a result of the policy of Dilma's first term, when she made an attempt to radicalize PT's neodevelopmentalism, deepening Brazil's integration into the BRICS group. The decline of economic growth was another key factor. In this new situation, international capital and the faction of the Brazilian bourgeoisie associated with it, alongside the U.S. government, decided that it was necessary to react and that it would be possible to win and went on the political offensive (Boito, 2021). Its first option was an electoral victory in 2014, something that it came close to achieving. The second option was impeachment, an idea that had been born in the upper-middle-class movement. Finally, during the second half of 2015, it managed to remove part of the internal big bourgeoisie from the base supporting the Dilma administration. The internal bourgeoisie showed an interest in resuming a neoliberal program of reforms that went against the interests of the masses and, moreover, imagined that it would be safe because with impeachment the PMDB instead of the PSDB would take power. With this shift the neodevelopmentalist political front went into crisis.

This conflict "at the top" was responsible for the politicized and polarized character of the 2014 election campaign, something that created and even stimulated unrest among those "at the bottom," and this is what made the middle class and the petty bourgeoisie a distinct reactionary social force. Organizations and intellectuals connected to these groups took the initiative to propose the impeachment of Dilma Rousseff and created new social movements focused on that effort. The PSDB spent months hesitating to take a stand, given that its leadership was divided over the drive for impeachment. One significant episode symptomatic of the difference between the social structure and political orientation of the PSDB and those of the impeachment movement was the removal of the main party leaders from a proimpeachment demonstration in the city of São Paulo.

The mass movement by the upper middle class to remove Dilma Rousseff can be considered the origin of the neofascist movement, first, because the motivation of the movement was reactionary. It expressed the revolt of the upper middle class and a small part of the lower classes motivated by PT economic and social policies. The upper- middle-class movement identified the PT and the left as an enemy that had to be fought and eliminated. Street demonstrations, battle cries, rude and aggressive references to supporters of the left and center-left, and threats to and attacks on leftists and intellectuals in public places by groups of this extreme right wing attest to this. Second, the whole reactionary movement of the middle class broke with the democratic charade when it argued for impeachment without even finding a reason to justify it and when some even advocated for a dictatorship. What they were asking for was military intervention. In polls taken before the election and in the 2018 calculations map, 8 or 9 out of 10 upper-middle-class voters favored the candidate who openly defended the military dictatorship, torture, torturers, machismo, and homophobia.

This movement was not then and is not now homogeneous, to the point that under the Bolsonaro administration the two aforementioned groups decided not to participate in the May 26, 2019, demonstration once they became aware of the force behind the calls for closing down Congress and the Supreme Court, but both groups mobilized their bases a month later, on June 30, for a demonstration in support of Bolsonaro's neofascist government. All of this appears to point to what many observers have said: that there is a solid core of Bolsonarism, which I am characterizing as neofascist, around which a broader periphery gravitates from various outer reaches of the right and far-right.

Two observations can be made in relation to the political-crisis element analyzed above. The first is that the reactionary mobilization of the middle class was linked to the emergence of political activism by the civil bureaucracy, especially the judiciary and the federal police, and this activism generated successive institutional crises. In other words, it is here, in the political activism of the state bureaucracy, that we find the third element of crisis highlighted by Poulantzas. Operation Car Wash involved a large part of the "justice system," with both passive and active involvement by the Supreme Court, the Superior and Regional Courts, and the Prosecutor General's Office. Federal police chiefs, prosecutors, judges, appeals court judges, and Supreme Court justices make up an integral part of the upper middle class. To be precise, their very high salaries and privileged working conditions actually place them at the top of that class. At the same time, they are officials of the state's repressive apparatus, making them responsible for maintaining the capitalist order. These two social realities contributed to the active support of these bureaucrats for neofascism or to a conniving attitude toward it. Throughout the crisis, Dilma Rousseff's administration and Congress found themselves under heavy pressure from the judiciary and even the armed forces. The military began to speak out, publicly demanding that the Supreme Court not allow Lula's presidential candidacy.

The second observation is that the upper-middle-class movement gained supporters during the 2018 election campaign when the Pentecostal and Neo-Pentecostal churches latched on to Bolsonaro's neofascist candidacy. Their support, especially because of the patriarchal, sexist, and homophobic values prevailing among them, ended up being key to Bolsonaro's late surge among the masses. He hid his extreme neoliberal program from these working-class supporters, but in the free elections, just as in Germany and Italy, the socialist and communist parties hung on to the electoral majority thanks to their ties to the working class (Poulantzas, 1976). Thus Lula and the PT were able to hold on to their electoral hegemony among the lower classes. This was clearly evidenced by the victory of Fernando Haddad in the Northeastern states in the 2018 presidential election that ended up being won nationwide by Bolsonaro.

The working class and other lower-class groups, as well as the democratic camp, suffered successive defeats from 2014 on and have clearly been on the political defensive since then. There was also an ideological crisis in the neodevelopmentalist field. Growth was slowing, and Dilma Rousseff's administration had decided to apply a heavy fiscal adjustment in addition to implementing or announcing measures that were at once expensive for big capital and unpopular among the general population. The ideological offensive of neoliberalism rounded out the picture. A discussion began on what was called the exhaustion of the neodevelopmentalist program. The Rousseff administration took the first step to the right and was succeeded by Temer's government, which went even farther and represented a change in the nature of governance. The administration that immediately preceded the neofascist government was already a conservative administration (similar to what happened with the original fascism). Contrary to what happened with the military dictatorships in Latin America's Southern Cone, neither fascism nor neofascism is a direct and immediate response to popular or reformist government.

To build on Poulantzas's comments, this change came in response to a series of defeats: abandonment of the neodevelopmentalist program by Dilma in 2015 in her second term; the crushing defeat in the impeachment vote in April 2016; approval of the constitutional amendment, freezing social investment, in December 2016; the final approval of labor reform in July 2017; the conviction and imprisonment of Lula da Silva, resulting from a clearly persecutory process, in April 2018; the challenge of Lula's candidacy; and, finally, Jair Bolsonaro's victory in the 2018 election. In each of these defeats, mobilization by the working and lower classes was weak at best. The neofascist demonstrations for Dilma's removal and Lula's arrest were much bigger than the demonstrations in defense of workers, democracy, and their political leaders. It almost seemed as if the wealthy middle class made up the majority of the population.

The political offensive intended to restore the associated bourgeoisie, the creation of a reactionary middle-class movement, the institutional crisis caused by the political activism of the state bureaucracy, and the defensive situation of the democratic and popular movement all added to the crisis of representation of traditional bourgeois parties, all working to create a dynamic that made the victory of neofascism possible.

The PSDB's electoral success had been on a downward spiral. The party's formidable performance in the 2014 presidential election was merely a passing reaction. In 2018 neither this nor any other bourgeois party showed electoral viability. The fight ended up centering on the PT candidate and Bolsonaro, who became a member of a micro-party that merely offered to host his candidacy. According to articles published mainly in *Valor Econômico*, the "market" tended to support the candidacy of the PSDB's Geraldo Alckmin. As Alckmin's candidacy proved to be electorally infeasible, the general business community transitioned to supporting the Bolsonaro candidacy, which, as mentioned earlier, until 2017 represented a candidacy for the upper middle class while enjoying the support of rural landowners. The candidates from the largest and most traditional bourgeois parties (the PSDB and the PMDB) combined received only 5.96 percent of the valid votes in the first round of the 2018 presidential election. Press reports showed the great fear that gripped the electoral market in the face of the possibility of the victory of someone commonly referred to as a populist PT candidate who would allegedly threaten the Temer government's program of neoliberal reforms. This was, in effect, an implicit recognition that the interests of big business and democracy had collided. In contrast to what had happened in the 1990s, the continuity of the neoliberal economic program seemed to require more radical and even reckless solutions. These included supporting the candidacy of an extreme-right-wing politician who defended a dictatorial regime, someone with no party base and no history that would point to his becoming president. Despite all of this, the dynamics of the crisis pushed big business interests to support the neofascist candidacy.

Beyond mere electoral calculations there was the dissatisfaction of the associated big bourgeoisie and foreign capital with what they understood to be the moderation of the neoliberalism of the traditional bourgeois candidates. In the press, certain business leaders were vocal about their desire for deeper and bolder neoliberal reforms, which opened up the transition to ultraliberalism. In a movement opposite to that of the prodemocratic and grassroots side of the equation, the big bourgeoisie also began to seek, if not a new program, a stronger dose of the same medicine it had been applying. In other words, we find here an indication of a generalized ideological crisis of the two political visions that, until then, had polarized the national political process. As we have seen, this is also one of the elements of a political crisis that typically precedes fascism. One major business leader told *Valor* that Alckmin was a good passenger-plane pilot but Brazil would need to elect a fighter-plane pilot to the presidency. The crisis of party representation therefore involved the erosion of ties between the representative and those represented. However, big business interests approached Bolsonaro not merely out of electoral pragmatism.

During the electoral campaign, Jair Bolsonaro became aware that the bourgeoisie had co-opted his candidacy and announced that he would appoint the ultraliberal Paulo Guedes as minister of the economy. He not only promised but is delivering ultraliberalism, once again opening up the nation to foreign capital, and his foreign policy reflects passive alignment with the United States. All of this goes hand in hand with a reduction in labor and social rights. Despite the fact that, as is typical in fascism, Bolsonaro and his social base are effectively at the service of the big bourgeoisie, they do not allow themselves to become passive instruments of the social class that opened up their access to government power.

FINAL CONSIDERATIONS

The aggravation of class conflicts and their repercussions for state institutions are part of any political crisis. Despite this, the conflict and repercussions vary from one type of crisis to another. In a revolutionary crisis, when the continuity of the capitalist mode of production is called into question, the contradictions that end up being aggravated are those that oppose the workers' movement to the bourgeois front. The effects of all this on state institutions often mean a reduction of the decision-making capacity of all branches of the state, favoring an alternative power structure organized outside of it: a guerrilla movement, a people's army, or a network of workers' and people's councils. In a crisis of bourgeois democracy rather than of the bourgeois state itself, the deepening conflicts may be of another kind. One example of this could be the worsening of conflicts between fractions of the ruling class, in which the response may be a head-on confrontation between institutions that make up the state apparatus. This last phenomenon, however, is just as likely to occur in a political crisis that precedes the introduction of a fascist dictatorship as in one that precedes the implementation of a military dictatorship. I have shown that what is specific about the prefascist political crisis may well be summarized by the five elements that I have examined here: a crisis of hegemony relating to the bloc in power, the formation of a reactionary middle-class movement, the political activism of the state bureaucracy, the political defensiveness of the workers' and lower-class movement, which made it impossible for them to offer their own solution to the crisis, and, finally, the crisis of representativeness of the bourgeois parties. In this situation the bourgeoisie, in its attempts to suppress gains made by the working class, finds itself facing both the need for and the possibility of opting for fascism. This option is not devoid of risks, as is reflected today by the demonstrations, albeit localized, of dissatisfaction with the Bolsonaro administration, whose middle-class social base remains active though not always following the direction desired by the ruling class, on the part of the Brazilian bourgeoisie,

NOTES

1. Gentile (2019), a historian of fascist Italy, rejects any general concept of fascism, and a similar position exists in the Marxist literature. I have criticized this position in a recent text (Boito, 2019).

2. The petty-bourgeois character of the original fascist movement is affirmed and demonstrated by countless Marxist writers on the basis of extensive documentation and statistics of various types—the geography of the vote, the composition of the fascist and Nazi parties, etc. In addition to the texts by Togliatti (2010) and Poulantzas (1970) are Gramsci's "I due fascismi" (1973a, originally published in 1921 in *Ordine Nuovo*), Trotsky's *Revolution and Counter-Revolution* (1968 [1933]), Guérin's (1965 [1936]) *Fascisme et grand capital*, and, working with other issues and theories, Reich's (1972 [1936]) work on the mass psychology of fascism and that of Moore Jr. (1987) on the social bases of obedience and revolt.

3. See his lecture to the Conservative Political Action Conference in São Paulo in October 2019. https://www.youtube.com/watch?v=ysSiSTBCG1w.

4. "One of the weakest aspects of the anti-fascist struggle of our parties lies in the fact that they react inadequately and too slowly to the demagogy of fascism, and to this day continue to look with disdain upon the problems of the struggle against fascist ideology. Many comrades did not believe that so reactionary a variety of bourgeois ideology as the ideology of fascism, which in its stupidity frequently reaches the point of lunacy, was capable of gaining a mass influence at all. This was a great mistake" (Dimitroff, 1935: 77–78).

5. I try to demonstrate this hypothesis in my book on the current Brazilian political process (Boito, 2021).

6. Gramsci (1973b: 105–107) describes a scenario that leads us to reflect on similarities between today's Brazil and Italy at the beginning of the past century, mentioning the widespread practice of homicide in Italy at the time, massacres of the poor population, the humiliating ways in which employers controlled their workers, and violence by landowners in the private sector.

7. The idea of the existence of conflict between what I am calling the domestic big bourgeoisie and international capital and the associated big bourgeoisie is a controversial idea, and critics of it have provided an anachronistic use of the literature in arguing for the nonexistence of a national bourgeoisie in Brazil. I call this "anachronistic" because to analyze today's Brazil it uses a literature that was created in the 1960s and 1970s (Prado Jr., 1966; Cardoso and Faletto, 1970; Fernandes, 1973;

Evans, 1980). Imperialism and dependency have entered a new period (Amin, 2002; Dumenil and Lévy, 2004), and in this new period, typical of neoliberal capitalism, the imposition of limits on capitalist development prevails. To determine whether there is conflict between national capital and foreign capital in Brazil, these critics resort to a literature that discusses something different and much deeper: whether Brazil has a national anti-imperialist bourgeoisie, something that was the subject of debate in the 1960s and 1970s. While there is no such bourgeoisie in Brazil, this does not mean that the entire Brazilian bourgeoisie has a uniform position vis-à-vis foreign capital.

REFERENCES

Adorno, Theodor W.
    2006 "A teoria freudiana e o padrão da propaganda fascista." *Margem Esquerda* 7 (May): 164–191.
Amin, Samir
    2002 *Oltre il capitalismo senile*. Milan: Punto Rosso.
Boito, Armando
    1999 *Política neoliberal e sindicalismo no Brasil*. São Paulo: Editora Xamã.
    2019 "O neofascismo no Brasil." *Boletim LIERI (UFRRJ)* 1 (May): 1–11.
    2021 *Reform and Political Crisis in Brazil: Class Conflicts in Workers' Party Governments and the Rise of Bolsonaro Neo-fascism*. Leiden: Brill.
Cardoso, Fernando H. and Enzo Faletto
    1970 *Dependência e desenvolvimento na América Latina*. Rio de Janeiro: Zahar Editores.
Cavalcante, Sávio and Santiane Arias
    2019 "A divisão da classe média na crise política brasileira (2013–2016)," pp. 97–127 in Paul Boufartigue, Armando Boito, Sophie Béroud, and Andréia Galvão (eds.), *O Brasil e a França na mundialização neoliberal: Mudanças políticas e contestações sociais*. São Paulo: Alameda.
Dimitroff, Georgi
    1935 *Working-Class Unity, Bulwark against Fascism: Seventh World Congress of the Communist International*. New York: Workers' Library Publishers.
Duménil, Gérard and Dominique Lévy
    2004 "O imperialismo na era neoliberal." *Crítica Marxista* 18: 11–36.
Eco, Umberto
    2017 *Il fascismo eterno*. Milão: La Nave di Teseo.
Evans, Peter B.
    1980 *A tríplice aliança: As multinacionais, as estatais e o capital nacional no desenvolvimento dependente brasileiro*. Rio de Janeiro: Zahar Editores.
Farias, Francisco P.
    2018 *Estado burguês e classes dominantes no Brasil (1930–1964)*. Curitiba: Editora CRV.
Fernandes, Florestan
    1973 *Capitalismo dependente e classes sociais na América Latina*. Rio de Janeiro: Zahar Editores.
Galvão, Andréia
    2016 "As classes médias na crise política brasileira." Blog Junho. http://blogjunho.com.br/as-classes-medias-na-crise-politica-brasileira (accessed August 2, 2019).
Gentile, Emilio
    2019 *Chi è fascista*. Rome and Bari: Editori Laterza.
Gramsci, Antonio
    1973a "I due fascismi," pp. 133–136 in Antonio Gramsci, *Sul fascismo*. Edited by Enzo Santarelli. Rome: Editori Riuniti.
    1973b "Forze elementari," pp. 105–107 in Antonio Gramsci, *Sul fascismo*. Edited by Enzo Santarelli. Rome: Editori Riuniti.
Guérin, Daniel
    1965 (1936) *Fascisme et grand capital*. Paris: François Maspero.
Guilmo, Nataly
    2019 "O capital internacional como agente político no Brasil." MS, Campinas.

Moore Jr., Barrington
    1987 *Injustiça: As bases sociais da obediência e da revolta*. São Paulo: Brasiliense.
Narciso, Pedro
    2019 "O pré-sal em disputa: petróleo e burguesia no segundo Governo Lula." Master's thesis, Universidade Federal de Pelotas.
Paxton, Robert O.
    2004 *The Anatomy of Fascism*. New York: Alfred A. Knopf.
Poulantzas, Nicos
    1968 *Pouvoir politique et classes sociales*. Paris: François Maspero.
    1970 *Fascisme et dictature*. Paris: François Maspero.
    1976 "A propos de l'impact populaire du fascisme," in Maria Antonietta Macciocchi (ed.), *Élements pour une analyse du fascisme*. Vol. 1. Paris: Union Générale d'Éditions.
Prado Jr., Caio
    1966 *A revolução brasileira*. São Paulo: Brasiliense.
Prandi, Reginaldo
    2019 "Os 12% do presidente—em que lugar da sociedade habita o bolsonarista convicto?" *Jornal da USP*. https://jornal.usp.br/?p=272283 (accessed September 20, 2019).
Reich, Wilhelm
    1972 (1936) *La psychologie de masse du fascisme*. Paris: Payot.
Riley, Dylan
    2010 *The Civic Foundations of Fascism in Europe: Italy, Spain, and Romania, 1870–1845*. Baltimore: Johns Hopkins University Press.
Togliatti, Palmiro
    2010 *Corso sugli avversari: Le lezioni sul fascismo*. Turin: Einaudi.
Trotsky, Leon
    1968 (1933) *Revolução e contra-revolução*. Rio de Janeiro: Laemmert.

The Social Base of Bolsonarism

An Analysis of Authoritarianism in Politics

by
Mariana Miggiolaro Chaguri and Oswaldo E. do Amaral

The cohesion and resilience of the social base supporting Jair Bolsonaro is backed by an authoritarian perception of politics and society. Support for the president runs through all sectors of Brazilian society and reflects a variety of demands. A multidisciplinary research strategy that articulates statistical analysis of data from an innovative national survey with a sociological approach to the construction of an authoritarian vision of politics and society in Brazil suggests that the authoritarian right is a political and electoral force that will persist and that it has several characteristics that distinguish it from conservative movements in the Global North.

A coesão e resistência da base social que apoia a Bolsonaro são baseadas numa visão autoritária da política e da sociedade porque o apoio ao presidente se estende por todas as classes na sociedade brasileira e traz à tona uma diversidade de exigências. Uma estratégia multidisciplinária de pesquisa que articula uma análise estatística de dados colhidos de um levantamento nacional inovador com base numa aproximação sociológica voltada para a construção de uma ótica autoritária da política e da sociedade no Brasil constata que a direita autoritária persistirá como força política e eleitoral e que tem várias características as quais lhe distingue dos outros movimentos conservadores localizados nos países do norte global.

Keywords: *Authoritarianism, Contemporary Brazil, Politics and society, Democracy, Jair Bolsonaro*

A year and a half after taking office, Jair Bolsonaro's administration was already facing a number of problems, among them low economic growth, high unemployment, defeats in the legislature, and corruption scandals involving two of the president's sons, Councilman Carlos Bolsonaro and Senator Flávio Bolsonaro, and his former adviser Fabrício Queiroz. To make matters worse, the country was one of the worst-hit in the world by COVID-19, with the highest death rates. The federal government's management of the crisis was severely

Mariana Miggiolaro Chaguri is a professor of sociology at the Universidade Estadual de Campinas and the university's Center of Contemporary Sociology. Oswaldo E. do Amaral is a professor of political science at the same institution and director of its Center for Studies on Public Opinion. They thank Bárbara Castro, Michel Nicolau Netto, Otávio Catelano, Sávio Cavalcante, and Vitor Vasques for suggestions made on the first version of the text and the Conselho Nacional de Desenvolvimento Científico e Tecnológico (313472/2020-3; 315411/2021-0) and the CAPES/Print Program for funding. Some of the findings contained in this article were presented at seminars held in February 2020 at Brown, Columbia, and Harvard Universities, and the authors are grateful to everyone who participated in those events.

LATIN AMERICAN PERSPECTIVES, Issue 248, Vol. 50 No. 1, January 2023, 32–46
DOI: 10.1177/0094582X231152245
© 2023 Latin American Perspectives

criticized both inside and outside of the country as the international press reported that Brazil was one of the nations that was worst at administering the pandemic.[1] Still, opinion surveys conducted in the first half of 2020 reflected that about 30 percent of Brazilians scored the Bolsonaro administration "excellent" or "good," according to data from the Datafolha Institute.[2] What explains this stability and resilient support for the president and his administration in such an adverse political and economic context?

To answer this question, we turn to a multidisciplinary research strategy in which we articulate the statistical analysis of data from the third phase of the national opinion poll "The Face of Democracy," still unpublished, which was conducted by the Instituto da Democracia[3] between May 30 and June 5, 2020, with a sociological approach regarding the construction and consolidation of an authoritarian vision of politics and society in Brazil.

The article is organized as follows: in the first section, we demonstrate how an authoritarian perception of politics is fundamental to understanding the most loyal base of support for President Jair Bolsonaro; in the second, we discuss how worldviews and authoritarian perceptions of social life organize ways of speaking and perceiving social differences and inequalities, organizing the ideological bases of authoritarianism, and to close we address the Brazilian case from a comparative perspective and point to the long-term implications of support for Bolsonaro for the nation's political scenario.

The concept of authoritarianism and the notion of transversality are key to our analysis. Authoritarianism as a social and political phenomenon is nothing new to Brazilian history and has been the subject of analysis by a long and varied series of writers. Among the essays addressing the Brazilian situation we have, for example, Buarque de Holanda (1936) on the difficulty of implementing both a stable and durable democratic order and the universalization of rights and citizenship in a social dynamic marked by privatism. Oliveira Vianna (1920; 1949), in turn, argued for the need to strengthen and centralize the state in order to limit the political influence of local oligarchies in the pursuit of an authoritarian modernization of the economy, legislation, and society itself.[4]

While, in the Brazilian case, the tensions between democracy and authoritarianism helped to shape ways of interpreting the relations between the state and society, especially between 1930 and 1950, in the post–World War II period (1939–1945) writers such as Lowenthal and Guterman (1949), Adorno et al. (1950), and Horkheimer (1959) conducted quantitative and qualitative research dedicated to investigating the correlations between ideology and the sociological and psychological factors of large-scale adherence to authoritarianism. In general terms, they observed that socially shared perceptions about the apparent decline of traditional patterns and the inability to deal with changes in society helped to foster hatred of various groups (Jews, blacks, women, sexual dissidents, etc.), preparing the social and political terrain for the authoritarian order. The defense of tradition against degeneration has thus emerged as one of the strongest mobilizing forces for political currents that include Nazism and fascism but also for racist and xenophobic discourse and practices in contexts that include North America.

The rise of far-right governments around the world in recent years has led various scholars to return to some of these theories and offer perspectives for understanding the emergence of the phenomenon in the twenty-first century. Works by writers including Brown, Gordon, and Pensky (2018) revisit debates on authoritarianism and seek out correlations between their contemporary emergence and the economic and social crises produced by neoliberalism and its impacts on crises of representation in liberal democracies. Writers such as Eatwell and Goodwin (2018) emphasize the importance of nationalism in the emergence of contemporary authoritarian populism in an effort to reframe the nativist, racist, homophobic, sexist, and antisecular symbols aimed at legitimizing far-right governments. As we draw from these debates, we begin to understand authoritarianism as a singular way of organizing the relationships between the state, society, and the market, undermining the legitimacy of conflict as a basic dimension of democracy and citizenship. As a result, we find it to be a question of transforming the state into an instrument for promoting the identification of ideas that include that of a national majority—who the people are and what their values are.

We argue that moral values, behavioral norms, and authoritarian ideas about society, politics, and the state do not come from a single group. Our data show that the social base of Bolsonarism is ideologically cohesive and significantly heterogeneous in terms of generation, levels of education and income, and occupation. Through this information, we will show that the social and political phenomenon of Bolsonarism is a pillar of contemporary Brazilian society, with support that runs through a wide range of groups.

THE AUTHORITARIAN PERCEPTION OF POLITICS AND THE SOCIAL FOUNDATIONS OF BOLSONARISM

Writings relating to the base supporting President Jair Bolsonaro have, to date, concentrated on the electoral period and factors that were key to his electoral victory in 2018. Hunter and Power (2019) point out that level of education, income, and religion help explain the retired captain's victory. With a strong anticorruption, political antiestablishment, and law-and-order discourse, Bolsonaro won over both the more stabilized middle class and the new middle class, a segment that benefited from the economic growth and inclusive policies of the Partido dos Trabalhadores (Workers' Party–PT) administrations (2003–2016). The conservative discourse on issues related to sexual traditionalism was a key factor in seducing another large group, evangelicals. Nicolau (2020), in an analysis that uses electoral data and polls, also highlights the importance of the evangelical vote and rejection of the PT, also known as "anti-PTism," in Bolsonaro's victory.

In a similar vein, Amaral (2020), using data from the 2018 Brazilian Electoral Study, shows that anti-PTism was one of the fundamental factors in the election results, and Duque and Smith (2019) make the same argument. Drawing on an analysis of panel-format research, Rennó (2020) shows that Bolsonaro voters were aligned with his conservative discourse on moral and social issues and his liberal approach on economic issues and says that this is a new phenomenon in Brazilian politics that is likely to persist.

Our analysis is different from these others in that it does not try to explain Bolsonaro's victory but examines which groups have formed the basis of stable support for him even after the severe economic and health crises that hit the country in the first half of 2020. We focus on the 25 percent of those interviewed in the "Face of Democracy" survey who said that they really liked Jair Bolsonaro. We will call this group "Bolsonarists" and address an issue that, until now, has been overlooked by empirical studies: the significantly authoritarian perception of politics and society that establishes cohesion within it and the stability and resilience of Bolsonarism as a social and political phenomenon.

Our hypothesis begins with the observation that Bolsonaro's leadership promotes a synergy of two political and social phenomena that have been well-described in the literature: (1) a conservative, right-wing discourse that openly defends authoritarian regimes like those between 1964 and 1985 in Brazil and between 1973 and 1990 in Chile, a discourse identified by Coppedge (1997) and Power (2000) in processes of democratization in Latin America throughout the 1980s and 1990s but, as mentioned by Luna and Rovira (2014), less important in the early 2000s, and (2) the global emergence of similar movements in other parts of the world in which, defending what they call "authentic democracy," leaders attack the political establishment and institutions that exercise any control over the president (Levitsky and Ziblatt, 2018; Norris and Inglehart, 2019).

We focus on the convergence of Brazil's long tradition of authoritarianism and the transnational rise of authoritarian populism as fertile ground for unifying and consolidating the Bolsonarist group and suggest that this is the breeding ground for electorally competitive authoritarian leaderships in Brazil that will continue for quite some time to come.

The data we have analyzed come from the third phase of the "Face of Democracy" survey, which was conducted amidst the spread of the COVID-19 pandemic in Brazil and a major economic downturn.[5] The survey consisted of 1,000 telephone interviews made to persons over the age of 16 and had a 3.1 percent margin of error (C.I. 95 percent). Initially, we created two multivariate statistical models to analyze the impact of authoritarian perceptions on the scores given to President Jair Bolsonaro. Both models allow us to analyze the impact of each variable separately, taking all the others as constants. Our dependent variable is taken from the following question: "On the basis of your feelings, how would you score the following politicians on a scale of 1 to 10, in which 1 means that you don't like them at all and 10 means you like them a lot?" For the analysis, we grouped the responses into three categories[6]: 1–3 (dislike), 4–7 (neither especially like nor dislike), and 8–10 (like considerably). The first category reflected 47.5 percent of those interviewed and the second and third categories 26.8 percent and 24.7 percent, respectively.

To assess the level of authoritarian perception of politics, we put together an authoritarianism index that involved three questions in relation to whether a military coup would be justified in any of the following situations: (1) very high unemployment, (2) high crime rates, and (3) lots of corruption. The possible answers were 0–3, with 0 being rejection in all cases and 3 representing agreement.[7] The same measurement was used as a continuous variable.

The models also included the following control variables: (1) age; (2) level of education (incomplete and complete primary, incomplete and complete middle school, incomplete and complete high school, incomplete and complete higher education, and graduate education), used as a continuous variable; (3) income

TABLE 1
Determining Factors of Support for Jair Bolsonaro in June 2020

	Model 1		Model 2	
	B	B(Exp)	B	B(Exp)
Age	.005	1.005	.006	1.006
Level of education				
Family income	−.006	.994		
Occupation (formal worker)				
Impoverished informal worker			−.223	.800
Not impoverished informal worker			−.033	.968
Not part of the EAP			−.205	.815
Housewife			−.067	.935
Unemployed and potentially not seeking employment			−.014	.986
Sex (female)	.346*	1.413	.356*	1.428
Authoritarianism index	.367*	1.443	.359*	1.432

Source: The Face of Democracy (2020).
Note: Model 1: $N = 908$. Dependent variable: Score given to Jair Bolsonaro (1–3, 4–7, 8–10). Reference category in parentheses. Ordinal regression with negative log-log function. −2LL = 1,748.500. R2 Nagelkerke = 0.109. Maximum VIF = 1.496.
Model 2: $N = 908$. Dependent variable: Score given to Jair Bolsonaro (1–3, 4–7, 8–10). Reference category in parentheses. Ordinal regression with negative log-log function. −2LL = 1,724.709. R2 Nagelkerke = 0.113. Maximum VIF = 1.089.
*($p < 0.05$)

(up to 1, 1–2, 2–3, 3–5, and more than 5 monthly minimum wages), also used as a continuous variable; (4) occupation (impoverished informal worker [employed with no registration, self-employed, independent professional, entrepreneur, assistant, and apprentice with family income less than two monthly minimum wages]; not impoverished informal worker [employed with no registration, self-employed, independent professional, entrepreneur, assistant, and apprentice with family income more than two monthly minimum wages]; not part of the economically active population; housewife; formal worker [registered employee and public servant]; potentially no longer seeking employment; and unemployed).[8] and (5) sex (female, male). Positive coefficients indicate a higher probability of belonging to a higher score category. Because the occupation variable was assembled taking into account the family income declared by the person interviewed, we used two models, with income the variable in one and occupation in the other. Given the ordered distribution of the dependent variable categories, we decided to use ordinal regression models.

The variations related to age, level of education, and income, along with the different occupations, have no association with whether someone likes Bolsonaro more or less (Table 1). None of these variables was shown to be statistically significant. In other words, the data show substantial cross-sectional support for Bolsonaro—support that is not directly related to homogeneous social groups, at least from the point of view of their occupation, incomes, levels of education, and ages. Since it is impossible to characterize Bolsonarism's political base in terms of social stratification, it can only be understood in terms of the cross-cutting support found throughout different positions in such stratification.

By pointing out this transversality, we are not trying to highlight the fragility of the president's social and political base and the random nature of its support for him. Rather, our argument is that the social heterogeneity of the persons and groups that make up his base is fundamental to the popularity, wide reach, and persistence of Bolsonarism as a social and political phenomenon. In other words, it is a political response to a wide variety of social demands and disputes. Expanding on our argument, we maintain that Bolsonarism is an authoritarian activism that needs to be repeatedly reworked and reaffirmed in practice, what we call a "performative *golpismo*."[9]

However, as far as the gender variable is concerned, this transversality is not observed. In both models, this variable was statistically significant. Men were 40 percent more likely to like the president than women. This is not surprising and reflects the findings of Amaral (2020) and Nicolau (2020) in relation to the 2018 elections, when, for the first time, the gender variable appeared as a good way to predict presidential votes. On the basis of the data available to us, it is difficult to say whether this is part of a broad political divide that is being created in terms of issues, struggles, and conflicts related to gender. Reading the data in context, it is more likely that this result is associated with the aggressive rhetoric against women of then-Congressman Jair Bolsonaro. During the elections, this rhetoric was the catalyst for the #NotHim movement, which was responsible for the largest street protests held in opposition to the candidate in 2018.

One of the most visible faces of the Bolsonaro candidacy and his administration so far concerns the almost omnipresent vocalization of issues related to the status of women, marriage, and sexuality. The Bolsonaro administration created the Ministry of Women, Family, and Human Rights, which was led by Damares Alves, one of the administration's most active ministers in international forums. For example, at the September 2019 Demography Summit in Hungary, Alves said that "Brazil is now a pro-family nation" and that the country was willing to "lead a pro-family bloc in the UN,"[10] defending "a resounding no against gender ideology."[11] Also under the Bolsonaro administration, Brazilian diplomacy promoted an unprecedented turnaround with respect to its position in the UN with its veto of the use of the term "gender" in the organization's resolutions. This shows that gender policy was an important pillar both for the Bolsonaro administration and in relation to the set of values that mobilizes his support base. In this context, women become targets of public policies or moral or religious judgments that aim to discipline them and subordinate them to the authority and universal control of heterosexual men.[12]

While the lower level of female support for Bolsonarism may not mean a permanent social divide, it does help us to understand the ideological context specific to Bolsonarism as an opportunity to use language about the gender roles associated with males and females and norms of sexuality that generates hierarchies and excludes certain groups from the world. This authoritarianism depends on the existence of conflict, since it aims at the symbolic and material exclusion of groups, public policies, and economic, political, and social agendas.

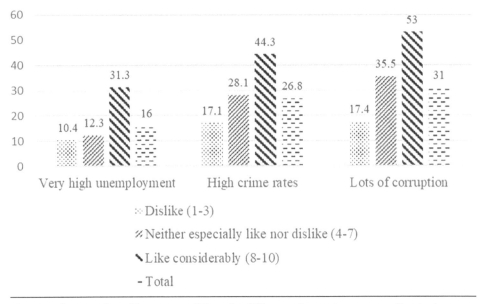

Figure 1. Support for military coups (%) under different circumstances according to degree of preference for Bolsonaro in June 2020 "Face of Democracy" survey. Those who did not answer or did not know how to answer were excluded from the results. N = 936, 942, and 936, respectively, for each intersection.

The authoritarianism variable, as expected, was statistically significant in both models. For each point above the index, the chance of a person's liking Bolsonaro increased by about 40 percent when all other social and demographic variables were held constant. This means that the authoritarian perception of politics is an important element in distinguishing among those who give higher scores to the retired captain.

With regard to the authoritarianism index, those who very much liked Bolsonaro reflected greater favorability to a coup than the other two groups, with the differences being statistically significant (C.I. 95 percent) (Figure 1). This means that the greater the support for Bolsonaro, the higher the index, with all the differences being statistically significant (C.I. 95 percent). Among those who very much liked Bolsonaro, the index average was 1.28; for those who somewhat liked him, it was 0.76, and for those who disliked him it was 0.44 (N = 915). In other words, on average, Bolsonarists supported at least one of the three alternatives mentioned in relation to a military coup.

The transversality of Bolsonarism can be explained in that it also corresponds to authoritarian activism[13] reinforced by elements that included limiting the state's role in the economy and anticorruption slogans. Is this really such a new phenomenon? If our argument is correct, there has always been a demand for leaders like Jair Bolsonaro in the postdemocratization period, but the political system that arose from the democratic transition barred the emergence of electorally viable right-wing populist-authoritarian alternatives. In recent years, the scenario has changed. The coincident discrediting of the political establishment through Operation Car Wash and the reduction of the constraints on electoral wins through the advance of new technologies and forms of political communication, as well as the international scenario, made the change possible.

THE TRANSVERSALITY OF BOLSONARISM:
POLITICS AND SOCIETY

The cohesion of the Bolsonarist group is based on an authoritarian activism that converges on the state, making it an active element in the modulation of different repertoires of political action, social struggle, and ways of reading, narrating, and interpreting the country, especially in the postdemocratization context. As a consequence, the transversality of the phenomenon refers to ideological content that remains constant and is repeatedly reinforced through Bolsonaro's performative *golpismo*. As examples of this tactic, we can cite the constant threats to democratic institutions, repeated positive mentions of the Brazilian civil-military dictatorship (1964–1985), and celebration of torture.

Bolsonarism has reorganized the ideological bases of authoritarianism in two main ways: rearranging the way in which social relations based on perceived differences between sexes, genders, races, and classes are expressed and catalyzing significant aspects of anticorruption agendas and actors. In the first three decades of postdemocratization, various activisms or union actions were focused on expanding social rights and the redistribution of wealth, promoting demands that were incorporated or recognized by the state in a variety of ways (Abers, Serafim, and Tatagiba, 2014). Taken together, institutional innovations and societal dynamics converged to establish new forms of negotiation with the state that influenced perceptions of social status and the material and symbolic differences that organize them (Penna and Rosa, 2015). The interaction between collective demands and institutional responses by the state was expressed, for example, in administrative mechanisms for land expropriation performed as part of agrarian reform, financing models for popular housing programs, legal changes that implemented ethnic-racial quotas, and national conferences to discuss public policies. This all helped to reorganize symbolic and material criteria and principles of social classification while focusing on the social and economic inequalities of Brazilian society (Bastos and Chaguri, 2017).

Whereas identification within the Bolsonarist group often arises out of negation or violent reaction to such dynamics and postdemocratization processes, Bolsonarism is a phenomenon that cuts across all parts of Brazilian society precisely because it reorganizes the imagination, solidarity, and individual and collective recognition in this society. In the terms used by Bolsonarism itself, "The world needs to be indivisible (*Brazil above all*), sexually binary (*boys in blue, girls in pink*), intellectually shallow (*stop whining*), and devoid of empathy and otherness (*majority rules*)" (Cavalcante, Chaguri, and Netto, 2019: 3). Through the construction of such antagonisms, Bolsonarism offers the cultural and material bases for an authoritarian view of both politics and society, connecting past and future to forge specific ties of solidarity and identification in the present. Bolsonarism as a social and political phenomenon affects the bases on which society recognizes itself, forging characteristic connections that lead to symbolic and material transformations in the postdemocratization period. These are expressed through the emergence and gradual institutional acceptance of policies like affirmative action in higher education, putting a real value on the minimum wage, and female ownership in income transfer programs that include the Bolsa Familia (Family Allowance).

Rather than deny such differences, which could reduce the reach and impact of Bolsonarist activism, Bolsonarism redrafts and reorganizes the social roles associated with men and women; this includes the grammar used to describe class relationships and the interaction with an authoritarian bias between the state and society. This bias is expressed, for example, in the rhetoric that the state and multilateral organizations like the UN, the World Trade Organization, and the World Health Organization use in the cause of limiting individual freedoms. Former Education Minister Abraham Weintraub summarized the issue by taking up a megaphone and saying, "Freedom is the most important thing in a democracy. And the first thing they will try to silence is freedom of expression." He made this statement to a group of activists who were waiting for the then-minister following his testimony to the Federal Police in an investigation of hate crimes. The activists' banners demanded "Out with Communism, Out with Globalism, Out with the New World Order."[14]

Our argument is that the notion of freedom is always affirmed in opposition to social pacts and the institutional rule of promoting collective life in the public sphere. The same applies, therefore, to the seeing the state as the enemy of individual freedom. However, it is not a question of eliminating the state but one of opposing public policies or legal and institutional rules that promote social protection, recognize the right to differences, and, especially, agree on the rallying of the public in relation to private ways of organizing the social aspect of life.

To explore the dimension of authoritarianism itself, we move on to the second point: the recurrence and the capacity for mobilization that the anticorruption agenda finds in Brazil, especially within the Bolsonarist group. We initially believed that authoritarianism and the mobilization generated by anticorruption agendas or demands did not coincide. On the contrary, we now point out that anticorruption mobilization is a key component of authoritarianism.

The "Face of Democracy" survey asked people what they thought was the country's biggest problem, and they were given the option to respond freely. Even in a context in which the novel coronavirus pandemic had already caused tens of thousands of deaths in Brazil, among those who liked Bolsonaro very much 29.6 percent said that the country's biggest problem was corruption. The pandemic was mentioned by 22.7 percent (Figure 2). The percentages of persons who found corruption to be the country's biggest problem increased alongside scores given to Bolsonaro, with a statistically significant difference between them (C.I. 95 percent).

Almost ubiquitous in discussion about the country, corruption has become the preferred way to talk about the impasse between public and private matters in contemporary Brazil. The tension of political order in a postdemocratization period apparently reached its peak in the process that led to Bolsonaro's winning the presidency. The ideological transversality of Bolsonarism is related to his offering a way of reorganizing the conflict between reproduction of inequality and the emergence of democratizing options. Historically, the stalemate between the public and private sectors has been expressed in terms of issues like corruption, patrimonialism, and conflicts between state, society, market, and family, a key repertoire through which ideas were produced, disputed, and put into circulation (Buarque de Hollanda, 1933; Faoro, 1957; Franco, 1969).

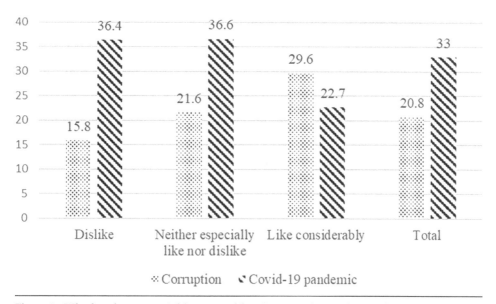

Figure 2. Whether the country's biggest problem is corruption or the pandemic (%) according to degree of preference for Bolsonaro in June 2020 "Face of Democracy" survey. Those who did not answer or did not know how to answer were excluded from the results. $N = 990$.

Bolsonarism is the electoral expression of a theoretical debate and a set of political conflicts that have been ongoing throughout Brazil's republican history, offering ethical, moral, and authoritarian policies for establishing relationships between the state, the society, and the market. Reflecting on the role of the anticorruption agenda in the mobilization of the middle classes in recent years, Cavalcante (2018) points out that the association between corruption and the distortion of free competition is one of the most effective ideas for sparking the political mobilization of these groups, building a social base around this agenda that defends "the *impartial* agents of the Judiciary, while distrusting the *populist* character of public servants' intentions" (Cavalcante, 2018: 118). Despite his three decades in Congress, Bolsonaro's rise was a product of the impression that he was an antiestablishment candidate committed to the anticorruption agenda. This impression helped to bring together part of his support base, which has continued mobilizing and producing an identity within the Bolsonarist group that we analyze here.

Once elected president, and with two of his children holding public office and involved in corruption charges and scandals, Bolsonaro found himself struggling to maintain associations between the anticorruption agenda and the morality of "good men," a symbolic pillar of, for example, the backing and reproduction of Operation Car Wash that was manifested in his support for the key role in it of his former minister of justice, Sérgio Moro. Without the option of being able to abandon the anticorruption agenda, he repositioned it to make his support base more cohesive and stable. As a result, symbolically and materially moving away from Operation Car Wash is far from abandoning the often-repeated idea that the Brazilian government is overrun by corrupt actors and has a long way to go to heal the nation.

Corruption here is not synonymous with the misappropriation of public assets; rather, it is associated with individual choices, ideological choices, or political positions, thereby offering ethical and moral justifications for authoritarianism. It has become associated with left-wing ideologies and public policies that promote the recognition of differences and the protection of the rights of women, blacks, or the LGBTQI+ population. Within the Bolsonarist group, this association is retranslated in terms of the need for honorable individuals to either restore morality to institutions or promote public policies capable of protecting the nation and the family.

The association between authoritarianism and the anticorruption agenda is one of the key points of support for Bolsonarism as a social and political phenomenon that cuts through all sectors of Brazilian society. The anticorruption agenda offers material and symbolic means of disqualification of difference and justification of inequality, operating to legitimize the fundamental reconversion led by authoritarianism: the reorganization of the state to promote policies and actions that can identify the Brazilian people and their values. Therefore, Bolsonarism offers renewed social and political bases for authoritarianism in the postdemocratization context.

FINAL CONSIDERATIONS: THE FUTURE OF BOLSONARISM

The existence of leaders and political parties with popular support combining social conservatism, political authoritarianism, and populist practices is far from a recent phenomenon that is exclusively Brazilian or Latin American. The list is long and has been growing in recent years in different parts of the world: Marine Le Pen in France, Viktor Órban in Hungary, Donald Trump in the United States, Geert Wilders in the Netherlands, and Rodrigo Duterte in the Philippines are examples of such leaders. In Europe alone, Norris and Inglehart (2019: 236–237) have counted up to 16 electorally competitive parties with these characteristics existing in 15 different countries. The combination of elements responsible for the political rise of these leaders and parties varies according to the institutional and social contexts of each country, but there are several recurrent characteristics: nationalism, disdain for civil rights, and the defense of tradition and stability, generally founded on unitary notions of Judeo-Christian religiosity, the family, and the nation and making conflicts and disputes into an issue of *us* against *them*.

Norris and Inglehart (2019), seeking to understand the phenomenon in Europe and the United States, developed the theory of "cultural backlash," pointing to an increase in levels of education and urbanization and circulation of ethnic groups that led to a silent revolution beginning in the 1970s favoring the debate and the eventual implementation of more inclusive, liberal policies, notably those with regard to gender equality and the protection of cultural, religious, or ethnic minorities (Taylor, 2007). This process ended up deepening cultural divides in these countries, producing a reaction led by groups that had lost their culturally hegemonic status in society. Feeling their social position to have come under threat, these groups began to defend agendas that were predominantly conservative in terms of social values and increasingly authoritarian in relation to politics, blaming the economic and political establishment for not listening to or for distancing itself from the real interests of the people. This generated a demand for socially conservative and politically authoritarian leaders and parties on the political scene (Norris and Inglehart, 2019: 32–64).

This theory only partly applies to Brazil. Although there is certainly an element of reaction to changes that have occurred in the past 30 years with regard to the inclusion of social groups and the recognition of their demands and rights, the Brazilian case has a component that is not found in Europe and North America. While in the older democracies postmaterialist political agendas (environmental conservation, gender equality, minority rights, etc.) gained strength after a generalized sense of material security had been achieved (Inglehart, 1977; 1993), in Brazil the past three decades have seen postmaterialist agendas come to overlap with the issue of material security itself. The extent of material inequality in Brazil is related to the dynamics of the creation of differences based on race and gender under slavery as a way of organizing the workforce and under patriarchy as a way of organizing the family and collective life. In other words, material inequalities are so deeply linked to gender and race issues, for example, that materialist and postmaterialist policy agendas have become practically indissociable, translating into the crosscutting nature of Bolsonarist support throughout society. As a result, Brazil's social and political dynamics are marked by an ongoing redistributive conflict that, in various ways and over time, produces and reproduces symbolic and material exclusions (and inclusions) of varied economic and social groups, policies, and agendas.

In the specific case of the rise of Jair Bolsonaro, Bolsonarists articulate an authoritarian political response to this conflict. Authoritarianism is a political option that seeks to justify and normalize inequalities and material and symbolic differences among groups and classes. This characteristic is responsible for an almost daily reiteration and reaffirmation of what we have called a performative *golpismo*—the mobilization of material and symbolic imagery such as that of the 1964 military coup and the capacity of the military to bring order to the state and cure the nation, implementing the popular will even if it means going beyond constitutional limits.

What does this mean for the future of Bolsonarism? First and foremost, it means that Brazil is facing something more complex than the essentially cultural divide seen in the older democracies. Beyond an issue of dominance in terms of values, the country is experiencing an intense dispute over the distribution of scarce resources during an economic crisis and reviewing the historical bases of the subordination of certain social groups. Secondly, it means that politically relevant and authoritarian conservative social bases have gained space in public debate and will be key in shaping the day-to-day political workings for some time to come. These bases had previously been dormant and merely needed a competitive political agent (Zechmeister, 2015) and a favorable international environment to come together. Blocked by institutional determining factors between 1989 and 2014, as well as by a world in which the silent revolution prevailed, this agent emerged from the crisis that hit the Brazilian political system after Operation Car Wash and from the international cultural backlash that we have mentioned. Resilient support for Jair Bolsonaro is something that goes beyond the "myth," charisma, or individual personality of the president. Bolsonarism reveals a consolidation of authoritarianism as a viable political option that could well survive any failures of his administration. The struggle will be long, and Bolsonarism is only a name.

NOTES

1. https://www.washingtonpost.com/opinions/global-opinions/jair-bolsonaro-risks-lives-byminimizing-the-coronavirus-pandemic/2020/04/13/6356a9be-7da6-11ea-9040-68981f488eed_story.html.

2. Data available at www.datafolha.com.br.

3. The Instituto da Democracia e da Democratização da Comunicação (Institute for Democracy and Democratization of Communication—IDDC) includes research groups from the Universidade Federal de Minas Gerais, the Universidade Estadual de Rio de Janeiro, the Universidade Estadual de Campinas, and the Universidade de Brasília with funding from the Conselho Nacional de Desenvolvimento Científico e Tecnológico, the Coordinação de Aperfeiçoamente de Pessoal de Nível Superior, and the Fundação de Amparo à Pesquisa do Estado de Minas Gerais.

4. For an overview of authoritarianism in Brazilian thinking and society, see Schwarcz (2020).

5. On June 5, 2020, the country had 35,047 deaths caused by COVID-19 and 646,006 cases. As of the end of May, according to data from the PNAD Contínua, the country had a 13.1 percent unemployment rate, the lowest employment level since the survey's origin in 2012. Data available at http://www.ibge.gov.br.

6. We chose to put the answers into categories because the distribution of answers was not normal.

7. The reliability test alpha was 0.827.

8. The original alternatives were the following: (1) informal worker living in poverty, (2) worker in the informal sector not living in poverty, (3) not part of the economically active population, (4) housewife, (5) worker in the formal sector, and (6) potentially no longer seeking work and unemployed. We thank Bárbara Castro for her help.

9. We owe the term "performative *golpismo*" to Amy Erica Smith, who wrote it in a personal letter. To understand its meaning, see Smith (2020).

10. https://noticias.uol.com.br/internacional/ultimas-noticias/2019/09/21/com-damares-cupula-da-demografia-ataca-onu-feminismo-e-homossexuais.htm.

11. https://jamilchade.blogosfera.uol.com.br/2019/09/14/governo-bolsonaro-articula-alianca-internacional-pro-familia/.

12. For example, this is the case of the national plan for the prevention of early sexual risk that was announced by Minister Damares Alves in January 2020. https://oglobo.globo.com/sociedade/damares-reconhece-abstinencia-sexual-como-politica-publica-em-construcao-1-24182738.

13. Steve Bannon, one of the most influential generators of far-right discourse and practices in the world, often reaffirms the need to foster right-wing populist activism. In a 2018 interview, he announced the creation of the movement, a political consultancy based in Brussels (Belgium), whose objective would be to provide "the infrastructure for the global populist movement." https://www.independent.co.uk/news/steve-bannon-moving-europe-movement-foundation-far-right-wing-politics-george-soros-a8458641.html.

14. https://noticias.uol.com.br/politica/ultimas-noticias/2020/06/04/weintraub-novo-recurso-stf.htm?cmpid.

REFERENCES

Abers, Rebecca, Lizandra Serafim, and Luciana Tatagiba
    2014 "Repertórios de interação estado-sociedade em um estado heterogêneo: a experiência na Era Lula." *Dados* 57: 325–357.
Adorno, Theodor W., Else Frenkel-Brunswik, Daniel J. Levinson, and R. Nevitt Sanford
    1950 *The Authoritarian Personality*. New York: Harper and Row.

Amaral, Oswaldo E. do
  2020 "The victory of Jair Bolsonaro according to the Brazilian electoral study of 2018." *Brazilian Political Science Review* 14 (1): 1–13.
Bastos, Elide Rugai and Mariana M. Chaguri
  2017 "A terra no Brasil contemporâneo: notas para um debate," pp. 123–140 in André Botelho and Heloísa Starling (eds.), *República e democracia: Impasses do Brasil contemporâneo*. Belo Horizonte: Editora UFMG.
Brown, Wendy, Peter E. Gordon, and Max Pensky
  2018 *Authoritarianism: Three Inquiries in Critical Theory*. Chicago: University of Chicago Press.
Buarque de Holanda, Sérgio
  1936 *Raízes do Brasil*. Rio de Janeiro: José Olympio Editora.
Cavalcante, Sávio Machado
  2018 "Classe média, meritocracia e corrupção." *Crítica Marxista* 46: 103–125.
Cavalcante, Sávio Machado, Mariana M. Chaguri, and Michel Nicolau Netto
  2019 "O conservadorismo liberal do homem médio." *Época on-line*. https://epoca.globo.com/artigo-conservadorismo-liberal-do-homem-medio-23358236.
Coppedge, Michael
  1997 *Strong Parties and Lame Ducks: Presidential Partyarchy and Factionalism in Venezuela*. Stanford, CA: Stanford University Press.
Duque, Debora and Amy Erica Smith
  2019 "The establishment upside down: a year of change in Brazil." *Revista de Ciencia Política* 39 (2): 165–189.
Eatwell, Roger and Matthew Goodwin
  2018 *National Populism: The Revolt against Liberal Democracy*. London: Penguin.
Faoro, Raymundo
  1957 *Os donos do poder: Formação do patronato político brasileiro*. Porto Alegre: Editora Globo.
Franco, Maria Sylvia de Carvalho
  1969 *Homens livres na ordem escravocrata*. São Paulo: Instituto de Estudos Brasileiros/USP.
Horkheimer, Max
  1959 "Authoritarianism and the family today," pp. 359–374 in Ruth Nanda Anshen (ed.), *The Family: Its Function and Destiny*. New York: Harper.
Hunter, Wendy and Timothy J. Power
  2019 "Bolsonaro and Brazil's illiberal backlash." *Journal of Democracy* 30 (1): 68–82.
Inglehart, Ronald
  1977 *The Silent Revolution: Changing Values and Political Styles among Western Publics*. Princeton: Princeton University Press.
  1993 "Democratização em perspectiva global." *Opinião Pública* 1 (1): 9–67.
Levitsky, Steven and Daniel Ziblatt
  2018 *How Democracies Die*. New York: Broadway Books.
Lowenthal, Leo and Norbert Guterman
  1949 *Prophets of Deceit: A Study of the Techniques of the American Agitator*. New York: Harper.
Luna, Juan Pablo and Cristóbal Rovira Kaltwasser
  2014 *The Resilience of the Latin American Right*. Baltimore: Johns Hopkins University Press.
Nicolau, Jairo
  2020 *O Brasil dobrou à direita: Uma radiografia da eleição de Bolsonaro em 2018*. Rio de Janeiro: Zahar.
Norris, Pippa and Ronald Inglehart
  2019 *Cultural Backlash: Trump, Brexit, and Authoritarian Populism*. Cambridge: Cambridge University Press.
Penna, Camila and Marcelo C. Rosa
  2015 "Estado, movimentos e reforma agrária no Brasil: reflexões a partir do Incra." *Lua Nova: Revista de Cultura e Política*, no. 95, 57–86.
Power, Timothy
  2000 *The Political Right in Postauthoritarian Brazil: Elites, Institutions, and Democratization*. University Park: Pennsylvania State University Press
Rennó, Lúcio
  2020 "The Bolsonaro voter: issue positions and vote choice in the 2018 Brazilian presidential elections." *Latin American Politics and Society* 62: 3–23.

Schwarcz, Lilia M.
　2020 *Sobre o autoritarismo brasileiro*. São Paulo: Companhia das Letras.
Smith, Amy Erica
　2020 "COVID vs. democracy: Brazil's populist playbook." *Journal of Democracy* 31 (4): 76–90.
Taylor, Charles
　2007 *A Secular Age*. Cambridge: Harvard University Press.
Vianna, Oliveira
　1920 *Populações meridionais do Brasil: História, organização, psicologia*. São Paulo: Monteiro Lobato.
　1949 *Instituições políticas brasileiras*. Rio de Janeiro: José Olympio Editora.
Zechmeister, Elizabeth
　2015 "Left-right identifications and the Latin American voter," pp. 195–225 in Ryan Carlin, Matthew Singer, and Elizabeth Zechmeister (eds.), *The Latin American Voter*. Ann Arbor: University of Michigan Press.

Bolsonaro, the Last Colonizer

by
Manuel Domingos Neto and Luis Gustavo Guerreiro Moreira
Translated by
Nick Ortiz

The traditional relationship between the Brazilian state and indigenous peoples is based on the state's "protection." Under the ultraconservative Bolsonaro government, the state has been taken over by elites with rural and extractive capital who plan on exploiting the Amazon rain forest at any cost and see indigenous peoples as an obstacle to their goal. The military also has a noteworthy position in this offensive, which strikes at the heart of what are considered human rights. The legislative and judiciary branches continue to confront this ambiguous policy, which is accompanied by laws, statutes, national agreements, and international conventions that lack clarity and precision. If Bolsonaro were to be reelected it might mean the extinction of surviving indigenous ethnicities.

A relação tradicional entre o Estado brasileiro e os povos originários é baseada na "tutela" do Estado. O governo ultraconservador de Bolsonaro reflete a captura do Estado pelas elites do capital agrário e extrativista que pretendem dispor da floresta amazônica a qualquer custo, considerando os povos originários como obstáculo à sua agenda. Os militares têm posição de destaque nesta ofensiva que afronta as noções elementares de direitos humanos. Ora, os poderes Legislativo e Judiciário lidam com essa política de maneira ambígua, acompanhando leis, estatutos e convenções nacionais e internacionais de forma pouco precisa e pouco clara. Se Bolsonaro for reeleito, isso poderá acelerar a extinção das etnias indígenas sobreviventes.

Keywords: Indigeneity, Indigenous peoples, Colonialism, Tutelary state, Bolsonaro regime

One of the main tenets of President Jair Bolsonaro's electoral campaign was a radical change in the Brazilian government's policy toward indigenous peoples. Now it is part of a neoconservative ideology supported by a large part of Brazilian society. With the backing of ruralists, the military, and evangelicals, Bolsonaro has put in place racist, ethnocentric, and anti-indigenous policies that threaten the very survival of indigenous peoples. He is the head of a state that has declared war against indigenous rights. This radical break with past

Manuel Domingos Neto is a retired professor from the Universidade Federal de Ceará and the Universidade Federal Fluminense and a former president of the Associação Brasileira de Estudos de Defesa and the Conselho Nacional de Desenvolvimento Científico e Tecnológico. Luís Gustavo Guerreiro Moreira has Ph.D. in public policy from the Universidade Estadual de Ceará and is an indigenist at the Fundação Nacional do Índio, a researcher at the Observatório das Nacionalidades, and the editor of *Tensões Mundiais*. Nick Ortiz is a writer, researcher, linguist, and translator with experience in translation relating to Latin American history and politics.

LATIN AMERICAN PERSPECTIVES, Issue 248, Vol. 50 No. 1, January 2023, 47–63
DOI: 10.1177/0094582X221147598
© 2023 Latin American Perspectives

policies supports the interests of farmers, loggers, and miners who see existing groups as a nuisance that must be eliminated.

A complex institutional arrangement has been established to curtail the powers of nongovernmental organizations (NGOs) and social movements. The Government Secretariat, which has the task of maintaining a dialogue and interaction with civil society organizations, has become an institution that supervises, coordinates, and monitors the activities of international bodies and NGOs. The role of these organizations in defending indigenous groups has long been denounced by the military as a threat to national sovereignty, and the same has occurred with various public agencies that are tasked with defending the environment. Government directives have a military orientation because of the number of military officers chosen to fill important positions in the state apparatus.

Soon after assuming the presidency, Bolsonaro signed Provisional Measure 870,[1] which transferred power from the Fundação Nacional do Índio (National Indian Foundation—FUNAI), the institution responsible for enforcing Brazilian policies toward indigenous peoples, to the Instituto Nacional de Colonização (National Institute for Land Settlement and Agrarian Reform—INCRA), a body subordinate to the Ministry of Agriculture that is charged with demarcating indigenous lands. The measure weakened FUNAI's ability to fulfill its primary goal, which was overseeing the demarcation process for indigenous lands.

This initiative was challenged in court, and in August 2019 the plenum of the Supreme Court terminated the provisional measure, citing Article 231 of the 1988 Constitution and International Labor Organization (ILO) Convention 169, of which Brazil is a signatory. Article 6 of the Convention requires that the government "consult the peoples concerned, through appropriate procedures and in particular through their representative institutions, whenever consideration is being given to legislative or administrative measures which may affect them directly," and Article 14 recognizes "the rights of ownership and possession of the peoples concerned over the lands which they traditionally occupy" (ILO, 1989).

The obsession of the current government with imposing a ruralist agenda on Brazilian policy with regard to indigenous peoples and the haste with which it did so generated a climate of political instability. The three branches of the Republic (executive, legislative, and judiciary) are the setting for disputes on a wide range of issues that end up judicializing politics and, in some cases, politicizing the judicial system. Many of these issues fall beyond the jurisdiction of the congressional courts and cabinet and therefore go to the Supreme Court and overload its docket. The rural sector connected with agribusiness is intent on halting the demarcation of indigenous lands.[2] According to FUNAI, 440 demarcation processes have so far been completed. These areas make up 12.6 percent of Brazil's territory, mainly in the Amazon, and are subject to strict environmental and social protection laws backed by international treaties and agreements.

Policies with regard to indigenous peoples are strategic actions taken by nation-states to impose their will on the way the cultures of these peoples are identified. Generally, their form and content are the product of demands made by indigenous peoples. Despite Brazilian legislation's having been updated since redemocratization (the product of years of struggle by indigenous movements), the institutions that enforce policies with regard to indigenous peoples have imposed on them a regime known as "monitored autonomy." The 1988 Constitution led to many important changes in these policies, among which was the full recognition of indigenous autonomy. This autonomy applied to indigenous social and political organizations, their cultures, and their ways of life. However, there were contradictions in it. The assimilationist and integrationist standard that dated to the colonial period had been continued by the Estado Novo (1937–1945) and the military dictatorship (1964–1985) and even survived the democratic advances of recent years.

The government's indigenous policy is officially based on the idea of an interethnic relationship that rejects the notion of forced integration on the pretext of "national communion." This relationship goes beyond the concept of a nation in which indigenous peoples must play the role of pacified "noble savage" in an unequal relationship with people who are not indigenous. Even the state claims to reject this ethnocentric view. Brazilian society envisions an exclusionary world that ignores the complexities of being human (Krenak, 2001).

The struggles of indigenous peoples influence the way in which they are governed rather than the way in which the state is organized. There is hardly talk of struggles for social emancipation. Instead, in the best-case scenario of political liberalism, the state is limited to creating conditions that resolve issues such as access to clean water, electric energy, or social benefits. It tends to play down the link between the fight for indigenous rights and its social and historical dimensions. The pursuit of immediate comfort in the context of a dominant social model is presented by liberal modernity as the only possible direction for state policy. Even with the rise of more leftist governments such as those of the period when the Partido dos Trabalhadores (Workers' Party— PT) dominated the presidency, little happened with regard to resolving the lingering issues associated with the way the state treats indigenous groups. Jair Bolsonaro's government represents a step in the wrong direction because it officially opposes the indigenous movement and its campaign for indigenous rights. The new way in which institutions are organized affects the ability of executive bodies to formulate policies with regard to indigenous peoples, and it reflects the wishes of the miners, farmers, fraudsters, and military officers who support this arrangement.

What differentiates the Bolsonaro government from its predecessors is its openly anti-indigenous orientation. In 2017, when Bolsonaro visited the state of Mato Grosso do Sul, he stated his opposition to the demarcation of new indigenous lands in Brazil: "There will not be another square centimeter demarcated." In making his position against the indigenous movement very clear, he was applauded by the most reactionary elements of Brazilian society. On various occasions, especially during a speech he gave at an event celebrating the inauguration of the Conselho da Amazônia (Amazonian Council), he denounced what he considered a "demarcation industry for indigenous lands" and alleged that the demarcation process was tied to corruption (Murukawa and Walendorff, 2020). Bolsonaro is a vigorous supporter of mineral exploration and agriculture on indigenous lands (through demarcation or occupying them through traditional means) without taking into account that the law requires that any activity in these areas be socially and environmentally sustainable.

As the recently elected president, he began to make racist comments and promised to "treat indigenous peoples as Brazilians" and to "provide means by which the Indians can be integrated into Brazilian society." Ignoring the constitution and the international treaties that Brazil had signed, he held firm on his promise to allow the leasing of indigenous lands for the purpose of expanding agribusiness (*Folha de São Paulo*, December 1, 2018). The president is a firm believer in an evolutionary ideology for Brazilian society and holds that being indigenous is a temporary condition between barbarism and civilization. This perception is a relic of a colonialist ideology that continues to influence Latin American societies and remains active in many institutions. The perception of an indigenous person as a second-class citizen was formally abandoned with the 1988 Constitution and ILO Convention 169. In practice, the idea persists that indigenous peoples are incapable of evolving without "de-Indianizing" or, rather, submitting to the norms of the dominant civilization. As Manuela Carneiro da Cunha (2012: 60) argues, this perception assigns to the laws of nature something that is essentially the product of politics. This "consolation" works for everyone except its victims.

COLONIALISM AND SELF-DETERMINATION

Pablo Gonzalez Casanova (1965: 27) argues that political boundaries directly or indirectly influence the formulation and use of sociological categories such as colonialism. Certain categories have emerged to address the internal problems of imagined nations and their demands for demarcation of their boundaries. Because this process has failed to acknowledge the interconnections of indigenous peoples, the possibility arises that these categories may also be used to explain international problems and vice versa. The concept of "colonialism" is an international phenomenon that explains the asymmetrical relationships between peoples and nations. According to Gonzalez Casanova, colonialism and the colonial structure as ideas promoted notions of domination and submission between groups in national projects as well as internationally, and indigenous peoples were among the most affected by power relations imposed by capitalist development.

Aníbal Quijano (2010) came up with the concept of "the coloniality of power" to classify and systematize the sociopolitical effects of colonialism. This concept allows a new understanding of colonial power structures as structures that did not disappear with the achievement of independence or national sovereignty but were constantly being reconstructed and redefined within the modern state. The notion of coloniality makes it impossible to discuss the modern without considering race and ethnicity. Modernity is intrinsically linked to the colonial experience. Colonialism is fundamental to the creation of a global capitalist system. Structures relating to power and subordination directed by mechanisms of the world system are reproduced in the construction of nation-states.

Boaventura de Sousa Santos (2004) argues that colonialism was among the greatest watershed moments in Western history and was seen as a civilizing mission. This argument is captured by Quijano, who sees the colonialism model as hegemonic since the conquest of the Americas. Ideas such as race, work, space, and the people are articulated through the need to obtain capital for the benefit of white Europeans. Colonialism is manifest not in the inclusion of non-Europeans in the process of modernization but in their exploitation to meet the demands of capital and produce the benefits expected by the upper classes presenting themselves as models for progress and civilization. The idea of the coloniality of power refers to the persistence of a colonial logic after the end of colonialism. The survival of a colonial mentality worldwide is seen in the exploitation by global capital of poor workers in the Global South who are considered racially and ethnically inferior to those from the North who led the capitalist expansion. States are forced to adopt public policies formulated by multilateral organizations such as the International Monetary Fund (IMF) and the World Bank in order to satisfy those with political and economic hegemony.

According to Grosfoguel (2008: 224), "Peripheral zones remain in a colonial situation, even though they are no longer under a colonial regime." He argues that the old idea that societies evolve according to a one-dimensional historical pattern that begins with precapitalist modes of production and ends with a capitalist system should be abandoned. Rather, everyone is imbedded in a world capitalist system that articulates different forms of work in accordance with a racial classification of the world population that determines "the social geography of capitalism" (Quijano, 2000: 208).

Quijano (2000: 234–235) argues that the idea of "a national social interest" relates to the existence of a national society dominated by a national bourgeoisie that controls the nation-state. A power structure is configured along these lines. He contends that the coloniality of self, knowledge, and power is characterized by an antihistoricity that ignores past occurrences of violence and tutelage. It underestimates the impact of civil and Eurocentric processes on the national space in an effort to legitimize the power disparity that these conflicts represent. In fact, social policies disregard ideas (such as culture, history, and territory) in order to impose demands that, in general, damage the groups that should be their beneficiaries.

The struggle of indigenous peoples has become more noticeable in the past 30 years. Once the nation-state became a universal entity and model for political development, indigenous demands for land, resources, rights, and self-governance became challenges to the hegemonic system imposed on them. Through the use of new modes of communication and cultural exchange, the political consciousness of indigenous peoples has increased both in the developed countries and in the periphery. Activists have perfected the use of legal tools in the international and domestic realm to defend indigenous populations.

The right of indigenous peoples to determine their own lives has been incorporated into various documents that led to the United Nations Declaration on the Rights of Indigenous Peoples in 2007[3] and were mostly established in the first article of the United Nations Charter: "All peoples have the right to self-determination. By virtue of that right they freely determine their political status and freely pursue their economic, social and cultural development." The concept of self-determination is one of the most misunderstood and obscure concepts in Brazilian society and the one most prone to rejection and sabotage by the state. Article 3 of the UN Declaration reads as follows: "Indigenous peoples

have the right to self-determination. By virtue of that right they freely determine their political status and freely pursue their economic, social, and cultural
development." Article 4 of ILO Convention 169 says, "Indigenous peoples, in
exercising their right to self-determination, have the right to autonomy or self-
government in matters relating to their internal and local affairs, as well as
ways and means for financing their autonomous functions." The idea of self-
determination and the legal precedents that established it have been used by
indigenous peoples throughout the world. The fight for separate rights has
meant the replacement of monolithic state structures with other structures that
are more open and oriented toward cultural plurality.

The concept has also been used as a form of resistance to coloniality, as it has
in the struggle surrounding the demarcation of indigenous lands and in the
opposition to the construction of large infrastructure projects such as hydroelectric plants and businesses in indigenous areas. The fight to empower minority ethnic groups requires that state actors and others recognize the demands
of indigenous activists and the consequent need for conflict resolution despite
the claims of political elites that these groups threaten national unity and sovereignty. Colonial domination demanded the elimination of spaces inhabited
by indigenous peoples and imposed a kind of working subordination that ele-
vated the interests of elites and forced indigenous peoples to conform to policies that were detrimental to their interests. Sometimes this subordinate
relationship was associated with organizational and decision-making autonomy for indigenous communities. Instead of recognizing indigenous autonomy, the state opted for a deliberate denial of cultural and indigenous
heterogeneity. In doing so it rejected Caio Prado Júnior's idea of an ongoing
historical process of transition from a colony to a nation that remains heavily
constrained by the colonial past. Cultural diversity persists by taking refuge in
organizational forms that are more or less isolated or different from the national
project. The old colony has continued to foster destructive behavior relating to
indigenous expressions of identity. The fight has continued for judicial-consti-
tutional recognition of indigenous autonomy in Brazil, and as a result some
state institutions have been able to preserve the principle of self-determination
to a certain extent.

STATE TUTELAGE OF INDIGENOUS PEOPLES

Brazilian policies with regard to indigenous peoples were originally organized according to positivist principles. Positivism was the guiding ideology of
the military after the Proclamation of the Republic in 1889 and remained influential into the first decades of the new regime. The Serviço de Proteção ao Índio
(Indian Protection Service—SPI), eventually the Serviço de Proteção ao Índio e
Localização de Trabalhadores Nacionais (Service for the Protection of Indians
and the Placement of National Workers—SPILTN)—was founded in 1910, and
its goal was to fulfill the government's responsibilities with regard to two
groups in Brazilian society that could not be more alien and distant from one
another: indigenous peoples and so-called national workers (Freire, 2007). The
objective was to "nationalize" the Indians (or "forest dwellers") and transform

them into peasants—to integrate them into the local economy and what was called the "national community." This was an expression that was frequently used by intellectuals who, before World War I, argued with each other about the political significance of nationality and the legitimacy of the state (see Neto and Martins, 2006). Foremost in the minds of policy makers was preventing indigenous peoples from living near the border or becoming isolated, the fear being that they might become rebellious and ally themselves with neighboring nation-states. In the 1930s the SPI was incorporated into the Special Department for Borders of the Ministry of War, which was headed by Marshal Cândido Rondon (Lima, 1992: 164–165), who claimed to be an expert in Brazil's rural interior. Over time, it fell under the purview of other ministries: the Ministry of Agriculture, Industry, and Commerce and the Ministry of the Interior. For these various institutions, indigenous peoples had to become part of the national community in formation. Considerable resources were spent on the integration of indigenous peoples into the capitalist system, which represented in practice their extinction as indigenous peoples.

The state developed various strategies for creating national workers, among them a generic classification of designated indigenous peoples as members of either the urban or the rural working class. The proletarianization of indigenous peoples was part of a project that sought to create an "imagined community." This idea establishes the notion of a collective "we" despite the intentions, inequalities, and hierarchies that lie behind its creation. The 1916 Civil Code recognized the "relative inability" of indigenous peoples to engage in the practices of civil life and the consequent need to subject them to a tutelary regime. A series of special laws and regulations was based on the degree to which indigenous peoples could become part of Brazilian "civilization" (Cordeiro, 1999: 5).

This trend was reinforced after the 1930 Revolution and even more so after the inauguration of the Estado Novo in 1937. This dictatorship, presided over by Getúlio Vargas and backed by the military, used every brutal and sophisticated resource at its disposal to build a Brazilian nation. Waves of Northeasterners, so-called rubber soldiers, were sent to the Amazon to take over control of the region. The colonization of the Amazon was even described using military terminology. The outbreak of World War II brought what was called "military patriotism," the idea that it was the sacred duty of all Brazilians to support the regime's dictatorial policies. The driving force behind Brazil's official indigenous policy reappeared with a vengeance with the military dictatorship in 1964. Among the principles of the national security doctrine of the War College was the binomial "development and security" (Dreifuss, 2006). Fully believing that they were the saviors of the nation, military officers removed by force any obstacle that stood in their way.

After the creation of FUNAI in 1967 and the passage of Law 6,001/73 (also known as the Indian Statute), the state established a more sophisticated relationship with indigenous peoples while preserving the old colonial mentality. Promulgated by sworn integrationists who lived by the mantra adopted by the dictators and generals of the time, "Integrar para não entregar" (Integrate rather than hand over), the statute was based on the principle established by the 1916 Brazilian Civil Code that Indians were "relatively incapable" and should be protected by the state. It contained clauses that promoted discrimination, assimilation, and expropriation based on the idea of the indigenous person's "transitoriness." Indigenous peoples were denied the right to own property and could be removed for reasons of national security or the conduct of public works projects or mining by state-owned companies or to allow the leasing of indigenous lands.

The 1988 Constitution abandoned the idea of assimilation and guaranteed the physical and cultural preservation of ethnic minorities. It also ratified ILO Convention 169. Articles 231 and 232 identified indigenous peoples as parties that could initiate legal action in defense of their rights and interests. This major innovation was based on applying the concept of self-determination to indigenous communities. Certain rights were granted them, among them autonomy with regard to their cultural organization and free, prior, and informed consent on issues that interfered directly or indirectly with their way of life. The goal was "interaction" rather than "integration." Although the constitution made important changes in the legal system, the fundamental rights of indigenous peoples continue to be constantly violated, especially with regard to the preservation of their territories and social, agricultural, health, and welfare policies. The view of indigenous peoples as incapable of defending or expressing themselves remains strong in all three branches of government, and institutions continue to recognize FUNAI's tutelage. The legal and constitutional recognition of the autonomy of indigenous peoples in Brazil did not put an end to the old notion of the Indian's being caught in a transitory state between barbarism and civilization. Instead, the assimilationist indigenous policies that dominated for decades were replaced by policies that sought to "de-Indianize" Brazilian society. Ethnocide was practiced either intentionally or unintentionally by the state for decades in the name of progress and economic development (Stavenhagen, 2010).

This colonialist vision survives in indigenous policy and is decisive in the way the state's tutelary policies with regard to indigenous peoples are formulated. Even FUNAI, on its website, officially recognizes a transitory status for indigenous peoples: "Despite the establishment in the 1988 Federal Constitution of a new paradigm on the rights of indigenous peoples in Brazil, putting an end to the tutelary and integrationist perspective remains a work in progress." According to Viveiros de Castro (1983: 235),

> While formally being a symmetrical guarantee at the heart of an asymmetrical relationship between Indians and Whites, the idea of tutelage has been invented by the government as a way to exercise its power over indigenous peoples despite its claim to protect indigenous peoples in our society—silence them, take away their power, reduce their territories, and stunt their movements.

Colonialism became a framework in which the ideological and cultural domination of Western modernity could be legitimized. The "rule of law" guarantees the privileges of certain groups. Indigenous peoples continue to occupy a space of ontological and political "exteriority" within the nation, and social programs and public policies are imposed on them without opposition. In fact, initiatives designed to help indigenous peoples obtain social benefits reproduce prejudices and reinforce the idea that indigenous peoples need to be protected. Perhaps the initiative that does the most to spread these preconceptions is the policy relating to access to welfare benefits. The National Social Security Institute specifies that indigenous policyholders must be approved by FUNAI and must demonstrate their rural status individually or within a family economy regime. For an organization in the public sector to require approval from FUNAI goes against Brazilian law. The constitution does not say anything about tutelage but instead focuses on the recognition of cultural differences and different modes of social organization. By demanding approval from FUNAI for access to social programs, the state not only illustrates its disregard for the self-determination of these peoples but also reproduces a colonial mentality.

A similar situation exists in the education system. In order to prove their identity and benefit from the quotas assigned to them in Brazilian universities, many indigenous students have to make long trips to FUNAI to ask for official recognition of a certificate stating that they are under its care (in other words, a certificate recognizing another certificate). This authority is formally exercised in the absence of constitutional norms, defending an idea on paper but doing the opposite in reality.

Indigenous tutelage is an expression of power that the Bolivian sociologist Luís Tapia calls the "monocultural state." Although he focuses on the Bolivian context, Tapia (2002, quoted by Walsh, 2009: 69) ends up describing the state structures that exist in Latin America as follows:

> The state, laws, government institutions, the regime governing politics and organizations are accountable only to culture, [in particular,] the culture that belongs to the society that conquered the continent. Soon afterward, under more modern guises, a subordinated integration was established. In this way, structurally and constitutionally speaking, it is a racist state even though it is not publicly seen as such.

THE GOVERNMENTS BEFORE BOLSONARO

The persistence of a tutelary, assimilationist, and integrationist model for indigenous peoples does not necessarily mean that every government behaves in the same way. There are characteristics that they have in common, but their relationships with indigenous peoples differ. There were social advances during the 13 years of the PT governments, among them income distribution programs, access to education at all levels of society, and job creation. Social programs such as Fome Zero (Zero Hunger) and the Bolsa Família (Family Allowance or Family Stipend) reduced the number of families that lived below the poverty line and had a substantial impact on the lives of indigenous peoples. Nonetheless, these social programs were characterized by discrepancies relating to certain ethnic traits and by the idea that their social inclusion was limited and temporary. Despite this weakness, the PT governments created and reestablished various committees that focused on national public policies, national conferences, and participatory processes, and indigenous

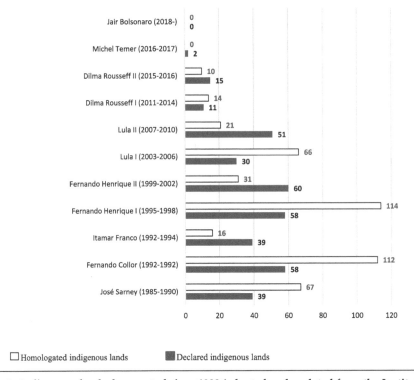

Figure 1. Indigenous lands demarcated since 1988 (adapted and updated from the Instituto Socioambiental [https://www.socioambiental.org/pt-br/noticias-socioambientais/com-pior-desempenho-em-demarcacoes-desde-1985-temer-tem-quatro-terras-indigenas-para-homo-logar (accessed January 19, 2020)]).

representatives took part in these committees, especially the national committee for indigenous policy and the local and district committees and national conference on indigenous health. Despite these advances, however, development and progress continued to be viewed from an ethnocentric perspective. The main concern of the indigenous movement, the demarcation of indigenous lands, has suffered increasing setbacks over time (Figure 1).

It was José Sarney's conservative government and those with a neoliberal orientation such as those of Fernando Collor de Mello and Fernando Henrique Cardoso that did the most to demarcate indigenous lands. Since Lula's second term, agribusiness elites have become a political force, and they gained even more influence after Dilma Rousseff was deposed in a parliamentary coup in 2016. The congressional proceedings on the issues of concern to the Frente Parlamentar Agropecuária (Congressional Agrarian Front—FPA) reveal the expansion of the anti-indigenous offensive in recent years (Figure 2).

The neoexpansionist agenda and the "productivity pact" of the PT governments represented a setback for the demarcation of indigenous lands. The Lula and Dilma governments were heavily criticized by the operators of large hydroelectric plants such as Belo Monte in Rio Xingu and the Tapajós Complex in Pará that are part of the Growth Acceleration Program. Despite the promising results of PT social programs in the fight against poverty,

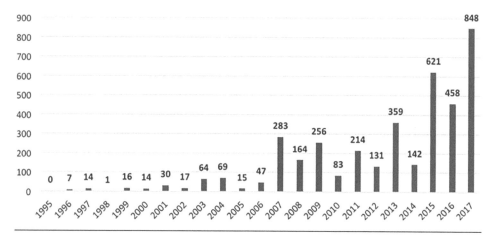

Figure 2. Anti-indigenous bills in Congress, 1995–2017 (data from Câmara dos Deputados, Conselho Indigenista Missionário, and FUNAI [https://outraspalavras.net/outrasmidias/congresso-os-numeros-da-grande-ofensiva-anti-indigena/ (accessed July 28, 2018)]).

larger structural issues remained unresolved, such as ensuring territorial access in an environment of ecological and cultural sustainability. Political accords in the congressional setting during the PT governments also indicated a growing number of lobbyists working for agribusiness, a sector of the Brazilian economy that greatly benefited from PT policies.

THE ANTI-INDIGENOUS TREND IN BRAZILIAN GOVERNMENT

Jair Bolsonaro's election in 2018 was a victory for a reactionary force in Brazilian politics that already had considerable influence in Congress. Formulated with the backing of major opponents to indigenous rights such as the FPA and supported by agribusiness, the political agenda of the current government seeks to hamper indigenous policies in several areas (such as education, social welfare, and ethnic development) with a special focus on curtailing the designation of indigenous lands. Bolsonaro's congressional record is full of racist remarks and attacks on indigenous peoples. In 2004, during a session of the Chamber of Deputies, he called indigenous people "smelly, uneducated, and people who do not speak our [Portuguese] language." In 2008, in front of the entire chamber, he called on the indigenous leader Jecinaldo Barbosa to "eat grass outside and remember where you came from." During his political campaign, Bolsonaro stated on various occasions that Brazil has a "demarcation industry" set up by FUNAI and the NGOs. During an interview he said, "If it were up to me, there would be no more demarcations of indigenous lands" (Resende, 2018). He frequently described indigenous peoples as groups with "an inferior background" and even compared them to zoo animals.

The institutional stance of Bolsonaro is not an isolated occurrence but a neocolonialist project aimed at dismantling Brazilian indigenous policies. This project is supported by three groups that have tremendous influence in Brazilian society—the ruralists, the military, and the evangelicals. The ruralists are interested in promoting the expansion of agribusiness on indigenous lands. The military continues to express concern about a supposed risk to national sovereignty if indigenous groups remain autonomous. The more radical evangelical churches are seeking to extend their sphere of influence through missionary activities. The confluence of these different agendas manifests itself in the fight for deregulation in the demarcation of indigenous lands, which also has an impact on policies relating to access to and exploitation of indigenous lands.

The FPA is the largest political force organized by Congress, with 257 deputies (of a total of 513) and 32 senators (of a total of 81) (*Congresso em Foco* UOL, 2019). The recent arrival of the ruralists as a political force has its roots in an ideological dispute between agribusiness and other modes of production (Schneider, 2010: 516–517). The FPA has taken a firm stance against the demarcation of indigenous lands, arguing that it means less space for agribusiness to expand and pointing out that 14 percent of Brazil's national territory is owned by ethnic groups that represent less than 0.5 percent of the population (FUNAI, 2017). Furthermore, it condemns the legal uncertainty created in cases where demarcations are not clearly defined. In May 2018, the then-federal deputy and presidential candidate Jair Bolsonaro promised, on his way to an exhibition of agricultural technology in Brasília, to allow and encourage landowners to be armed: "If it were up to me, every farmer would have a gun on his property." He also said that to leave farmers unarmed was "foolish and irresponsible" and would mean leaving them "at the mercy of the Movimento dos Trabalhadores Sem Terra [Landless Workers' Movement—MST] and other types of bandits."

Jair Bolsonaro's government is apparently acting in concert with the large rural producers, but it has disrupted agricultural exports in some respects. A few hours after becoming president, Bolsonaro signed Provisional Measure 870, an administrative reform that transferred control of FUNAI to the Ministry of Women, Family, and Human Rights, whose head was the evangelical pastor Damares Alves. The ministry did not plan on annulling previous demarcations of indigenous lands but, rather, allied itself with missionary organizations that sought to evangelize indigenous peoples at any cost. However, under pressure from the indigenous movement, progressive sectors of the population, and members of Congress, FUNAI was returned to the Ministry of Justice and Public Security. The dismantling of indigenous policies also included the adoption of a provisional measure transferring FUNAI's power to demarcate indigenous lands to INCRA, but the Supreme Court reversed it. The reissuing of the measure was judged by Justice Luis Roberto Barroso as "an unacceptable affront to the supreme authority of the Federal Constitution" and "an inadmissible and dangerous transgression of the fundamental principle of separation of powers stated in Article 2 of the Federal Constitution" (STF, 2019).

Besides the attacks on policies demarcating indigenous lands, pressure was exerted by ruralist groups and others to reverse the status of areas whose control had already been legally established. This effort was led by sectors linked to mining companies, which want to weaken the laws regulating environmental and ethnic protection. Their main goal is to mine the subsoil of indigenous lands in areas that are also environmentally protected. Indigenous lands are owned and used by indigenous peoples, but they are also the property of the federal government.

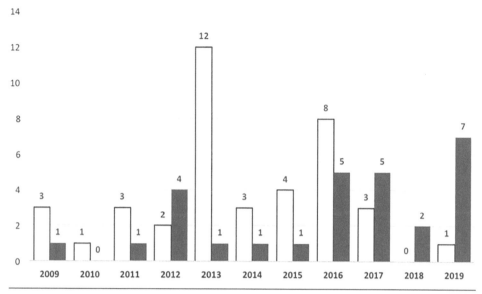

Figure 3. Assassinations of indigenous people (*white bars*) and leaders (*black bars*), 2009–2019 (data from Centro de Documentação Dom Tomás Balduino and Comissão Pastoral da Terra, 2020).

The FPA is also fighting environmental protection and sustainable agricultural practices on indigenous lands. Using a proposed constitutional amendment that would change certain provisions of the 1988 Constitution, rural lobbyists, in league with Bolsonaro, sought permission for nonindigenous Brazilians to mine on indigenous lands. This measure plans on returning Brazil to an integrationist and assimilationist model and is incompatible with ILO Convention 169. In February 2020, Bolsonaro said, "Indians are the same as us in that they are human beings and have a heart." He said this with the intention of sending to Congress a proposal to permit mining on indigenous lands, but he was doing nothing less than questioning the humanity of indigenous peoples, a process that dates back to Brazil's colonial past (*Folha de São Paulo*, January 23, 2020). The presidency of FUNAI was turned over to a representative of the Federal Police, whose various regional departments are controlled by military officers. Control of technical and strategic sectors such as the Department of Isolated Indians and Recent Contact was given to a fundamentalist evangelical missionary. These officials brought indigenous policy in line with the agendas of evangelical and ruralist lobbyists.

Bolsonaro's public attacks on indigenous peoples took place in a context in which *grilagem* (falsification of property documents for the illegal possession of lands), timber theft, mining, and invasions of indigenous lands were increasing dramatically.[4] The scale of the disputes for control of these areas is very worrisome. These disputes have led to the largest number of indigenous leaders' dying in conflicts in the countryside in 11 years, according to the Catholic Comissão Pastoral da Terra (Pastoral Land Commission—CPT). In 2019, seven indigenous leaders were assassinated, compared with two in 2018 (Figure 3).

According to a 2019 survey done by the Conselho Indigenista Missionário (Indigenous Council of Missionaries—CIMI) (2020), "[It has come] to our attention that within the first nine months of 2019, there were 160 cases of invasion on 153 indigenous lands located in 19 states and throughout 2018 there were 111 [similar] cases on 76 indigenous lands in 13 states." The indigenous peoples themselves were the first to launch protests after Bolsonaro's inauguration. The Articulação dos Povos Indígenas do Brasil (Liaison for Indigenous Peoples in Brazil—APIB) made headway at UN headquarters and in the Organization of American States (OAS) with the goal of condemning the violence and violations committed by the current government. The indigenous leader Dinaman Tuxá of the APIB summarized the situation: "Our prospects are the worst they have ever been. Now that FUNAI is under the control of the Ministry of Justice again, we will continue to find ourselves the target of a policy of extermination. . . . There is a deliberate attempt to weaken and suffocate FUNAI. As things stand, FUNAI does not meet the minimum requirements for functioning properly" (UOL, 2019).

The recent weakening of environmental defense organizations such as the Instituto Brasileiro do Meio Ambiente e dos Recursos Naturais Renováveis (Brazilian Institute for the Environment and Renewable Natural Resources—IBAMA), the Instituto Chico Mendes de Conservação da Biodiversidade (Chico Mendes Organization for the Preservation of Biodiversity—ICMBio), and FUNAI reveals an agenda that seeks to open these territories so that they can be exploited for their natural resources. The recent reissuing of Provisional Measure 910, which allows property speculators, trespassers, and miners to own property on public lands, gives the green light to others who would repeat these criminal practices.

In the wake of the COVID-19 pandemic, the health system is unable to promote policies that mitigate COVID's spread even though indigenous peoples are among the most vulnerable to the pandemic's effects.

CONCLUSION

The demands of the indigenous movement for more democracy have resulted in institutional gains, the recognition of their political equality, and the constitutionalization of their social rights. The 1988 Constitution was a watershed moment for the fight for indigenous rights. The principle of self-determination (written into the constitution and reaffirmed in ILO Convention 169) became an important source of legal support for the indigenous movement. Even with the onset of redemocratization, indigenous peoples fought for a different standard in the relationship between the state and Brazilian society in which the former would become more reflective of the diversity present in the latter. Furthermore, they fought so that indigenous peoples could shape and influence state actions and participate in the formulation of public policies.

Although the constitution signified a fundamental rupture that included all of Brazilian society (with popular participation at every political level), the governments elected did not implement any real changes regarding the relationship between the state and society. The primary demands of indigenous peoples (especially the demarcation of their lands) were answered only in specific instances dependent on the circumstances of the time. Situated in a context that saw a slight improvement during the 13 years of the PT governments, the Brazilian political system frustrated the advance of indigenous rights in Brazil.

The desire for indigenous lands because of the mineral resources they contain is the main motivation for the offensive against the 305 different ethnicities that are recognized by the Brazilian government. The collusion of public officials with private interests (led by those who represent the interests of agribusiness and landowners) is evident in the way this bloc has spread its tentacles to occupy important positions in many institutions. The emergence of statements and policies against indigenous peoples is the result.

The current government's stance against indigenous peoples has two fundamental aspects. The first is a confusion of the government with the state in which the current group in power seeks to circumvent republican values and impose a form of government based on personal relationships that keeps Bolsonaro in power. The second is a worldview based on ethnocentric dichotomies, the main one in this case being "civilized" vs. "primitive." It is a tragic situation not only for indigenous peoples but also for Brazilian society, since demarcated lands represent close to 14 percent of the national territory and, coincidentally, are the most environmentally protected in all of Brazil (FUNAI, 2017). Protecting these lands is not only essential for preserving an ecological balance but also important for agribusiness.

An ethnocentrism that supports arguments for reducing indigenous territories and for the cultural and physical extinction of indigenous peoples is also based on an idea that indigenous peoples are incapable of modernizing. This idea is not new. It has played a pivotal role in Brazilian history and continues to influence Brazilian society. Bolsonaro's government is the product of a colonialist and ethnocentric perspective in the guise of neoliberalism. This perspective continues to wield tremendous influence, even on progressive governments. Bolsonaro's government is very different from its predecessors because of the radical way in which it applies exclusionary policies. The anti-indigenous bloc wants to exploit indigenous resources, take away indigenous rights, and exploit indigenous peoples for its own political and economic benefit. Bolsonaro is an ally of this bloc who is more than willing to break the law and impose his will by force in order to appease it. The president is making progress toward his goal of exterminating indigenous peoples.

NOTES

1. A provisional measure is a politico-judicial instrument used by the president of the Republic in cases of urgency. It has the force of law and has immediate effects, but it depends on the approval of Congress to become law. Its period of application is 60 days with a single extension for another 60.

2. Among the main goals of the rural sector are the paralysis and termination of demarcation processes that are in progress or finalized, mining on indigenous lands, farming on a mass scale on indigenous lands for the purposes of expanding agribusiness, and the forced "cultural integration" of indigenous peoples.

3. https://www.un.org/esa/socdev/unpfii/documents/DRIPS_pt.pdf (accessed August 23, 2019).

4. *Grilagem* consists of planting a falsified document in a box of crickets to give it an aged appearance.

REFERENCES

Centro de Documentação Dom Tomás Balduíno e Comissão Pastoral da Terra
2020 *Conflitos no campo/Brasil 2019*. Edited by Antônio Canuto, Cássia Regina da Silva Luz, and Paulo César Moreira dos Santos. Goiânia: CPT Nacional.

Congresso em Foco UOL
2019 "Com 257 parlamentares, bancada ruralista declara apoio à reforma da Previdência: reunião do setor rural definiu apoio da maior bancada do Congresso à pauta." https://congressoemfoco.uol.com.br/economia/com-257-parlamentares-bancada-ruralista-declara-apoio-a-reforma-da-previdencia/.

Conselho Indigenista Missionário
2020 *A violência contra os povos indígenas no Brasil: Dados de 2019*. Brasília: CIMI.

Cordeiro, Enio
1999 *Política indigenista brasileira e promoção internacional dos direitos das populações indígenas*. Brasília: Instituto Rio Branco.

da Cunha, Manuela Carneiro
2012 *Índios no Brasil: História, direitos e cidadania*. São Paulo: Claro Enigma.

Dreifuss, René Armand
2006 *1964, A conquista do Estado: Ação política, poder e golpe de classe*. Petrópolis: Vozes.

Freire, Paulo
2007 *The Pedagogy of the Oppressed*. New York: Continuum.

FUNAI (Fundação Nacional do Índio)
2017 "Terras indígenas." http://www.funai.gov.br/index.php/indios-no-brasil/terras-indigenas.

Gonzalez Casanova, Pablo
1965 "Internal colonialism and national development." *Studies in Comparative International Development* 1: 27–37. https://doi.org/10.1007/BF02800542.

Grosfoguel, Ramón
2002 "Colonial difference, geopolitics of knowledge, and global coloniality in the modern/colonial capitalist world-system." *Utopian Thinking* 25: 203–224.
2008 "Para descolonizar os estudos de economia política e os estudos pós-coloniais: transmodernidade, pensamento de fronteira e colonialidade global." *Revista Crítica de Ciências Sociais* 80: 115–147.

ILO (International Labor Organization)
1989 "International Labour Conference Convention 169 of the ILO on indigenous and tribal peoples." https://www2.camara.leg.br/legin/fed/decleg/2002/decretolegislativo-143-20-junho-2002-458771-convencion169-pl.pdf (accessed March 14, 2018).

Krenak, Aílton
2001 "Uma vista inesperada," pp. 71–78 in Luís Donisete Grupioni, Lux Boelitz Vidal, and Roseli Frischmann (eds.), *Povos indígenas e tolerância: Construindo práticas de respeito e solidariedade*. São Paulo: Editora da Universidade de São Paulo.

Lima, A. C.
1992 "O governo dos índios sob a gestão do SPI," pp. 155–172 in M. M. C. Cunha (ed.), *História dos Índios no Brasil*. São Paulo: Companhia das Letras/Secretaria Municipal de Cultura/FAPESP.

Murakawa, Fabio and Rafael Walendorff
2020 "Bolsonaro vê 'uma indústria das demarcações de terra indígena.'" *Valor Econômico*, February 11.

Neto, M. D. and M. D. Martins
2006 "Significados do nacionalismo e do internacionalismo." *Tensões Mundiais* 2 (1): 80–138.

Quijano, Aníbal
2000 "Colonialidad del poder, eurocentrismo y América Latina," in Edgardo Lander (ed.), *La colonialidad del saber: Eurocentrismo y ciencias sociales, perspectivas latinoamericanas*. Buenos Aires: CLACSO/UNESCO.
2010 "Colonialidade do poder e classificação social," pp. 84–130 in Boaventura de Sousa Santos and Maria Paula Menezes (eds.), *Epistemologias do Sul*. São Paulo: Cortez.

Resende, Sarah Motta

2018 "'No que depender de mim, não tem mais demarcação de terra indígena', diz Bolsonaro a TV." *Folha de São Paulo*, November 5.

Santos, Boaventura de Sousa

2004 "Do pós-moderno ao pós-colonial: e para além de um e de outro." Paper presented at the opening session of the Eighth Luso-Afro-Brazilian Congress of Social Sciences, Coimbra, Portugal, September 16–18. http://www.ces.uc.pt/misc/Do_pos-moderno_ao_pos-colonial.pdf.

Schneider, Sergio

2010 "Situando o desenvolvimento rural no Brasil: o contexto e as questões em debate." *Brazilian Journal of Political Economy* 30: 511–531. https://doi.org/10.1590/S0101-31572010 000300009.

Stavenhagen, Rodolfo

2010 *Los pueblos originarios: el debate necesario*. Edited by Norma Fernández. Buenos Aires: Ediciones CLACSO/Instituto de Estudios y Formación de la CTA.

STF (Supremo Tribunal Federal)

2019 "Plenário referenda liminar que suspendeu medida provisória que transferia demarcação de terras indígenas para Ministério da Agricultura." https://portal.stf.jus.br/noticias/verNoticiaDetalhe.asp?idConteudo=418183 (accessed February 22, 2020).

Tapia, Luis

2002 *La producción del conocimiento local: Historia y política en la obra de René Zavaleta*. La Paz: CIDES/UMSA/Muela del Diablo.

UOL

2019 "FUNAI sob fogo." https://noticias.uol.com.br/ultimas-noticias/deutschewelle/2019/06/13/a-funai-sob-fogo.htm.

Viveiros de Castro, Eduardo B.

1983 "A autodeterminação indígena como valor." *Anuário Antropológico*, no. 81, 233–242.

Walsh, Catherine

2009 *Interculturalidad, estado y sociedad: Luchas (de)coloniales de nuestra época*. Quito: Abya Yala.

Between Markets and Barracks

The Economic Policy Narrative of Brazilian Authoritarianism

by
Niels Søndergaard

In recent years, a series of right-wing populists has ascended to power in both the Global North and the Global South. While these leaders frequently have provided challenges to liberal democracy, neoliberal modes of economic governance have often been part of their agendas. Analysis of the economic policy narrative of the Brazilian President Jair Bolsonaro's electoral campaign in 2018 through the theoretical lens of authoritarian neoliberalism reveals that it has worked by the relegation of economic matters to technocratic management outside the sphere of democratic debate and the instrumentalized estrangement of groups and institutions opposed to his political views.

Recentemente, uma série de populistas direitistas têm chegado ao poder tanto nos países do norte como naqueles do sul. Enquanto estes lideres frequentemente apresentam desafios às democrâcias liberais, modos neoliberais de governança econômica muitas vezes desempenham um papel nas suas agendas. Uma análise da narrativa da política econômica na campanha presidencial do Presidente Jair Bolsonaro no Brasil em 2018 mediante uma visão teorética de neoliberalismo autoritário indica que ela funcionou pela relegação de assuntos econômicos a gestores tecnocrâticos que ficam fora da esféra de debate democrâtico e pelo afastamento instrumentalizado de grupos e instituições que se opõem às idéias políticas de Bolsonaro.

Keywords: *Authoritarian neoliberalism, Brazil, Bolsonaro, Policy narratives*

Jair Bolsonaro's election as Brazil's thirty-eighth president on October 28, 2018, concluded an electoral campaign that had been marked by unprecedented polarization and incendiary rhetoric. The elections took place as the country was immersed in an economic and institutional crisis that had spurred popular discontent and disenchantment with the political system. This provided a fertile context for the far-right-wing populist Jair Bolsonaro to reach power by appealing to the reestablishment of order and political renewal. While the severity of the crisis undoubtedly facilitated his ascent to power, Bolsonaro's election should also be viewed as part of a wider global trend of right-wing populists' reaching power by electoral means (Capelovitch and Pevehouse, 2019; Ikenberry, 2018; Levitsky and Ziblatt, 2018). In spite of their

Niels Søndergaard is an assistant professor at the Institute for International Relations of the Universidade de Brasilia. His interests span various areas of international political economy, in particular critical approaches to natural-resource production, governance, and trade.

LATIN AMERICAN PERSPECTIVES, Issue 248, Vol. 50 No. 1, January 2023, 64–79
DOI: 10.1177/0094582X231154226
© 2023 Latin American Perspectives

commonalities, these different political projects have been marked by great variety in their emphasis on market orientation as opposed to political authoritarianism. While they have been advanced on a heterodox economic platform in some countries, such as Hungary and Poland (Buzogány and Varga, 2018; Nölke, 2017; Toplišek, 2019), in others, such as Turkey, authoritarian leaders have combined free-market orientation with repressive and antidemocratic politics conceptualized as authoritarian neoliberalism (Bozkurt-Gungen, 2018; Bruff, 2014; Tansel, 2018). That the situation of dubious democratic legitimacy surrounding the Temer government's implementation of neoliberal economic reforms has also been termed authoritarian neoliberalism (Saad-Filho, 2019) underscores the need to maintain awareness of the diversity of these politics depending on both the temporal and the spatial locus of their concretization. While the overtly authoritarian nature of Bolsonaro's rhetoric has often drawn much international attention, the market fundamentalism that permeated his campaign and characterized his election promises has gone relatively unnoticed. Considering Brazil's extreme inequality and the severity of the current economic and social crisis, it becomes imperative to examine how the intersection with authoritarian populism fueled a neoliberal policy agenda in this context. This study therefore analyzes the economic policy narrative of the Bolsonaro campaign from the point of view of recent contributions in the field of authoritarian neoliberalism. This perspective provides an understanding of how the insulation of economic policy making from democratic scrutiny, the instrumentalization of populism, and the strategic estrangement of groups and institutions provided a path for the electoral success of neoliberalism. The narrative analysis focuses on the central story lines of *antisocialism*, *antistatism*, and ultraconservative *moralism* and the underlying emplotment structure that supported them. Public statements by Bolsonaro and his campaign staff in the three months preceding the final elections are systematically examined and provide the basis for the analysis of the narrative structure. In the following, the article proceeds with a conceptual review of the notion of authoritarian neoliberalism, a section presenting the narrative approach adopted, an analysis of the Bolsonaro campaign's economic policy narrative, an analysis of market actors' support for Bolsonaro campaign, and some conclusions.

THE POLITICS OF AUTHORİTARIAN NEOLIBERALISM

Combining a clearly authoritarian discourse and admiration for Brazil's military dictatorship (1964–1985) with a neoliberal economic orientation, Bolsonaro's ascent to power becomes a relevant object of study through the lens of the burgeoning literature on authoritarian neoliberalism. This approach helps to make sense of recent Brazilian events in light of contemporary global political developments and provides conceptual tools for understanding the specific character of authoritarian neoliberalism in a Brazilian context. While authoritarian practices and rationalities have been associated with neoliberal governance both globally and within Latin America, contemporary authoritarian neoliberal political projects imply characteristics that go beyond any inherently nondemocratic traits of capitalism (Bruff and Tansel, 2018: 7). Since "neoliberalism" can be viewed as a "loose and shifting signifier" (Brown, 2015: 20), it becomes imperative to evaluate how this ideology molds state-society configurations in the particular temporal and spatial loci of their concretization (Ismail, 2018: 848). Because neoliberalism has been treated in recent decades as an ideological force that permeates highly diverse global policies and polities (Anderson, 1995; Zhang, 2018: 866–868), attention should be paid to the concrete form of its present authoritarian turn (Clua-Losada and Ribera-Almendoz, 2017: 29). Thus, while a distinctive global trend of authoritarian neoliberalism can be identified in recent years (Bruff and Tansel, 2018: 5), this concept's most fruitful renderings appear to derive from its specific contextual application(s).

Tansel (2018: 119) defines authoritarian neoliberalism as "a disciplinary statecraft that closes off key decision-making processes to popular pressures . . . with a view to protecting the circuits of capital accumulation" and accentuates its repressive nature by "deploying the coercive, legal and administrative state apparatuses to marginalise democratic opposition and dissident social groups." The first aspect has been treated in terms of the "insulation" of policy-making processes from wider popular inputs and meaningful participation (Bozkurt-Gungen, 2018: 220; Bruff, 2014: 115). This clearly reflects the "structural limits" of capitalism that rein in political control over economic spheres (Ayers and Saad-Filho, 2015: 4), resulting in the imposition of a conceptual and practical separation between the economic and the political realms that eventually produces tension between liberal democracy and the market (Cozzolino, 2019). The second fundamental aspect relates to the particular political results of the intersection between neoliberalism and authoritarianism. Harrison (2019: 4) defines authoritarian neoliberalism as a "subspecies" of the wider notion of authoritarianism and as "a bundle of practices and institutions that construct states that use bureaucracy and coercion in the attempt to construct, enforce and discipline societies into marketised forms." In line with this political rationale, strategies of accumulation and strategies of repression are not parallel but intertwined (Jenss, 2019: 11). The role of the state thereby becomes law enforcement and the guaranteeing of contractual relations on the concrete level and in a more general sense the imposition of a market rationality in social spheres and realms of human activity. This is underpinned by a cultural transformation of civil society—an increasing acceptance of authoritarian responses to a variety of social problems and societal dilemmas (Gonzales, 2018: 82).

For the purpose of the present study, which focuses not on effectuated policies but on the narrative propelling the emergence of an authoritarian neoliberal political project, the mechanisms of consent production are of central importance. By pitting "the people" against "unions" and "the nation" against "class" or through combined appeals to "individual responsibility" and "family values," neoliberalism can be advanced through populist morals and even serve to dismantle social institutions benefiting a broad spectrum of society (Bruff, 2014: 117–118; Hall, 1988). With a point of departure in the Turkish context, Bilgic (2018: 260) stresses that authoritarian neoliberalism is nurtured by references to a supposed "national will" that serves to coerce critical voices. This draws attention to the highly heterogeneous concretizations deriving from the current wave of authoritarian populism, which has resulted in both challenges to and new political vehicles for the advancement of neoliberalism

(Kiely, 2017). Antiestablishment populism may in some cases adopt extreme orthodox economic precepts (Havertz, 2019). Conceptual similarities between right-wing populism and market fundamentalism can be identified through a strict categorical division of the world into two countervailing parts, the first based on identity-related factors and the second on the socioeconomic ordering (Pühringer and Ötsch, 2018: 193). The illiberal commonalities of these dichotomizations underlie different contemporary authoritarian neoliberal political currents (200).

A NARRATIVE APPROACH

While economic policy debates often occur in terms of supposed factuality and assessments of plausible causalities, they have a dimension of values and unspoken collective beliefs about the present and the future that is frequently neglected. Economic discourses therefore lend themselves to interpretation of these underlying and intangible elements, and their moral expectations and identity-related inclinations have been the object of narrative analysis (Anson, 2016; Sackley, 2015). This approach serves to identify the specific way in which authoritarian neoliberalism has been embedded within the economic policy narrative of the campaign resulting in Bolsonaro's election in late 2018.

Narratives are accounts presented by political figures to connect events and developments and imbue them with a pattern of meaning that supports their ideas (Bacon, 2012: 15–16). They simplify complex and highly contextual stories and align them with the articulation of certain identities (Tonra, 2011: 1193–1194). Their successful proliferation therefore hinges on the way they resonate with value systems and institutional conventions (Olsen, 2014: 251). In the following analysis, attention is directed toward story lines and plots as components of the economic policy narrative of the Bolsonaro campaign. Story lines identify the social time of the narrative, which does not necessarily follow a linear pattern. They help to make sense of the past, the present, and the future and provide an integrated explanation of how these are connected while identifying social expectations according to this explanation (Godart and White, 2010: 575). They link events and lead to normative preferences through which the story influences social behavior (Seabrooke and Thomsen, 2016: 252). Plots construe significant events and produce characterizations that serve as moral markers shaping the narrative. They structure the episodes of the narrative and identify its inflection points (Czarniawska, 2010: 64; Polletta, 1998: 421). Rather than chronological or categorical ordering, emplotment offers an alternative arrangement for the narrative account (Somers, 1994: 616). It is based on the inclusion and exclusion of specific elements of a wider and complex reality—the selective appropriation of the parts of the social world that help to sustain and reproduce the narrative (Baker, 2005: 8–9).

The Bolsonaro campaign's economic policy narrative was identified in different sources through which it was communicated to the wider public from his nomination on July 22, 2018, to the second round of the presidential elections on October 28, 2018. Pronouncements made in this period by central figures such as Bolsonaro himself and his prospective minister of finance, Paulo

Guedes, provide the main material for analysis. In some cases, these are supplemented by statements made by other members of the campaign staff or in the government plan (the candidate's stated goals in a variety of issue areas). Keyword searches (*Bolsonaro* and *economía*) of digitalized news articles in the archives of the two main newspapers with nationwide circulation, *Folha de São Paulo* and *O Globo*, resulted in 773 hits, and 111 articles were found to reproduce/cite statements made by the Bolsonaro campaign related to economic issues. A search of Bolsonaro's Twitter account in this period resulted in a more limited number of hits, since economic issues did not gain much attention in this sphere. Statements made during televised participation in official presidential debates and interviews with nationwide broadcasters were also transcribed and included in the study.

NARRATIVES OF AUTHORITARIAN NEOLIBERALISM IN THE BOLSONARO CAMPAIGN

The elections in 2018 took place in a context that was strongly marked by a crisis of political legitimacy, institutional disarray, and a period of prolonged economic stagnation based upon a profound economic recession from 2015 to 2016. Yet, the analysis of the Bolsonaro campaign's treatment of economic issues nonetheless reveals a remarkably superficial and often contradictory approach to this theme. The reasoning presented by the presidential candidate himself often escaped conventional logics of causation and basic economic assumptions and frequently resorted to anecdotal evidence and moralistic argumentation. While not impeding the identification of an economic policy narrative, the neglect of economic questions calls for study of the positioning of this issue in the campaign's communication strategy.

The highly superficial way in which economic policy was approached may to some extent be explained by Bolsonaro's frequently admitted lack of knowledge regarding this issue. He often recognized his economic illiteracy, denying that it would be of any significance and referring to Guedes on the subject. On one occasion he bluntly asked, "Am I going to take a college entrance exam or am I on a political campaign?" (Grillo, Menezes, and Prado, 2018). As a Chicago-trained neoliberal economist, Guedes thereby gained central significance within the campaign in that economic questions were largely "outsourced" to him (Tavares, 2018). He is said to have persuaded Bolsonaro to abandon his inclination toward economic *dirigisme* and proved a significant figure in gaining political support from the Brazilian business community (Gielow, 2018). While Bolsonaro's adversaries dedicated much time to problems related to health care, education, and the economy, he himself focused mainly on value-related issues and controversies such as criticism of the press, discrediting of his opponents, and alerting about the alleged perils of sexual education in public schools (*Folha de São Paulo*, August 16, August 30, and September 27, 2018). This meant that on the eve of his election very little was known about the specifics of the economic strategy that he intended to pursue (Leitão, 2018a).

In the run-up to the elections, the Bolsonaro campaign appears to have been marked by a certain degree of disarray concerning its economic strategy.

Statements about the need for sweeping privatizations of public enterprises on the order of R$2 trillion (approximately US$500 billion) were made by Guedes in the course of the campaign. When asked about these plans, Bolsonaro either denied them or sought to avoid the issue (Boghossian, 2018). As Guedes was confronted with strong criticism of such extensive privatizations as unrealistic, he adopted a more generic discourse concerning the need to "think outside the box" (*GloboNews*, August 23, 2018). Bolsonaro's aversion to commenting on the issue was interpreted as a tactic to conceal the lack of substantive proposals (Leitão, 2018b). Similar inconsistencies and contradictory statements from within the campaign could be observed with regard to Guedes's intention to reinstitute a tax on all financial transactions and a flat income tax of 20 percent. Apart from the fact that Bolsonaro previously had been fiercely opposed to the former (Fernandes and Seto, 2018), the negative repercussions of the proposal made him distance himself from it. The course of events even indicates that Bolsonaro, who was in the hospital at the moment of their presentation, appears not to have been informed about these plans (*Folha de São Paulo*, September 21, 2018).

Beyond the simple lack of coordination within the campaign, it is interesting to observe the interplay between the presentation of policy proposals and their repercussions; whenever the economic policy discourse reached even a minimal degree of specificity, the negative public reaction prompted its return to a generic state at which it eventually remained. In the first round of the vote, Guedes's economic team was ultimately inhibited from making any public statements (Gielow, 2018). The extensive use of Twitter and other social media platforms within the Bolsonaro campaign appears to have had two major and mutually reinforcing effects: on the one hand, it allowed assertions and ideas to be presented without any sort of contestation or critical feedback, which undoubtedly contributed to the lack of a thorough development of economic policy proposals in the few instances in which they were presented. On the other hand, the lack of filtering and the instantaneous nature of the social media meant that contradictory messages were constantly being emitted by different campaign staff members, to the point that the identification of a more coherent economic program became infeasible.

Considering the socially unbalanced character of the Bolsonaro campaign's economic policy proposals, their concealment behind moral and identity-based issues amounted to the introduction of neoliberalism by way of the elimination of distributive questions from public debate. The outsourcing of central economic dilemmas to technocratic management by Guedes reflects the division between politics and economics upon which contemporary authoritarian neoliberalism is based.

The somewhat confused signals emitted by the Bolsonaro campaign and the lack of specificity of its economic policy proposals to some extent blurred its economic policy narrative but by no means concealed it. Although they may be relatively detached from more pragmatic observation of social and economic realities, the populist framings of this narrative nonetheless provided a series of internally converging story lines about contemporary Brazil. These were strongly based on an estrangement from the social forces that have shaped the country's recent past. A central element of this narrative was the antisocialist story line. This relied on an account of the post-redemocratization period (1985–) as a time in which the prevalence of social liberalism undermined the country's social and economic fabric. In a televised debate on August 18, Bolsonaro attributed the economic chaos and unemployment to the successive administrations of the Partido dos Trabalhadores (Workers' Party—PT) and the Partido da Social Democracia Brasileira (Brazilian Social Democratic Party—PSDB) (RedeTV, August 18, 2018). The same conviction was stated in the campaign's government plan: "During the past 30 years, cultural Marxism and its derivatives such as Gramscianism have united corrupt oligarchies in order to undermine the values of the nation and the Brazilian family" and, furthermore, "after 30 years in which the left has corrupted democracy and caused the stagnation of the economy, we will make an alliance for order and progress." In a similar vein, Guedes emphasized that after successive center-left governments in recent decades had raised taxes and increased the size of the state, it was now time for a center-right government (Corrêa, 2018).

Although a clear opposition to the political forces adhering to the principles of the liberal democracy in power since the 1980s can be detected in this story line, a particularly antagonistic relationship becomes evident regarding the PT. Bolsonaro's use of the metaphor of the "ghost of communism" to explain the corruption, dishonesty, and inefficiency of the state constituted an important plot within this story line (RedeTV, August 18, 2018). An economic section of Bolsonaro's government plan stated that "the problem is the Workers' Party's legacy of inefficiency and corruption" and proceeds to point to the staggering public deficits. Economic ills were categorically ascribed to the PT administration, in relation to which Bolsonaro appeared to seek a diametrically opposite position whenever possible (Fernandes and Bilenky, 2018). In the runoff with the PT's candidate, Fernando Haddad, the Bolsonaro campaign also reinforced the *ghost-of-communism* plot with televised spots displaying the fall of the Berlin Wall and the Venezuelan crisis (*Folha de São Paulo*, October 13, 2018). The radicalized rhetoric employed by Bolsonaro even reached the point of attributing the economic problems of ordinary Brazilians to the "thieving" PT (Band, August 10, 2018). The radical hostility toward the PT invokes a suggestive framing of the solution to the economic crisis as the dismantling of institutions and organizations associated with the left. This is not least the case with regard to labor rights, as Bolsonaro highlighted in an interview in which he stated that one day the wage worker would have to choose between fewer rights and entitlements and unemployment (*O Globo*, August 28, 2018). The same confrontational position was adopted with regard to social movements by one of Bolsonaro's campaign managers, who stressed the need to confront "nongovernmental organizations and civil society" to protect the economic interests of agribusiness (D'Avila, 2018).

Another central story line in the Bolsonaro campaign's economic policy narrative was that of antistatism. This story line was based on a representation of the public sector as a superinflated entity that strangled economic activity, as is reflected in comments made by Bolsonaro upon winning the first round, "We will remove the state from the backs of those who produce. . . . We will remove the [onerous] contributions from the paycheck" (L. Carvalho, 2018). The same line of thought was presented in the government plan; "The public administration has been inflated in an uncontrolled manner in recent years. . . . As a result, we see a slow, politically appropriated, and inefficient public sector." The underlying antagonistic relationship expressed in this story line extended beyond Brazil's recent political leadership to confront the country's developmentalist past. Guedes thus painted a picture of Brazil's current economic ills as similar to those that had brought about the downfall of the French monarchy in the late eighteenth century, the collapse of the Soviet Union, or the economic crises of the Figueredo government (1979–1985) and the end of the military regime. The common denominator of these events was said to be rising public spending that eroded the political order (*GloboNews*, August 23, 2018). The alleged solutions for this situation were framed as a transition toward a minimal state, even with regard to sensitive areas such as health care and other social functions undertaken by the public sector (Barbosa et al., 2018). The need to conduct "a frontal attack" on the supposedly dysfunctional state was highlighted as a necessary strategy on the path to economic recovery (*GloboNews*, August 23, 2018).

The antistatist story line was supported by the *excessive-tax-burden* plot, which from Guedes's perspective had produced a "Hobbesian machine state" and warranted a transition to a "Rousseau-ian state, based on the will of the people." In more concrete terms, this emplotment identified a set of policy prescriptions that precluded any new taxes (Cintra, 2018) and called for the elimination of progressive taxation through the institution of a flat income tax. According to Bolsonaro, "The Union would lose income, yes, but the incentive that you would give to companies, rural producers, to employ people, by reducing the paycheck taxation, completely compensates for this" (M. Carvalho, 2018). Another fundamental element within this story line may be characterized as the *cumbersome-bureaucracy* plot. In line with this plot, the businessman became a victim who suffered under an unbearable load of red tape and regulation, as reflected in Bolsonaro's observation "Being an entrepreneur in Brazil is a hell. . . . Who wants to be an entrepreneur?(!)" (interview, TV Cultura, July 30, 2018). Generic references to debureaucratization, deregulation, and simplification were thus presented by different exponents of the campaign as fast tracks to economic prosperity (Band, August 10, 2018). Thus this emplotment structured the expectation that, as long as public economic intervention was assertively confronted, economic stability would inevitably come about. The opening statement in the government plan coupled the inviolability of private property, which was "sacred, and must not be stolen, invaded, or expropriated," and the family, which likewise was deemed "sacred" and outside the legitimate scope of state intervention. This interplay between conservative values and neoliberalism permeated the Bolsonaro campaign, which thereby sought an antipodal position to the social redistribution and political tolerance of previous years.

The depiction of Brazilian politics as morally decadent, leaving the country in a situation of severe economic crisis, was central to the moralist story line. This story line was heavily laden with assumptions of links between individual virtue, righteousness, and prosperity, which resulted in a near-messianic representation of Bolsonaro as an individual upon whom the capacity to save the nation had been bestowed. As he stated in an interview, "During the past 20 years, two parties have sunk Brazil into the most profound ethical, moral, and economic crisis. Let us change this together, but in order to do that, it is necessary to elect a president of the republic who is honest, who has God in his heart, [is] patriotic, and who respects the family" (*O Globo*, August 28, 2018). The moralist story line was strongly based on the *pork-barrel-politics* plot. The belief in moral misconduct as the cause of the crisis became apparent in Bolsonaro's Twitter communications during the first round of the elections. Herein he sought to distance himself from the traditional party system, promiscuous relations with the business sector, and the negotiation of political positions (Twitter, January 10, 2018). He thereby associated his opponents with these practices, claiming that "the only one who can change this—the establishment, the machine, the system—is Jair Bolsonaro. Because we have the morality, and the honesty to complete that mission" (Band, August 10, 2018). There was a very close link between the pork-barrel-politics plot and the *corruption* plot, which to a large measure also characterized the moralist story line. Brazil's long-standing problems with corruption of different sorts and on varying levels of society were appropriated by the Bolsonaro campaign and applied as an overarching explanation for the country's problems. This became apparent in one of Bolsonaro's televised appearances, in which he ascribed the 14 million unemployed to the corruption of previous governments (RedeTV, August 18, 2018). When asked how he would find the means to confront a series of more specific problems with a yellow fever epidemic and a high rate of infant mortality if he planned to lower taxes, he responded that "there should be more scrutiny of public means; it's the corruption!" (interview, TV Cultura, July 30, 2018). A link between the antistatism story line and the moralist story line was made by Guedes, who stressed corruption as a consequence of pork-barrel politics and an inflated public sector, resulting in a situation that could only be solved through a market economy (*GloboNews*, August 23, 2018). The moralist story line also implied suggestive framings calling for the reinstitution of order through clampdowns on crime and social activism as a necessity to improve economic performance. Couplings between violence, social stability, and economic performance are evident in the government plan and from Bolsonaro's Twitter communications (September 4, October 10, and October 20, 2018), which on several occasions stressed combating crime as a path to economic recovery. Classification of social movements as terrorists was also proposed by Bolsonaro as a means to benefit the agribusiness sector by protecting property rights and enforcing its juridical security (Marcello, 2018). The intertwining of the assertion of repressive authority and the installation of neoliberal economic measures was made explicit by Guedes. In an interview, he conveyed what he viewed as a current popular plea for order and a general societal clamor for market-oriented reform and privatizations (*GloboNews*, August 23, 2018). This observation thus expressed an almost teleologically rooted perception of the political forces behind Bolsonaro as acting upon an indisputable social imperative and popular mandate to pursue the politics of the market and of order.

THE MARKET'S DARLING?

In their *How Democracies Die*, Levitsky and Ziblatt (2018) emphasize the role of elites in "filtering" candidates with authoritarian inclinations before they reach power by way of popular election. While a more exhaustive analysis of how the different political and economic elites acted in relation to Bolsonaro's election is beyond the scope of this study, it is interesting to assess the extent to which the Brazilian financial markets "bought" his economic policy narrative through an evaluation of their oscillation during the electoral campaign. In addition to this, it is interesting to evaluate the extent to which the populist appeal of neoliberalism gave the Bolsonaro candidacy traction within the poorer social segments, which traditionally voted for more left-leaning parties.

In spite of his previous record of supporting interventionist economic measures during his 28 years in Congress, Bolsonaro's partnership with Guedes from late 2017 on appears to have won him a great measure of confidence within the Brazilian business community. Thus, when a group of investors in August 2017 was asked about the likely consequences of Bolsonaro's election, 88 percent said a fall in the stock market, while 89 percent pointed to a devaluation of the real. When asked the same question in July 2018, after Guedes had become the economic campaign manager, 62 percent pointed to a rise in the stock market and only 28 percent to a devaluation (Gentile and Pagnan, 2018). Bolsonaro had become positioned within a field of candidates that many market actors would deem tolerable. Yet, in the early stages of the campaign, the more centrist and economically liberal PSDB candidate Geraldo Alckmin was still seen to enjoy the favor of the many economic actors (Kastner and Sodré, 2018). This had changed by September, when Alckmin failed to take off in the opinion polls in spite of holding nearly half of the mandatorily allocated TV time because of his web of political alliances and when Bolsonaro was stabbed by a mentally disturbed individual. Upon the news of the attack on Bolsonaro on September 6, which at first was reported to be a superficial wound, the stock exchange jumped instantly, since this course of events was generally interpreted as improving his chances of winning (*Folha de São Paulo*, September 6, 2018; Kastner, 2018a). From the moment that Bolsonaro suffered the attack, the market systematically responded positively to all news that hinted at his election. This became evident as opinion polls shortly before the first round of the elections showed that a gap was opening up between the leading Bolsonaro and his adversaries (Kastner, 2018b). After he gained a surprisingly large number of votes in the first round, the stock exchange took a very positive turn (Kastner, 2018c). The market also responded to his mixed signaling, as is illustrated by the fall of 2.8 percent in the stock exchange after he asserted the need to limit the privatization of certain public assets (Kastner, 2018d). Similarly, individual companies were also quick to call for caution when sporadic comments such as his negative statements about Chinese investments caused concern (Pamplona, 2018). Even so, upon Bolsonaro's final victory in the second round on October 28, 2018, the Brazilian stock exchange surged to a historic high (Kastner, 2018e).

In spite of the lack of specificity, internal coordination, and technical elaboration, the economic policy narrative that Bolsonaro's campaign adopted appears to have convinced large swathes of the market. This might seem a conundrum, especially considering that four or five other candidates presented economic policy proposals that made similar appeals to the business community, albeit through much more elaborated plans. In this regard, Bolsonaro's versatile signaling, lack of interest in economic issues, and history of voting in favor of interventionist measures should have made him a less attractive alternative for economic actors. Yet, the political context in which the elections were held and the discrediting of the political class more generally should be taken into account in this regard. By 2018, this situation had granted Bolsonaro a very strong initial momentum as a supposed outsider whose candidacy was promoted by conservative forces that very skillfully made use of the increasingly influential social media platforms. Bolsonaro's sudden adoption of a neoliberal economic policy program therefore quickly made him a highly competitive alternative and thus provided a more realistic chance for economic elites to see a president supportive of their general agenda elected. At the same time, it is very likely that the credibility provided by Guedes made it possible for Bolsonaro to obtain endorsement beyond the narrower radical segments of his core supporters.

The somewhat heterogeneous composition of Bolsonaro's support base might suggest that some of the poorer but socially conservative segments would be reluctant to embrace a neoliberal economic policy agenda. Yet, it is possible that the neoliberal agenda was presented in such a way that it attracted groups beyond the economic elites and was therefore introduced "through the backdoor" in a campaign with a strong focus on moralistic rhetoric. The populist appeal of neoliberalism, based on the belief in individual entrepreneurship, is presented by Stuart Hall (1988) as highly compatible with social conservatism, especially in a societal context in which traditional class identities and affinities between the working class and established leftist parties have been weakened. In this regard, examination of the economic policy inclinations of the rapidly expanding and increasingly influential Neo-Pentecoastal evangelical churches is instructive. Although many of these congregations had up until 2014 engaged in strategic alliances with the PT, the wave of right-wing conservatism that emerged from 2015 on changed this picture. The "theology of prosperity," based on values of market entrepreneurship and individual social mobility, provides the basis for the adoption of neoliberal economic ethics (de Antonio and Lahuerta, 2014). This has been evident not least in the peripheral urban favelas, where residents, often beyond the reach of sufficient social coverage, have internalized a belief in individual economic fulfillment as a remedy for their precarious situation. This trend has been closely coupled with a certain loss of support for the PT in peripheral urban areas, which previously had been electoral strongholds for the party (Arruda, 2013). A significant intersection between conservative values and neoliberal ideology could therefore be detected in some otherwise highly disadvantaged groups that appear to have been drawn by the policy narratives of the Bolsonaro campaign.

The version of an authoritarian neoliberal political project that crystallized around the Bolsonaro campaign may also have been more than a "marriage of convenience" that led economic elites to accept an essentially authoritarian candidate. It is therefore worth considering whether certain economic elites may have held an instrumental preference for Bolsonaro precisely because of his autocratic inclinations. His assertive rhetoric and bigotry in relation to groups and social forces opposed to his vision of progress may have been very welcome to economic sectors aligned with this vision. This appears to have been the case with certain segments of agribusiness, which were very positive with regard to his confrontational rhetoric in relation to landless peasants, indigenous populations, and environmentalists. Strategies of accumulation and strategies of repression thereby appear to be interconnected and mutually enforcing (Jenss, 2019: 11). In a similar vein, the Bolsonaro campaign's lack of specificity in its policy proposals may not have been a concern for many market actors: as long as there was general confidence in Bolsonaro's and Guedes's commitment to pursue profound neoliberal reform, the absence of any detailing of highly unpopular policy measures appears to have been met with a high degree of understanding. The strict division sought between the realms of politics and economics that was personified in the very different figures of Jair Bolsonaro and Paulo Guedes and constantly accentuated throughout the campaign is in line with the tendency to depoliticize economic issues that has been highlighted in the literature on authoritarian neoliberalism (Ayers and Saad-Filho, 2015; Bozkurt-Gungen, 2018; Bruff, 2014). Thus, paradoxically, in spite of the country's being immersed in economic stagnation, Bolsonaro was elected without having to present any minimally detailed plans about how to confront this situation. The hostile climate in which the elections were held and the successful populist diversion of the public debate toward moralistic issues framed by disinformation from the blogosphere meant that democratic discussions about problems essential to most Brazilians' lives were largely circumvented.

CONCLUSION

Analysis of the economic policy narrative of Jair Bolsonaro's electoral campaign reveals a clear tendency to treat this issue in a generic and ad-hoc manner, without presenting detailed proposals. An effort was made to compensate for the presidential candidate's lack of personal knowledge of or engagement with economic matters by outsourcing to the economist Paulo Guedes. While this did not result in a more substantial elaboration of the campaign's economic policy program, it did have the effect of depoliticizing a series of important distributive matters while insulating the supposed policies from public scrutiny and critique. The economic policy narrative presented by the Bolsonaro campaign relied on three overlapping and mutually reinforcing story lines. The antisocialist story line was antagonistic toward the social redistribution and liberal democratic principles that to varying degrees had been pursued by administrations in the redemocratization period, and a central plot within it framed the PT and social movements as the cause of Brazil's economic problems. The antistatist story line sought a radical elimination of institutions rooted in Brazil's developmentalist past and stressed an allegedly inflated public sector as the reason for the present economic crisis, with plots revolving around an excessive tax burden and a cumbersome bureaucracy. Finally, the moralist story line sought to connect ethics and ideals of honesty and individual virtue with economic performance and stressed pork-barrel politics and corruption in presenting Bolsonaro as an outsider who would clean up Brazilian politics. This story line led to a call for the reestablishment of order through assertive and often even ostensibly repressive measures. The Bolsonaro campaign's economic policy narrative appears to have been positively received by the markets, partly because he appeared to be the candidate likely to adopt a neoliberal policy agenda as the electoral campaign progressed. Yet, there also seems to have been a yearning for a candidate who would be committed to defending the interests of capital, even if this meant going beyond the bounds of democracy. In relation to some poorer groups, the populist framings of neoliberalism as a path to economic self-fulfillment also appears to have been somewhat effective in ensuring support for a market-oriented candidate in the context of economic stagnation and institutional crisis.

REFERENCES

Anderson, Perry
   1995 "Balanço do neoliberalismo," pp. 9–23 in Emir Sader and Pablo Gentili (eds.), *Pós-neoliberalismo: As políticas sociais e o Estado democrático*. Rio de Janeiro: Paz e Terra.
Anson, Ian G.
   2017 " 'That's not how it works': economic indicators and the construction of partisan economic narratives." *Journal of Elections, Public Opinion and Parties* 27 (2): 213–234.
Arruda, Roldão
   2013 "PT perde apoio na periferia paulistana, seu 'núcleo duro' eleitoral." *Estado de São Paulo*, July 14.
Ayers, Alison J. and Alfredo Saad-Filho
   2015 "Democracy against neoliberalism: paradoxes, limitations, transcendence." *Critical Sociology* 41 (4-5): 1–22.
Bacon, Edwin
   2012 "Public political narratives: developing a neglected source through the exploratory case of Russia in the Putin-Medvedev era." *Political Studies* 60 (4): 1–19. https://doi.org/10.1111/j.1467-9248.2011.00939.
Baker, Mona
   2005 "Narratives in and of translation." *SKASE Journal of Translation and Interpretation* 1 (1): 4–13. https://doi.org/10.1017/CBO9781107415324.004.
Band
   2018 "Debate with the Brazilian presidential candidates." August 10.
Barbosa, Flávia, Cassia Almeida, Danielle Nogueira, and Marcello Corrêa
   2018 "Agenda de Guedes esbarra na resistencia do Bolsonaro." *O Globo*, September 23.
Bilgiç, Ali
   2018 "Reclaiming the national will: resilience of Turkish authoritarian neoliberalism after Gezi." *South European Society and Politics* 23 (2): 259–280.
Boghossian, Bruno
   2018 "O candidato e o presidente." *Folha de São Paulo*, August 29.
Bozkurt-Güngen, Sümercan
   2018 "Labour and authoritarian neoliberalism: changes and continuities under the AKP governments in Turkey." *South European Society and Politics* 23 (2): 219–238.
Brown, Wendy
   2015 *Undoing the Demos: Neoliberalism's Stealth Revolution*. New York: Zone Books.
Bruff, Ian
   2014 "The rise of authoritarian neoliberalism." *Rethinking Marxism* 26 (1): 113–129.
Bruff, Ian and Cemal B. Tansel
   2018 "Authoritarian neoliberalism: trajectories of knowledge production and praxis." *Globalizations* 16: 233–244. https://doi.org/10.1080/14747731.2018.1502497.
Buzogány, Aron and Mihai Varga
   2018 "The ideational foundations of the illiberal backlash in Central and Eastern Europe: the case of Hungary." *Review of International Political Economy* 25: 811–828.
Capelovitch, Mark and Jon C. W. Pevehouse
   2019 "International organizations in a new era of populist nationalism." *Review of International Organizations* 14 (2): 169–186.

Carvalho, Laura
  2018 "Promesa e dívida." *Folha de São Paulo*, October 18.
Carvalho, Mario Cesar
  2018 "Reforma tributária de Bolsonaro provocaria rombo de R$27 bilhões." *Folha de São Paulo*, October 24.
Cintra, Marcos
  2018 "Reforma tributária e movimentação financeira." *Folha de São Paulo*, September 20.
Clua-Losada, Mónica and Olatz Ribera-Almandoz
  2018 "Authoritarian neoliberalism and the disciplining of labour," pp. 29–45 in Cemal Burak Tansel (ed.), *States of Discipline: Authoritarian Neoliberalism and the Contested Reproduction of Capitalist Order*. London: Rowman and Littlefield International.
Corrêa, Marcello
  2018 "Bolsonaro me convenceu de que não entendo de política." *O Globo*, September 22.
Cozzolino, Adriano
  2019 "Reconfiguring the state: executive powers, emergency legislation, and neoliberalization in Italy." *Globalizations* 16: 336–352. DOI: 10.1080/14747731.2018.1502495.
Czarniawska, Barbara
  2010 "The uses of narratology in social and policy studies." *Critical Policy Studies* 4 (1): 58–76.
D'Avila, Frederico
  2018 "O Brasil precisa de Bolsonaro." *Folha de São Paulo*, September 5.
de Antonio, Gabriel H. B. D. and Milton Lahuerta
  2014 "O neopentecostalismo e os dilemas da modernidade periférica sob o signo do novo desenvolvimentismo brasileiro." *Revista Brasileira de Ciência Política*, no. 14, 57–82. http://dx.doi.org/10.1590/0103-335220141403.
Fernandes, Talita and Thais Bilenky
  2018 "Bolsonaro propõe fundir ministérios da área econômica." *Folha de São Paulo*, August 15.
Fernandes, Talita and Guilherme Seto
  2018 "Bolsonaro votou contra a CPMF e ligou-a a cubanização." *Folha de São Paulo*, September 19.
Gentile, Rogério and Rogério Pagnan
  2018 "Bolsonaro venceu descrédito de aliados, e mudou a forma de se fazer campanha," *Folha de São Paulo*, October 6.
Gielow, Igor
  2018 "Estatizante, Bolsonaro se diz convertido ao liberalismo." *Folha de São Paulo*, October 7.
Godart, F. C. and H. C. White
  2010 "Switchings under uncertainty: the coming and becoming of meanings." *Poetics* 38: 567–586.
Gonzales, Alfonso
  2018 "Neoliberalism, the homeland security state, and the authoritarian turn." *Latino Studies* 14: 80–98.
Grillo, Marco, Maiá Menezes, and Thiago Prado
  2018 "Exclusivo: 'Não entendo mesmo de economia' afirma Jair Bolsonaro." *O Globo*, July 22.
Hall, Stuart
  1988 *The Hard Road to Renewal: Thatcherism and the Crisis of the Left*. London: Verso Books.
Harrison, Graham
  2019 "Authoritarian neoliberalism and capitalist transformation in Africa: all pain no gain." *Globalizations* 16: 274–288. DOI: 10.1080/14747731.2018.1502491.
Havertz, Ralf
  2019 "Right-wing populism and neoliberalism in Germany: the AfD's embrace of ordoliberalism." *New Political Economy* 24: 385–403.
Ikenberry, Jon
  2018 "The end of liberal international order?" *International Affairs* 94 (1): 7–23.
Ismail, Salwa
  2011 "Authoritarian government, neoliberalism and everyday civilities in Egypt." *Third World Quarterly* 32: 845–862.

Jenss, Alke
    2019 "Authoritarian neoliberal rescaling in Latin America: urban in/security and austerity in Oaxaca." *Globalizations* 16: 304–319. DOI:10.1080/14747731.2018.1502493.
Kastner, Tássia
    2018a "Após atentado a Bolsonaro, bolsa dispara e dólar recua para R$4,10." *Folha de São Paulo*, September 7.
    2018b "Dólar cai a R$3,94 e Bolsa dispara após pesquisa Ibope vantajosa para Bolsonaro." *Folha de São Paulo*, October 2.
    2018c "Apos primeiro turno, Bolsa bate recorde em giro financeiro e dollar cai para 3,77." *Folha de São Paulo*, October 9.
    2018d "Bolsa cai 2,8% apos Bolsonaro falar em limite a privatizações." *Folha de São Paulo*, October 11.
    2018e "Bolsa fecha na máxima histórica com exterior positivo e otimismo com Bolsonaro." *Folha de São Paulo*, November 1.
Kastner, Tássia and Eduardo Sodré
    2018 "Mercado espera que dólar oscile mais principalmente entre 1 e 2 turno." *Folha de São Paulo*, September 17.
Kiely, Ray
    2017 "From authoritarian liberalism to economic technocracy: neoliberalism, politics and 'de-democratization.'" *Critical Sociology* 43 (4-5): 725–745.
Leitão, Míriam
    2018a "Do pouco que até agora se sabe." *O Globo*, October 18.
    2018b "Bolsonaro e o vazio de ideias." *O Globo*, September 20.
Levitsky, Stephen and Daniel Ziblatt
    2018 *How Democracies Die*. New York: Crown.
Marcello, Maria Carolina
    2018 "Bolsonaro diz não enviará nada ao Congresso sem conversa prévia; quer tipificar atos do MST como terrorismo. " *Reuters*, October 21.
Nölke, Andreas
    2017 "Brexit: Towards a new global phase of organized capitalism?" *Competition and Change* 21 (3): 230–241.
Olsen, Kristine A.
    2014 "Telling our stories: narrative and framing in the movement for same-sex marriage." *Social Movement Studies* 13 (2): 248–266.
Pamplona, Nicola
    2018 "Após Bolsonaro criticar China, vale disse que disputa não é boa." *Folha de São Paulo*, October 16.
Polletta, Francesca
    1998 "Contending stories: narrative in social movements." *Qualitative Sociology* 21: 419-446.
Pühringer, Stephan and Walter O. Ötsch
    2018 "Neoliberalism and rightwing populism: conceptual analogies." *Forum for Social Economics* 47 (2): 193–203.
Saad-Filho, Alfredo
    2019 "Varieties of neoliberalism in Brazil (2003–2019)." *Latin American Perspectives* 47 (1): 9–27.
Sackley, Nicole
    2015 "The road from serfdom: economic storytelling and narratives of India in the rise of neoliberalism." *History and Technology* 31: 397–419. https://doi.org/10.1080/07341512.2016.1142633
Seabrooke, Leonard and Rune R. Thomsen
    2016 "Making sense of austerity: everyday narratives in Denmark and the United Kingdom." *Politics* 36 (3): 250–261. https://doi.org/10.1177/0263395716652413.
Somers, Margaret R.
    1994 "The narrative constitution of identity: a relational and network approach." *Theory and Society* 23: 605–649.
Tansel, Cemal B.
    2018 "Authoritarian neoliberalism and democratic backsliding in Turkey: beyond the narratives of progress." *South European Society and Politics* 23 (2): 197–217.

Tavares, Joelmir

2018 "Criadores da campanha do posto Ipiranga comemoram apelido de guru de Bolsonaro." *Folha de São Paulo*, August 25.

Tonra, Ben

2011 "Democratic foundations of EU foreign policy: narratives and the myth of EU exceptionalism." *Journal of European Public Policy* 18: 1190–1207. https://doi.org/10.1080/13501763.2011 .615209.

Toplišek, Alen

2019 "The political economy of populist rule in post-crisis Europe: Hungary and Poland." *New Political Economy* 25: 388–403. DOI:10.1080/13563467.2019.1598960.

Zhang, Chenchen

2018 "Governing neoliberal authoritarian citizenship: theorizing *hukou* and the changing mobility regime in China." *Citizenship Studies* 22: 855–881.

Development Projects, Models of Capitalism, and Political Regimes in Brazil, 1988–2021

by
Carlos Eduardo Santos Pinho
Translated by
Nick Ortiz

The Bolsonaro government combines authoritarianism with a model of capitalism that destroys social rights. Despite the expansion of the neoliberal reforms put in place during the 1990s and the decline of the inclusionary policies of the 2000s, there is a causal link between the content of neoliberal public policies, the drop in the level of political participation in their implementation, the militarization of the Bolsonaro government, and the decay of democratic institutions in Brazil.

O governo Bolsonaro combina o autoritarismo com um modelo de capitalismo destruidor de direitos sociais. Além do aprofundamento das reformas neoliberais dos anos 1990 e da regressão das políticas de inclusão dos anos 2000, há uma relação de causalidade entre o conteúdo de políticas públicas neoliberais, a redução do nível de participação política em sua implementação, a militarização do governo Bolsonaro e a degeneração de instituições democráticas no Brasil.

Keywords: *Development projects, Models of capitalism, Political regimes, Austerity, Brazil*

The goal of this article is to explain the causes of the various phases of the implementation of development projects and models of capitalism in Brazil and their impact on political regimes from the ratification of the 1988 Federal Constitution to the Jair Bolsonaro government. It seeks to build upon the lit-

Carlos Eduardo Santos Pinho is a professor in the postgraduate program for social sciences at the Universidade do Vale do Rio dos Sinos and an associate of its Centro Internacional Celso Furtado de Políticas para o Desenvolvimento. He is a researcher at the Interinstitutional Think Tank on the Futures of Social Protection led by Sonia Fleury. This article is the end result of research he conducted as a postdoctoral student at the Instituto Nacional de Ciência e Tecnologia em Políticas Públicas, Estratégias e Desenvolvimento (INCT/PPED). A scholarship was also provided by the Coordenação de Aperfeiçoamento de Pessoal de Nível Superior (CAPES) under the supervision of Renato Raul Boschi. A preliminary version of this article was presented at the Eleventh Meeting of the Brazilian Association of Political Science, July 31–August 3, 2018, at the Universidade Federal de Paraná (Curitiba). The author thanks the anonymous reviewers for valuable and constructive comments, criticisms, and suggestions that contributed a great deal in strengthening the arguments proposed in this article. Nick Ortiz is a writer, researcher, linguist, and translator with experience in translation relating to Latin American history and politics.

LATIN AMERICAN PERSPECTIVES, Issue 248, Vol. 50 No. 1, January 2023, 80–97
DOI: 10.1177/0094582X221147595
© 2023 Latin American Perspectives

erature on the relation between development projects, models of capitalism, and political regimes in Brazil (Draibe, 1985; Fernandes, 1976) by highlighting the recent Brazilian political/economic crisis in public and academic debates and placing it in comparative perspective. Particular emphasis will be given to events and policies of the 1990s and 2000s that remain relevant today. Instead of focusing strictly on institutional traits, this article will include Brazil's democratic political regime and the context in which it operates. By analyzing the projects and processes associated with Brazil's political economy and the central role it plays in broad coalitions, the article will examine not only the interests of political/economic elites but also those of social groups and classes.

Regarding the end of the period (2003–2016) that witnessed the emergence of development schemes associated with policies of social inclusion, the main questions posed in this article will be structured as follows: How do the "structural reforms" laid out in *Uma ponte para o futuro* (A Bridge to the Future) (Fundação Ulysses Guimarães/PMDB, 2015) and swiftly implemented by the Michel Temer and Jair Bolsonaro governments differ from the promarket reforms (1990–2002) and those put in place as part of a program known as the new democratic developmentalism (2003–2016)? Is there a causal link between the framework for the implementation of neoliberal public policies, the erosion of the level of political participation in the decision-making process behind these policies, the militarization of the Brazilian state, and the collapse of Brazil's democracy? This article argues that there is such a link, which runs parallel to the radicalization of neoliberal reforms of the 1990s and the decline of the inclusionary policies of the 2000s. The ties between neoliberalism and authoritarianism become more and more apparent in this process.

The article first examines the literature of the political economy of development and varieties of capitalism and then seeks to modernize its focus, which is fundamentally Eurocentric and business-centered. It revitalizes the role of the state in that it considers the unique qualities of capitalist development in Brazil in the context of financial hegemony and cuts in social spending. It also explores the differences between the varieties of neoliberalism of the 1990s and those that have been implemented since the 2016 coup and the subsequent breakdown of Brazil's democracy (Bastos, 2017; Boschi, 2011; 2013; Boschi and Pinho, 2019a; 2019b; Carvalho, 2018; Hall and Soskice, 2001; Ianoni, 2018; Pinho, 2019; 2020; Singer, 2018; Vasileva-Dienes and Schimidt, 2019). Then, treating the Brazilian case as an empirical object, it attempts to appropriate and systematize contemporary theories of democracy that analyze the emergence of authoritarian leaders through the ballot box. The goals of these "incidental rulers" (Abranches, 2020) are based on a morality that is tied to resentment, the decline of institutions that promote social solidarity, the rejection of scientific knowledge and academics, and neofascist characteristics founded on a disdain for minority rights. These rulers seek to overturn elections, encourage constant attacks on the democratic political system, and promote de-democratization. They express their discontent with the freedom of the press and work to destabilize public policies that are based on the practice of participative democracy as a tool for political representation (Abranches, 2018; 2020; Avritzer, 2019; Brown, 2019; Couto, 2021; Dahl, 1997; Fraser, 2019; Levitsky and Ziblatt, 2018; Miguel, 2019; 2014; Mounk, 2019; Pogrebinschi and Santos, 2011; Przeworski, 2020; Santos, 2017; Snyder, 2019; Tatagiba, 2021; Tilly, 2007).

This article analyzes the underlying tensions that emerge when resources are distributed among various actors and coalitions. These tensions are mediated by the same state institutions in which they are situated, and they are located at the center of an endemic conflict between capitalist markets and political democracy (Streeck, 2011: 6). This conflict is exacerbated by the increasing financialization of the economy (Davis and Kim, 2015). After this introduction, the second section will examine the unique qualities of the 1988 Constitution and the promarket reforms (1990–2002). The third section will investigate the rise and fall of the progressive coalition that led the wave known as the new democratic developmentalism (Pinho, 2019) and what led to the failure of reforms that sought to liberalize the Brazilian economy in terms of economic growth, job creation, and income distribution. The fourth section will explore the austerity measures put in place by the Temer and Bolsonaro governments when Brazil's democracy began to break down in 2016 and conduct a retrospective and situational analysis of the causal mechanisms that link austerity policies to the deficit of democracy that exists in Brazil today. The last section will present some final thoughts.

THE 1988 CONSTITUTION AND THE PROMARKET REFORMS (1990–2002)

The 1988 Constitution constitutes the framework for the institutional architecture of citizenship and the democratic transformation of the state and society. It also creates a system of social protections inspired by the values that lie at the heart of the social welfare state (a model that is seen in past and present European social democracies). These protections include universality, social security, and the law as opposed to others such as focalization, social safety, and welfarism. Its fundamental traits include a highly decentralized system and a decision-making process that incorporates a federal system and a society organized around areas of political participation. This process creates new intergovernmental relations and changes the relationship between the state and social actors (Fagnani, 2017; Fleury, 2014).

The sociologist Florestan Fernandes offers a more skeptical analysis in his study of the political/institutional context behind the transition from authoritarianism to democracy. According to him, when the "New Republic" was being constructed, the dominance of the Partido do Movimento Democrático Brasileiro (Brazilian Democratic Movement—PMDB) was decisive regarding the adoption of an electoral college. It was in this way that it acted as a "party of order." He further argues that the supremacy of the conservative parties (the Partido Democrático Social, the Partido da Frente Liberal, the Partido do Movimento Democrático Brasileiro, and the Partido Trabalhista Brasileiro) was geared toward carrying out the agenda of private interests. The 1987 constituent assembly that preceded the promulgation of the 1988 Constitution represented an unequal balance of power. Conservative parties dominated this assembly to the detriment of political groups that represented Brazilian workers (the Partido dos Trabalhadores, the Central Única dos Trabalhadores, and the Confederação Geral dos Trabalhadores). This conservative pact represented a shift toward an ultraconservative and counterrevolutionary orientation by the bourgeoisie that allowed it to exert its political power using authoritarian methods (Fernandes, 1989).

On the one hand, there was an effort at political redemocratization that included policies to reduce the social debt incurred as part of the authoritarian national developmentalism of the military dictatorship (1964–1985). On the other hand, Brazil's weakened financial system, the foreign debt crisis, hyperinflation, and the haphazard way in which liberalizing policies were implemented limited the ability of the state to rectify the situation (Pinho, 2019; 2020). According to Fleury (2014: 22), "In other words, there were two concurrent movements going in opposite directions: one expressed by the macroeconomic adjustment measures and the other by demands for assuring social rights and institutionalizing the [welfare state]."

After the failure of various monetary stabilization plans implemented by the José Sarney government (1985–1989), the Fernando Collor de Mello government did not follow the logic of "coalition presidentialism." Unable to navigate between the different fragmented political parties and interests that occupied Congress, officials in Collor de Mello's government could not form the majority coalition that was necessary to govern effectively (Abranches, 2018). This experiment was an inauspicious and disastrous beginning to an era of promarket reforms and ill-fated monetary stabilization policies such as Collor Plans 1 and 2. These policies deprived many middle-class families of their savings and undermined the concept of private property (Pinho, 2019). At the cost of destabilizing Brazil's bureaucracy, the Collor de Mello government carried out an administrative restructuring that involved the modernization of the state, economic adjustments, deregulation, privatization, and liberalization of the Brazilian economy. This restructuring led to the removal of 112,000 civil servants, including officials from lower levels in the public sector and those who held commissions and high-level advisory positions (Diniz and Boschi, 2014; Lima Jr., 2014).

The contradictions between neoliberalism and democracy became apparent during the Collor and Fernando Henrique Cardoso (1995–2002) governments. These contradictions were largely the result of dependence on the revision of provisional measures by Congress. These efforts were thwarted in September 2001, near the end of Cardoso's second term, with the ratification of Constitutional Amendment 32/2001, which prevented the reintroduction of these measures within the same legislative session (a year). According to Pessanha (2002), during Cardoso's two terms in office, 5,036 provisional measures were issued (65.9 per month) compared with 363 for Itamar Franco, 70 for Collor, and 22 for Sarney.

Cardoso relied on a political coalition that enabled him to "reform the state" with a managerial, entrepreneurial, and decentralized approach, seeking to overcome the bureaucracy of the civil service that was typical of the national developmentalism practiced by past governments such as that of Getúlio Vargas. He himself had been minister of the interior under Franco when the 1994 Real Plan for countering hyperinflation and ensuring macroeconomic stabilization was implemented. Under Cardoso, the government minimized the role of the state in the economy. In addition, it undertook administrative reforms that included more flexibility in economic stabilization policies, dismissal for lack of performance, an end to isonomy and the Uniform Administrative Law, and modification of the social security system. It even passed an amendment of the law on reelection (Boschi and Lima, 2002; Diniz and Boschi, 2014; Lima Jr., 2014).

Brazilian industrialists were negatively affected by these liberalizing reforms and appeared to be frustrated with the changes that they entailed, among them high interest rates, uncontrolled liberalization of the economy, the overvaluation of the real, the denationalization of many Brazilian industries, and deindustrialization. Two anchors were used to stabilize Brazil's currency, the stock exchange and high exchange rates. The first anchor tied the real to the dollar. Constant assistance from the Central Bank was necessary to keep the real at an artificially low level, and assistance came at a high cost for the currency. The second anchor maintained exchange rates that were much higher than the global average, and this caused the federal public debt to increase exponentially. In order to compensate for the costs of implementing the Real Plan, large numbers of federal assets were privatized in places such as Vale do Rio Doce, and 40 percent of the federal assets in Petrobras were privatized, along with government stocks in Light São Paulo e Rio and all of the country's telephone companies, petrochemical plants, and steelworks. The government ended up spending US$109 billion to cover recurrent costs and interest payments alone. When it eventually ran out of assets to sell, the expenses and interest payments continued to pile up (Araújo, 2017).

During the 1990s, the government adopted liberalizing measures that went hand in hand with the main ideology of the time: the financialization of the economy. This ideology imposed structural obstacles to industry, public investment, and the expansion of social policies. Integrating Brazil into a global financial system required not only opening up its economy but also reducing the amount of regulation of capital flows. This created the conditions for a mass accumulation of wealth that altered the behavior of bankers, entrepreneurs, and financial speculators alike. These liberalizing measures established an economic model that was favorable to the interests of the large banking corporations that had lost their inflationary profits as a result of the Real Plan. When a drop in inflation led to monetary stabilization policies, one of the measures taken by the state was swapping the concept of "hyperinflation" for "hyperinterest" based on the Central Bank's activities (Bruno, 2015). This measure was a violation of the 1988 Constitution, which stated in Article 192 (later removed) that real interest could not exceed 12 percent per year.

The government attached considerable importance to the credibility and confidence that were promoted by risk-rating agencies and international financial investors. This led to the private appropriation of public policies by large financial groups that reaped significant profits from the increase in the public debt. In 1999, a proposal to amend the constitution (PEC 53/1999, later known as Constitutional Amendment 40/2003) removed several paragraphs from Article 192 in the 1988 Constitution that regulated the national financial system. As a result, investment in government bonds that were paid for with taxpayer money suddenly became more profitable to intermediaries and financial agents. This sudden profitability of government bonds was detrimental to investment in public policies and infrastructure that sought to diversify Brazil's production structure and boost the country's economy (Bruno, 2015; Corrêa, Lemos, and Feijo, 2017; Dowbor, 2017).

DEVELOPMENT PROJECTS AND STATE-DIRECTED CAPITALISM IN THE NEW DEMOCRATIC DEVELOPMENTALISM

In 2002, pressure from the global financial system, fears of an increase in inflation, noncompliance with contracts, and the rise in the public debt compelled Luiz Inácio Lula da Silva and the Partido dos Trabalhadores (Workers' Party—PT) to release their "Letter to the Brazilian People" during the presidential election. In this document, they expressed their support for a macroeconomic policy that rested on three principles: a system of inflation targets, a floating exchange rate, and a primary surplus. Despite the high degree of macroeconomic instability that year, Lula won the election thanks to a coalition composed of workers, unions, social movements, and industrialists that were dissatisfied with the austerity policies implemented by Cardoso's governments (Pinho, 2019; 2021).

Once he took office, President Lula adopted a restrained macroeconomic policy that proposed raising the goal of the primary surplus for the public sector from 3.75 percent in 2003 to 4.25 percent of Brazil's gross domestic product (GDP). This was a testament to the hegemony of the three principles of the PT's economic program, which became known as the *tripé rígido* (rigid tripod) (Ianoni, 2018). Two economic approaches clashed at the end of Lula's first term: neoliberalism and developmentalism. By 2006 the latter had become hegemonic. Flexibility of macroeconomic policies was causally linked with a social developmentalist coalition based on the interests of the productive sector (industrialists, agribusiness owners, and workers), but this coalition did not represent a break with fiscal orthodoxy. Flexibility in the tripod reached its height during this period. Although it led to important changes in the economy, it proved ineffective in strengthening manufacturing industry in an age of globalization (Ianoni, 2018).

In the first decade of the twenty-first century, a developmentalist agenda was clearly beginning to take shape. This agenda was composed of directives identified in 2004–2006 and strengthened during Lula's second term. The implementation of the 2004–2007 multiyear plan, "A Brazil for Everyone: Sustainable Growth, Employment, and Social Inclusion," was based on a framework composed of a number of public policies: credit expansion, valuation of the minimum wage, increase of formal employment, wide-ranging social policies such as the Bolsa Família (or Family Stipend) and consigned credit, a more assertive industrial policy, environmentally sustainable growth and the reduction of regional disparities, and strengthening of the role in the economy of the Banco Nacional de Desenvolvimento Econômico e Social (National Bank for Economic and Social Development—BNDES). This coincided with the Growth Acceleration Plan of 2007 and the productive development policy of the following year. As far as fiscal policy was concerned, there was a withdrawal of investment by the Union (Brazil's political/administrative apparatus) based on calculations of the primary surplus target. This same process began to be applied to planned investment in the Growth Acceleration Plan after July 2009. In 2007, despite its efforts to promote public investment, the Lula government also initiated a series of tax breaks to encourage private investment and develop a mass consumer market (Diniz, 2016).

In 2010 Lula's chief of staff, Dilma Rousseff, was elected president. After an initial fiscal adjustment in 2011, she reinforced this developmentalist shift in the government's macroeconomic policy with a vigorous fiscal policy that awarded large subsidies and tax breaks to Brazilian industrialists. With the goal of promoting more investment in the productive sector via industrialization policies (Boschi and Pinho, 2019a), she implemented the controversial new macroeconomic matrix, which sought to counter past rentier policies and reduce the negative impact on the economy of the 2008 global financial crisis. It was based on the following interventionist measures: reducing interest, relying heavily on the BNDES for reindustrialization, tax breaks, reforming the power sector, devaluating the real, monitoring capital flows, and promoting domestic production through government purchases. In contrast to Lula, Rousseff sought to eliminate the rentierism that viewed the public debt as simply an instrument for accumulating capital (Bastos, 2017; Carvalho, 2018; Pinho, 2019; Singer, 2018).

Significant changes in the global economic system following the 2008 financial crisis prevented a convergence of interests between different levels of Brazil's bourgeoisie. Its economic policies during Dilma Rousseff's first term had had mixed results and led to a cyclical slowdown of the economy and growing dissatisfaction among the country's business owners, who complained about the large amount of invoicing they were required to produce in order to pay their workers. Thus, even though one of the goals of Rousseff's macroeconomic policy was to support Brazilian businesses and entrepreneurs, it ended up having the opposite effect by turning them against the government's interventionist policies (Bastos, 2017; Singer, 2018). As a result, a group of business owners formed a "single, bourgeois front" in 2013 that adopted a neoliberal platform and opposed the Rousseff government's "developmentalist experiment" (Singer, 2018: 39). This platform promoted cuts in public spending and the reform of Brazil's labor and welfare policies. The measures that were previously demanded by industrialists (such as reducing interest rates and payroll tax exemption) did not have the desired effect and instead created a profound distrust of Rousseff's economic policies among business owners and entrepreneurs.

Shunned by Brazil's industrialists, Rousseff dismissed the unconventional economist Guido Mantega from his post as minister of the interior and replaced him with the traditional economist Joaquim Levy in a desperate attempt to please the rentier coalition that had opposed her during her presidential campaign in 2014. After Mantega's dismissal, she launched a bold fiscal and monetary adjustment that included cutting government spending and raising interest rates (Boschi and Pinho, 2019a; 2019b; Carvalho, 2018; Pinho, 2019; 2021; Singer, 2018). Despite this shift, many of Brazil's unconventional economists saw Dilma Rousseff's policies as not developmentalist enough because of their focus on private instead of public investment during a time when household debt and the acquisition of consumer durables had reached their peak. According to Laura Carvalho (2018), the 2011–2014 period marked the end of a cycle of expansion of public investment in infrastructure. It was replaced with an agenda of tax reductions, concessions, and other incentives for the private sector that caused a severe decline in revenue just as the annual cost of tax waivers (R$140 billion in 2010) rose to R$250 billion in 2014. Regardless of the tax breaks that were put in place during this period, the cost of these policies rose from R$45.5 billion in 2012 to R$74.8 billion in 2013 and R$101.3 billion in 2014, amounting to 1.8 percent of the GDP (Carvalho, 2018).

In addition to the collapse of its political/entrepreneurial support base, the turn toward a traditional economic orientation, the deterioration of public accounts, the loss of credibility of the government's macroeconomic policies, and a combination of other causal mechanisms led to the end of the new democratic developmentalism, the expansion of austerity policies (Pinho, 2019), and a phase of democratic backsliding that is still under way. First, Rousseff's fiscal adjustment came at the cost of her support base and generated unemployment and a decline in revenue in 2014–2015. Secondly, it made her presidency extremely unpopular in the eyes of many Brazilians. Thirdly, a Congress emerged from the 2014 elections that was the "most conservative of any in the post-1964 period" (*O Estado de São Paulo*, 2014). This shift to the right was followed by a decline in the number of seats (from 86 to 46) held by unions and their allies in Congress. The data collected by the Inter-Union Department for Congressional Assistance show that the Congress elected in 2014 reflected "a party shakeup and a shift toward a liberal economic and socially conservative orientation that represents a step back when it comes to human rights and environmental issues" (DIAP, 2014: 13).

Fourthly, Congress's conservative orientation served to embolden an "ultraliberal counteraudience" that manifested itself in social media networks and in the impeachment protests against Dilma Rousseff. This "counteraudience" consisted of young liberal university students and professors who shared an identity centered on a radical defense of the free market as the foundation for social and economic organization. Although they were not socially oppressed, they nonetheless saw themselves as marginalized in the public sphere (Rocha, 2019).

Lastly, the implementation of the Lava Jato (Car Wash) operation, an investigation of corruption launched by the Federal Police in Rio de Janeiro in 2014, had catastrophic effects on the economy. It disrupted industrial policies that sought to strengthen production chains relating to oil, gas, infrastructure, and shipbuilding. It also created an opportunity for many officials to practice a "justicialism of exception" (Boschi and Pinho, 2019a: 305)— the collusion of politics and justice previously seen in the authoritarian policies of Juan Perón in Argentina during the 1940s and 1950s. This economic downturn had serious effects on Petrobras and Pre-Salt operations in Brazil and their ability to attract global investors. It also had a negative impact on the creation of parafiscal resources used to finance Brazil's educational, scientific, and technological infrastructure (Bastos, 2017).

THE 2016 COUP, AUSTERITY, AND DEMOCRATIC DECAY

In line with contemporary democratic political theory, Wanderley Guilherme dos Santos (2017: 180) describes the Brazilian "parliamentary coup" as a tacit agreement between officials in Brazil's legislative and judicial systems. It involved systematically sabotaging presidential actions in order to disrupt income distribution policies and create a "coalition that would support a conservative power grab." After Rousseff's impeachment, Brazil went through an unprecedented process of destabilization with regard to constitutionally protected social rights, the radicalization of neoliberal reforms from the 1990s, and the resurgence of authoritarianism in the government (Boschi and Pinho, 2019a; 2019b; Fleury and Pinho, 2019; Pinho, 2021).

In carrying out the PMDB's austerity program, Michel Temer gained approval for his labor reforms even when they interfered with his own reforms of Brazil's welfare state. They created disruptions of regulatory institutions with regard to labor and the implementation of CLT/1943 and Constitutional Amendment 95/2016, compelling policy makers to pursue drastic budget cuts and criminalize social policies by capping public primary spending. The fluctuation for this spending was set at 20 years according to the inflation index used at the time, and the result was a reduction in Brazil's budget per capita. This emergency measure was a clear violation of Article 6 of Chapter 2 of the 1988 Constitution, which states that education, health, work, transport, security, welfare, food, housing, leisure, maternity and child protection, and aid to the poor are social rights that must be protected.

According to a study conducted by the Instituto de Pesquisa Econômica Aplicada (Institute for Applied Economic Research—IPEA), during the first year in which these policies were implemented the new fiscal regime allotted only R$79 billion instead of the usual R$85 billion necessary to sustain Brazil's social protection policies—an 8 percent reduction. At this rate, the cuts in the financing of those policies by 2036 will amount to 54 percent, around R$868 billion (Paiva et al., 2016). In addition to ignoring past countercyclical policies aimed at bolstering public investment and aggregated demand, these austerity measures were put in place during a period (2015–2016) that was witnessing a severe recession. The GDP declined by 7.2 percent (*Valor Econômico*, 2017) and then suffered a slow recovery. During the first year of Jair Bolsonaro's term, the number of people waiting for support from the Bolsa Família rose from zero to 494,229 families (*O Globo*, 2020). This sudden increase was part of a pattern that has intensified to this day. After a cycle (2003–2014) of growth and social inclusion, these austerity policies represented a shift toward the radical liberal/traditional policies typical of the Old Republic (1889–1930).

Jair Bolsonaro waged a radicalized electoral campaign that was based on fake news and an ambiguous political platform. He came to power with the aid of "epistemic communities in support of fiscal austerity" (Pinho, 2021)—a powerful liberal/conservative coalition composed of media oligopolies, agribusiness owners, industrialists, traditional economists, liberal organizations, and sections of the middle and upper classes that had helped impeach Dilma Rousseff. Bolsonaro awarded considerable decision-making powers to his minister of the economy, Paulo Guedes, who had a doctorate from the

University of Chicago and was one of the economists who supported Augusto Pinochet's austerity policies in Chile during the country's military dictatorship (1973–1990).

Despite Bolsonaro's inability to coordinate and manage a congressional majority, his welfare reforms were approved thanks to the support of Congress in establishing and negotiating the country's economic policy. These reforms raised the contribution time and minimum age and reduced welfare benefits to the minimal thresholds established by the government. Thus the austerity agenda of the Bolsonaro government united the political/economic elites and served as a warning to the financial market that fiscal balance and cuts in public spending would be necessary to save the economy. During the third year of a turbulent term that witnessed the catastrophic management of the COVID-19 pandemic and a massive drop in his popularity, Bolsonaro became a prisoner of the Centrão (Core), a bloc of self-interested political parties and politicians lacking any clear ideological program or agenda. Made up of congresspeople whose only desire was for political positions, public funds, and amendments, it has supported every Brazilian government since redemocratization regardless of political orientation.

In terms of the principle of including participatory practices in public policy making, this framework is contradictory to that of the new democratic developmentalism. During the period between 2002 and 2010, modes of interaction between the state and society were established that encouraged the democratization of public policies and promoted social participation as a method for managing areas such as social protection, infrastructure, the environment, and economic development (IPEA, 2012: 3). Participatory and deliberative practices coincided with the emergence of new actors in the management of public policies. This combination enhanced political representation and strengthened Brazil's democratic system (Pogrebinschi and Santos, 2011). In contrast to the state's tradition of bureaucratic isolation (Nunes, 2003), the Lula government established a dialogue with civil society, unions, and social movements, and this dialogue intensified under the PT governments. Despite Rousseff's centralizing tendencies, preference for isolation, and distaste for negotiations, there was more dialogue under Rousseff than under Temer. Temer's government did not establish the mechanisms with which to consult civil society regarding the implementation of its austerity measures.

The decline of participatory policies began with the congressional resistance to Decree 8,243 of May 23, 2014 (Miguel, 2019), which established the National Policy for Social Participation "with the goal of strengthening and defining democratic mechanisms and institutions and [encouraging] joint action between the federal civil service and civil society" (Presidência da República, 2014). In a decision that characterized his first 100 days in office, Bolsonaro issued Decree 9,759/2019, which abolished the managing councils, participatory institutions, and conferences that previously had helped formulate public policies. However, the Supreme Court formed a majority to suspend the decree that extinguishes councils (*Congresso em Foco*, 2019).

This suggests that Jair Bolsonaro's election was part of a worldwide phenomenon characterized by the emergence of autocratic leaders who seek to undermine democratic institutions from within. However, while individual rights continue to be respected to a degree, citizens/constituents of this type of political system suffer a considerable decline in the amount of influence they can exert on public policies. Social inequality can have an impact on the way a democracy functions (Miguel, 2014). Bolsonaro's radical constituents view Brazil's military dictatorship and Institutional Act 5 (issued to solidify the military's position in the government through the repression of political rights) with nostalgia. They also show a clear disdain for democratic institutions such as Congress, the Supreme Court, and the Superior Electoral Court. Bolsonaro himself has tried to undermine these institutions through private means. He has also infringed upon the rights of religious and ethnic minorities. His actions are characteristic of an "illiberal democracy," a democracy without rights (Mounk, 2019). The state under Bolsonaro distanced itself from the sociologist Peter Evans's (2014) "twenty-first century developmentalist state," in which deliberative and participatory institutions are constructed while allowing business interests to act independently.

The question of the causal mechanisms that link austerity policies with the recent decline in Brazilian democracy requires a complex response. The goal here is to explore the historically comprehensive relationship between political regimes, coalitions, and public policies based on the following factors:

1. The decision of the defeated Partido da Social Democracia Brasileira (Brazilian Social Democracy Party—PSDB) candidate Aécio Neves to challenge the 2014 election results. Neves, who was supported by the president of Brazil's Chamber of Deputies, Eduardo Cunha, pursued a "bombshell agenda" that included outsourcing labor, making it difficult for the government to implement its fiscal adjustments, and approving the petition to impeach Dilma Rousseff written by the legal experts Janaina Paschoal and Miguel Reale Jr. This hostile legislative environment served to exacerbate the political instability and gridlock that already existed within Congress.

2. The election in 2014 of a Congress with the most conservative orientation of any Congress in the post-1964 period and the election in 2018 of a Congress with a similar conservative orientation. Both Congresses had promarket platforms and were composed of evangelicals, landowners, arms manufacturers, and elements of the extreme right that opposed human rights, environmental policies, women, black Brazilians, quilombolas (descendants of Brazilian slaves who had sought refuge in fugitive slave communities known as quilombos), indigenous peoples, the LGBTQIA + community, universal social policies, and labor regulation. The dominance of right-wing actors in Brazil's Congress coincided with a sharp decline in the number of seats held by unions and lobbyists who represented the interests of Brazilian workers.

3. Dilma Rousseff's granting of substantial subsidies and tax breaks to business. These policies ruined the public accounts, failed to generate new jobs, and led many Brazilians to lose faith in macroeconomic policy. As a result, Michel Temer, Jair Bolsonaro, and his minister of the economy, Paulo Guedes, argued that austerity was the only path forward in order for the Brazilian state to avoid fiscal insolvency. These austerity measures reduced the size of public banks such as the Banco do Brasil, the Caixa Econômica Federal, and the BNDES and limited investment in infrastructure.

4. The shift toward neoliberal policies during Dilma Rousseff's second term, a desperate attempt to gain the support of business and attract financial capital that led to cuts in public policies, a rise in unemployment, a drop in revenue, and growing discontent among the poorer sectors of the electorate. These factors shook the foundations of Rousseff's popularity and cost her her support base. Shattered hopes and disillusionment among the electorate caused many Brazilians to cast their votes for Bolsonaro. A proponent of violent rhetoric against political parties, traditional politicians, the "communist left," and representative democracy, he promised to resist the dissolution of the traditional family, restore the economy, and preserve the free market, meritocracy, and private property.

5. The failure of the developmentalist governments to propose any effective public policies for reducing violence and improving public security. Bolsonaro filled this void with a demagogic discourse that revealed his intent to repress his political enemies, persecute religious and ethnic minorities, and rebuild Brazil's arsenal.

6. The Petrobras corruption scandal, which in addition to disrupting the production chain for petroleum, gas, civil engineering, infrastructure, shipbuilding, and the GDP delegitimized the state's policies for the productive sector and its role as a provider of public services. This helped in spreading an antipolitics rhetoric promoting the idea that the market was not only efficient and virtuous but also immune to corruption.

7. The suppression of Luiz Inácio Lula da Silva's political rights, which had a considerable impact on the results and legitimacy of the 2018 presidential election. Banning Lula from independently launching his candidacy was a clear violation of republican rules for democratic electoral competition. Cleared of all Lava Jato accusations, Lula won the 2022 election against Bolsonaro but in the face of several antidemocratic acts, vigils by Bolsonaro supporters in front of armed forces barracks calling for a military coup, roadblocks across the country, vandalism, and use of firearms by scammers.

8. The widespread exposure in the digital media of the 2013 protests, the diverse platform of which stemmed as much from their opposition to the government's raising bus fares as from their effort to fight corruption. The mobilization of the upper and middle classes in 2015–2016 in favor of the Lava Jato operation, the impeachment of Dilma Rousseff, and the involvement of the military demonstrate the seriousness of the political crisis and the significance of the increase in conservatism in the country. The radical protests (many of them attended by Bolsonaro himself) supporting Institutional Act 5, military intervention, closing down Congress and the Supreme Court, and eliminating the Superior Electoral Court and the electoral court system took place during the pandemic and were characterized by their aggression toward health officials, journalists, and the press.

9. The crucial role of the military in undermining Lula's candidacy, helping Bolsonaro get elected, and occupying important posts in his government. It led to the broad militarization of ministries and key positions in the public bureaucracy and state enterprises. The appointment of a general, General Walter Braga Netto, as chief of staff had not happened since Golbery do Couto e Silva left the post in 1981 during the military dictatorship. For the first time

since redemocratization, the armed forces are extending their role in Brazil's political and administrative institutions, actively attacking the various branches of the government), praising the 1964 military dictatorship, and delivering cryptic speeches against the democratic regime (*Folha de São Paulo*, 2021). General Eduardo Villas Bôas had a fundamental role in this process as commander of the army (2015–2019). On the eve of the habeas corpus ruling that allowed Lula to run for president, he threatened the Supreme Court on Twitter. Soon after this incident, he was sent to prison for 580 days. Despite this, a period of veiled military activism followed the publication of the final report of the National Truth Commission, its main figure being a general, Sérgio Etchegoyen, the leader of the recently created Gabinete de Segurança Institucional (Cabinet of Institutional Security—GSI). Bolsonaro himself recognized the fundamental role Villas Bôas had played in his victory, and the general considered Bolsonaro's election the beginning of a new era.

10. The central role of the mainstream press in the emphatic defense of austerity reforms and the criminalization of political activity. This biased coverage heightened the disdain for political representation that allowed Bolsonaro to assume power. In an article that served as his mea culpa, Pedro Cafardo (2020), the former executive editor of *Valor Econômico*, argued that the elites (judges, attorney generals, industrialists, agribusiness owners, financial investors, and churches) knew what electing Bolsonaro would mean when they went to the polls. According to him, journalists could not "escape their responsibilities" and "should have looked more closely at what they wrote in the recent past."

11. The pressure that was brought to bear on the rule of law and the legal process and the systematic attempts of Bolsonaro to undermine the independence of executive institutions of control such as the Federal Police, the Public Prosecutor's Office, the judiciary, the Attorney General's Office, and the Solicitor General's Office were intended to save members of his family involved in corruption scandals or connected to militias (the armed groups formed paralegally by Brazilian police officers and others to fight drug trafficking and maintain order).

The recent efforts to derail Brazil's democracy are due as much to politics as to a perspective centered on development and a model of predatory capitalism that destroys social rights. They are motivated by a reactionary ideology that seeks to dismantle institutions built during the post-1988 period. The powerful coalition that supports Bolsonaro is made up of sectors of Brazil's industrialists, agribusiness owners, arms manufacturers, and evangelical churches. One of its leaders is the media owner Edir Macedo, ranked 177 on *Forbes*'s (2019: 110) list of billionaires with a net worth of R$1.41 billion. Bolsonaro's supporters look down on minority rights, oppose state regulation, and adhere to a ultraliberal capitalism that represses social rights. This is evident in the phrase used by the former environment minister Ricardo Salles during a ministerial meeting on April 22, 2020 (*Folha de São Paulo*, 2020), "[We should] keep taking advantage of this unique opportunity [and] continue to change and simplify every rule and regulation [we come across]."

Here one can see the synergy that exists between moral conservatism, reactionary politics, economic ultraliberalism, political authoritarianism, and disdain for democratic institutions. The empirical data systematized in this article support the following conclusions with regard to the Bolsonaro government: As seen through his words and deeds, Bolsonaro refuses to play by the democratic rules of the game. He denies the legitimacy of his rivals. He encourages and is flippant about the use of violence to goad his captive electorate into attacking his opponents and others who defend democracy, and he is willing to curtail the civil liberties of his adversaries, especially those in the press (Levitsky and Ziblatt, 2018). The challenge that confronts Brazilians today is uniting the democratic forces in defense of a young and embattled Brazilian democracy.

FINAL THOUGHTS

Combining a theoretical/conceptual model with an empirical analysis, I have examined the causes of the various phases of development projects and models of capitalism and their relationship to events that had a significant impact on Brazil's political regime. The 2016 coup and Bolsonaro's election as president inaugurated a model of ultraliberal capitalism that reduces public participation in the development of policy and constantly attacks democratic institutions. This reality contradicts the established argument of various scholars that there was no chance of an institutional crisis in Brazil—that "Brazil's democracy had been consolidated" (Bresser-Pereira, 2014: 374). The evidence in this study points to the idea that Brazil is undergoing profound institutional change and an abrupt transition from a model of coordinated, democratic, and regulated capitalism to a model of capitalism that is more radical, ultraliberal, antidemocratic, and intent on destroying social rights (Boschi and Pinho, 2019a). The new model of capitalism is isolated from economic and political institutions and has not the slightest regard for democracy and its representative, participatory, and governing institutions. The terms "ultraliberal," "antidemocratic," and "radical" in this article are observations based on an analytic reinterpretation the purpose of which is to bring to light the authoritarian features of the government's current economic measures that are less well known to the Brazilian public.

The model of capitalism under Bolsonaro qualifies as ultraliberal capitalism in that it seeks to intensify a neoliberal agenda that dates from the 1990s. A case in point is the new fiscal regime, an emergency measure that is unlike anything seen elsewhere in the world today. It is antidemocratic in that it refuses to allow public scrutiny of the decision making that underlies its austerity measures and disregards constitutional principles of social participation and the monitoring of public policies. It is radical in the haste, depth, and reach with which it has been carried out by political and economic elites with ties to globalized financial interests. This socially destructive model of capitalism is based on state regulation that either violates or eliminates constitutional protections.

In contrast, the privatizing governments were heavily interventionist and made significant contributions toward increasing the national debt. Through the broad use of provisional measures, the Collor de Mello and Cardoso governments sought to bury the national-developmentalist and institutional legacy of the Vargas era. By pursuing these promarket reforms, they only deepened the contradictions between capitalism and democracy. The Lula da Silva and Dilma Rousseff governments not only oversaw a process of unprecedented economic growth that included more opportunities for social inclusion, expansion of the domestic market, and mass consumption but also formed a coalition of the most archaic, parasitic, and conservative segments of Brazil's political economy that initiated the construction of a national popular democracy. After having practically put an end to extreme poverty in Brazil and allowing the country to reach a prominent position on the international stage, this model of development and its project for national development were discarded after the 2016 coup. The rise of Bolsonaro included austerity measures, a decline in social indicators (such as unemployment, extreme poverty, and hunger), the militarization of state institutions, the dismantling of public policies that had a successful track record, and the vilification of democracy through systemic attacks on the freedom of the press and republican institutions.

REFERENCES

Abranches, Sérgio
    2018 *Presidencialismo de coalizão: Raízes e evolução do modelo político brasileiro*. São Paulo: Companhia das Letras.
    2020 *O tempo dos governantes incidentais*. São Paulo: Companhia das Letras.
Araújo, André
    2017 "O ninho da recessão: como a economia brasileira perdeu o rumo." August 15. *Dinâmica Global*. https://dinamicaglobal.wordpress.com/2017/08/15/o-ninho-da-recessao-como-a-economia-brasileira-perdeu-o-rumo/.
Avritzer, Leonardo
    2019 *O pêndulo da democracia*. São Paulo: Todavia.
Bastos, Pedro P. Z.
    2017 "Ascensão e crise do governo Dilma Rousseff e o golpe de 2016: poder estrutural, contradição e ideologia." *Revista de Economia Contemporânea* 21 (2): 1–63.
Boschi, Renato
    2011 "Instituições, trajetórias e desenvolvimento: uma discussão a partir da América Latina," pp. 7–30 in Renato Boschi (ed.), *Variedades de capitalismo, política e desenvolvimento na América Latina*. Belo Horizonte: Ed. UFMG.
    2013 "Politics and trajectory in Brazilian capitalist development," pp. 123–143 in Uwe Becker (ed.), *The BRICs and Emerging Economies in Comparative Perspective: Political Economy, Liberalisation and Institutional Change*. London: Routledge.
Boschi, Renato and Carlos Eduardo Santos Pinho
    2019a "Crisis and austerity: the recent trajectory of capitalist development in Brazil." *Contemporary Politics* 25 (3): 292–312.
    2019b "Crise fiscal, pensamento empresarial e financeirização no Brasil: a desconstrução da ordem corporativa no século XXI," pp. 65–94 in Rita Giacalone (ed.), *Pensamiento empresarial latinoamericano en el siglo XXI*. Bogotá: Editorial Universidad Cooperativa de Colombia.
Boschi, Renato and Maria Regina Soares de Lima
    2002 "O executivo e a construção do Estado no Brasil: do desmonte da Era Vargas ao Novo Intervencionismo Regulatório," pp. 195–253 in Luiz Werneck Vianna (ed.), *A democracia e os três poderes no Brasil*. Belo Horizonte and Rio de Janeiro: Ed. UFMG/IUPERJ/FAPERJ.
Bresser-Pereira, Luiz C.
    2014 *A construção política do Brasil: Sociedade, economia e estado desde a independência*. São Paulo: Editora 34.
Brown, Wendy
    2019 *Nas ruínas do neoliberalismo: A ascensão da política antidemocrática no Ocidente*. São Paulo: Editora Filosófica Politeia.

Bruno, Miguel
2015 "Ortodoxia e pseudodesenvolvimentismo: nunca antes uma receita foi tão infeliz." *Insight Inteligência* 69: 94–105.
Cafardo, Pedro
2020 "Mea culpa, mea culpa, mea maxima culpa." *Valor Econômico*, June 15.
Carvalho, Laura
2018 *Valsa brasileira: Do boom ao caos econômico*. São Paulo: Todavia.
Congresso em Foco
2019 "STF proíbe Bolsonaro de extinguir com decreto conselhos criados por lei." June 13. https://congressoemfoco.uol.com.br/justica/stf-proibe-bolsonaro-de-extinguir-com-decreto-conselhos-criados-por-lei/ (accessed January 30, 2020).
Corrêa, Mariana F., Pedro Lemos, and Carmem Feijo
2017 "Financeirização, empresas não financeiras e o ciclo econômico recente da economia brasileira." *Economia e Sociedade* 26: 1127–1148.
Couto, Cláudio G.
2021 "Do governo-movimento ao pacto militar fisiológico," pp. 35–49 in Leonardo Avritzer, Fábio Kerche, and Marjorie Marona (eds.), *Governo Bolsonaro: Retrocesso democrático e degradação política*. Belo Horizonte: Autêntica.
Dahl, Robert. A.
1997 *Poliarquia: Participação e oposição*. São Paulo: Ed. USP.
Davis, Gerald F. and Suntae Kim
2015 "Financialization of the economy." *Annual Review of Sociology* 41: 203–221.
DIAP (Departamento Intersindical de Assessoria Parlamentar)
2014 "Radiografia do novo Congresso: Legislatura 2015–2019." December. https://www.diap.org.br/index.php/publicacoes?task=download.send&id=414&catid=13&m=0 (accessed September 26, 2021).
Diniz, Eli
2016 "Desenvolvimento e estado desenvolvimentista: Tensões e desafios da construção de um novo modelo para o Brasil do século XXI," pp. 33–55 in Eli Diniz and Flavio Gaitán (eds.), *Repensando o desenvolvimentismo: Estado, instituições e a construção de uma nova agenda de desenvolvimento para o século XXI*. São Paulo and Rio de Janeiro: Hucitec Editora/INCT/PPED.
Diniz, Eli and Renato Boschi
2014 "Reforma administrativa no Brasil dos anos 90: projeto e processo," pp. 69–110 in Glaucio Soares and Antonio Lavareda (eds.), *A relevância da ciência política: Comentários à contribuição de Olavo Brasil de Lima Júnior*. Rio de Janeiro: Revan.
Dowbor, Ladislau
2017 *A era do capital improdutivo*. São Paulo: Autonomia Literária.
Draibe, Sonia M.
1985 *Rumos e metamorfoses: Um estudo sobre a constituição do Estado e as alternativas da industrialização no Brasil (1930–1960)*. Rio de Janeiro: Paz e Terra.
Evans, Peter
2014 "The developmental state: divergent responses to modern economic theory and the twenty-first-century economy," pp. 220–240 in Michelle Williams (ed.), *The End of the Developmental State?* New York: Routledge.
Fagnani, Eduardo
2017 *O fim do breve ciclo da cidadania social no Brasil (1988–2015)*. Instituto de Economia da UNICAMP Texto para Discussão 308.
Fernandes, Florestan
1976 *A revolução burguesa no Brasil: Ensaio de interpretação sociológica*. Rio de Janeiro: Zahar Editores.
1989 *A Constituição inacabada: Vias históricas e significado político*. São Paulo: Estação Liberdade.
Fleury, Sonia
2014 "Building democracy in an emerging society: challenges of the welfare state in Brazil," pp. 11–31 in Jan Pieterse and Adalberto Cardoso (eds.), *Brazil Emerging: Inequality and Emancipation*. New York: Routledge.
Fleury, Sonia and Carlos Eduardo Santos Pinho
2019 "La deconstrucción de la democracia social y de la ciudadanía urbana en Brasil." *Medio Ambiente y Urbanización* 90 (1): 271–304.

Folha de São Paulo
    2020 "Ministro do Meio Ambiente defende aproveitar crise do coronavírus para 'passar a boiada.'" May 22. https://www1.folha.uol.com.br/ambiente/2020/05/ministro-do-meio-ambiente-defende-aproveitar-crise-do-coronavirus-para-passar-a-boiada.shtml?origin=folha (accessed June 19, 2020).
    2021 "Entenda a militarização do governo Bolsonaro e as ameaças que isso representa." February 28. https://www1.folha.uol.com.br/poder/2021/02/entenda-a-militarizacao-do-governo-bolsonaro-e-as-ameacas-que-isso-representa.shtml (accessed September 27, 2021).

Forbes
    2019 *Bilionários brasileiros—o ranking definitivo dos mais ricos do país.* 71 (special edition).

Fraser, Nancy
    2019 "Neoliberalismo progressista versus populismo reacionário: a escolha de Hobson," pp. 77–89 in Heinrich Geiselberger (ed.), *A grande regressão: Um debate internacional sobre os novos populismos e como enfrentá-los.* São Paulo: Estação Liberdade.

Fundação Ulysses Guimarães and PMDB (Partido do Movimento Democrático Brasileiro)
    2015 "Uma ponte para o futuro." October 29. http://pmdb.org.br/wp-content/uploads/2015/10/RELEASE-TEMER_A4-28.10.15-Online.pdf, (accessed February 11, 2020).

Hall, Peter and David Soskice
    2001 *Varieties of Capitalism: The Institutional Foundations of Comparative Advantage.* London: Oxford University Press.

Ianoni, Marcus
    2018 *Estado e coalizões no Brasil: Social-desenvolvimentismo e neoliberalismo.* Rio de Janeiro: Contraponto.

IPEA (Instituto de Pesquisa Econômica Aplicada)
    2012 "Participação social como método de governo: um mapeamento das 'interfaces socioestatais' nos programas federais." *Comunicados do IPEA* 132. http://www.ipea.gov.br/portal/images/stories/PDFs/comunicado/120125_comunicadoipea132.pdf (accessed January 27, 2019).

Levitsky, Steven and Daniel Ziblatt
    2018 *Como as democracias morrem.* Rio de Janeiro: Zahar.

Lima Jr., Olavo B.
    2014 "As reformas administrativas no Brasil: modelos, sucessos e fracassos," pp. 41–67 in Gláucio Soares and Antonio Lavareda (eds.), *A relevância da ciência política: Comentários à contribuição de Olavo Brasil de Lima Júnior.* Rio de Janeiro: Revan.

Miguel, Luis F.
    2014 *Democracia e representação: Territórios em disputa.* São Paulo: Editora UNESP.
    2019 *O colapso da democracia no Brasil: Da Constituição ao golpe de 2016.* São Paulo: Fundação Rosa Luxemburgo.

Mounk, Yascha
    2019 *O povo contra a democracia: Por que nossa liberdade corre perigo e como salvá-la.* São Paulo: Companhia das Letras.

Nunes, Edson
    2003 *A gramática política no Brasil: Clientelismo e insulamento burocrático.* Rio de Janeiro: Zahar.

O Estado de São Paulo
    2014 "Congresso eleito é o mais conservador desde 1964, afirma Diap." October 6. https://politica.estadao.com.br/noticias/eleicoes,congresso-eleito-e-o-mais-conservador-desde-1964-afirma-diap,1572528 (accessed January 29, 2020).

O Globo
    2020 "Bolsa Família volta a ter fila, com 500 mil inscritos em apenas um ano." January 27. https://oglobo.globo.com/economia/bolsa-familia-volta-ter-fila-sao-quase-500-mil-familias-espera-do-beneficio-1-24212924 (accessed September 25, 2021).

Paiva, Andrea et al.
    2016 "O Novo Regime Fiscal e suas implicações para a política de assistência social no Brasil." *Nota Técnica IPEA* 27 (September). http://www.ipea.gov.br/portal/images/stories/PDFs/nota_tecnica/160920_nt_27_disoc.pdf (accessed August 13, 2017).

Pessanha, Charles F.
    2002 "O poder executivo e o processo legislativo nas constituições brasileiras: teoria e prática," pp. 141–194 in Luiz Werneck Vianna (ed.), *A democracia e os três poderes no Brasil.* Belo Horizonte and Rio de Janeiro: Ed. UFMG/IUPERJ/FAPERJ.

Pinho, Carlos E. S.
2019 *Planejamento estratégico governamental no Brasil: Autoritarismo e democracia (1930–2016).* Curitiba: Appris.
2020 "The responses of authoritarian national developmentalism to the structural economic crisis (1973–1985)." *Brazilian Journal of Political Economy* 40: 411–431.
2021 "Welfare state and epistemic communities of fiscal austerity in Brazil: from Lula da Silva to Jair Bolsonaro (2003–2020)." *Sociedade & Estado* 36 (1): 195–216.
Pogrebinschi, Thamy and Fabiano Santos
2011 "Participação como representação: o impacto das conferências nacionais de políticas públicas no Congresso Nacional." *DADOS: Revista de Ciências Sociais* 54 (3): 259–305.
Presidência da República
2014 "DECRETO Nº 8.243, DE 23 DE MAIO DE 2014. Institui a Política Nacional de Participação Social (PNPS) e o Sistema Nacional de Participação Social (SNPS), e dá outras providências." http://www.planalto.gov.br/ccivil_03/_ato2011-2014/2014/decreto/d8243.htm (accessed January 27, 2019).
Przeworski, Adam
2020 *Crises da democracia.* Rio de Janeiro: Zahar.
Rocha, Camila
2019 " 'Imposto é Roubo!' A formação de um contrapúblico ultraliberal e os protestos Pró-*Impeachment* de Dilma Rousseff." *DADOS: Revista de Ciências Sociais* 62 (3): 1–42.
Santos, Wanderley G. dos
2017 *A democracia impedida: O Brasil no século XXI.* Rio de Janeiro: FGV Editora.
Singer, André
2018 *O lulismo em crise: Um quebra-cabeça do período Dilma (2011–2016).* São Paulo: Companhia das Letras.
Snyder, Timothy
2019 *Na contramão da liberdade: A guinada autoritária nas democracias contemporâneas.* São Paulo: Companhia das Letras.
Streeck, Wolfgang
2011 "The crisis of democratic capitalism." *New Left Review,* no. 71, 5–29.
2018 *Tempo comprado: A crise adiada do capitalismo democrático.* São Paulo: Boitempo.
Tatagiba, Luciana
2021 "Desdemocratização, ascensão da extrema direita e repertórios de ação coletiva," pp. 441–452 in Leonardo Avritzer, Fábio Kerche, and Marjorie Marona (eds.), *Governo Bolsonaro: Retrocesso democrático e degradação política.* Belo Horizonte: Autêntica.
Tilly, Charles
2007 *Democracy.* Cambridge: Cambridge University Press.
Valor Econômico
2017 "PIB do Brasil cai 7,2% em dois anos, pior recessão desde 1948." March 7.
Vasileva-Dienes, Alexandra and Vivien A. Schimidt
2019 "Conceptualising capitalism in the twenty-first century: The BRICs and the European periphery." *Contemporary Politics* 25 (3): 255–275.

Opening Pandora's Box

The Extreme Right and the Resurgence of Racism in Brazil

by
Joaze Bernardino-Costa
Translated by
Heather Hayes

The emergence of Bolsonarism as a face of the extreme right in Brazil has come out of the articulation of several groups mobilized on social networks around a handful of key ideas including moral conservatism, economic liberalism, patriotism, public security, and a common enemy. Research on social networks and articles in the press shows that Bolsonarism has opened a Pandora's box, releasing behavior that combines racist antiracialism and racist racialism and that aims to dismantle the recent achievements of black and indigenous groups.

A emergência do Bolsonarismo como manifestação da extrema direita no Brasil deve sua origem à articulação de vários grupos que se mobilizaram nas redes sociais em torno de um conjunto de idéias chaves que inclui um inimigo comum, um conservadorismo moral, um liberalismo econômico, o patriotismo e a segurança pública. Estudos sobre as redes sociais e artigos nos jornais mostram que o Bolsonarismo tem abrido uma caixa de Pandora, fomentando um comportamento que combina o antiracialismo racista com um racialismo racista que almeja desmontar os sucessos recentes conseguidos por grupos negros e indígenas.

Keywords: *Bolsonarism, Far right, Social networks, Racism, Antiracism*

Jair Bolsonaro's rise to the Presidency of the Republic in Brazil was accompanied by, on the one hand, the threat of the destruction of the antiracist policies adopted by previous governments and, on the other, the creation of incentives for racist behavior that until recently had not been publicly admitted in Brazil.[1] His election led to the emergence of Bolsonarism, "a phenomenon that transcends the very figure of Jair Bolsonaro and is characterized by an ultraconservative worldview, preaching a return to traditional values and assuming a nationalist and patriotic rhetoric deeply critical of everything that

Joaze Bernardino-Costa is an associate professor of sociology at the Universidade de Brasília and author of *Saberes subalternos e decolonialidade: Os sindicatos das trabalhadoras domésticas no Brasil* (2015) and *Decolonialidade e pensamento Afrodiaspórico* (2018). He thanks the anonymous reviewers of *Latin American Perspectives*, Sales Augusto do Santos, and Emerson Ferreira Rocha for their comments. This work has been supported by the Swedish Research Council (Vetenskapsrådet) research project "Principles and Practice in Approaches to Deracialization: Countering the Social Dynamics of Contemporary Racialization in Brazil, South Africa, Sweden, and the United Kingdom" (2016-04759). Heather Hayes is a translator living in Quito, Ecuador.

LATIN AMERICAN PERSPECTIVES, Issue 248, Vol. 50 No. 1, January 2023, 98–114
DOI: 10.1177/0094582X221147596
© 2023 Latin American Perspectives

is minimally identified with the left and progressivism" (Freixo and Pinheiro-Machado, 2019: 19). From a racial point of view, Bolsonarism is equivalent to the enthronement of whiteness, the mistaken belief in the superiority of white people over other racial groups and, at the same time, the belief that the white man represents universality—a group that has no social markers. Within this logic, it is proposed that race be eliminated from our lexicon, given that only blacks and indigenous people possess social markers. Meanwhile, whiteness is seen as the default identity, making it universal. Although there are black people in the government apparatus, they exist there only to deny the antiracist agenda.

While until Bolsonaro's election it was believed that Brazil was a cordial, tolerant, and friendly country, today we are faced with an image of a country that for a long time we refused to recognize. Just as Pandora's box, in Greek mythology, when opened, let all the evils of the world escape, Bolsonarism revealed an intolerant, racist, homophobic, sexist, misogynist, antirefugee, denialist, antiscientific country that has proved to be a defender of dictatorship, the military, and torture. Bolsonaro's election campaign slogan "Brazil above everything, God above everyone" is but one example of his refusal to mention particular groups. When it comes to racial issues, he has apparently chosen to understand the Brazilian people as an amorphous and homogeneous mass made up simply of Brazilians instead of recognizing the existence of racial distinctions. In concrete terms, the refusal to recognize the existence of race as a social category is equivalent to the refusal to recognize racism in the country and the need to develop antiracist policies.

In these efforts to generate an image of the country as a nation free of racial problems, thereby reinforcing the myth of racial democracy, the president and his supporters have produced an antiblack, anti-indigenous, and antiquilombola racist discourse. This tone of the Bolsonaro government constitutes an "authoritative" attitude toward its supporters. To a certain extent, the government's behavior is a conduit for the manifestation of racism by other Brazilians who identify with its ideology. What we have seen in recent years is the opening of Pandora's box through the ongoing manifestation of racist speeches and practices in a country that, until recently, imagined itself as nonracist and tolerant. Part of the explanation for this phenomenon lies in Bolsonarism. This is the most palpable expression of the extreme right, characterized by the confluence and consolidation of a variety of groups that mobilize mainly on social networks around certain key ideas including the perception of a common enemy (the left, in general, and the Partido dos Trabalhadores [Workers' Party—PT], in particular), moral conservatism (defense of the traditional family, patriarchy, and a Christian nation), economic liberalism (neoliberalism, the theology of prosperity, the inviolability of private property, and entrepreneurship), patriotism (Brazil above everything), and public safety (as in the saying that the only good criminal is a dead criminal).

Jair Bolsonaro's and Bolsonarism's modus operandi has numerous consequences when it comes to what we would call an egalitarian agenda and respect for human rights. One of the dimensions strongly affected and under threat is antiracism. In this article, I will discuss the threat of destruction of an antiracist agenda that has been gradually coming together since the redemocratization of the country, a process that has had an important role in the black movement and gained ground in the PT administrations. I will also look at the possibility of racism's resurging as a result of the behavior of Brazil's president and that of his followers, who, in practice, back up and authorize racism.

My analysis is based on observations made in everyday life as conveyed by the traditional media and on observations taken from the social media accounts of social groups identified with the extreme right and Bolsonarism. In recent years, the effectiveness and centrality of social networks in people's lives has become evident not only because it has become a catalyst for political mobilization but also because of its importance in forming the opinion of a community of readers and supporters of specific political projects.

After this introduction, the article is divided into five sections that address theories about the racial state, the racial formation of Brazil, progress on racial issues during the PT administrations, the impeachment of Dilma Rousseff and the rise of the extreme right, and the racism of Bolsonarism.

THE RACIAL STATE AND THE RACIAL FORMATION OF BRAZIL

Understanding the threat of Bolsonarism to the country's recent antiracist achievements and the risk of the resurgence of racism requires understanding the racial background of Brazil over the past century (Omi and Winant, 1994; Goldberg, 2002) and the antiracist agenda built by the black movement and implemented in recent government administrations. Therefore I will begin with some brief comments on the way race has been lived, negotiated, and contested in Brazil and its role in the construction of policies and interpretations of the nation. Focusing on the period from the twentieth century to the present, I will use the following concepts: "racialism," "antiracialism," "racism," and "antiracism." By "racialism" I mean a system of social classification that presupposes the existence of race as a category that exists only on the plane of social relations. "Antiracialism" is the denial of the existence of races. Both of these can give rise to "racist" or "antiracist" behaviors and attitudes. Thus, "racism" is a doctrine that hierarchizes racial groups and motivates prejudiced and discriminatory attitudes, while understanding "antiracism" is a political action in opposition to the system of racial hierarchy (Guimarães, 1999).

In racial terms, the twentieth century began with the shadow of scientific racism that had been cultivated by the Brazilian political and intellectual elite in the previous century. Scientific racism was triggered, mainly from the 1870s on, when the issue of replacing African labor in response to the impending end of slavery (in 1888 [Skidmore, 1975]) took hold of the country's political agenda. At that time, the racist notions of the Brazilian political elite were becoming clear. Shortly thereafter, explicit declarations were made of a preference for European immigrants, believing them to belong to a superior race.

However, while there was certainty about the status of black people in the supposed evolutionary hierarchy, the same was not true of those who became known as mestizos, because a good part of Brazilian intellectuals, academics, and politicians were themselves at the time considered mestizos. The theories created in the European context were not fully accepted by the Brazilian intelligentsia, and there was indecision as to whether miscegenation degraded pure races or was a positive factor. If miscegenation was seen as something positive, it was because it could be used to turn Brazil into a white country. According to predictions of the time, mestizos and blacks would end up disappearing (Lacerda, 2012 [1911]). The idea of whitening was then introduced as a solution to Brazil's racial problems and, later, as a way of making Brazil into a civilized nation. This was because the political equation of the time—using the nomenclature of the era— held that a superior race corresponded to a civilized nation and an inferior race to a primitive nation. Between the 1870s and the 1920s, then, the hegemonic political thinking about race formation was racist racialism, meaning that race, which at the time was understood to be a natural category, was mobilized to produce racist public policies and behaviors.

The whitening model coexisted with a narrative in which relationships between ex-slaves and ex-masters had not been as sour as in other places, especially the United States, and that we had developed a model of civilization in which racial barriers were of little relevance (da Costa, 1998). Almost 50 years after the end of slavery, Gilberto Freyre (1992 [1933]) summarized the myth of racial democracy in his book *Casa-Grande & Senzala*. This book provided a brilliant construction of the idea that we had no barriers between racial groups and that there was a fluid miscegenation between whites, blacks, and indigenous people. Freyre described Portuguese men's propensity for miscegenation in their relations with indigenous and African women. This was his formula for making miscegenation a positive concept and a pillar of the nation. Thus, the miscegenation of whites, indigenous, and blacks apparently gave rise to a single world ("the world that the Portuguese created") characterized by a reality in which race was not relevant in determining social relations or the social mobility of individuals, which were understood to be based merely on personal effort. Freyre's ideas were the standard for Brazilian politics and culture until practically the end of the twentieth century. On the basis of these ideas, the exaltation of miscegenation, combined with the model of whitening, created an idealization of Brazil as a paradise nation, a racial democracy, where there were no conflicts or racial problems. These ideas continue to permeate all dimensions of Brazilian social life, from state institutions to popular culture.

The myth of racial democracy was the belief that a social system had been inaugurated in Brazil in which race was not a relevant element in social relations, especially when it came to moving up the social ladder. According to this explanation, black people, especially mestizos, apparently had no barriers to their social rise. This "paradisiacal" character of Brazilian society was contrasted, above all, with U.S. society, which had created numerous barriers for the black population (Bernardino, 2002). The myth of racial democracy functioned as a regulator of social relations, while in other countries social relations were regulated by segregation (Goldberg, 2002). Through the exaltation of miscegenation and the assertion that there were no racial barriers to blacks' moving up the social ladder, the myth of racial democracy moved the debate on racism from the public sphere to the private one. In other words, experiences of racism and racial discrimination in Brazil have always been seen as specific to individual behavior.

If we characterize the previous period as marked by racist racialism, the subsequent period, beginning in the 1930s, can be characterized as one of racist antiracialism, in which the denial of the existence of race in the state's and even society's hegemonic discourse existed alongside daily racist practices. All of this led to a continuation of racial inequalities and the marginalization of the black population. As a general rule, cases of racism were treated as racial prejudice, something always relegated to the private sphere, and such occurrences were treated as if their perpetrators were merely being impolite. Instances of racism were treated as features of individual behavior and not the responsibility of social institutions.

While official discourse and even intellectuals and cultural producers were propagating the myth of racial democracy, black intellectuals and the black movement have produced a different narrative about racial relations in Brazil since at least the Black Convention of 1950, specifically in the Teatro Experimental do Negro of Abdias Nascimento and the Teatro Popular Brasileiro of Solano Trindade and in the demonstrations that led to creation of the Unified Black Movement in the 1970s. Continued development of the discussion that had been generated within the wide-ranging organizations of the black movement found success in the next decade, most notably in the 1988 Constitution. Among these successes were the creation of the Fundação Cultural de Palmares (Palmares Cultural Foundation) and Article 68 of the Transitional Constitutional Provisions Act, which recognized the right of landownership for the remaining black quilombos. In addition to these constitutional rights, also in the 1980s, the black movement managed to achieve other progress—the declaration of November 20 as Black Consciousness Day, the designation of Serra da Barriga (the site of the historic quilombo of Palmares) as a national heritage site, and the recognition of Zumbi dos Palmares as a national hero (Pereira, 2005; Gonzalez and Hasenbalg, 1981; Andrews, 1998).

The counternarrative originating from the black movement, which was registering important symbolic-cultural achievements in the 1980s, gained further traction in the following decade, when on November 20, 1995, the historic Zumbi dos Palmares March against Racism, for Citizenship, and for Life brought together more than 30,000 protesters in Brasília. On that occasion, President Fernando Henrique Cardoso was presented with a document entitled the "Program to Overcome Racism and Racial Inequality" that contained a series of demands, including not only symbolic-cultural claims, as in the previous decade, but policies to promote racial equality in the labor market, affirmative action policies in universities, the granting of land titles to quilombos, etc. The following year, in Brasília during the inauguration of an international seminar on multiculturalism and racism, for the first time in the country's history a president, Cardoso, recognized that Brazil was a racist country (Souza, 1997).

Although timidly, the Cardoso administration (1995–1998, 1999–2002) began to adopt a series of racially oriented policies that included the first experiments with affirmative action in the Ministry of Foreign Affairs, the Ministry of Agrarian Development, the Ministry of Justice, and elsewhere (Silva, 2019). However, it was only during the PT administrations, which began in 2003, that the antiracist agenda that had been built by the black movement began to act with true boldness. Despite questioning and limited conviction within the PT itself when it came to an antiracist agenda, and given the fact that within the party there was strong opposition to this agenda, with accusations of generating class struggle, we can identify a victory for the counternarrative of the black movement both within the broader society and within the party itself (Bernardino-Costa, 2019).

The creation of the Secretaria Nacional de Políticas de Promoção de Igualdade Racial (National Secretariat for Racial Equality Policies—SEPPIR) three months into President Lula's first term was much more the result of the action of black party loyalists than the result of any structural political component within the PT (Bernardino-Costa, 2019). In any case, despite infighting within the party and government, SEPPIR played an unparalleled role in the fight against racial inequality and racism. This new look at the racial issue was the direct result of black activism within the PT and in the federal government and of an important coincidence: the discussions that simmered in the country before and after the Third UN World Conference against Racism, which took place in 2001 in Durban, South Africa. Those discussions put the need to confront racism and racial inequalities on the agenda (Pereira, 2005; Silva, 2019). The achievements of the black movement since the 1980s may lead us to conclude that we were seeing an antiracist racialism that recognized the importance of race as a structural dimension of social life and therefore a social category to be taken into account when generating public policies aimed at reversing the effects of racism and racial discrimination.

PROGRESS ON RACIAL MATTERS DURING THE PT GOVERNMENT: ANTIRACIST RACIALISM

Even though the PT adopted a "weak reformism" as a result of its coalition policy (Singer, 2012; Bernardino-Costa, 2019), the creation of SEPPIR and the adoption of an antiracist racialism can be seen as a 13-year spark of progress in the face of more than 500 years of structural, routine racism. Despite its low budget and minimal staff, SEPPIR was behind numerous extremely positive and significant policies to combat racism and promote racial equality. Various instances of progress on racial matters in the 2000s were a direct result of black activism within the government.

Laws 10,639/2003 and 11,645/2008 modified the elementary and high school curricula, making Afro-Brazilian history and culture and then Afro-Brazilian and indigenous history and culture mandatory subjects. Law 12,711/2012 forced all public and federal universities in the country to adopt a quota for prospective students from public schools, low-income communities, and black, brown, and indigenous people. Law 12,990/2014, similar to the affirmative action policies applied to students in higher education, reserved 20 percent of public jobs for black candidates. Decree 4,887/2003 established the procedure for the identification, recognition, delimitation, and titling of lands occupied by the remaining members of quilombo communities. Law 12,288/2010, known as the Racial Equality Statute, established guidelines for confronting racial inequalities in the spheres of health, education, culture, sports, access to land, the media, etc.

In addition to this progress, several universalist policies implemented during the PT administrations had a significant and positive impact on the black population: the income transfer policy (Bolsa Família), the real increase in the minimum wage, and, most important, the law that gave domestic workers the same rights as all other formal workers. Even considering that much more could have been done if the PT had adopted a more radical left-wing political project instead of a coalition policy, we can recognize significant progress on an antiracist agenda that promotes racial equality, especially when compared with other administrations.

This "weak reformism" (Singer, 2012) was enough to provoke reactions from part of the upper middle class, which had never seen so many poor and black people aspiring to middle- and upper-class status. A numerically significant part of the black and poor population now had access to goods and services that had been exclusive to the middle class, such as owning a car, traveling by plane, and studying at a public university. The backlash against the PT administrations gained intensity with the accusations that some of the party leaders were involved in corruption. It is in this context that we have seen a weakening of the left's agenda and a significant strengthening of the discourse of the extreme right.

OPENING PANDORA'S BOX: DILMA ROUSSEFF'S IMPEACHMENT AND THE RISE OF THE FAR-RIGHT

The roots of what we call Bolsonarism began to form in the first term of President Dilma Rousseff, specifically in the June 2013 demonstrations. Those demonstrations, organized by the Free Fare Movement (an autonomist social movement) against the increases in bus fares in the city of São Paulo, began with a progressive battle cry defending the right to the city. Soon other demonstrations followed, speaking out against the "Lulista or PT model" of governing, which had been characterized by an increase in distributive policies and a larger state apparatus (Miguel, 2018; Freixo and Pinheiro-Machado, 2019). The anticorruption battle cry became the great force that acted to unify various segments of the right. While until then, especially since the country's redemocratization in 1985, the streets had been the stage for protests by the left and its progressive agenda, beginning in June 2013 they became home to conservative groups ranging from monarchists to middle-class citizens with an anticommunist discourse, religious conservatives, and even defenders of the military dictatorship (Freixo and Pinheiro-Machado, 2019). That process, which began the day after Dilma Roussseff's electoral victory was announced, would culminate in her impeachment. When her second term began on January 1, 2015, the crisis was already under way. There was a mix of dissatisfaction with the country's poor economic performance, accusations of corruption, and criticism of a progressive agenda in the field of human rights that ranged from income redistribution, women's rights, and sexual rights to the rights of black and indigenous populations.

Dilma Rousseff was removed from the presidency on August 31, 2016. Michel Temer took over as president of Brazil, and a succession of events strengthened the mobilizations of the extreme right both on social networks and in the numerous demonstrations organized during this period. During the weakened Temer administration, the right-wing agenda within the government was restricted to economic matters, with the government adopting several pro-market measures. A far-right agenda when it came to traditional cultural issues was coming together on the social media in terms of public demonstrations against the PT and against corruption. However, all this saw the full light of day only when the Bolsonaro administration rose to power.

As for racial policies, on the government's part an antiracist racialist agenda existed up through Dilma's impeachment. Under this agenda, race as a social category was mobilized to produce antiracist policies in order to promote equality and social justice. With the Temer administration, this agenda began to be dismantled. For example, in the ministerial reform proposed by Temer, SEPPIR was downgraded to a secretariat lacking any resources. Under Bolsonaro, there has been a mix of racist antiracialism and racist racialism. The government produces an official discourse in which race is not a category in public policies (antiracialism) because there are supposedly no divisions among Brazilians (Brazil above everything). Meanwhile, the president makes statements that promote a biological racialism with racist content. However, the fact is that both the antiracialism and the racialism of the Bolsonaro administration have fostered racism. Beyond Bolsonaro's statements, whiteness is the hallmark of his administration. Only blacks, indigenous people, and quilombos are named and socially marked, while whiteness is unidentified and therefore universal (Schucman, 2014).

This combination of racist antiracialism and racist racialism is not just a characteristic of the state but is also present from time to time in society, especially among the sectors that identify with the right-wing agenda. People declare themselves to be antiracialists, since under the Brazilian ethos they do not see themselves as racist or, at most, believe that racism is found in the other, never in themselves (Fernandes, 1978; Datafolha, 1995; Telles, 2003). Therefore, this mix of racist antiracialism and racist racialism is something that we find not only in Jair Bolsonaro but also in the phenomenon that we call Bolsonarism.

Bolsonarism is racist antiracialist when it insists, in connection with the rhetoric of the myth of racial democracy, that everyone is equal and that there is no distinction in terms of color and race among Brazilians. Within this logic, there is no way to politicize and treat acts of racism as a public issue. Therefore, when they occur, they are treated not as structural racism but rather as circumstantial racism, since ultimately they are the exclusive and individual responsibility of the perpetrator of a racist act. Now, if everyone is equal and if racism is an individual and private matter, there is no reason to have racial equality policies. Bolsonarism is also characterized by its attempt to dismantle quota policies because, in its mistaken conception, they corrupt the principle of equality and meritocracy. That said, at the same time as it defends this supposed (formal) equality, Bolsonarism also produces an openly racist discourse. This leads us to identify the presence of a racist racialism, a racialism that mobilizes a notion of race very close to the biological sense of race found in the nineteenth century, as a foundation for racist conceptions and attitudes. Before examining the racist racialism in the president's discourse, let us first look at two sets of events in which the combination of racist anti-racialism and racist racialism of Bolsonarism occurs: everyday events and demonstrations on social networks.

BOLSONARISM, THE FAR-RIGHT, EVERYDAY EVENTS, AND SOCIAL NETWORKS

Through everyday events that have been reported in recent years, we can see the emergence of an ultraconservative mentality with embryonic far-right components.

1. Because of the country's income redistribution policies, many black people began to enjoy services that had been perceived as almost exclusive to white people belonging to the middle class. One such service was air travel. The reaction of the white middle class (Souza, 2019) was seen in comments that Brazilian airports were full of poor and black people and therefore similar to bus stations, which are traditionally identified as spaces for poor and black people.

2. In late 2013 and early 2014, young people—mostly blacks—from the outskirts of large cities used the social media to organize *rolezinhos* (slang for taking a walk with friends) in shopping centers in large cities (Erber, 2019). After several successful rolezinhos brought together approximately 6,000 young people, some shopping centers in the main Brazilian cities, especially those that are practically exclusive to rich white people, closed their doors to avoid having such events happening there. These gatherings were understood by many as manifestations of "savages who spit on civilization" and "barbarians incapable of recognizing their own inferiority" (Constantino, 2014).

3. In 2013, Dilma Rousseff's administration launched the Mais Médicos (More Doctors) program, which had the objective of placing doctors in the public health network in the interior of the country and in the peripheral regions. The open positions were primarily intended for newly graduated Brazilian doctors and those trained abroad. After that target group, the positions went to foreign doctors. In order to encourage the arrival of foreign professionals, the Brazilian government set up an agreement with the Cuban government in which more than 15,000 Cuban doctors came to participate in the program. This program was strongly criticized by the opposition, which claimed that the program veiled indirect financing of the communist government of Cuba, since part of the salary paid to the professionals went directly to the Raúl Castro administration. However, this was not the only reaction to the program. What was surprising was the reaction of the Brazilian population to black Cuban doctors. During the orientation course they were required to take, Cuban doctors were harassed by Brazilian doctors and journalists (Pragmatismo Político, 2013). The most explicit racism came from a journalist who posted the following on the social media: "Forgive my prejudice, but these Cuban doctors look like maids. Are they really doctors? How terrible. Doctors tend to have a doctor's attitude, a doctor's face, and command respect based on their appearance alone. What a shame for our people. Do these doctors even know what dengue is? Yellow fever? God protect our people!" (G1 RN, 2013).

In addition to these horrifying examples of the conservative reaction to the expansion of the rights of the black and poor population, we have examples that include the affirmative action policies for admission into Brazilian universities and public service, the Racial Equality Statute, and the immigration of Haitians and Venezuelans, all of which were the subject of criticism. In this last example, some such immigrants were even physically attacked. This set of policies and transformations in Brazilian society—although identified as a "weak reformism"—represented a threat to the patterns of social distinction to which the middle class was accustomed. At a time when policies of income redistribution and racial equality were being implemented in Brazil, discomfort was generated among the white middle class and anti-PT sentiment was strengthened.

Along with the anticorruption agenda and hostility against the PT and the left, there was also an agenda related to national customs, particularly relating to the traditional values of Brazilian society that went against progress on the antiracist agenda. Social networks became the silent space for propagating those values and worldview. This meant that such ideas were not restricted to a small group but won over a significant portion of the population, which ended up giving Jair Bolsonaro 55.13 percent of the vote in the presidential election in 2018.[2]

This gave us a scenario marked by a strong congressional opposition to President Dilma, with the press and the judiciary clearly taking the side of Operation Car Wash, which accused and convicted the PT and former President Lula before any trial took place. On the social media, the warped mind-set of the extreme right was built to become stronger and stronger as the days went by, leading millions of Brazilians to accept that agenda, which included racism.

Social networks would provide the necessary fuel for Bolsonarism, a phenomenon that expresses an ultraconservative moral and neoliberal economic worldview. From a moral point of view, Bolsonarism defends a return to traditional values, assuming a nationalist rhetoric and enthroning a type of white masculinity. From an economic point of view, it denies any obstacles arising from social pacts (such as the rights of workers, indigenous peoples, quilombos, and the forest code).[3] Both Bolsonarism and the extreme right bring together diverse groups with fluid borders and an intercommunicable agenda whose union is motivated by the perception of a common enemy: the left (Miguel, 2018).

Over the past decade, and more intensely beginning in June 2013, groups identified as belonging to the extreme right began to organize and take action, especially on the social media. Something that was fundamental to every such organization was the construction of a common enemy: the left, in general, and the PT in particular. If there is a common denominator in all far-right opinion makers, it is the creation of a polarization on the Internet between "us" and "them," with "us" being the standard bearers of all the country's restorative virtues and "them" the enemies responsible for both the economic crisis and the moral degeneration of the country. Far-right opinion makers disseminate arguments on their social media that identify the PT as responsible for corruption in the country, with the entire left being the incarnation of dishonesty and evil and Lula as the gang's leader (Miguel, 2018; Ribeiro, 2018; Freixo and

Pinheiro-Machado, 2019; Messemberg, 2017). As if that were not enough, the bipolarity of the Cold War is also restored in this discourse, making the PT representative of communism in Brazil. There was even talk of a plot engineered by Marxists to end all of Western culture and civilization. This conspiracy theory revolved around a concept of cultural Marxism that was said to be omnipresent in public education, especially in public universities, the media, among civil rights activists, and in the entertainment industry (Miguel, 2018).

Anti-PT sentiment is like a big tent with four posts, all of them articulated and intercommunicable: patriotism/anti-corruption, moral conservatism, economic liberalism, and public security. Racist implications can be found in each of these. The patriotism/anticorruption theme is strongly intertwined with anti-PT rhetoric and gained a lot of strength when associated with Operation Car Wash, which served to turn into common knowledge the idea that the country's corruption began with the PT administrations and that the country's economic crisis was fallout from the related corruption. It includes statements relating to the indivisible and homogeneous character of the homeland, which is allegedly under threat from globalist forces (the UN, the World Health Organization) and from discourses produced in international contexts such as North American antiracism. The moral conservatism theme is characterized by the defense of moral and Christian values, bringing together Neo-Pentecostal leaders with activities in the world of virtual networks, in the media, and in Congress. A strong position against a progressive agenda in the field of cultural traditions includes statements to the effect that Brazilian society is connected to a Greco-Roman-Christian tradition. The economic liberalism theme is characterized by identifying the state as a source of corruption and privilege and therefore an enemy, either because it regulates economic relations or because it is being co-opted by political groups that corrupt it. The solution to avoid corruption, therefore, would be the privatization of public companies. Meanwhile, adherents criticize social income transfer policies, arguing that they discourage economic competition, violate the principle of meritocracy, and encourage laziness (Casimiro, 2018; Rocha, 2015; 2018). The theme of public security, strongly identified with what has come to be known as the bullet caucus in Congress, defends people's right to carry weapons as a self-defense strategy against increasing urban violence and to prevent the land invasions promoted by the Movimento Sem Terra (Landless Workers' Movement—MST). Another issue here is reducing the age of criminal responsibility to 16 years. The narrative of virtual social stakeholders can be summarized in words such as "Don't feel sorry for a thief, because the thief doesn't feel sorry for you."

Drawing on an analysis of the values and ideas shared among the communities of readers that are formed in relation to these themes, I find the following ideas relevant to understanding the racial policy proposed by Bolsonarism: (1) rejection of the relevance of race in the belief that the Brazilian population is homogeneous, devoid of racial distinctions; (2) aversion to religions of African origin and any positive mention of Africa, reiterating the Greco-Roman and Christian tradition of Brazilian society and underestimating any African and indigenous contribution; (3) the portrayal of the state as the source of corruption, making it necessary to reduce its size by eliminating income transfer policies and quota policies; (4) support for the criminalization and mass incarceration of the black population by reducing the age of criminal liability and normalizing conflict by defending the right to carry weapons—implying that the Brazilians in question are the "good citizens," a group represented by middle-class white males. The construction of Bolsonarism and the consolidation of the extreme right that we can observe in everyday events and in social networks leads to a combination of antiracialism and racist racialism.

What we find here is the transition from an antiracist racialist agenda created beginning in 1988, when the nation's new constitution was being drafted, to an agenda with a combination of racist antiracialism and racist racialism—between the option of avoiding naming race and actually naming it. However, one dimension is quite evident: whether or not race is actually named, the Bolsonaro administration threatens a number of antiracist policies that were achieved by the black movement. This ambiguity of Brazilian racial politics took on its most complete form under Jair Bolsonaro, who is seen by his supporters as uncouth but authentic, far from the figure of the traditional politician. In fact, he has used his uncouth and supposedly authentic personality to excuse himself from the numerous accusations of racism that have marked his political career.

UNLEASHING THE EVILS OF PANDORA'S BOX: BOLSONARO'S AND HIS ADMINISTRATION'S RACISM

Bolsonaro's statements about the black and indigenous population exhibit an undisguised racism. While at times there is no mention of race—for example, in the government program of the then-candidate that was filed with the Superior Electoral Court or in his electoral slogan "Brazil above everything, God above everyone"—on numerous other occasions throughout his political career his statements have cast a bright light on his racism. In fact, racism transcends his entire persona and is the very mark of what makes Bolsonarism what it is. The strategy of not mentioning the terms "black" or "indigenous" is very much in line with his campaign slogan. It is fundamental to the racist antiracialism of Bolsonarism.

What "Brazil" is this? What "God" is this? As we can infer from both the electoral campaign and the government's actions, this Brazil is the Brazil of whiteness (Schucman, 2014), which sees no need to name itself, and this God is a sectarian, partisan god who does not respect beliefs and religiosities of African origin. From an institutional point of view and in practical terms, the slogan "Brazil above everything, God above everyone" led to a weakening and dismantling of SEPPIR, which turned into nothing more than a secretariat within the Ministry of Human Rights without a course of action or any specific projects and devoid of resources and personnel. At the same time, it has been used as a ploy for making attacks on the black, quilombo, and indigenous movement.

Bolsonarism is also racist racialist. Blacks are accused of being leftists, profiteers, victimists, antinationals, and "damned scum," to name just a few of the epithets used against them. Not only the discourse but also the actions taken by Bolsonaro's administration point to an antiblack, anti-indigenous, antiquilombo racialism. Demands made by the black movement are seen as coming from foreign sources and as being accompanied by divisive actions. The demarcation of indigenous and quilombo territories is seen, above all, as an obstacle to the megaprojects proposed by transnational capitalism to exploit the forest and the subsoil. This explains the government's eagerness to disregard these groups' position as groups claiming their collective right to land. To counter this, the government argues that indigenous groups are already well-established in modern society (asserting that the quilombolas are lazy) and can therefore be integrated into global capitalism through projects aimed at exploiting the natural resources found on their lands.

The president's racist racialism functions as a type of "hall pass" for the rest of Brazil to express its own racism and identify with the extreme right. Bolsonaro himself is at once the figure and the symbol that opens Pandora's box, revealing and fostering a country that breaks from preexisting pacts of coexistence and civility. Below are several illustrative instances of Bolsonarism: In 2008, in the context of discussions on the demarcation of the Raposa Terra do Sol Indigenous Reserve, he said, "If I make it [to the office of the president], there won't be a demarcated corner for an indigenous reserve or a quilombo." In 2011, on a television program, he said, "Anyone who makes use of a quota, in my opinion, is putting an 'unqualified' next to his signature. I would not get on a plane in which the pilot got his job thanks to a quota, nor would I accept being operated on by a doctor who earned his position through a quota." In a lecture at the Clube Hebraico in Rio de Janeiro during the presidential campaign in 2018, he said, "I went to a quilombo, in Eldorado Paulista. The lightest Afro-descendant there weighed something like seven arrobas.[4] They don't do anything! I don't think they can even reproduce themselves anymore." During the election campaign, the then-candidate told an audience of approximately 1,000 financial executives at the Banco BTG Pontual that he had a solution for Rocinha, the largest favela in Rio de Janeiro, with approximately 70,000 inhabitants. He would send helicopters to drop flyers warning the drug dealers that if they didn't surrender within six hours he would machine-gun the whole favela. The proposal was applauded by the bankers in attendance (Jardim, 2018). Does this type of discourse go uncontested because these favelas are largely made up of black bodies?

Since his taking office as president, the frequency of Bolsonaro's racist statements seems to have subsided. However, in July 2021, while greeting his supporters in front of the Planalto Palace, Bolsonaro addressed one of his supporters, a young black man with black-power hair, saying, "How are the cockroaches growing in there? Look at the cockroach breeder here!" (making direct mention of a black person's hair). These demonstrations by Bolsonaro make use of well-known rhetorical devices, turning racist comments into jokes, but behind this rhetoric is a discourse and a practice of dehumanization and animalization of black and indigenous people, identifying them as dirty, stupid, incapable, and therefore unworthy of having their territory demarcated (in the case of indigenous people and quilombolas) and undeserving of quota policies (in the case of urban black people).

The government's racist manifestations continue to date thanks to Sérgio Camargo, president of the Fundação Cultural Palmares. The foundation was established in 1988 with the mission of promoting and preserving the cultural, historical, economic, and social values of the black population, and until 2018 its presidency was always held by a person committed to antiracism. However, under Bolsonaro it turned into an authoritative source for the government's racist discourse, since Camargo's comments are not rebuked. In April 2020, in a meeting with advisers, he referred to the black movement as "a bunch of bums" and "damned scum" (G1, 2020). A few months earlier he had declared on Twitter that slavery had been beneficial to people of African descent. He also tends to express prejudice against the practitioners of Afro-Brazilian religions. His most recent and controversial statement was made in September 2021, at an event for a conservative audience, when he said that the Fundação Cultural Palmares "has in its DNA the gene for victimization, grudges, and resentment. . . . [It is] a Marxist slave quarters or, if you prefer, a victimist slave quarters." He continued: "Unfortunately, I don't see the possibility of recovering this idiotic black militancy, blacks on a leash. What black people need to do is free themselves, turn their backs on this movement, seek strength to overcome the difficulties, and this can only be done through study, discipline, merit, work, family, country, and religion." Finally, after a meandering discourse, he said that racism against whites was what has emerged in the country: "Black people have a certain immunity when it comes to insulting white people. . . . We are witnessing the birth of a new type of racism, racism by the victim. This type of racist cannot be criminalized because he is, in theory, oppressed because his ancestor was enslaved" (*Correio Braziliense*, 2021).

This political performance is illustrative of Bolsonarism and the opening of Pandora's box. Camargo, a self-styled right-wing black man appointed by Bolsonaro in 2019, became the main spokesperson for racism during his presidency. (In March 2022 he was removed from office in order to run for the post of federal deputy for São Paulo.)

Examples of racist racialism by the president himself, his administration, and Bolsonarism in general can be identified almost daily. What we see in the daily life of Brazilian society is a racial tension in the air in which the president and his government indirectly authorize racist discourse and practices by any citizen who aligns himself with his government project. This is not to say that Bolsonaro is creating racist behavior in Brazil or that such behavior did not previously exist; the fact of the matter is that this type of behavior is reinforced by the president's own behavior. In addition to structural and institutional racism, there is attitudinal racism.

CONCLUSION

Built under the banner of whiteness, a place of symbolic and material privilege that is seen as a nonplace devoid of any social markings (Schucman, 2014), the current administration brings true threats and risks to the black, indigenous, and quilombola population. From the point of view of contemporary racial politics, we have what I characterize as a racist racialism combined with a racist antiracialism, something that jeopardizes the political achievements of antiracist movements. The evils that were once trapped inside of Pandora's box have been released.

The aggressive way in which Bolsonarism is imposed, however, not only affects the black, indigenous, and quilombola populations but threatens the entire social pact built since 1988, when we had not only a social-democratic constitution but an entire social-democratic society. The long-term success (or failure) of the extreme right will eventually be the result of the political game that has been taking place on a daily basis in the country. This game threatens and puts at risk the gains made by feminists, environmentalists, the working class, religious minorities, and others. As a result, resistance to the evils that have escaped from Pandora's box seems to me not simply a task to be undertaken by black, indigenous, and quilombola actors but one for all those who defend the dignity of each and every person as a basic condition for social existence.

While this analysis of today's government points to desolation, some events signal the resurgence of hope and resistance. In the Black Lives Matter movement or the removal of statues of slave-owning figures from the past, the formation of coalitions for democracy in the country is beginning in the form of efforts to reposition antiracism as a central issue. This, for example, is the tone of the document *Com racismo não há democracia*[5] of the Coalizão Negra por Direitos (Black Coalition for Rights), which represents more than 100 Brazilian black organizations. Documents like this one point to the importance of understanding the centrality of race for understanding and rebuilding the country. If racism is a structural phenomenon in Brazilian society, then we need structural public policies to overcome the harm it has caused.

While the Pandora's box opened by Bolsonarism reveals evils that have always been present in Brazilian society, it also provokes a response from this society's democratic and antiracist actors. Only by recognizing race will we be able to challenge the racism present in the state, in civil society, and even in ourselves as individuals. Closing Pandora's box is the job of all social actors committed to antiracism.

NOTES

1. This article was written in mid-2020, during the second year of the Bolsonaro administration. At that time, not everything explained herein was as evident as it is today. Over time, the evils that came out of Pandora's box became part of the country's daily news.

2. In the second round of the elections, Bolsonaro obtained 55.13 percent of the valid votes, winning 57,796,986 votes, while Fernando Haddad obtained 44.87 percent of the votes, equivalent to 47,038,963 votes. Abstentions totaled 21.3 percent (31.3 million votes), blank votes, 2.14 percent (2.4 million votes), and null votes, 7.43 percent (8.6 million votes). http://www.tse.jus.br/eleicoes/eleicoes-2018/votacao-e-resultados/resultados-eleicoes-2018.

3. In putting this section together, I visited Facebook, Instagram, and Twitter pages of social movements, legislators, and journalists connected with the new right between April and July of 2020. Some of the key Facebook and Twitter pages visited were the Free Brazil Movement, Revoltados Online, Enright Brazil, the New Party, the Social Liberty Party, the Alliance for Brazil, Jair Messias Bolsonaro, Sérgio Camargo, Carlos Bolsonaro, Major Olímpio, Olavo de Carvalho, Felipe Moura, and Rodrigo Constantino.

4. An arroba is a unit of measurement used to weigh animals, especially cows. In other words, this is racist language that animalizes and dehumanizes the quilombola population.

5. https://comracismonaohademocracia.org.br/.

REFERENCES

Andrews, George Reid
   1998 *Negros e brancos em São Paulo (1888–1988)*. Bauru: EDUSC.
Bernardino, Joaze
   2002 "Ação afirmativa e a rediscussão do mito da democracia racial no Brasil." *Estudos Afro-Asiáticos* 24 (2): 247–273.
Bernardino-Costa, Joaze
   2019 "The Worker's Party and the racial agenda in 21st-century Brazil: the need for a new project of the left against racial inequality?" pp. 159–181 in Vladimir Puzone and Luis Felipe Miguel (eds.), *The Brazilian Left in the 21st Century: Conflict and Conciliation in Peripheral Capitalism*. London: Palgrave Macmillan.
Casimiro, Flávio Henrique Calheiros
   2018 "As classes dominantes e a nova direita no Brasil contemporâneo?" pp. 42–47 in Esther Solano Gallego (ed.), *O ódio como política: A reinvenção das direitas no Brasil*. São Paulo: Boitempo.
Constantino, Rodrigo
   2014 "O 'rolezinho' da inveja, ou A barbárie se protege sob o manto do proconceito?" https://www.gazetadopovo.com.br/rodrigo-constantino/artigos/o-rolezinho-da-inveja-ou-a-barbarie-se-protege-sob-o-manto-do-preconceito/ (accessed June 10, 2020).
Correio Braziliense
   2021 "Sergio Camargo: Sou o terror dos 'afromimizentos' e da negrada vitimista." https://www.correiobraziliense.com.br/politica/2021/09/4947634-sergio-camargo-sou-o-terror-dos-afromimizentos-e-da-negrada-vitimista.html (accessed November 15, 2022).
da Costa, Emilia Viotti
   1998 *Da monarquia à república: Momentos decisivos*. São Paulo: Editora da UNESP.
Datafolha
   1995 *Racismo cordial: A mais completa análise sobre preconceito de cor no Brasil*. São Paulo: Editora Ática.
Erber, Pedro
   2019 "The politics of strolling." *Latin American Perspectives* 46 (4): 37–52.
Fernandes, Florestan
   1978 *A integração do negro na sociedade de classes*. Vol. 1. São Paulo: Editora Ática.
Freixo, Adriano de and Rosana Pinheiro-Machado
   2019 *Brasil em transe: Bolsonarismo, nova direita e desdemocratização*. Rio de Janeiro: Oficina Raquel.
Freyre, Gilberto
   1992 (1933) *Casa-Grande & Senzala: Formação da família brasileira sob o regime de economia patriar-cal*. Rio de Janeiro: Record.
G1
   2020 "Sergio Camargo, Presidente da Fundação Palmares, chama movimento negro de 'escória maldita' em reunião." https://g1.globo.com/politica/noticia/2020/06/02/sergio-camargo-presidente-da-fundacao-palmares-chama-movimento-negro-de-escoria-maldita-em-reuniao.ghtml (accessed Novermber 15, 2022).
G1 RN
   2013 "Jornalista diz que médicas cubanas parecem 'empregadas domésticas.'" http://g1.globo.com/rn/rio-grande-do-norte/noticia/2013/08/jornalista-diz-que-medicas-cubanas-pare-cem-empregadas-domesticas.html (accessed June 10, 2020).
Goldberg, David Theo
   2002 *The Racial State*. Oxford: Blackwell Publishers.
Gonzalez, Lélia and Carlos Hasenbalg
   1981 *Lugar de negro*. Rio de Janeiro: Marco Zero.
Guimarães, Antônio Sérgio Alfredo
   1999 *Racismo e anti-racismo no Brasil*. São Paulo: Editora 34.
Jardim, Lauro
   2018 "A solução de Bolsonaro para a Rocinha." https://blogdacidadania.com.br/2018/02/desmascarando-bolsonaro-no-caso-da-rocinha/ (accessed June 10, 2020).

Lacerda, João Batista de
  2012 (1911) "The metis, or half-breeds, of Brazil," pp. 377–382 in G. Spiller (ed.), *Papers on Interracial Problems Communicated to the First Universal Races Congress*. London: Forgotten Books.
Messenberg, Debora
  2017 "A direita que saiu do armário: a cosmovisão dos formadores de opinião dos manifestantes de direita brasileiros." *Sociedade e Estado* 32: 621–648.
Miguel, Luís Felipe
  2018 "A reemergência da direita brasileira?" pp. 17–26 in Esther Solano Gallego (ed.), *O ódio como política: A reinvenção das direitas no Brasil*. São Paulo: Boitempo.
Omi, Michael and Howard Winant
  1994 *Racial Formation in the United States: From the 1960s to the 1990s*. New York and London: Routledge.
Pereira, Amauri Mendes
  2005 *Trajetória e perspectiva do Movimento Negro Brasileiro*. Belo Horizonte: Editora Nandyala.
Pragmatismo Político
  2013 "Médicas 'patricinhas' envergonham o Brasil." https://www.pragmatismopolitico.com.br/2013/08/medicas-patricinhas-envergonham-o-brasil.html (accessed June 10, 2020).
Ribeiro, Márcio Moretto
  2018 "Antipetismo e conservadorismo no Facebook?" pp. 87–93 in Esther Solano Gallego (ed.), *O ódio como política: A reinvenção das direitas no Brasil*. São Paulo: Boitempo.
Rocha, Camila
  2015 "Direitas em rede: think tanks de direita na América Latina?" pp. 261–278 in Sebastião Velasco Cruz, André Kaysel, and Gustavo Codas (eds.), *Direita, volver! O retorno da direita e o ciclo político brasileiro*. São Paulo: Fundação Perseu Abramo.
  2018 "O boom das novas direitas brasileiras: financiamento ou militância?" pp. 48–54 in Esther Solano Gallego (ed.), *O ódio como política: A reinvenção das direitas no Brasil*. São Paulo: Boitempo.
Schucman, Lia Vainer
  2014 "Branquitude e poder: revisitando o medo branco no século XXI." *Revista da ABPN* 6 (13): 134–147.
Silva, Tatiana Dias
  2019 "Mudança, discurso e instituições: uma análise sobre políticas públicas de igualdade racial no Brasil de 2000 a 2014." Ph.D. diss., Universidade de Brasília.
Singer, André
  2012 *Os sentidos do Lulismo: Reforma gradual e pacto conservador*. São Paulo: Companhia das Letras.
Skidmore, Thomas
  1975 *Preto no branco: Raça e nacionalidade no pensamento brasileiro*. Rio de Janeiro: Paz e Terra.
Souza, Jessé
  1997 *Multiculturalismo e racismo: Uma comparação entre Brasil e Estados Unidos*. Brasília: Paralelo 15.
  2019 *A elite do atraso: Da escravidão a Bolsonaro*. São Paulo: Estação Brasil.
Telles, Edward
  2003 *Racismo à brasileira: Uma nova perspectiva sociológica*. Rio de Janeiro: Relume Dumará.

Radical Reorganization of Environmental Policy

Contemporaneous Evidence from Brazil

by
Mauro Guilherme Maidana Capelari, Ana Karine Pereira, Nathaly M. Rivera,
and Suely Mara Vaz Guimarães de Araújo

An overview of environmental policy in Brazil since President Jair Bolsonaro took office in January 2019 suggests that the rise to power of a new political elite has led to a radical change in Brazil's trajectory of climate change initiatives and environmental protection. The new elite is associated with the disruption of two factors historically relevant for the design of environmental policy: the participation of civil society in the governance of public policy and multilateralism in matters of environment policy.

Uma análise das políticas ambientais brasileiras desde a tomada de posse de Jair Bolsonaro da presidência da República em Janeiro 2019 constata que o aparecimento de uma nova elite política acarretou em uma alteração radical na trajetória do Brasil com respeito às suas iniciativas sobre a mudança climática e a preservação ambiental. Houve uma perturbação de dois fatores por causa desta elite política que eram historicamente importantes pela elaboração de políticas ambientais: a participação de organizações de sociedade civil na governança de políticas públicas e o multilateralismo.

Keywords: Civil society, Multilateralism, Environmental policy, Radical change, Brazilian politics

An unquestionable and inherent conflict characterizes the design of environmental policy around the world (Dryzek, 1992; Shahar, 2019). The interaction at various temporal and spatial scales, the myriad of actors involved, and the general lack of internalization by some productive sectors of the negative externalities for the environment (Dryzek, 2013; Duit, Feindt, and Meadowcroft, 2016) increase the strains in the process of regulating the use and protection of environmental resources. In developing countries this conflict is exacerbated by their efforts to increase industrialization and urbanization and by the land degradation that is common in agricultural countries (Hochstetler, 2019). This is the case with Brazil, the largest democracy in Latin America, whose environmental agenda is of worldwide importance. Constant improvements of its environmental institutions have made Brazil known for having one of the best-developed environmental policy structures in the world (Moura, 2016). In January 2019, however, a new political elite was elected, and this led to a radical

Mauro Guilherme Maidana Capelari and Ana Karine Pereira are assistant professors at the Centro de Desenvolvimento Sustentável of the Universidade de Brasília. Nathaly M. Rivera is a postdoctoral research fellow at the Universidade de São Paulo, and Suely Mara Vaz Guimarães de Araújo is a full professor at the Instituto Brasileiro de Ensino, Desenvolvimento e Pesquisa.

LATIN AMERICAN PERSPECTIVES, Issue 248, Vol. 50 No. 1, January 2023, 115–132
DOI: 10.1177/0094582X221148714
© 2023 Latin American Perspectives

reorganization of the country's environmental institutions (Meeus, 2019) and a potential reduction of the quality of its public policies (Araújo, 2020). While recent works address the relationship between radical governments and the environment in developed countries (e.g., Bomberg, 2017; Lachapelle and Kiss, 2018; Lockwood, 2018; Huber, 2020), we still lack a good understanding of this relationship in developing countries. By characterizing the recent reorganization of Brazil's environmental institutions, we fill a gap in the study of the relationship between radical politics and environmental policy in developing-country settings.

Environmental policy conflicts in Brazil have historically been complex (Drummond and Barros-Platiau, 2006), mainly because of the existence of various groups trying to insert their beliefs and views on the environment into the country's environmental agenda (Capelari et al., 2020). Drawing from the institutional literature (Mahoney and Thelen, 2009; Thelen, 2002), we suggest that Brazil's environmental policy was shaped over time through conflicts around the distribution of resources that allowed some of these political coalitions to regulate access to and the transformation of natural resources according to their immediate interests (Guimarães, 1991). During the past few years, however, more systematic and thorough environmental concerns have prevailed (Dean,1997; Rochedo et al., 2018), and improvements in the environmental agenda have been sustained by the balance among the several political coalitions involved in struggles over power and over the resources made available by the environmental policy subsystem (Issberner and Léna, 2016). In this paper, we argue that this balance was historically supported by two sometimes overlapping factors that have been disrupted with the rise of the new political elite: (1) a close relationship between civil society and the state with regard to environmental policies implemented in institutional and noninstitutional settings that produced significant results in the quality of the state's bureaucracy and public policies (Jacobs, 2002; Pádua, 2018) and (2) environmental multilateralism materialized through international pressures and cooperation that turned into specific regulatory conditions in exchange for funding, the encouragement of stricter environmental rules or the enforcement of existing ones, and the country's willingness to be part of global environmental initiatives and agreements (Margulis and Unterstell, 2016). The disruption of this balance may have irreparable consequences for the environment. The remainder of this paper is organized as follows: the next section identifies recent changes in legislation and organization of environmental policy in Brazil since 2019, and the following section characterizes these changes. A fourth section concludes.

THE REORGANIZATION OF ENVIRONMENTAL POLICY

One of the most notorious changes in Brazil's environmental policy is the Environmental Licensing Bill 3.279/2004 (Brasil, 2004), proposed in 2004 but put into discussion again in 2019 in the wake of the disastrous failure of the B1 tailing dam at the Córrego do Feijão mine in Brumadinho (state of Minas Gerais), considered one of the biggest dam-related environmental catastrophes in the past 25 years (BBC, 2019c). The precarious condition of this dam and others in Minas Gerais at the time of the accident raised the alarm regarding the issuance and renewal of environmental licenses in the country. Despite the concerns that followed the Brumadinho disaster, the bill's proposal was left to Congress in the face of the resistance of the executive to proposing a debate on concrete recommendations. The House of Representatives took the lead and, during 2019, held 12 public hearings and consultations with stakeholders, including technicians and representatives of civil society. Despite the numerous hearings and four different versions of the proposal, no consensus was reached. The bill is still undergoing debate in Congress. Controversy is centered mostly around three issues: the degree of regulation needed at the national level, whether it is possible to obtain a license without an environmental analysis that supports the request, and the degree of participation that organizations dealing with indigenous territories, protected areas, and cultural heritage may have during the licensing process. Incidentally, the executive has stated its position in favor of reducing the number of regulations, in line with the guidelines set by the 2019 Economic Freedom Law (Brasil, 2019f). During this discussion, the government tried unsuccessfully to impose the automatic approval of environmental licenses after the expiration of the term. A second attempt to include this possibility as a provisional measure (by executive order) was also obstructed by Congress.

A second bill is the Indigenous Lands Bill 191/2020 (Brasil, 2020e) sponsored by the executive and fully supported by President Jair Bolsonaro. This bill aims at regulating mining on indigenous lands. According to the country's constitution, mining on tribal lands is not ruled out but is currently prohibited because it is not regulated. The plan to regulate these activities on indigenous reservations was a campaign promise of Bolsonaro and was stressed in many of his speeches during the first year of his administration (Agência Brasil, 2019a). After several meetings of the executive in 2019, the bill was introduced to the House of Representatives in February 2020. Currently it would regulate mining and the use of hydrocarbons and water resources in indigenous homelands and is predicted to provide revenues that will benefit native communities, but it contains several provisions that have created a strong reaction from society (APIB, 2020). Among other things, it prioritizes mining and free access to exploration for resources, ignoring the traditions of native communities and ruling out environmental regulation during this stage. Motivated by society's negative reaction, the House Speaker stated that the bill would not move forward in the legislative process during his term (*Correio Braziliense*, 2020), postponing its discussion until 2021.

A third bill, the Land Grabbing Bill 2633/2020 (Brasil, 2020d), is currently in Congress. Also one of Bolsonaro's campaign promises, it aims to regulate the tenure of public lands.[1] It seeks to extend the concept of "occupation," increase the area of occupied public lands that may be regulated, and facilitate the sanction of irregular land occupations throughout the entire country and especially in the Amazon basin, which has the most publicly owned lands.

Relying on arguments such as the government's recurring efforts to regulate mining, occupation of publicly owned lands, and land grabbing, both the Indigenous Lands Bill and the Land Grabbing Bill have been widely criticized by civil society and by the state's magistrates (Agência Pública, 2020b).

Additional considerations regarding the feasibility of these projects include the willingness of the Brazilian state to transfer state-owned lands to private developers. Another possibility is that these bills are intended to materialize the government's ideas about the environment, protected areas, and the role in society of native communities. Since the electoral campaign, the focus of the current administration has been on the idea that the country has too many protected areas (Jovem Pan, 2018) and the belief that indigenous communities are the country's largest landowners (Agência Envolverde, 2018) and are willing to be integrated into the market economy (Agência Brasil, 2019b). Moreover, Bolsonaro has repeatedly stated that "no one takes better care of the environment than Brazil" (Brasil, 2020f), which could justify bringing land use in the Amazon basin closer to economic development without proper environmental protection and thus weaken the country's position in the global discussion of worldwide environmental and climate governance.

In addition to these bills, a massive number of regulations and procedures has been issued. In 2019, the approval of more than a dozen regulations by the Ministério da Agricultura, Pecuária e Abastecimento (Ministry of Agriculture, Livestock, and Supply—MAPA) increased the number of agricultural pesticides allowed in the country. This raised concerns from Congress, civil society, and Brazil's Public Prosecutor's Office (Duprat, 2019). More than 475 new pesticides were released for use in Brazil, a historical record for permits issued in a given year (G1, 2019b). Estimates from January to May indicate that an additional 150 products were released, representing a 53 percent increase relative to the previous year (Agência Pública, 2020a). Several of these products are restricted overseas (e.g., in Europe), and some of them are associated with detrimental effects on ecosystems and wildlife (*National Geographic*, 2019). Other examples come from the Ministério do Meio Ambiente (Ministry of the Environment— MMA). For instance, there was an attempt to relax the existing Atlantic Forest Law 4.410/2020 (Brasil, 2006), which deals with the protection of the Atlantic Forest biome by limiting deforestation. This initiative was promptly rejected by civil society, by Congress, and by the Public Prosecutor's Office (MPF, 2020). Later on, the minister of the environment declared his intention to act through regulations or procedures instead of new environmental laws because of the difficulty of getting such laws through Congress.

Regarding the organization of the public agencies charged with environmental policies, there is Law 13.844/2019 (Brasil, 2019e). The persistent threat of the transformation of the MMA into an internal secretariat of the MAPA (*O Eco*, 2018) was eventually frustrated by MAPA's own staff, which considered the existence of the MMA as forestalling possible retaliation by the developed countries in the area of purchases of Brazil's commodities (*Época Negocios*, 2018). Though the MMA continued to have ministerial status and to be part of the cabinet, its responsibilities were significantly reduced (*Época Negocios*, 2019). The transfer of the Forest Service's duties to the MAPA led to a modification in the supervision of the Rural Environmental Registry, one of the main mechanisms derived from the Protection of Native Vegetation Law 12.651/2012, which was approved after more than 10 years of discussion (Brasil, 2012; Soares-Filho et al., 2014) and is still awaiting implementation. The recurring postponement of the implementation of this law is criticized by environmentalists, who now fear more delays because of the transfer (BBC, 2019b). A second movement aimed at reducing the responsibilities of the MMA was the removal of water resources management from its agenda. The Agência Nacional de Águas (National Water Agency—ANA), with responsibility for the implementation of the national water resources policy, was transferred from the MMA to the Ministério do Desevolvimento Regional (Ministry for Regional Development). This transfer was criticized by the public and by the managers in the states mainly because of the absence of prior consultation with stakeholders and the potential for a modification of the definition of "water resources." A third action that reduced the MMA's importance was the elimination of the Secretariat for Climate and Forest Change, which was responsible for the implementation of Brazil's agenda to reduce its carbon footprint under the Paris agreement. The MMA is no longer in charge of the country's climate agenda, which remains halted, and some of its staff members have been dismissed from strategic positions (Reuters, 2020b). Indeed, the new MMA structure contains five departments—biodiversity, forest and sustainable development, environmental quality, ecotourism, and international relations—with no direct link to climate change or the Paris agreement (Brasil, 2019a).

ANALYSIS OF A RADICAL CHANGE

Recent changes in the country's environmental policy are perceived as radical alterations in its institutions that may result in the aggravation of current environmental problems and the undermining of their management. This disruption has been publicly condemned by eight former ministers of the environment (*Guardian*, 2019b), the association of public environmental officials, the public ethics commission, and the Public Prosecutor's Office (Congresso em Foco, 2019a). Two aspects of this radical reorganization that have historically been part of the legal and organizational processes of environment policy are civil society participation and multilateralism.

CIVIL SOCIETY PARTICIPATION

The role of civil society in shaping Brazilian environmental policy was prominent even before the creation of governmental institutions on the subject (Hochstetler, 2019; Hochstetler and Keck, 2007; Pádua, 2018). To a large extent, the importance of nongovernmental actors is explained by the expertise developed by environmental nongovernmental organizations (NGOs) and researchers' associations, which have made Brazilian society widely aware of their issues (Losekann, 2012). They have long had close relations with the government in the creation and reshaping of environmental institutions and the design of environmental protection policies (Abers, 2019; Abers and Von Bulow, 2019). Brazil's environmental movement has gone through three periods characterized by an increasingly close relationship between civil society and the state (Hochstetler and Keck, 2007). The first period, called "scientific and nationalist" (1950–1970), sought to warn the public about the unrestrained use of natural resources and the need for long-term planning of local productive activities.

The second, called "confrontation" (1970–1990), had a more political content, rejecting the military regime and its energy policies, especially its hydro and nuclear energy projects. During this period, there was a massive creation of NGOs throughout the country as a result of the campaign slogan "From Protest to Engagement." The third period, called "active" (post-1990), is characterized by professionalization and provision of services, lobbying, and the dissemination of information. The slogan of this third period is "From Protest to Project." Various forms of dialogue between the government and civil society, ranging from informal relationships to more institutionalized and collaborative practices, occurred throughout these three phases (Abers and Von Bulow, 2019). Relations between state and society in this area were made possible mainly by the creation of participatory settings (Hochstetler and Keck, 2007; Jacobi, 2003; Viola, 2002), budget allocations, the design of public policy by environmental NGOs (Alonso, Costa, and Maciel, 2007), and the hiring of environmental activists for positions in the middle- and upper-level bureaucracy (Abers, 2019; Oliveira, 2020; Pereira, 2021). This relationship was also driven by the close relations between the environmental movement and political parties (Loureiro and Pacheco, 1995; Pádua, 1991; 2012), some left-wing (Viola, 1987) and others center-right (Oliveira, 2016).

During Bolsonaro's administration, however, there has been a weakening of these traditional forms of interaction, with a deliberate attempt by the government to exclude civil society from the design of environmental policy. For instance, it repeatedly insists that too much public funding is allocated to NGOs (*Folha de São Paulo*, 2018a). Immediately after taking office, Bolsonaro put an end to the conversion program for environmental violation fines, which aimed at allocating the substantial resources generated by fines to environmental recovery projects that might include NGOs as operators. Instead, the government opted for a settlement strategy between violators and environmental agencies *(Estadão*, 2019). Additionally, there is evidence of an attack on the formal participation of civil society in environmental management. For instance, the government excluded representatives of civil society entities from the deliberative council of the Fundo Nacional de Meio Ambiente (National Environment Fund) through Decree 10.224/2020 (Brasil, 2020b). Funded by the government and private donations, this fund sponsors projects aimed at the rational and sustainable use of natural resources, and with its restructuring representatives of NGOs, socio-environmental movements, municipalities, scientists, and the Conselho Nacional do Meio Ambiente (National Environmental Council—CONAMA) were all removed from its deliberations. The government argued that it wanted more rationality and objectivity in the management of this fund (G1, 2020a). Nowadays, the fund is no longer sponsoring projects, since it is deadlocked (Agência Brasil, 2020).

Another example is the restructuring of the CONAMA itself through Decree 9.802/2019 (Brasil, 2019c). Brazil's main collegiate body for environmental policy since 1981, it was suddenly, citing reasons of efficiency, reduced from 96 to 23 members, only 4 of whom represent civil environmental organizations (the rest representing businesses and the government). This downsizing of civil society's participation in the design of Brazilian environmental policy has been criticized by researchers and experts (UOL, 2019). One more action that reveals

the suppression of civil society in environmental policy discussions is its elimination by the government from the country's delegations to climate change
negotiations (Reuters, 2019a), citing alleged but never demonstrated irregular
exchanges between NGOs and the Amazon Fund, a national funding mecha-
nism aimed at reducing emissions from deforestation and forest degradation
of the Amazon (*Folha de São Paulo*, 2019b). Charges of NGOs' being responsible
for fires in the Amazon region (G1, 2019a), oil spills on the country's coast
(Congresso em Foco, 2019b), and even the beginning of the burning of the
Amazon biome (*El País*, 2019) were among the other arguments offered to justify this removal (*Folha de São Paulo*, 2019a).

Furthermore, the defense of civil society's socio-environmental interests
through the assignment of activists to public administration positions or the
defense of these demands by career government employees committed to
socio-environmentalism was weakened by the adoption of new criteria for the
appointment and dismissal of high- and medium-level bureaucrats from the
MMA and related organizations. Our analysis of the academic and professional
profiles of the MMA's members obtained from its website[2] reveals a strong
recent presence of actors linked to the armed forces, a significant number of
appointees lacking experience in environmental issues, and a large number of
vacant positions. The number of appointees from the armed forces is especially
significant in the Minister's office; its chief of staff and the ombudsperson are
both trained in military sciences and have experience in military agencies. Also
noteworthy is the fact that at the highest level there is no one with experience
in the environmental area. For instance, the executive secretary, the undersec-
retary of planning, budget, and administration, and the general budget and
finance coordinator are all military personnel. Additionally, all of the MMA's
departments, especially the Forest and Sustainable Development and the
Ecotourism Secretariats, have significant numbers of vacant positions, and the
other three departments have officials with no experience in the area. For
instance, the secretary of biodiversity is a physician specialized in aerospace
medicine with experience in the armed forces, while the secretary of ecotourism is a public administrator with a background in the financial market.

The presence of military actors is also recorded in agencies linked to the
MMA. The Instituto Chico Mendes de Conservação da Biodiversidade (Chico
Mendes Institute for Biodiversity Conservation—ICMBio) was militarized in
May 2020, when military personnel took over the directorship of four of its five
regional offices. Nowadays the institute's president is a military man (Reuters,
2019c). A similar militarization took place at the Instituto Brasileiro do Meio
Ambiente e dos Recursos Naturais Renováveis (Brazilian Institute of the
Environment and Renewable Natural Resources—IBAMA). In April 2020, its
environmental protection director and two career employees were dismissed
from an operation to combat illegal mining in indigenous lands in the state of
Pará (G1, 2020b).

These new appointment criteria disrupted the history of the environmental
policy area, which has been traditionally characterized by the presence of activists with strong experience in environmental protection and, more recently,
technicians with expertise in the area (Abers and Oliveira, 2015). One of the
consequences of these appointments is the sector's inability to solve concrete

problems in the area, revealed for instance by the failure of military operations to contain deforestation in the Amazon region (Reuters, 2020a)—a failure acknowledged by Brazil's vice president and head of the Amazon Council, Hamilton Mourão (Reuters, 2020a). Another consequence is the reduction of civil society's representation, since a significant portion of the new high-level officers has no links to social movements and does not identify with their causes.

MULTILATERALISM AND THE ENVIRONMENT

In addition to having a close relationship with civil society, environmental policy in Brazil has traditionally been characterized by adherence to and the incorporation of, albeit partially and reluctantly, international environmental demands (Pádua, 1991). International pressures established since the 1972 United Nations meeting, later enhanced by the Club of Rome's *Limits to Growth* (Meadows et al., 1972), were responsible for the creation of a more rigorous environmental agenda in the country (Bursztyn and Bursztyn, 2018). One example of Brazil's reaction to these pressures was the creation of the Special Secretariat for the Environment (SEMA) (Brasil, 1973), a subcabinet agency under the Ministério do Interior (Ministry of the Interior). Among SEMA's main duties were the setting of pollution control standards and the regulation of the industrial activity that was taking place mostly in South and Southeast Brazil. During the 1980s, the country's environmental agenda was once again shaped around international discussions. For instance, the term "sustainable development" was included in Article 225 of the 1988 Constitution (Brasil, 2020a) shortly after it was officially presented in the Brundtland (1988) report. In 1992 the country had an additional positive reaction to international environmental movements with the transformation of SEMA into the Ministério do Meio Ambiente (Ministry of the Environment—MMA) (Brasil, 1992), which became the first cabinet-level institutional body exclusively charged with managing environmental policy (Ganem, 2019).

The formation and national structuring of the climate change and biodiversity agendas during the early 2000s were also a result of progress in international relations and the depiction of Brazil as a key nation in the preservation of current environmental conditions (Viola and Franchini, 2017). Though there was initial resistance to implementing these agendas, the country managed to produce legal frameworks on these issues through the creation of the National Policy on Climate Change (Brasil, 2009b), the National Fund on Climate Change (Brasil, 2009a), and the Biodiversity Law (Brasil, 2015), three important examples of the internal understanding regarding the need for global cooperation on climate change and biodiversity protection.

The break of Brazil's current political elite with this tradition of environmental multilateralism and global cooperation regarding environmental management (Viola and Gonçalves, 2019) can be dated to the 2018 presidential campaign (Pereira and Viola, 2019), when the current president and his sons openly questioned the reality of climate change, calling it a "hoax" (*Folha de São Paulo*, 2018b) and "an act of extreme activists" (*El País*, 2018). The candidate Bolsonaro threatened to pull Brazil out of the Paris climate agreement (Reuters, 2019d).

Two important actions taken during Bolsonaro's administration are clear evidence of this break. The first was the country's withdrawal as host of the 2019 UN Climate Change Conference (Reuters, 2018). Led by the president, the decision was read as a change in the country's stand on climate policy (CAT, 2019). This denoted the end of Brazil's image as an important player in the discussion of climate change and the beginning of its role as a global threat as perceived by other nations (*Foreign Policy*, 2019). The second was the appointment as chancellor of Ernesto Araújo, a climate change denier (*Guardian*, 2018). The minister considers climate change and globalization part of a communist and anti-Christian plan to impose economic regulations on nations that reduce their autonomy and economic growth (Araújo, 2018). His anti-climate-change and antiglobalist discourse (Brasil, 2019d) led to the elimination of the climate change division of the ministry and the abandonment of Brazil's position as a leader in the discussion of climate change (*Guardian*, 2019a).

Three other situations are worth mentioning to illustrate the break with multilateralism in the environmental arena. First, there was an attempt to restructure the management of the Amazon Fund. Dissatisfied with the use of the fund's resources, both the chief executive and the minister of the environment tried to reorganize the orientation committee of the Amazon Fund, seeking to increase Brazil's autonomy in the management of these resources. After failing to reach an agreement, the government publicly attacked the fund's sponsoring countries (DW, 2019). The fund's activities were briefly suspended after Germany and Norway—its largest donors—suspended their transfers, with negative impacts on the states located in the Amazon region (Reuters, 2019b). Notwithstanding, the Amazon Fund still has roughly R\$2 billion (more than US\$300 million) in its budget awaiting implementation (*O Globo*, 2019).

A second situation occurred in the context of the resonation overseas of the 2019 Amazon fire season (BBC, 2019a). France's President Emmanuel Macron called the attention of the G7 to the fires and labeled them an international crisis that developed countries needed to act on (*France 24*, 2019b). The government replied verbally, attacking him and his wife through the social media (*New York Times*, 2019). Though the G7 responded to Macron's call by offering Brazil US\$20 million to fight the fires, Brazil's answer was to accept the offer only if Macron apologized, which did not happen (*France 24*, 2019a). A similar chain of reactions took place in response to Greta Thunberg's post on social media regarding the deaths of indigenous people in the Amazon region, when Bolsonaro made derogatory comments about her (CNN, 2019). These two examples illustrate the fact that the break with multilateralism includes an aggressive attitude toward international leaders who express their opinions on Brazil's environmental management (Casarões and Flames, 2019).

Lastly, there is the removal of climate-related topics from the MMA's priority agenda and the promotion of local pollution-related topics such as solid waste and the urban environment (MMA, 2019). This abrupt change in the MMA's goals probably explains the relaxation of environmental inspections and the consequent increase in deforestation in both the Amazon and Cerrado biomes (*Science*, 2019) due to the lack of planning to meet the country's nationally determined contributions of greenhouse gases (SGEE Brasil, 2019), the elimination of the interministerial committee on climate change (Brasil, 2019b), the reduction of the budgets involved (Araújo, 2020), and the country's inability to meet the 2020 goals established in the Paris agreement (Angelo and Rittl, 2019).

The break with multilateralism happened concurrently with a reduction of the quality of environmental policy and a deterioration of the country's image in the eyes of the global community, particularly in the case of countries that ratified the Paris agreement. Though the country's vice president and Congress have tried to appease the international community, their efforts have been unsuccessful, as is shown by current signs of international boycotts of Brazilian products and continuing budget cuts to the Amazon Fund (*Guardian*, 2019c), not to mention the withdrawal or dwindling of foreign investment. If Brazil pursues its deficient environmental policy and climate governance, it remains to be seen how the international community will react.

CONCLUSION

Despite the history of conflicts in the overall design of Brazilian environmental policy, its progress over time was noticeable. The balance of power between different political coalitions was always coupled with intense pressure from civil society and strong collaboration from the international community in the design of policies aimed at protecting the country's natural environment. The creation of the Forum of Brazil's Former Environment Ministers in Defense of Democracy and Sustainability and its indictment of the course of environmental policy in the Bolsonaro era reflect the historical consensus on the subject (*Folha de São Paulo*, 2020b). Since 2019, however, Brazil's new political elite in power has been making an effort to break away from this tradition. This disruption is marked by an increased imbalance among related coalitions and the consolidation of those with limited concerns with the protection of the natural environment. This has translated into a rapid and profound deterioration of the country's environmental quality indicators. For example, in the Amazon there was a 34.4 percent increase in deforestation between August 2018 and July 2019 relative to the same months of the previous 12-month period—the highest annual regional deforestation rate in 10 years (Reuters, 2020c). The Cerrado saw a 15 percent increase in deforestation of protected areas during the same period (*Folha de São Paulo*, 2020a), which threatened the international appeal of some of the area's main agricultural commodities (Rajão et al., 2020). Enforcement activities by environmental agencies have become lax, and increased violence in rural areas has affected indigenous and traditional communities. With this dismantling under way (Nobre, 2020), along with the undermining of civil society and the rejection of multilateral commitments, Brazil's environmental policy is in need of help.

Several avenues remain open for future research. First, one could study how civil society can politically advocate for a better environmental policy agenda in the context of radical politics. Future research could reflect on and explore the historical and new forms of action and the various tools and resources that civil society has available to become a more engaged player in the design of environmental policy in the present context. One could dig deeper into the professional profiles of the personnel in public positions that relate to the design of environmental policy and management. Finally, the international community could exert pressure to guide certain local behaviors aimed at increasing environmental protection in Brazil during the Bolsonaro era. The new political elite's response to these eventual international constraints and the potential political and economic consequences for Brazil of these radical answers remain open research questions.

NOTES

1. The bill replaced Provisional Measure 910/2019.
2. https://www.mma.gov.br/o-ministerio/quem-e-quem.html.

REFERENCES

Abers, Rebecca
> 2019 "Bureaucratic activism: pursuing environmentalism inside the Brazilian state." *Latin Americ an Politics and Society* 61 (2): 21–44. doi:10.1017/lap.2018.75.

Abers, Rebecca and Marília Oliveira
> 2015 "Nomeações políticas no Ministério do Meio Ambiente (2003–2013): interconexões entre ONGs, partidos e governos." *Opinião Pública* 21: 336–364. doi:10.1590/1807-01912015212336.

Abers, Rebecca and Marisa Von Bulow
> 2019 "Social movement and the state: conventional and contentious politics," pp. 105–118 in Barry Ames (ed.), *Routledge Handbook of Brazilian Politics*. New York and London: Taylor & Francis Group.

Agência Brasil
> 2019a "Bolsonaro anuncia PL que regulamenta exploração de terras indígenas." https://agenciabrasil.ebc.com.br/politica/noticia/2020-02/bolsonaro-envia-projeto-que-regulamenta-exploracao-de-terras-indigenas.
> 2019b "Bolsonaro defende mineração e agropecuária em terras indígenas." http://agenciabrasil.ebc.com.br/politica/noticia/2019-04/bolsonaro-defende-mineracao-e-agropecuaria-em-terras-indigenas.
> 2020 "Conselho do Fundo Nacional do Meio Ambiente tem mova composição." https://agenciabrasil.ebc.com.br/politica/noticia/2020-02/conselho-do-.

Agência Envolverde
> 2018 "As ameaças de Bolsonaro ao papel central do Brasil no meio ambiente." https://envolverde.cartacapital.com.br/as-ameacas-de-bolsonaro-ao-papel-central-do-brasil-no-meio-ambiente/.

Alonso, Angela, Valeriano Costa, and Débora Maciel
> 2007 "Identidade e estratégia na formação do movimento ambientalista Brasileiro." *Novos Estudos CEBRAP*, no. 79, 151–167. doi:10.1590/S0101-33002007000300008.

Angelo, Claudio and Carlos Rittl
> 2019 "Is Brazil on the way to meet its climate targets?" Observatório do Clima. http://www.observatoriodoclima.eco.br/wp-content/uploads/2019/09/Is-Brazil-on-the-way-to-meet-its-climate-targets_-1.pdf.

APIB (Articulação dos Povos Indigenas do Brasília)
> 2020 "Statement in condemnation of Draft Law no. 191/20 on the exploration of natural resources on indigenous lands." http://apib.info/2020/02/12/statement-in-condemnation-of-draft-law-no-19120-on-the-exploration-of-natural-resources-on-indigenous-lands/?lang=en.

A Pública
> 2020a "Em meio à pandemia, governo Bolsonaro aprova 118 agrotóxicos em dois meses." https://apublica.org/2020/05/em-meio-a-pandemia-governo-bolsonaro-aprova-96-agrotoxicos-em-dois-meses/.

2020b "PL da Mineração: 'É como se o Estado decidisse legalizar o homicídio por não saber controlar,' diz subprocurador-geral da República." https://apublica.org/2020/02/pl-da-min-eracao-e-como-se-o-estado-decidisse-legalizar-o-homicidio-por-nao-saber-controlar-diz-sub-procurador-geral-da-republica/.

Araújo, Ernesto
2018 "Sequestrar e perverter." Metapolítica 17: Contra o Globalismo. https://www.metapo-liticabrasil.com/post/sequestrar-e-perverter?fbclid=IwAR2yJ9k5BJzaHGjjYrVwRdTNyX53D HT1Ng6e4MtnV-sA1xvD-MloWv84hMU.

Araújo, Suely Mara Vaz Guimarães de
2020 "Environmental policy in the Bolsonaro government: the response of environmentalists in the legislative arena." Brazilian Political Science Review 14 (2): 1–20.

BBC
2019a "Amazon fires: what's the latest in Brazil?" https://www.bbc.com/news/world-latin-america-49971563.
2019b "Em ano de alta do desmatamento na Amazônia, Meio Ambiente perde quase 20% dos técnicos." https://www.bbc.com/portuguese/brasil-50412828.
2019c "Tragédia com barragem da Vale em Brumadinho pode ser a pior no mundo em 3 déca-das." https://www.bbc.com/portuguese/brasil-47034499.

Bomberg, Elizabeth
2017 "Environmental politics in the Trump era: an early assessment." Environmental Politics 26: 956–963.

Brasil
1973 "Decreto n° 73.030, de 30 de Outubro de 1973." https://www2.camara.leg.br/legin/fed/decret/1970-1979/decreto-73030-30-outubro-1973-421650-publicacaooriginal-1-pe.html.
1990 "Medida Provisória n° 150, de 15 de Março de 1990." http://www.planalto.gov.br/ccivil_03/MPV/1990-1995/150.htm.
1992 "Lei n° 8.490, de 19 de Novembro de 1992." http://www.planalto.gov.br/ccivil_03/LEIS/L8490.htm.
2004 "Projeto de Lei n° 3.729, Licenciamento Ambiental." https://www.camara.leg.br/proposicoesWeb/fichadetramitacao?idProposicao=257161.
2006 "Lei n° 11.428, de 22 de dezembro de 2006." http://www.planalto.gov.br/ccivil_03/_Ato2004-2006/2006/Lei/L11428.htm.
2009a "Lei n° 12.114, de 9 de dezembro de 2009." https://www2.camara.leg.br/legin/fed/lei/2009/lei-12114-9-dezembro-2009-596941-norma-pl.html.
2009b "Lei n° 12.187, de 20 de Dezembro de 2009." https://www.camara.leg.br/proposicoesWeb/prop_mostrarintegra?codteor=841507&filename=LegislacaoCitada+-.
2012 "Lei n° 12.651, de 25 de Maio de 2012." http://www.planalto.gov.br/ccivil_03/_ato2011-2014/2012/lei/l12651.htm.
2015 "Lei n° 13.123, de 20 de Maio de 2015." http://www.planalto.gov.br/ccivil_03/_Ato2015-2018/2015/Lei/L13123.htm.
2019a "9.672, de 2 de Janeiro de 2019." http://www.planalto.gov.br/ccivil_03/_ato2019-2022/2019/decreto/D9672.htm.
2019b Decreto n° 9.759, de 11 Abril de 2019." http://www.planalto.gov.br/ccivil_03/_Ato2019-2022/2019/Decreto/D9759.htm.
2019c "Decreto n° 9.806, de 28 de Maio de 2019." http://www.planalto.gov.br/ccivil_03/_Ato2019-2022/2019/Decreto/D9806.htm.
2019d "Discurso do ministro Ernesto Araújo na Conferência Brazil Day in Washington da Câmara de Comércio Brasil-Estados Unidos." http://www.itamaraty.gov.br/pt-BR/acontece-no-exterior/20177-discurso-do-ministro-ernesto-araujo-na-conferencia-brazil-day-in-wash-ington-da-camara-de-comercio-brasil-estados-unidos-washington-estados-unidos-18-de-marco-de-2019.
2019e "Lei n° 13.844, de 18 de Junho de 2019." http://www.planalto.gov.br/ccivil_03/_ato2019-2022/2019/Lei/L13844.htm.
2019f "Lei n° 13.874, de 20 de setembro de 2019." http://www.planalto.gov.br/ccivil_03/_ato2019-2022/2019/lei/L13874.htm.
2020a "Constituição da República Federativa do Brasil, atualizada até 2019." http://www2.senado.leg.br/bdsf/bitstream/handle/id/566968/CF88_EC105_livro.pdf.

2020b "Decreto n° 10.224, de 5 de Fevereiro de 2020." http://pesquisa.in.gov.br/imprensa/jsp/visualiza/index.jsp?data=06/02/2020&jornal=515&pagina=21.

2020c "Projeto de Lei n° 4162, Marco Legal do Seneamento." https://www25.senado.leg.br/web/atividade/materias/-/materia/140534.

2020d "Projeto de Lei n° 2.633, Regularização Fundiária." https://www.camara.leg.br/propostas-legislativas/2252589.

2020e "Projeto de Lei n° 191, Terras Indígenas." https://www.camara.leg.br/proposicoesWeb/fichadetramitacao?idProposicao=2236765.

2020f "Entrevista com Jair Bolsonaro: Nenhum outro país cuida mais que o Brasil do meio ambiente." http://www.itamaraty.gov.br/pt-BR/discursos-artigos-e-entrevistas-categoria/presidente-da-republica-federativa-do-brasil-entrevistas/21234-nenhum-outro-pais-cuida-mais-que-o-brasil-do-meio-ambiente-entrevista-jair-bolsonaro-die-weltwoche-suica-15-01-2020.

Brundtland, Gro Harlem
1988 *Nosso futuro comum*. Rio de Janeiro: Fundação Getúlio Vargas.

Bursztyn, Maria and Marcel Bursztyn
2018 *Fundamentos de política e gestão ambiental: Caminhos para a sustentabilidade*. Rio de Janeiro: Editora Garamond.

Capelari, Mauro Guilherme Maidana, Suely Mara Vaz Guimarães de Araújo, Paulo Calmon, and Benilson Borinelli
2020 "Large-scale environmental policy change: analysis of the Brazilian reality." *Revista Brasileira de Administração Pública* 56: 1691–1710.

Casarões, Guilherme and Daniel Flames
2019 "Brazil first, climate last: Bolsonaro's foreign policy." GIGA Institute for Latin American Studies. https://www.gigahamburg.de/en/publication/brazil-first-climate-last-bolsonaros-foreign-policy.

CAT (Climate Action Tracker)
2019 "Climate Action Tracker: Brazil—country summary." https://climateactiontracker.org/countries/brazil/2019-06-17/.

CNN
2019 "Greta Thunberg labeled a 'brat' by Brazilian President Jair Bolsonaro." https://edition.cnn.com/2019/12/11/americas/bolsonaro-thunberg-brat-intl- scli/index.html.

Congresso em Foco
2019a "Bolsonaro será denunciado à ONU por associação de servidores ambientais." https://www.oeco.org.br/blogs/salada-verde/bolsonaro-sera-denunciado-a-onu-por-associacao-de-servidores-ambientais/.

2019b "Salles sugere que navio do Greenpeace derramou óleo no Nordeste." https://congressoemfoco.uol.com.br/especial/noticias/salles-sugere-que-navio-do-greenpeace-derramou-oleo-no-nordeste/.

Correio Braziliense
2020 "Maia diz que projeto sobre mineração em terras indígenas não terá urgência." https://www.correiobraziliense.com.br/app/noticia/politica/2020/02/18/interna_politica,828887/maia-diz-que-projeto-sobre-mineracao-em-terras-indigenas-nao-tera-urge.shtml.

Dean, Warren
1997 *A ferro e fogo: A história da devastação da mata atlântica brasileira*. Rio de Janeiro: Companhia das Letras.

Drummond, José Augusto and Ana Flávia Barros-Platiau
2006 "Brazilian environmental laws and policies, 1934–2002: a critical overview." *Law & Policy* 28 (1): 83–108. doi:10.1111/j.1467- 9930.2005.00218.x.

Dryzek, John
1992 "Ecology and discursive democracy: beyond liberal capitalism and the administrative state." *Capitalism, Nature, Socialism* 3 (2): 18–42. doi:10.1080/10455759209358485.

2013 *The Politics of the Earth: Environmental Discourse*. London: Oxford University Press.

Duit, Andreas, Peter Feindt, and James Meadowcroft
2016 "Greening Leviathan: the rise of the environmental state?" *Environmental Politics* 25 (1): 1–23. doi:10.1080/09644016.2015.1085218.

Duprat, Deborah
 2019 "Agrotóxicos: subsídios para a análise das medidas de fiscalização." http://www.mpf.
 mp.br/pfdc/manifestacoes-pfdc/anexo-ao-oficio-470-2019-pfdc-mpf.
DW
 2019 "Bolsonaro: Germany can learn 'a lot' from Brazil about environment." https://www.
 dw.com/en/bolsonaro-germany-can-learn-a-lot-from-brazil-about-environment/a-49384095.
El País
 2018 "Bolsonaro acha que a mudança climática é coisa de ativistas que gritam." https://brasil.
 elpais.com/brasil/2018/11/30/internacional/1543584550_559566.html.
 2019 "Juiz estende prisão de voluntários de ONG de Alter do Chão em meio a protestos de
 ativistas." https://brasil.elpais.com/brasil/2019-11-28/juiz-estende-prisao-de-voluntarios-
 de-ong-de-alter-do-chao-em-meio-a-protestos-de-ativistas.html.
Época Negocios
 2018 "Ministros e ex-ministros da Agricultura e do Meio Ambiente falam em prejuízos comerciais e ambientais com fusão das pastas." https://epocanegocios.globo.com/Economia/noti-
 cia/2018/10/ministros-e-ex-ministros-da-agricultura-e-do-meio-ambiente-falam-
 em-prejuizos-comerciais-e-ambientais-com-fusao-das-pastas.html.
 2019 "Bolsonaro mantém Ministério do Meio Ambiente, mas esvazia pasta." https://epocane-
 gocios.globo.com/Brasil/noticia/2019/01/bolsonaro-mantem-ministerio-do-meio-ambiente-
 mas-esvazia-pasta.html.
Estadão
 2019 "Decreto de Bolsonaro muda conversão de multas e cria núcleos de conciliação." https://
 sustentabilidade.estadao.com.br/blogs/ambiente-se/decreto-de-bolsonaro-muda-con-
 versao-de-multas-e-cria-nucleos-de-conciliacao/.
Folha de São Paulo
 2018a "Bolsonaro critica ONGs e põe em xeque R$ 1 bi de projetos ambientais." https://www1.
 folha.uol.com.br/ambiente/2018/11/bolsonaro-critica-ongs-e-poe-em-xeque-r-1-bi-de-proje-
 tos-ambientais.shtml.
 2018b "Hostilidade de filhos de Bolsonaro a aquecimento global preocupa cientistas." https://
 www1.folha.uol.com.br/ambiente/2018/11/hostilidade-de-filhos-de-bolsonaro-a-aqueci-
 mento-global-preocupa-ambientalistas.shtml?origin=folha.
 2019a "Especialista indica 2 pontos que 3º setor deve estar atento no novo governo." https://
 www1.folha.uol.com.br/empreendedorsocial/2019/02/especialista-indica-2-pontos-que-
 3o-setor-deve-estar-atento-no-novo-governo.shtml.
 2019b "Ministro diz que encontrou problemas em contratos de ONGs com Fundo Amazônia."
 https://www1.folha.uol.com.br/ambiente/2019/05/ministro-diz-que-encontrou-problemas-
 em-contratos-de-ongs-com-fundo-amazonia.shtml.
 2020a "Desmatamento no Cerrado se Mantém alto e cresce 15% em áreas protegidas." https://
 www1.folha.uol.com.br/ambiente/2019/12/desmatamento-no-cerrado-se-mantem-alto-e-
 cresce-15-em-areas-protegidas.shtml.
 2020b "Ex-Ministros do Meio Ambiente pedem à PGR que investigue Salles por crimes de
 responsabilidade." https://www1.folha.uol.com.br/ambiente/2020/06/ex-ministros-do-
 meio-ambiente-pedem-a-pgr-que-investigue-salles-por-crimes-de-responsabilidade.shtml.
Foreign Policy
 2019 "Brazil was a global leader on climate change. Now it's a threat." https://foreignpolicy.
 com/2019/01/04/brazil-was-a-global-leader-on-climate-change-now-its-a-threat/.
France 24
 2019a "Bolsonaro makes accepting millions in G7 aid for Amazon contingent on apology from
 Macron." https://www.france24.com/en/20190827-brazil-Jair-Bolsonaro-g7-aid-wildfires-
 amazon-rainforest-emmanuel-macron.
 2019b "Macron spearheads pressure on Bolsonaro over Amazon fires." https://www.france24.
 com/en/20190824-macron-france-brazil-bolsonaro-amazon-fires.
G1
 2019a "Bolsonaro diz que ONGs podem estar por trás de queimadas na Amazônia para
 'chamar atenção' contra o governo." https://g1.globo.com/politica/noticia/2019/08/21/
 bolsonaro-diz-que-ongs-podem-estar-por-tras-de-queimadas-na-amazonia-para-chamar-
 atencao-contra-o-governo.ghtml.

2019b "Governo federal sorteia novos integrantes do Conselho Nacional do Meio Ambiente." https://g1.globo.com/natureza/noticia/2019/07/17/governo-federal-sorteia-novos-inte-grantes-do-conselho-nacional-do-meio-ambiente.ghtml.

2020a "Bolsonaro exclui participação da sociedade civil de conselho do Fundo Nacional do Meio Ambiente." https://g1.globo.com/natureza/noticia/2020/02/06/bolsonaro-exclui-participacao-da-sociedade-civil-de-conselho-do-fundo-nacional-do-meio-ambiente.ghtml.

2020b "Governo exonera chefes de fiscalização do Ibama após operações contra garimpos ilegais." https://g1.globo.com/natureza/noticia/2020/04/30/governo-exonera-chefes-de-fiscalizacao-do-ibama-apos-operacoes-contra-garimpos-ilegais.ghtml.

Ganem, Roseli Senna
2019 *Legislação brasileira sobre meio ambiente*. Brasília: Câmara dos Deputados.

Guardian
2018 "Brazil's new foreign minister believes climate change is a Marxist plot." https://www.theguardian.com/world/2018/nov/15/brazil-foreign-minister-ernesto-araujo-climate-change-marxist-plot.

2019a "Brazilian diplomats 'disgusted' as Bolsonaro pulverizes foreign policy." https://www.theguardian.com/world/2019/jun/25/brazilian-diplomats-disgusted-bolsonaro-pulverizes-foreign-policy.

2019b "'Exterminator of the future': Brazil's Bolsonaro denounced for environmental assault." https://www.theguardian.com/world/2019/may/09/jair-bolsonaro-brazil-amazon-rainfor-est-environment.

2019c "UK firms urge Brazil to stop Amazon deforestation for soy production." https://www.theguardian.com/environment/2019/dec/03/uk-firms-urge-brazil-to-stop-amazon-defores-tation-for-soy-production.

Guimarães, Roberto
1991 *Ecopolitics of Development in the Third World: Politics and Environment in Brazil*. Boulder: Lynne Rienner.

Hochstetler, Kathryn
2019 "Environmental politics and policy," in Barry Ames (ed.), *Routledge Handbook of Brazilian Politics*. New York and London: Taylor & Francis Group.

Hochstetler, Kathryn and Margaret Keck
2007 *Greening Brazil: Environmental Activism in State and Society*. Durham, NC: Duke University Press.

Huber, Robert
2020 "The role of populist attitudes in explaining climate change skepticism and support for environmental protection." *Environmental Politics* 29: 1–24.

Issberner, Liz-Rejane and Philippe Léna (eds.)
2016 *Brazil in the Anthropocene: Conflicts between Predatory Development and Environmental Policies*. London: Taylor & Francis.

Jacobi, Pedro Roberto
2003 "Espaços públicos e práticas participativas na gestão do meio ambiente no Brasil." *Sociedade e Estado* 18 (1-2): 315–338. doi:10.1590/S0102-69922003000100015.

Jacobs, Jamie
2002 "Community participation, the environment, and democracy: Brazil in comparative per-spective." *Latin American Politics and Society* 44 (4): 59–88. doi:10.1111/j.1548-2456.2002.tb00223.x.

Jovem Pan
2018 "Em RO, Bolsonaro critica número de áreas florestais protegidas no país: 'atrapalha o desenvolvimento.'" https://jovempan.com.br/programas/jornal-da-manha/em-ro-bolson-aro-critica-numero-de-areas-florestais-protegidas-no-pais-atrapalha-o-desenvolvimento.html.

Lachapelle, Erick and Simon Kiss
2019 "Opposition to carbon pricing and right-wing populism: Ontario's 2018 general election." *Environmental Politics* 28: 970–976.

Lockwood, Matthew
2018 "Right-wing populism and the climate change agenda: exploring the linkages." *Environmental Politics* 27: 712–732.

Losekann, Cristiana
　2012 "Participação da sociedade civil na política ambiental do Governo Lula." *Ambiente &*
　　Sociedade 15 (1): 179–200. doi:10.1590/S1414-753X2012000100012.
Loureiro, Maria Rita and Regina Silvia Pacheco
　1995 "Formação e consolidação do campo ambiental no Brasil: consensos e disputas (1972–
　　92)." *Revista de Administração Pública* 29: 137–153. http://bibliotecadigital.fgv.br/ojs/index.
　　php/rap/article/view/8267/7052.
Mahoney, James and Kathleen Thelen
　2009 *Explaining Institutional Change: Ambiguity, Agency, and Power*. Cambridge: Cambridge
　　University Press.
Margulis, Sérgio and Natalie Unterstell
　2016 "Shaping up Brazil's long-term development considering climate change impacts," in
　　Liz-Rejane Issberner and Philippe Léna (eds.), *Brazil in the Anthropocene: Conflicts between*
　　Predatory Development and Environmental Policies. London: Routledge.
Meadows, Donella, Dennis Meadows, Jorgen Randers, and William Behrens
　1972 *The Limits to Growth*. New York: United Nations.
Meeus, Ben
　2019 "Politiques environnementales au Brésil: analyse historique et récents développements
　　sous Jair Bolsonaro." *La Pensée Écologique*, no. 2, 45–61. https://lapenseeecologique.com/poli-
　　tiques-environnementales-au-bresil-analyse-historique-et-recents-developpements-sous-jair-
　　bolsonaro-ben-meeus/.
MMA (Ministério do Meio Ambiente)
　2019 "Qualidade de vida da população que vive nas cidades é prioridade para o MMA."
　　https://www.mma.gov.br/informma/item/15715-qualidade-de-vida-da-população-que-
　　vive-nas-cidades-é-prioridade-para-o-mma.html.
Moura, Adriana Maria Magalhães
　2016 "Environment policy and governance in Brazil: challenges and prospects," in Liz-Rejane
　　Issberner and Philippe Léna (eds.), *Brazil in the Anthropocene: Conflicts Between Predatory*
　　Development and Environmental Policies. London: Routledge.
MPF (Ministério Público Federal)
　2020 "MPF propõe ação para anular despacho do Ministério do Meio Ambiente que coloca em
　　risco a preservação da Mata Atlântica." http://www.mpf.mp.br/df/sala-de-imprensa/noti-
　　cias-df/mpf-propoe-acao-para-anular-despacho-do-ministerio-do-meio-ambiente-que-col-
　　oca-em-risco-a-preservacao-da-mata-atlantica.
National Geographic
　2019 "Liberação recorde reacende debate sobre uso de agrotóxicos no Brasil." https://www.
　　nationalgeographicbrasil.com/meio-ambiente/2019/07/liberacao-recorde-reacende-debate-
　　sobre-uso-de-agrotoxicos-no-brasil-entenda.
New York Times
　2019 "Dispute over Amazon gets personal for Bolsonaro and Macron." https://www.nytimes.
　　com/2019/08/26/world/europe/bolsonaro-macron-g7.html.
Nobre, Marcos
　2020 *Ponto-final: A guerra de Bolsonaro contra a democracia*. São Paulo: Todavia.
O Eco
　2018 "Bolsonaro confirma promessa: Ministério do Meio Ambiente deixará de existir." https://
　　www.oeco.org.br/noticias/bolsonaro-confirma-promessa-ministerio-do-meio-ambiente-de-
　　ixara-de-existir/.
O Globo
　2019 "Fundo Amazônia fecha 2019 com R$ 2,2 bilhões parados." https://oglobo.globo.com/
　　sociedade/fundo-amazonia-fecha-2019-com-22-bilhoes-parados-24121515.
Oliveira, Marília Silva
　2016 "Movimento para as instituições: ambientalistas, partidos políticos e a liderança de
　　Marina Silva." Ph.D. diss., Universidade de Brasília.
　2020 "Movimentos sociais, ocupação de cargos públicos e políticas públicas, uma relação de
　　sucesso: o caso da produção do Plano de Prevenção e Combate ao Desmatamento na
　　Amazônia—PPCDAM,"in Rebecca Abers (ed.), *Ativismo institucional: Criatividade e luta de buro-*
　　cracia brasileira. Brasília: Editora UnB.

Pádua, José Augusto

1991 *O nascimento da política verde no Brasil: Fatores endógenos e exógenos*. Rio de Janeiro: Vozes.

2012 "Environmentalism in Brazil: a historical perspective," in J. R. McNeill and Erin Stewart Mauldin (eds.), *A Companion to Global Environmental History*. New York: Wiley-Blackwell.

2018 "Civil society and environmentalism in Brazil: the twentieth century's great acceleration," in Ravi Rajan and Lise Sedrez (eds.), *The Great Convergence: Environmental Histories of BRICS*. New Delhi: Oxford University Press.

Pereira, Ana Karine

2021 "Ativismo institucional em empreendimentos de infraestrutura: autonomia e discricionariedade no caso da hidrelétrica Belo Monte," pp. 189–219 in Rebecca Abers (ed.), *Ativismo institucional: Criatividade e luta da burocracia brasileira*. Brasília: Editora UnB.

Pereira, Joana Castro and Eduardo Viola

2019 "Catastrophic climate risk and Brazilian Amazonian politics and policies: a new research agenda." *Global Environmental Politics* 19 (2): 93–103. doi:10.1162/glep_a_00499.

Rajão, Raoni, Britaldo Soares-Filho, Felipe Nunes, Jan Borner, Lilian Machado, Débora Assis, Amanda Oliveira, Luis Pinto, Vivian Ribeiro, Lisa Rausch, Holly Gibbs, and Danilo Figueira

2020 "The rotten apples of Brazil's agribusiness." *Science* 369 (6501): 246–248. doi:10.1126/science.aba6646.

Reuters

2018 "Decisão de cancelar COP no Brasil teve participação minha, diz Bolsonaro em meio a desencontros da transição." https://br.reuters.com/article/topNews/idBRKCN1NX2RW-OBRTP.

2019a "Brazil's climate negotiators in dark on Bolsonaro's aims: sources." https://www.reuters.com/article/us-climate-change-accord-brazil/brazils-climate-negotiators-in-dark-on-bolsonaros-aims-sources-idUSKBN1Y617N.

2019b "Brazilian states bypass Bolsonaro to discuss rainforest protection funding directly." https://www.reuters.com/article/us-brazil-environment/brazilian-states-bypass-bolsonaro-to-discuss-rainforest-protection-funding-directly-idUSKCN1V91TS.

2019c "ICMBio centraliza gestão e põe militares para coordenar unidades de conservação ambiental." https://br.reuters.com/article/domesticNews/idBRKBN22Q3J2-OBRDN.

2019d " No longer the host, Brazil still aims for key role at U.N. climate talks." https://www.reuters.com/article/us-climate-change-brazil/no-longer-the-host-brazil-still-aims-for-key-role-at-u-n-climate-talks-idUSKBN1WU2YF.

2020a "Brazil acted too late to halt deforestation this year, vice president says." https://www.reuters.com/article/us-brazil-environment-enforcement/brazil-acted-too-late-to-halt-deforestation-this-year-vice-president-says-idUSKBN24B2PU.

2020b "Brazil Environment Ministry fires top climate change officials." https://uk.reuters.com/article/uk-brazil-environment-climatechange/brazil-environment-ministry-fires-top-climate-change-officials-idUKKCN20L2A6?il=0.

2020c "Desmatamento da Amazônia aumenta 34,4% em 2019 e é o maior desde 2008, diz Inpe." https://br.reuters.com/article/topNews/idBRKBN23H1ON-OBRTP.

Rochedo, Pedro, Britaldo Soares-Filho, Roberto Schaeffer, Eduardo Viola, Alexandre Szklo, André Lucena, Alexandre Koberle, Juliana Davis, Raoni Rajão, and Regis Rathmann

2018 "The threat of political bargaining to climate mitigation in Brazil." *Nature Climate Change* 8: 695. doi:10.1038/s41558-018-0213-y.

Science

2019 "Brazil's deforestation is exploding—and 2020 will be worse." https://www.sciencemag.org/news/2019/11/brazil-s-deforestation-exploding-and-2020-will-be-worse.

SGEE (System Gas Emissions Estimation Brazil)

2019 "Análise das emissões brasileiras de gases do efeito estufa e suas implicações para as metas do Brasil (1970–2018)." http://www.observatoriodoclima.eco.br/wp-content/uploads/2019/11/OC_SEEG_Relatorio_2019pdf.pdf.

Shahar, Dan

2019 "Environmental conflict and the legacy of the Reformation." *Environmental Politics* 28: 1–21. doi:10.1080/09644016.2019.1631114.

Soares-Filho, Britaldo, Raoni Rajão, Marcia Macedo, Arnaldo Carneiro, William Costa, Michael Coe, Hermann Rodrigues, and Ane Alencar
    2014 "Cracking Brazil's forest code." *Science* 344 (6182): 363–364. doi:10.1126/science.1246663.
Thelen, Kathleen
    2002 "The explanatory power of historical institutionalism," in James Mahoney and Dietrich Rueschemeyer (eds.), *Comparative Historical Analysis in the Social Sciences*. New York: Cambridge University Press.
UOL
    2019 "Decreto de Bolsonaro atinge a diversidade da representação popular." https://entendendobolsonaro.blogosfera.uol.com.br/2019/04/13/decreto-de-bolsonaro-atinge-a-diversidade-da-representacao-popular/?cmpid=copiaecola.
Viola, Eduardo
    1987 *O movimento ecológico no Brasil, 1974–1986: do ambientalismo à ecopolítica*. Florianópolis: Universidade de Santa Catarina.
    2002 "O movimento ambientalista brasileiro de Rio a Joanesburgo: as dificuldades da marcha do utopismo ao realism," in Samira Crespo (ed.), *O que pensa o brasileiro do meio ambiente e da sustentabilidade*. Rio de Janeiro: ISER.
Viola, Eduardo and Matias Franchini
    2017 *Brazil and Climate Change: Beyond the Amazon*. New York: Routledge.
Viola, Eduardo and Veronica Korber Gonçalves
    2019 "Brazil ups and downs in global environmental governance in the 21st century." *Revista Brasileira de Política Internacional* 62 (2). doi:10.1590/0034- 7329201900210.

The Far-Right Takeover in Brazil

Effects on the Health Agenda

by
Maíra S. Fedatto

On October 28, 2018, the far-right populist Jair Bolsonaro won Brazilian elections against the Partido dos Trabalhadores (Workers' Party—PT) candidate Fernando Haddad after a vigorous social-media campaign reinforced by fake news. In a context of economic crisis, escalating violence, and corruption scandals and a polarized population, Bolsonaro's authoritarian inclinations and reactionary rhetoric were concerns from several perspectives, mainly regarding the environment, education, human rights, health, and even the young Brazilian democracy. In particular, the Mais Médicos program, the national drug policy, and the HIV/AIDS Department have all been negatively influenced by his anticommunist rhetoric and the alarming escalation of evangelical conservatism. The militarization of his supporters in terms of moral values challenges the future of the secular state and therefore its substantial gains in international cooperation for health. With his approval rate falling and an international health crisis under way, Bolsonaro may not have an easy path ahead of him, and neither will the Brazilian population.

No dia 28 de outubro de 2018, o populista da extrema direita, Jair Bolsonaro, ganhou as eleições contra o candidato do Partido dos Trabalhadores (PT), Fernando Haddad, depois uma campanha enérgica baseada em redes sociais e reforçada por notícias falsas. Num âmbito que inclui uma crise econômica, uma escalada de violência, escândalos de corrupção e uma população polarizada, as tendências autoritárias e retórica reacionária de Bolsonaro apresentam desafios com respeito a muitos temas como o meio ambiente, a educação, direitos humanos, a saúde, e mesmo a democracia jovem do Brasil. O programa Mais Médicos, a política antidrogas e o Departamento de VIH/Sida, em particular, foram negativamente influenciados pela retórica anticomunista e pela alarmante expansão do conservadorismo evangélico. A militarização dos seguidores de Bolsonaro em termos de valores morais ameaça o futuro do estado secular e, por conseguinte, seus ganhos significativos na área de cooperação internacional com relação à saúde. Com sua índice de aprovação em declínio e uma crise internacional de saúde que está atualmente em curso, não podendo ser fácil para Bolsonaro e nem para a população brasileira nos anos a seguir.

Keywords: Brazil, Health, Bolsonaro, HIV/AIDS, Drug policy

Health and international relations have been predominantly distinct academic fields and policy arenas, but in recent years health has increasingly become a subject studied by experts in international relations and political

Maíra S. Fedatto is a global health researcher and consultant. She holds a joint Ph.D. in international relations from King's College London and the Universidade de São Paulo and a Master's from the Universidade de Brasília. She has been a specialized consultant for UNESCO and a researcher for the Núcleo de Estudos sobre Bioética e Diplomacia em Saúde (NETHIS/FIOCRUZ/PAHO).

LATIN AMERICAN PERSPECTIVES, Issue 248, Vol. 50 No. 1, January 2023, 133–148
DOI: 10.1177/0094582X221149026
© 2023 Latin American Perspectives

science. Throughout history, health studies adopted an epidemiological approach while international relations were mainly dominated by concerns about war and peace that reflected security-focused foreign agendas. The undeniable importance of the social and economic determinants of health[1] and awareness of the key role of collective action against disease and improvements in health have developed research and practice accordingly. Health has therefore begun to be seen as part of foreign policy. In 2007, for example, the foreign ministers of Brazil, France, Indonesia, Norway, Senegal, South Africa, and Thailand launched the Oslo Ministerial Declaration on global health. Because of the perception that global health should have a strategic place on the international agenda, 10 priority areas were chosen: preparedness and foreign policy, control of emerging infectious diseases and foreign policy, human resources for health and foreign policy, conflict, natural disasters and other crises, response to HIV/AIDS, health and the environment, health and development, trade policies and measures to implement and monitor agreements, and governance for global health security (Amorim et al., 2007).

With regard to Brazil, in the past 20 years, health has turned into a central and strategic topic for international relations and diplomacy, predominantly under Luiz Inácio Lula da Silva's governments (2003–2010). By promoting in multilateral forums positions such as access to medicine as a human right and social inclusion, Brazil has sought to strengthen in the international sphere principles that underlie the constitutional right to health. Since 1988 the Brazilian constitution has enshrined health as a citizens' right and given rise to a public, universal, and decentralized health system, the Sistema Único de Saúde (SUS). Massuda et al. (2018) point out that the system was conceived by civil society as part of the health reform movement and played a key role in the redemocratization of Brazil and the reinstatement of citizens' rights after 21 years of military dictatorship. Although underfunded from its creation and challenged by a private health care sector that accumulates considerable fiscal incentives, the system is widely acknowledged as having contributed to significant enhancements of Brazilian health service coverage and access and of health outcomes.

Under Lula, Brazil became a much-admired protagonist in South-South cooperation driven by local ownership, nonconditionality, and noninterference in partners' internal policies, and the health sector was seen as key for the country's development ambitions. Along these lines Brazil developed numerous cooperation initiatives in health such as establishing breast-milk banks, training human resources, strengthening primary health care, tackling HIV/AIDS and viral hepatitis, strengthening epidemiological surveillance, and promoting food and nutritional security. In 2010 a survey conducted by the Instituto de Pesquisa Econômica Aplicada (Institute of Applied Economic Research—IPEA) estimated the value of Brazilian development cooperation between 2005 and 2009 at US$1.43 billion, of which almost US$33 million were allocated to health projects on the African continent. Lula's foreign policy was used as a soft-power tool combining national development and autonomy to seek alliances and partnerships that would best serve both domestic and international objectives. Although without conditionality, Brazilian cooperation was guided by self-interested perspectives in which costs and benefits were precisely calculated. Cooperation was a tool of Lula's government for achieving economic outcomes and international bargaining power (Fedatto, 2013).

After eight years, Lula left the presidency with a personal approval rating of 87 percent and then, in conjunction with the Partido dos Trabalhadores (Workers' Party—PT), launched Dilma Rousseff as his successor. After her victory, it was expected that South-South cooperation would continue to be a foreign policy priority. However, Rousseff's first foreign minister, Antônio Patriota stated that "continuity did not mean repetition."[2] Thus, despite initial continuity, changes in foreign policy focus influenced international cooperation in health. Gómez and Perez (2016) argue that the decline of proactivity in foreign health policy during Rousseff's administration came primarily from her lack of personal interest in international affairs and emphasis on national economic and social development. Moreover, economic and political difficulties played an essential role in this foreign policy shift.

In 2016, Rousseff suffered a shady impeachment process less than two years after her reelection. Michel Temer, her vice president and successor, chose José Serra, a senator from the main opposition party, and Rousseff's past adversary, as minister of foreign affairs. This was an odd turnaround, since in the past 31 years (1985–2016) only three foreign ministers had been political party members. All the others were career diplomats trained at the Instituto Rio Branco, the Brazilian diplomatic academy. Under the Temer administration, South-South relationships—predominantly with Latin American governments aligned with the PT such as Venezuela, Bolivia, and Ecuador—lost steam.

Health was not included in any of the 10 foreign policy guidelines presented by Serra in May 2016. The only highlight of Temer's government in health was an adjustment to an existing agreement between Brazil and Argentina on the provision of emergency assistance and civil defense cooperation in border regions. The adjustment opened up the possibility for emergency services professionals to cross the border to act in specific cases.[3] Moreover, in 2016, the Congress approved a controversial constitutional amendment (PEC 55) that limited increases in public spending to inflation for the next 20 years. At that time, the United Nations special rapporteur on extreme poverty and human rights, Philip Alston, described it as "the most socially regressive austerity package in the world."[4] According to the Conselho Nacional de Saúde (National Health Council),[5] from 2018 to 2020 the health system lost some US$4.3 billion. Given the ongoing COVID-19 pandemic, the council called for the immediate repeal of the constitutional amendment, which never happened.

The election of Jair Messias Bolsonaro as the thirty-eighth president of Brazil and the consequent shift to the far right has raised concerns among various sectors of Brazilian society, including the health community. Elected through a polarizing narrative embedded in Neo-Pentecostal[6] values, Bolsonaro's supporters include the armed forces, from which he was judicially removed in the 1980s with the rank of lieutenant and afterward promoted to captain. The army had previously had nine presidents, including the 21-year civilian-military authoritarian regime (1964–1985), a dictatorship that has not undergone any process of transitional justice.[7] As Brazil has never reflected on the ideas underpinning past authoritarian tendencies, when Bolsonaro rose to power, the army's salvationism[8] reemerged.

During the electoral campaign Jair Bolsonaro presented himself as an out-sider (despite his having been a federal deputy for 27 years) and the only one capable of changing a "corrupted and economically devastated" country. The salvationist political movement is one of his most reliable supporters and is linked to the evangelical community represented in Congress. Together, their explicit goal is to renew the Brazilian policy dominated by corruption and the loosening of conventional morality and religious principles. The Pentecostal influence in Brazil, however, is neither contemporary nor accidental. It has been increasing for half a century, making evangelicalism the second-largest religious group in the country, behind only Catholicism. While in the 1940s evangelicals accounted for only 2.6 percent of the population, according to the last census, they represent 31 percent nowadays (Datafolha, 2020). Pentecostalism's advance, however, is significant not only on the religious and demographic levels but also in the media and politics (Mariano, 2004).

The influence of religion on both domestic and foreign policy is worrisome, and it has affected health. A survey released by Instituto Brasileiro de Opinião Pública e Estatística (Brazilian Institute of Public Opinion and Statistics—IBOPE) on December 13, two weeks before Bolsonaro took office, revealed health as the biggest concern of Brazilians, prevailing over unemployment, corruption, and violence. In his inaugural speech, Bolsonaro was the first pres-ident since the end of the military dictatorship not to mention the need to address poverty and inequality. Not surprisingly, after six months, while other ministries were in the spotlight for their controversies more than for projects, health seemed forgotten.

As we have seen, foreign policy is designed to achieve both domestic and international goals, and it is essential to understand how governments behave internally before analyzing its impact on the international scenario. Since 2009, as a result of a solid partnership between the Ministry of Health and the Ministry of International Affairs, the concept of "structural cooperation" was developed to characterize international cooperation intended to strengthen the health systems of partner countries. Bolsonaro's Minister of Health, Luiz Henrique Mandetta, was considered a technician and a moderate politician, although he had faced accusations of irregularities when he was head of the Secretariat of Health in Campo Grande, Mato Grosso do Sul. A member of the Democratas (Democrats) party, he had been a federal deputy between 2010 and 2018, and as soon as he took office he declared that his focus would be "the total reorganization of basic health in Brazil,"[9] including reducing expenses "considered unnecessary" and reformulating the public health database.

The religious and salvationist rhetoric that marked Bolsonaro's election cam-paign was translated into concrete measures and actions that threatened and violated human rights in Brazil. This paper is therefore divided into three sec-tions aiming to analyze how the beginning of Bolsonaro's far-right administra-tion influenced health policies. The first section is devoted to the consequences of the departure of the 8,517 doctors that Cuba had deployed to poor and remote regions of Brazil as part of the Mais Médicos (More Doctors) coopera-tion agreement. The second section deals with the new national drug policy, which introduced a more punitive approach including compulsory rehabilita-tion and added therapeutic communities to the national structure of drug addiction treatment. The third section is devoted to the widely recognized response to HIV and AIDS and what changed.

THE MAIS MÉDICOS PROGRAM

International cooperation was historically consolidated after World War II, both through the United Nations and as a consequence of the socioeconomic devastation caused by the war and the need for financial recovery. Therefore, according to the Article 1 of the Charter of the United Nations, one of the organization's purposes was "to achieve international co-operation in solving international problems of an economic, social, cultural, or humanitarian character, and in promoting and encouraging respect for human rights and for fundamental freedoms for all without distinction as to race, sex, language, or religion" (UN, 1945). Since then, despite some conceptual disagreements, international cooperation for development has become central to the field of international relations with regard to both academic research and decision-making forums beyond the UN system such as the World Bank and the Organization for Economic Co-operation and Development (OECD). According to Amado Cervo (1994), international cooperation became part of the country's foreign policy and began to mobilize a large number of internal and external entities. According to the Agência Brasileira de Cooperação (Brazilian Cooperation Agency—ABC) technical cooperation can contribute significantly to "the socioeconomic development of the country and the construction of national autonomy."

Despite the shrinkage of the so-called self-reliant and active foreign policy[10] conducted by President Lula da Silva and his foreign minister Celso Amorim, it was under Dilma Rousseff's government that Mais Médicos program was established. It was a technical cooperation agreement promoted by the federal government with the political and operational support of states and municipalities to expand the access of the Brazilian population to primary health care, particularly in small counties and remote areas. Signed in August 2013, the agreement was a triangular cooperation between the Pan American Health Organization (PAHO), Brazil, and Cuba and ultimately became well-known as Mais Médicos. According to the PAHO (2018), the main goal was to reduce the shortage of doctors in remote and vulnerable areas and health inequities, to strengthen health care infrastructure, and to increase medical school admissions and the specialization of health workforces.

To understand Mais Médicos program, one must first understand the severe inequalities in the distribution of the medical workforce across Brazil. Despite the evolving role played by Brazil in the field of health through cooperation programs focusing on development that reflected the advances of domestic public policies, enormous health disparities persist in the country. To illustrate, Brazil's most deprived and remote regions, which include the 34 special indigenous health districts, include five states with fewer than 1 physician per 1,000 inhabitants and 700 counties without a doctor. Girardi et al. (2011) have reported that despite the high density of doctors in big cities and wealthier regions of the country, severe shortages exist elsewhere. They estimate that some 7 percent of

Brazilian municipalities have no resident doctors and around 25 percent have only 1 doctor for every 3,000+ inhabitants. The North and Northeast, with 8 percent and 28 percent of the country's population respectively, have 4.3 percent and 18.2 percent of the physicians, while the Southeast, with 42 percent of the population, has 60 percent of the doctors. In 2012, the Maranhão, in the Northeast, had 0.58 physician per 1,000 inhabitants while Rio de Janeiro had 3.44. Given the scarcity of doctors in some regions and the struggle to keep professionals practicing in deprived areas, in January 2013 the Frente Nacional de Profeitos (National Mayors' Front) shared a document called *Where Is the Doctor?* that was signed by 4,600 mayors[11] and supported by the Conselho Nacional de Secretarias Municipais de Saúde (National Council of Municipal Health Secretariats). The document was presented to Alexandre Padilha, Rousseff's health minister. The lack of doctors has been pointed to by municipal health managers and opinion polls as one of the most significant health problems in the country. The pressure exerted by the mayors culminated in Mais Médicos program.

According to the FAQ of the Ministry of Health website,[12] priority to join Mais Médicos program was given to Brazilian doctors trained in Brazil and then foreigners trained in Brazil and Brazilians or foreigners trained outside Brazil who had legalized their credentials. If any vacancies remained, Cuban doctors would be called through the international cooperation agreement. Since the beginning of the program, the physicians have been assigned to counties with high rates of extreme poverty, 84 percent of them from the North and Northeast (PAHO, 2018). The presence of Cuban physicians in Brazil, however, triggered controversy. The Brazilian medical council dogmatically rejected the agreement. Bolsonaro not only questioned the quality of the Cuban health workers but also recurrently called them slaves because part of their wages went to the Cuban government. De Vos et al. (2007) emphasize that, despite economic difficulties in the 1990s, Cuba's national health system has gained worldwide recognition for its performance and results. Its health indicators are among the best in the world, and it has a well-known background in international aid in the health field dating to shortly after the 1959 Revolution and in 2007 reaching 69 countries.

According to the World Bank when it comes to the health workforce density of countries worldwide,[13] Brazil has 2.3 doctors per 1,000 inhabitants while Cuba has 8.4. The Cuban health system is described as highly structured, focused on prevention, innovative, and efficient (Campion and Morrissey, 2013) and is capable of sending health professionals overseas without negatively impacting the access to health care of Cuba's own population. Almost a year after the first case of *Ebola* the UN and the World Health Organization (WHO) requested international medical collaboration to assist with the medical crisis and the social disaster that had devastated West Africa. Chaple and Mercer (2016) emphasize that the Cuban authorities responded immediately and sent 256 doctors, nurses, and other health professionals.

Given this scenario, the cooperation agreement between Brazil and Cuba becomes understandable. Thus, one must ask why the program was attacked from the beginning not only by representatives of the Conselho Federal de Medicina (Federal Medical Council—CFM) but by the population. Aside from the political-ideological views of the program's opponents, the two main arguments against it were the salaries of the Cuban doctors and the medical revalidation process. Under the terms of the cooperation agreement, the Cuban doctors' salaries were paid by the Brazilian government to the PAHO, which passed them on to the Cuban government for payment. Counties were responsible for providing housing and food. The Brazilian government therefore did not establish individual contracts with the Cuban doctors, who were civil servants hired through a private company, Comercializadora de Servicios Médicos Cubanos S.A. In 2017, according to several national newspapers, 154 suits were brought in the Brazilian courts by 194 Cuban doctors to stay in the country and receive their full salaries. Given that some 14,000 Cubans had participated in the program, these complaints represented less than 2 percent of the participants. Regarding the medical revalidation process, the doctors in the program used to be assessed by both the Ministry of Health and the Ministry of Education. According to the federal government's *Diário Oficial da União*, upon arriving in Brazil the foreign health professionals underwent a period of preparation focused on the health system, health issues, and Portuguese. After four weeks of classes, they were evaluated and, on passing an admissions test, received provisional authorization to practice under the supervision of educational institutions.

According to the PAHO, in its first year (2013–2014) primary health care coverage in Brazil increased from 10.8 percent to 24.6 percent. Likewise, the UN Office for South-South Cooperation report points to a significant increase in the availability of primary health care doctors, benefiting approximately 63 million people in 4,058 counties and contributing to the reduction of infant mortality rates and hospitalizations (UNOSSC, 2016). Similarly, according to the Secretaria Especial de Saúde Indígena (Special Secretariat for Indigenous Health), indigenous districts experienced a 79 percent increase in physician availability within the first two years of the program, and 90 percent of the doctors who worked in these areas were from Cuba.

In November 2018, Cuba unilaterally declared the country's withdrawal from the cooperation agreement, citing constant threats, diplomatic disrespect, and lack of recognition of its humanitarian medical cooperation by the future president of Brazil. Considering that more than 8,000 Cuban doctors were at that time assigned to some 3,000 counties, the Confederação Nacional de Municípios (National Confederation of Counties— CNM) declared that approximately 28 million Brazilians would be affected, what could amount to a major public health disaster.[14] The newly elected government, however, played down the incident, assuring the population that Brazilian professionals would fill all the vacant positions. After the departure of the Cuban doctors, the Ministry of Health issued an edict to fill the 8,517 vacancies, of which 7,120 were subsequently occupied by doctors trained in Brazil. However, around 19 percent (1,325) withdrew from participating in the program until May 2019, resulting in almost 3,000-person decrease in the health workforce. Given the low salaries compared with those in private hospitals, the poor working conditions, and the lack of career prospects, filling vacancies in the most vulnerable and remote regions is one of Brazil's most significant challenges.

With COVID-19 pandemic sweeping the world and coronavirus-related deaths increasing sharply in Brazil, the minister of health announced that the country's health system could collapse in April 2020. Therefore, on March 25, 2020, the Ministry of Health through the Secretariat of Primary Health Care made an extraordinary call for Cuban health professionals who had remained in Brazil after the end of the triangular cooperation in November 2018. Considering the priority regions, which include counties with a high percentage of the population in extreme poverty, economic and social vulnerability, and heavy demand for health services due to the pandemic, more than 500 health professionals from Cuba were rehired.

THE NEW DRUG POLICY

International control over narcotics and psychotropic substances goes back to the early twentieth century. Following the first control strategies, the diversification of drugs, and the increasing capacity for synthesizing narcotics and psychotropic substances, the countries within the UN framework signed three conventions on drugs: the Single Convention on Narcotic Drugs of 1961, the Convention on Psychotropic Substances of 1971, and the Convention against Illicit Traffic in Narcotic Drugs and Psychotropic Substances of 1988. Every 10 years there are reviews of the treaties, but in 2016 a special session of the UN General Assembly was requested by three countries (Colombia, Guatemala, and Mexico). Despite being highly anticipated, no significant advances took place at this session, but the 193 member states unanimously established "drug addiction as a complex multifactorial health disorder characterized by chronic and relapsing nature" that is preventable and treatable and not the result of moral failure or criminal behavior. Moreover, the UN holds that drug addicts can be held in compulsory confinement or treatment by judicial order only if they have refused medical treatment and only for short periods of time or when they are considered an imminent threat to themselves and/or others. The shift from criminal justice to a public health approach was a hard-won advance for the multilateral institutions, but Brazil has always been more attuned to conservative and repressive positions on the issue of illicit drugs.

Thiago Rodrigues, director of institutional relations of the Associação Brasileira de Estudos de Defesa (Brazilian Defense Studies Association), clarifies that, mainly inspired by the Netherlands, at the beginning of the 1990s Brazil had introduced the limited harm-reduction policies employed in Europe since the 1980s, but they were aimed at vulnerable populations such as homeless people who injected drugs and shared syringes and therefore were more exposed to HIV, hepatitis, and other communicable diseases. The first attempt at a harm-reduction policy in Brazil was in Santos (São Paulo) in 1989 under the administration of Telma dos Santos, which became known for its focus on health. But it met with strong opposition from those who considered it an incentive for drug abuse. Subsequently, during Lula's first administration, the Ministry of Health was influenced by more progressive ideas and advanced the discussion of a new law—which had been under debate since the 1990s—to replace the extremely repressive Law on Toxics of 1976. With support from both progressive and conservative sides, Law 11.343 was approved in 2006 inaugurating a new era in the Brazilian legal system for dealing with drugs. The previous laws (Law 6.368 /76 and Law 10.409/02) had adopted a more criminal than sociological/public health approach. Rodrigues points out, however, that despite having a more progressive intention, such as setting alternative penalties for users, the new law has increased the penalty for drug traffickers and left the designation of who is a drug dealer and who is a user to the police (interview, London, July 4, 2019).

Although attached to the myth of being a racial democracy because of the historical absence of constitutional racial segregation, Brazilian society was built upon racial discrimination and inequalities. Structural violence combined with a corrupted police that became the main authority for identifying dealers and users led to an explosion of imprisonments in 2007–2008. Brazil has the world's third-largest proportion of the population incarcerated, behind only the United States and China, and this became a problem during the ongoing COVID-19 pandemic. The Conselho Nacional de Justiça (National Council of Justice—CNJ) recommended preventive measures to limit the spread of the new coronavirus in the prison system, but they were not welcomed by Bolsonaro's minister of justice, Sergio Moro.

A fierce defender of the "war on drugs" and the criminalization of drug use, in June 2019 Bolsonaro sanctioned Law 13.840, which authorized the compulsory hospitalization of the chemical-dependent without judicial authorization. The narrative supporting the law was the government's belief, based on no evidence, that the country was experiencing a drug epidemic. A US$1.5 million study on the consumption of licit and illicit substances in Brazil conducted by the Fundação Oswaldo Cruz (Fiocruz) did not confirm this belief, but the results were never released by the Secretaria Nacional de Políticas sobre Drogas (National Secretariat for Drugs Policies—SENAD), the agency responsible for commissioning the research. Researchers accused the government of censoring the survey, and the minister of citizenship and later COVID-19 denier Osmar Terra declared the study biased because the foundation had historically supported the liberalization of drug policy. The veto of the publication surprised scientific circles and worried public health experts.

Demoralizing and disempowering research institutes was a persistent strategy of Bolsonaro's government and supporters. A fake-news engine known as the hate office, was established and led by Bolsonaro's son, the city councilman for Rio de Janeiro Carlos Bolsonaro, and the international affairs adviser Filipe Martins was behind the government's aggressive tone and conspiracy theories. Through daily reports detailing their versions of the facts in Brazil and around the world, the hate office encourages virtual militias to attack political opponents and anyone who disagrees with the government's positions. This was what occurred with Fiocruz's drug study and afterwards during the COVID-19 pandemic. Fiocruz's experts have warned that increasing dependence on nonprescription opioids is a real cause for concern. They have also explained that cannabis is the most-used illicit drug, followed by cocaine, and that, while smoking rates have been falling in recent decades, alcohol is the drug most consumed. Crack cocaine users have become very common on Brazil's streets, but specialists maintain that the current numbers are not alarming enough to be considered an epidemic. Only 0.9 percent of the population have used crack once in their lives, 0.3 percent have used it in the past year, and only 0. 1 percent have used it in the past 30 days.

"Deny science and use strength" is the way Aldo Zaiden, a psychologist and a specialist in human rights and drug policy, summarizes Bolsonaro's new drug policy. He also warns that the therapeutic communities attached to evangelical churches are behind this tougher approach (interview, London, June 25, 2019). The therapeutic community is an intensive and comprehensive treatment model originated in 1958, when other approaches such as psychiatry and general medicine were proved unsuccessful in treating alcohol and other drug addictions. According to Perrone (2014), therapeutic communities were idealized in the wider context of the Psychiatric Reform Law (10.216/2001)., but because of the alarming escalation of drug use in Brazil and the lack of public policies to address the problem a proliferation of chemical-dependency internment locations occurred.

Ribeiro and Minayo (2015) describe three categories of therapeutic community— religious-spiritual, scientific, and mixed. In Brazil, Catholic and evangelical institutions predominate. According to a survey done by the IPEA in 2017, Brazil has some 2,000 therapeutic communities, of which some 64 percent receive money from one or more governmental spheres. Aldo Zaiden warned that Bolsonaro's administration aimed to create 30,000 more places in evangelical therapeutic communities similar to psychiatric hospitals, where inhuman treatment such as abuse, forced labor, and torture are habitual (interview, London, June 25, 2019). Therapeutic communities are supposed to follow the rules of the Conselho Nacional de Políticas sobre Drogas (National Drug Policy Council—CONAD) Resolution 01/2015, which establishes that treatment should be voluntary and any form of controlling patients with physical force and remedies is prohibited. Although explicitly prohibiting punishment, the resolution is vague on how treatments should be conducted. Moreover, according to the IPEA, 93 percent of Brazilian therapeutic communities use labor therapy, a method that has been criticized by the Conselho Federal de Psicologia (Federal Council of Psychology) for being used to maximize the profit of these communities.

Therapeutic communities perfectly exemplify the way politics and religion are increasingly intertwined in Brazil. *Intercept* has denounced regular meetings of representatives of therapeutic communities with drug policy makers in Brasilia. At the end of 2018, the former president Michel Temer announced a federal investment of R$90 million (USD17.5 million) to finance hospitalizations. The federal deputy Osmar Terra introduced House Bill 37/2013 on the conditions of care for users or drug-dependents and the financing of drug policy. Apart from facilitating involuntary hospitalizations, the bill strengthened therapeutic communities by making them eligible to receive tax-exempt money. People and businesses can allocate up to 30 percent of their income tax to these institutions. The bill had been in the Senate for six years, and it was approved less than six months after the beginning of Bolsonaro's government. The new law turns therapeutic communities into protagonists in the care of drug users by increasing public funding to them without addressing mechanisms for monitoring or evaluating the treatment offered.

Instead of strengthening the public health system, the new drug policy encourages private religious institutions. According to SUS guidelines, the drug-addicted patient has the right to medical attention, to be treated with the least invasive means, and to be treated by community mental health services if feasible. Drug abusers are also encouraged to attend the Rede de Atenção Psicossocial (Psychosocial Care Network). The Brazilian health system offers free social, psychological, and psychiatric assistance, while therapeutic communities force rehabilitation through religious conversion, a practice at odds with any public health policy.

THE STRUGGLE AGAINST AIDS

In 1985, still under the military regime, a program to control AIDS was created to coordinate epidemiological surveillance at the national level. The disease was recognized as an emerging public health problem. In 1996, Law 9.313/96 ensured that all patients infected with HIV who needed antiretroviral therapy would receive it free of charge through the public health system. Brazil started to be recognized for its strong response to the HIV epidemic through an equitable approach including prevention, treatment, and care. The active participation of civil society in shaping the Brazilian response to HIV and AIDS, mainly through several decision-making forums, was not only essential to governmental accountability but recognized as one of the key elements of the Brazilian success. Since the 1980s, the country has implemented campaigns including massive distribution of condoms and campaigns targeting vulnerable populations such as sex workers, injecting drug users, and homosexuals. In 2001, a survey conducted by the School of Public Health of the Universidade of Sao Paulo verified the effectiveness of the free distribution of syringes to drug users to reduce the spread of AIDS in Santos. Brazil buys and distributes more condoms than any other country in the world, and since 2013 free antiretroviral treatment through the health system has been available for all HIV-positive adults regardless of the stage of the disease. HIV/AIDS in Brazil was gradually ceasing to be a highly lethal disease and turning into a potentially controllable chronic one (Fedatto, 2017).

In the 2000s, Brazil threatened to break international patent laws on antiretroviral drugs, even in the face of economic sanctions from the United States, and denounced the profit-driven Western pharmaceutical companies that required low-income countries to pay full price for antiretroviral prescriptions. Along with India, Brazil led the discussions that culminated in the Doha Declaration on the TRIPS Agreement and Public Health at the World Trade Organization (WTO) fourth ministerial conference in 2001. The declaration states that "the agreement can and should be interpreted and implemented as supportive of WTO members' right to protect public health and, in particular, to promote access to medicines for all" (WTO, 2001). Likewise, Brazil challenged big pharmaceutical companies by producing generic versions of overpriced antiretroviral drugs, which ended up reducing prices globally. Through diplomacy, Brazil sought to shift the discussions of the agreement from the WTO to the WHO. In line with the priority of South-South cooperation under

Lula's government, in 2012 Brazil established an antiretroviral drug factory in Mozambique. The original objective, however, was not accomplished, since the drug nevirapine, which was supposed to be produced in the factory, is no longer used in HIV treatment. Domestically, the national STD/AIDS program aimed at the development of public policies to reduce transmission and to promote better health conditions for people living with AIDS. The focus was on early diagnosis, treatment and prevention of combined infections, training of health professionals, and research.

Despite its recognized global role in the fight against the epidemic, HIV/AIDS remains a significant challenge in Brazil as new infections have increased since 2010. According to UNAIDS (2019), 900,000 people were living with HIV in 2018 compared with 640,000 in 2010. Moreover, progressive agendas, including HIV-related policies, have been blocked since 2014 as conservative evangelical representatives have gradually been elected. Nowadays, of 594 deputies and senators, 90 have links with evangelical churches, representing 15 percent of the Congress. Under Bolsonaro's administration, their influence is considerable, with public health experts worrying that hard-won gains on HIV could be reversed.

One of the first signs of this was the dismissal of the public health physician Adele Benzaken from her post as director of the STD/AIDS and Viral Hepatitis Department in the first week of the new government. According to Minister of Health Mandetta, the pre-exposure prophylaxis approach could encourage high-risk behavior, despite its reducing the risk of getting HIV from sex by about 99 percent and from injection drug use by 74 percent. For the newly appointed minister, HIV/AIDS policies and prevention initiatives were to be carefully conducted so as not to affront families and sex education was to be addressed basically within the family environment. Moral and religious views were ruling the public health policies of a secular country.

The conservative evangelical movement, which was always an important part of Bolsonaro's government, started to filibustered any harm-reduction policy. Notwithstanding the new national drug policy, which no longer focused on harm reduction and was promoting abstinence, Brazil witnessed a reinforced stigma and prejudice against drug users and other vulnerable populations such as the LGBTQI community.

Agostini et al. (2019: 4601) call attention to the way notions such as family, God, and good morals have affected the HIV/AIDS program. They point out that, anti-agendas were built to question gender, sexual diversity, and harm reduction policies, which were historically key to HIV prevention in Brazil. Likewise, the fight against *gender ideology* and the *school without a party* proposal have been promoting an inquisitorial hunt for internationally recognized theorists such as Paulo Freire and Judith Butler. Additionally, Bolsonaro, Mandetta, and Minister of the Economy Paulo Guedes decided to merge tuberculosis, leprosy, sexually transmitted infections, AIDS, and viral hepatitis into a single department within the Ministry of Health—adding two diseases unrelated to sexual contagion that used to be under the umbrella of the Department of Surveillance of Communicable Diseases. Therefore, the former Department of STD/AIDS and Viral Hepatitis became the Department of Chronic Illnesses and Sexually Transmitted Diseases. According to several nongovernmental organizations and public health specialists, this change has the potential to weaken policies to combat AIDS by reducing its importance and diluting it in a department with different demands. Besides, the department will have to deal with two additional diseases without an increase in the budget.

Finally, despite the recognized strategic role of civil society in the Brazilian response to HIV/AIDS, Decree 9750 of April 11, 2019, essentially eradicates at least 650 participatory councils envisioned by former President Dilma Rousseff in 2014. These councils were seen as channels for "strengthening and articulating mechanisms and democratic instances of dialogue and joint action between the federal public administration and civil society." According to a preliminary survey by the CSN, the main areas affected will be human rights, racial equality, indigenous peoples, LGBTQI, and environment.

During his presidency Bolsonaro said that a person with HIV is "an expense for everyone in Brazil," and national campaigns focused on the postponement of sexual activity as a method for preventing pregnancy among young people. By ignoring the use of condoms and other contraceptive methods in nationwide campaigns and a number of other initiatives, the government has not only interrupted a successful history of raising awareness but also severely undermined key aspects of HIV/AIDS response, increasing potential stigma, prejudice, fear, and violence. Jair Bolsonaro's religious and moral-driven administration put at risk a program recognized worldwide and weakened evidence-based actions and activities. The consequences of his nefarious policies for HIV prevalence in Brazil have yet to be disclosed.

FINAL CONSIDERATIONS

In the period before his inauguration on January 1, 2019, and during his tenure as president of Brazil, Bolsonaro issued a number of declarations and executive orders with potential influence on domestic and international affairs. This paper has analyzed three of them: the withdrawal of the Cuban doctors who were part of the Mais Médicos program, the new national drug policy, and the significant changes in the country's HIV/AIDS policy, all influenced by anticommunist rhetoric and an alarming escalation of religious conservatism in Brazil.

The Neo-Pentecostal approach of Bolsonaro's government has effectively militarized supporters on the basis of moral values. The "God, fatherland, and family" legacy will challenge the future of the Brazilian secular state and, therefore, its substantial gains and leading role on human rights, environmental protection, and international cooperation for health. Brazilian politics is now poised to be deeply influenced by conservative religious ideals. The implementation of a policy of morality can be observed, for example, in the restructuring of the Department of HIV/AIDs, the modification of public health education packages that deal with the human body and sex education for teenagers, and a significant reduction in the budget for STDs. Bolsonaro's government completely ignored that health challenges must be understood as shared problems that require collective efforts and the maintenance of partnerships free of ideological views.

The ideological approach was similar to the approach to the COVID-19 pandemic, which caused almost 700,000 deaths in Brazil. Despite having a structured and decentralized health system, the Brazilian response to the coronavirus crisis had two main problems. First, epidemics, in most cases, affect the rich and the poor in different ways. Therefore, socioeconomic vulnerabilities that range from lack of access to clean water and sanitation services to limited access to health care are significant variables. Brazil has substantial spatial heterogeneity in terms of demography, access to public health, and poverty indexes. Pandemics such COVID-19 require a multisectoral and coordinated response at all levels. Second, Bolsonaro himself posed a threat to the country's response to the outbreak. All countries that have been intensely affected by COVID-19 have testified that the substantial number of infected patients who need to be hospitalized may lead to the collapse of the country's health care system. The minister of health has estimated that, while around 85 percent of coronavirus cases will require basic care at home, approximately 15 percent will involve being admitted to a hospital—a colossal burden on the public health system. If health facilities become compromised during an outbreak, this may both fuel the epidemic and affect broader health services.

Instead of working together with governors and mayors, Bolsonaro constantly attacked the isolation measures taken by states and counties, repeatedly referring to COVID-19 as a "little flu" surrounded by "hysteria" sustained by the media. He defied all recommendations from the WHO and fired two health ministers for not following his denial behavior. A former army general with no background in public health or medicine was the health minister during most of the pandemic. General Eduardo Pazuello quickly surrounded himself with other military men without health expertise and fired knowledgeable personnel. Jair Bolsonaro's response to the COVID-19 pandemic is therefore is seen by many international relations and public health pundits as a concrete example of "necropolitics," and he was judged and condemned by the symbolic Permanent People's Tribunal.

Preserving and strengthening the country's health system is the clear way to prevent and respond to unknown diseases. Jair Bolsonaro saw his popularity fade away in the battle between science and fanaticism he promoted. It is apparent from the results of the 2022 elections that, pointed to as the worst leader to tackle the ongoing pandemic, he shot himself in the foot.

NOTES

1. According to the World Health Organization, the social determinants of health are employment conditions, social exclusion, health systems, globalization, early child development, gender equity, public health programs, and urbanization. https://www.who.int/social_determinants/en/ (accessed June 20, 2019).

2. http://www.itamaraty.gov.br/pt-BR/discursos-artigos-e-entrevistas/ministro-das-relacoes-exteriores-entrevistas/4573-continuar-nao-e-repetir-veja-09-01-2011 (accessed June 23, 2019).

3. http://www2.planalto.gov.br/mandatomicheltemer/acompanhe-planalto/noticias/2017/02/brasil-e-argentina-assinam-atos-em-comercio-diplomacia-e-saude (accessed July 5, 2019).

4. Brazil's 20-year public expenditure cap will violate human rights, a UN expert warns. https://www.ohchr.org/EN/NewsEvents/Pages/DisplayNews.aspx?NewsID=21006 (accessed April 6, 2020).

5. The CNS is a deliberative and permanent body of the health system and part of the Ministry of Health. Created in 1937, its mission is to inspect and monitor public health policies, taking the demands of the population to the policy makers. It includes social movements, governmental and nongovernmental institutions, bodies of health professionals, the scientific community, and bodies of service providers and businesses in the health area.

6. Neo-Pentecostalism emerged in Brazil in the 1970s with the Nova Vida Church and gained visibility over the following decades. Some of the main Neo-Pentecostal churches in Brazil are Universal do Reino de Deus, Internacional da Graça de Deus, Cristo Vive, Sara Nossa Terra, and Comunidade da Graça. This generation of churches is different from the previous two in defending prosperity, being constantly at war with the devil, and not following traditional customs. Additionally, there is a great expansion in radio and TV. Universal do Reino de Deus is considered a "Neo-Pentecostal phenomenon" because of its appearances in biased news, its attacks on religions of African origin, and its huge public visibility, which leads to success in politics (Mariano, 2004).

7. Transitional justice is rooted in accountability and redress for victims. It recognizes their dignity as citizens and as human beings. From 1964 to 1985, Brazilians lived under a military dictatorship that suppressed unionists and young political activists. More than 400 people were killed or disappeared, and thousands were tortured or subjected to other severe abuse. While in power, the regime sought to protect itself. A 1979 amnesty law allowed exiled activists to return but was also used to shield human rights violators from prosecution. Those perpetrators have never faced criminal justice.

8. A political movement whose objective was to control Brazil's fate through the defense of moralistic and traditionalist demands such as "law and order," "morality and decency," "sexual morality," and family protection. Led by evangelical pastors with or without elective mandates, this movement played a key role in the 2018 Brazilian elections, which elected the ultraconservative federal deputy Jair Bolsonaro. Through political activism and a massive media structure, a "new policy" was proposed to religious voters and socially conservative groups.

9. https://www.valor.com.br/brasil/6045625/ministro-da-saude-pretende-reorganizar-atencao-basica (accessed July 1, 2019).

10. The expression coined by the former chancellor Celso Amorim (2003–2011) to identify the approach of Brazilian foreign policy during the Lula period. The objectives were mainly to promote Brazilian protagonism and to defend a strong multilateralism. In addition, Lula and Amorim focused on intense executive and technical participation in international negotiations and on active political coordination with relevant actors in world politics, generally independent partners in the developing world, with emphasis on India, South Africa, and China in addition to the neighboring countries of South America.

11. http://cadeomedico.blogspot.com/2013/01/ (accessed April 14, 2020).

12. http://www.maismedicos.gov.br/perguntas-frequentes (accessed July 1, 2019).

13. data.worldbank.org/indicator/SH.MED.PHYS.ZS (accessed December 15, 2022).

14. https://www.cnm.org.br/index.php/comunicacao/noticias/saida-de-cubanos-do-mais-medicos-afeta-28-milhoes-de-brasileiros-a-maioria-de-areas-vulneraveis (accessed July 1, 2019).

REFERENCES

Agostini, Rafael, Fátima Rocha, Eduardo Melo, and Ivia Maksud
    2019 "The Brazilian response to the HIV/AIDS epidemic amidst the crisis." *Ciência & Saúde Coletiva* 24: 4599–4604.
Amorim, Celso et al.
    2007 "Oslo Ministerial Declaration—global health: a pressing foreign policy issue of our time." *The Lancet* 369: 1373–1378.
Campion, Edward W. and Stephen Morrissey
    2013 "A different model—medical care in Cuba." *New England Journal of Medicine* 368: 297–299.
Cervo, A.
    1994 "Socializando o desenvolvimento: uma história da cooperação técnica internacional do Brasil." *Revista Brasileira de Política Internacional* 37 (1): 37–63.

Chaple, E. B. and M. A. Mercer
   2017 "The Cuban response to the *Ebola* epidemic in West Africa: lessons in solidarity." *International Journal of Health Services* 47 (1): 134–149.
De Vos, P., W. de Ceukelaire, M. Bonet, and P. Van der Stuyft
   2007 "Cuba's international cooperation in health: an overview." *International Journal of Health Services* 37: 761–776.
Fedatto, Maíra S.
   2013 "A Fiocruz e a cooperação para a África no Governo Lula." Master's thesis, Universidade de Brasília.
   2017 "The AIDS epidemic and the Mozambican Society of Medicines: an analysis of Brazilian cooperation." *Ciência & Saúde Coletiva* 22: 2295–2304.
Girardi, Sábado Nicolau et al.
   2011 "Índice de escassez de médicos no Brasil: estudo exploratório no âmbito da atenção primária," pp. 171–186 in C. R. Pierantoni, M. Dal Poz, and T. O. França (eds.), *O trabalho em saúde: Abordagens quantitativas e qualitativas.* Rio de Janeiro: CEPESC/IMS/UERJ-ObservaRH.
Gómez, Eduardo and Fernanda Aguilar Perez
   2016 "Brazilian foreign policy in health during Dilma Rousseff's administration (2011–2014)." *Lua Nova: Revista de Cultura e Política*, no. 98, 171–197.
Mariano, Ricardo
   2004 "Expansão pentecostal no Brasil: o caso da Igreja Universal." *Estudos Avançados* 18 (52): 121–138.
Massuda, A., T. Hone, F. A. G. Leles, et al.
   2018 "The Brazilian health system at a crossroads: progress, crisis, and resilience." *BMJ Global Health* 3 (4):e000829.
PAHO (Pan American Health Organization)
   2018 *Marco para el monitoreo y la evaluación del Proyecto de Cooperación Mais Médicos OPS/OMS.* 2d edition. Brasília, DF: OPAS.
Perrone, Pablo Andrés Kurlander
   2014 "The therapeutic community for recuperation from addiction to alcohol and other drugs in Brazil: in line with or running counter to psychiatric reform?" *Ciência & Saúde Coletiva* 19 (2): 569–580.
Ribeiro, Fernanda Mendes Lages and Maria Cecília de Souza Minayo
   2015 "As comunidades terapêuticas religiosas na recuperação de dependentes de drogas: o caso de Manguinhos." *Interface: Comunicação, Saúde, Educação* 19 (54): 515–526.
UN (United Nations)
   1945 "Charter of the United Nations." http://www.unwebsite.com/charter (accessed July 2, 2019).
UNAIDS
   2019 "UNAIDS data 2019." https://www.unaids.org/sites/default/files/media_asset/2019-UNAIDS-data_en.pdf (accessed April 30, 2020).
UNOSSC (United Nations Office for South-South Cooperation)
   2016 "Good practices in South-South and triangular cooperation for sustainable development." https://www.unsouthsouth.org/2016/05/30/good-practices-in-south-south-and-triangular-cooperation-for-sustainable-development-2016 (accessed June 25, 2019).
WTO (World Trade Organization)
   2001 "Declaration on the TRIPS agreement and public health." https://www.wto.org/english/thewto_e/minist_e/min01_e/mindecl_trips_e.htm (accessed April 30, 2020).

The Fight against Hunger in Brazil

From Politicization to Indifference

by
Lourrene Maffra
Translated by
Heather Hayes

Federal administrations have been addressing the problem of hunger in Brazil since the days of Lula da Silva. An extensive review of the literature shows that the fight against hunger reached its highest level of priority during the Lula da Silva administrations (2003–2010), where it was organized with an institutional structure and seen as an international model for public policy. Every subsequent government since then has given less attention to it, ending in the complete neglect of the issue under the Bolsonaro administration.

Governos federais têm abordado o problema da fome no Brasil desde a época de Lula da Silva. Uma revista exhaustiva da literatura aponta que a luta contra a fome atingiu o seu apogeu quando lhe foi atribuída máxima proridade na agenda política federal durante os governos Lula da Silva (2003–2010) onde era organizada com base numa estrutura institucional que é hoje celebrada como modelo internacional de política pública. Desde então, cada governo sucessivo prestou cada vez menos atenção à fome, acabando no descaso completo do assunto sob o governo Bolsonaro.

Keywords: Hunger, Brazil, Policy, Lula, Bolsonaro

Hunger is nothing new in Brazil and is perhaps one of the clearest products of the country's underdevelopment. However, over the years successive administrations have given hunger varying levels of priority. Hunger in Brazil has been addressed by public policy since the 1940s but has long been treated as a problem the solution to which was increasing food production, and the policies for dealing with it have had a welfare focus such as donating food baskets. It was not until 2003, with Lula da Silva, that hunger was recognized as a political problem. This led to progress in confronting the matter, since it had an impact on the type of policy envisioned at the federal level.

This article addresses the position that hunger occupied on the federal government's agenda from 2003 to 2020, a period covering the administrations of Lula da Silva (2003–2010), Dilma Rousseff (2011–2016), Michel Temer (2016–2018), and Jair Bolsonaro (2019–). I have performed a bibliographic review of public policies relating to food and nutrition security, looking at the programs that were implemented or reestablished and the roles of the parties involved. I

Lourrene Maffra is a doctoral student at the University of Seville and an assistant professor of international relations at the Universidade Federal de Amapá. Heather Hayes is a translator living in Quito, Ecuador.

LATIN AMERICAN PERSPECTIVES, Issue 248, Vol. 50 No. 1, January 2023, 149–164
DOI: 10.1177/0094582X231152905

have also used data provided by ministries, government statistical research agencies, and reports from international organizations on the subject. The article has three sections. In the first section, I address the Lula da Silva administration, in the second section what I have called the "transitional governments," the administrations of Dilma Rousseff and Michel Temer, and in the third the current Jair Bolsonaro administration.

LULA DA SILVA'S FOME ZERO: THE POLITICIZATION OF THE FIGHT AGAINST HUNGER IN BRAZIL

In his speech launching the Fome Zero (Zero Hunger) program and reestablishing the Conselho Nacional de Segurança Alimentar e Nutricional (National Council of Food and Nutrition Security—CONSEA), on January 30, 2003, the newly elected president of Brazil, Luís Inácio Lula da Silva, set the tone for the way hunger would be addressed by his government: as a political problem and as something given priority. Assigning a political character to hunger in Brazil was part of the strategy for combating it. The idea was to include the structural and causal aspects of the problem, including poverty and inequality, in addition to working on its immediate aspects. With the inauguration of his government on January 1, 2003, legal, institutional, and political structures were created that resulted in the Fome Zero program.

The first of these structures was the Extraordinary Ministry of Food Security and the Fight against Hunger.[1] During its 20 months of existence, it was under the leadership of the agronomy engineer José Graziano da Silva, who is considered the intellectual father of Fome Zero because, together with other professors at the Universidade Estadual de Campinas including Walter Belik and Maya Takagi, he participated in the development of the program, establishing its methods, evaluation measures, and budget. Fome Zero had a substantial legal structure covering everything from the target audience to the operationalization of the program in Brazilian municipalities. Law 10,683 of May 28, 2003, recreated the CONSEA; Law 10,696 of July 2, 2003, created the Programa de Aquisição de Alimentos (Food Acquisition Program—PAA); Law 10,836 of 2004 combined all the previous income transfer programs in the country into a single benefit, creating the Bolsa Família (Family Allowance Program); Law 11,346 of 2006 regulated food and nutrition security; Law 11,947 of 2009 specified that 30 percent of the funding for the Programa Nacional de Alimentação Escolar (National School Feeding Program—PNAE) would be purchased from family farmers; and Constitutional Amendment 64 of February 4, 2010, incorporated the human right to food into the list of Brazilians' social rights. The CONSEA was responsible for articulating the demands of civil society and academics with those of policy makers and actively participated in the negotiations to implement several programs that accompanied or followed it, including the PAA, the Bolsa Família program (which made payments to families with school-age children), and the PNAE.

The institutionalization process also involved structural changes in the ministries and special secretariats of the federal government. When the Extraordinary Ministry of Food Security and Fight against Hunger was eliminated, its activities were transferred to the newly created Ministry of Social Development and the Fight against Hunger, with some of them going to the Ministry of Agrarian Development[2] (Medeiros and Grisa, 2020). Other ministries, such as education, and special secretariats such as Human Rights and Women's Policies also acted indirectly in achieving Fome Zero in the country's municipalities.

A key milestone was the creation in 2004 of the Coordenação-Geral de Cooperação Humanitaria e Combate a Fome (General Coordination of Humanitarian Cooperation and Fight against Hunger—CGFome) under the Ministry of Foreign Affairs. This office was in charge of coordinating the actions of the government to fight hunger on the international stage. CGFome's actions followed the Food and Agriculture Organization's strategy for fighting hunger, called the twin-track approach, which sought structural changes alongside immediate action (IPEA and ABC, 2018: 227–228). It was responsible for supporting responses from the international community in cases of food insecurity and/or chronic hunger associated with economic crisis, war, civil conflict, and environmental disaster.[3] It was also responsible for the medium- and long-term administration and coordination of programs to improve the quality of life of the local population in efforts at sustainability such as PAA Africa (Purchase from Africans for Africa), inspired by the PAA program.

The federal government's actions under the Fome Zero program followed three lines: structural policies, specific policies, and local policies (Graziano da Silva, Grossi, and França, 2010). Structural policies involved medium-to-long-term actions to create a permanent and sustainable environment for combating the causes of hunger, including reducing the food vulnerability of families by increasing family income, universalizing social rights, providing access to quality food, and reducing income inequality, in particular by generating employment, increasing the minimum wage, and promoting family farming. Alongside these were specific policies designed to promote food security and directly combat hunger and malnutrition among the most vulnerable population groups on an emergency basis, including the food stamp program, emergency food basket donations, the creation of reserves, and the expansion of school meals. The local policies that rounded out these strategies were policies that were implemented by states and municipalities in partnership with civil society, among them municipal food security programs and policies for rural areas.

The Fome Zero program, as originally envisioned, was to operate for only a year, but other programs working toward the same objectives replaced it. The PAA promoted family farming under the Bolsa Família program, increased the minimum wage, and provided cash to purchase staples, and the PNAE promoted family farming in that 30 percent of food purchases for schools had to come from family farms. According to Vaz and Balsadi (2004: 109), Fome Zero articulated a set of public policies aimed at tackling the problem of food access in the short term and creating security conditions for the country's vulnerable families in the medium and long term. The objective was to implement different policies for family farming and build basic legislation for the national food and nutrition security policy (Cassel, 2010: 8).

This set of public policies was considered successful at the time. First, Brazil was removed from the hunger map of the Food and Agriculture Organization

(FAO) in 2014.[4] Second, its policies were adopted by other countries. Osório (2015) reports that Chile's cash transfer policy was borrowed from the Bolsa Família program, and Grisa and Sabourin (2018) say that Brazilian policies relating to family farming served as a model for other Latin American countries. In a broader sense, Milhorance (2013) has described the implications of the transfer of Brazilian agricultural policy to the African continent, and Maffra and Boza (2020) have discussed the influence of Brazil on the recently instituted government procurement policy for family farming in Chile.

The government took advantage of the visibility of these public policies and turned them into a foreign policy strategy. Pinheiro and Milani (2012: 335–336) identify this policy diffusion as "internationalization," something very different from exporting because it presupposes a high degree of acceptance and legitimacy generally stimulated by a real or constructed affinity between the parties involved (a more common experience in South-South cooperation) rather than as an imposition by outsiders. The Latin America and the Caribbean without Hunger Initiative, the Parliamentary Front against Hunger in Latin America and the Caribbean, PAA Africa, and the Zero Hunger programs for West African countries are all examples of this initial Brazilian influence (Graziano da Silva, Del Grossi, and França, 2010; Martín López, 2012; Fillol, 2014).

Third, Brazil often received congratulations from international organizations and foreign countries for its progress in the fight against hunger,[5] and two Brazilians were elected top authorities of two important international institutions on the issue of hunger: José Graziano da Silva to the FAO in 2011 and Roberto Azevedo to the World Trade Organization (WTO) in 2013. These elections were possible only with African support as part of what Oliveira (2005: 263) called a broad front of South-South cooperation in the defense of shared interests against the developed world—an alternative to the traditionally vertical relations between the developed North and the underdeveloped South. Taking advantage of the international situation and the optimism emerging from the positive results of its economic and social policies, Brazil presented itself as the "natural leader" of the region (Souza, 2002; Lafer, 2001) and of the developing countries (Lima, 2005), promoting discussions of expanding the permanent membership of the UN Security Council, representing the interests of developing countries in the Doha Round of the WTO, and negotiating an agreement between Mercosur and the European Union.

Lula da Silva served two terms as president, from 2003 to 2010, and in 2010 managed to get his successor elected. Dilma Rousseff, who was from the same political party (Partido dos Trabalhadores [Workers' Party—PT]), took over in 2011, maintaining essentially all of her predecessor's programs and establishing new ones such as Brasil sem Miséria (Brazil without Extreme Poverty).

THE TRANSITIONAL GOVERNMENTS AND THE BEGINNING OF THE DECAY OF THE AGENDA TO FIGHT HUNGER IN BRAZIL

The Rousseff and Temer administrations were "transitional" in that they marked the beginning of a slowdown in the national agenda to combat hunger. Rousseff was elected for two four-year terms (2011–2014, 2014–2018), but the second was interrupted in 2016, when she was impeached. For the last two years she was replaced by her vice president, Michel Temer. During her first term, most of the programs described earlier continued and poverty was more seriously addressed as a key element in achieving zero hunger. The Brasil sem Miséria plan was created in June 2011 through Presidential Decree 7,492; its main objective was to eradicate extreme poverty in the country by guaranteeing a minimum family income, improving access to public health services and education, and promoting productive inclusion to improve job opportunities for families. The plan was implemented between 2011 and 2014 and coordinated by the Ministry of Social Development and the Fight against Hunger through the Extraordinary Secretariat for Overcoming Extreme Poverty. Despite being directly under the responsibility of that agency, the plan was carried out in partnership with other ministries (Campello, Falcão, and Costa, 2014).

On the key point of guaranteeing a minimum income for Brazilian citizens, there was expanded funding for the Bolsa Família program (and an increase in the number of families served) and the creation of two new programs, Brasil Carinhoso, aimed at financing families with children from 0 to 48 months enrolled in day care centers, and Bolsa Verde, aimed at financing families that perform environmental conservation activities. For Rousseff the eradication of extreme poverty was a priority: "The eradication of poverty will benefit not only the poor, but society as a whole" (quoted in Campello and Mello, 2014: 37). According to the poverty data for 2010, 59.07 percent of Brazil's extremely poor lived in the Northeast, 16.75 percent in the Southeast, 16.34 percent in the North, 4.40 percent in the South, and 3.43 percent in the Central-West. The plan considered the extremely poor to be all persons earning a monthly per capita income of up to R$70 (at the time equivalent to approximately US$40, currently around US$13).[6] According to Campello and Mello (2014:44), the identification of the extreme poverty line made it possible to create a point of reference for selecting the target audience for the Brasil sem Miséria program with the assistance of the Cadastro Único.[7]

Although the policies and programs put together during the Lula da Silva administration had remained under Rousseff and other goals had been set, the country had begun to feel the belated effects of the 2008 world crisis, and this generated pressure for effective responses from the federal government, especially for the most affected sectors, which included industry and services. According to the Instituto Brasileiro de Geografía e Estadística (Brazilian Institute of Geography and Statistics—IBGE), the gross domestic product (GDP) that year shrank by 3.5 percent and household consumption (the main component of GDP demand) declined by 3.2 percent (IBGE, 2015). All of this translated into reduced tax collection during the Rousseff administration, which ended up making it necessary to give priority to certain programs over others. Those that won out were the ones aimed at economic recovery, which meant a capital increase for the Banco Nacional de Desenvolvimento Econômico e Social (Brazilian Development Bank) to subsidize financing of large national companies, favoring the interests of large Brazilian companies in the conduct of Brazilian foreign policy (mainly civil construction, oil and gas exploration, and naval matters), and an increase in public investment in infrastructure, with emphasis on the Growth Acceleration Program—all under a macroeconomic policy focused on sustaining domestic demand at the height of the international financial crisis (Queiroz, 2018: 141).

Another component of the economic crisis of 2015 was the mass protests of June 2013. Initially, their agendas demanded an increase in public investment in social issues and opposed the abusive increases in local bus fares. These demonstrations were later taken over by the middle class, which turned them into a springboard for its own demands. Many political analysts identify them as the seeds of dissent that ended up forcing Rousseff out of office in 2016. According to Singer (2018), Rousseff had displeased her government's political base by replacing former political patrons with technical staff in state-owned companies. This generated pressure from the parties with the most representatives in Congress, in particular the party to which her vice president belonged, the Partido do Movimento Democrático Brasileiro (Brazilian Democratic Movement Party—PMDB). Added to this was the eruption of the aforementioned demonstrations and investigations of corruption.

The scenario at the beginning of Rousseff's second term was complicated and required attention to the economic crisis that lay ahead (Corsi, 2018). It ended up causing a reduction of budgets for practically all social programs in 2015 in a frustrated attempt to balance the country's accounts.[8] These programs included Bolsa Família and the Programa Nacional de Fortalecimento da Agricultura Familiar (National Program for Strengthening Family Agriculture—PRONAF), part of the original Fome Zero strategy. At the same time, no adjustment was made to the prices paid for school food in the education network through the PNAE between 2010 and 2017, according to 2009 data published by the Confederação Nacional de Municipios (National Confederation of Municipalities).[9] The price per student remained the same as when the program was implemented in its current format in 2009, resulting in a major lag of prices behind inflation.

Starting at the end of Dilma's first and the beginning of her second term, social issues in general, alongside concern about hunger and poverty, began to lose ground among the government's priorities. This national decline was reflected on the international level, as pointed out by Cervo and Lessa (2014). This national context led to a political crisis that resulted in the impeachment and subsequent exit of Dilma Rousseff. The process began on December 2, 2015, when the Speaker of the Chamber of Deputies accepted that his legislative body would begin processing the impeachment, and it ended on August 31, 2016, when Dilma was impeached and Vice President Michel Temer assumed power.

Martuscelli (2020: 70) argues that, despite Congress's having followed all the procedures required by law, in the voting on the impeachment on April 17, 2016, "the declarations made by the vast majority of federal representatives did everything but focus on the process's legal aspects." Most representatives voted for personal reasons ("for family and for God"). Along with Martuscelli, Santos (2016), Ramos and Moreira (2016), Grabois and Cavalcante (2016), Alves (2016), Löwy (2016), and Jinkings (2016), I consider Rousseff's removal from office a coup. While her ouster was characterized by the use of legal and fiscal justifications, the practices cited had been common under previous administrations and had never before served as a basis for impeaching anyone. Her impeachment became possible only because of political considerations. According to the former president's defense report, Rousseff was the victim of a "neo-coup" (Cardozo and Franco, 2016, quoted by Martuscellli, 2020: 4):

> In these coups, tanks, bombs, cannons, or machine guns are not used, as they would be in military coups. False and deceptive legal arguments are used in an attempt to replace the violence of armed actions with the hollow and hypocritical words of those who pretend to be democrats to trample on democracy when it best serves their interests. The Constitution is invoked only to be elegantly and silently torn up.

Despite this rather questionable situation, Michel Temer assumed the Brazilian presidency with a discourse focused on austerity when it came to economic matters, saying that political interests needed to be redirected to overcome the serious crisis that the country was going through. He appealed to greater participation by the business sector in this economic recovery, speaking of the need to "downsize" (reduce) the state apparatus, in addition to emphasizing the importance of Operation Car Wash[10] in the fight against corruption, and to guarantee that this would allow social programs to remain and be improved.[11] However, when sending the national budget proposal for the following year, 2017, to Congress, Temer set the tone of his administration on social matters. Budget planning for the coming year included a cut of about 30 percent in the federal government's main social programs (Costa, 2016). The areas most affected were regional development, housing, agrarian reform, racial equality, women, indigenous people, and major programs such as Bolsa Família.[12]

Another important point in understanding the slowdown in investment and, consequently, the deterioration of the agenda to fight hunger in the country is the elimination of a large part of the institutional structure created during Lula da Silva's first term. Beginning with Provisional Measure 726, issued on May 16, 2016, the Ministry of Agrarian Development and the Ministry of Women, Racial Equality, Youth, and Human Rights were both eliminated. The Ministry of Social Development and the Fight against Hunger was transformed into the Ministry of Social and Agrarian Development and initially incorporated the functions of the Ministry of Agrarian Development. However, according to Mattei (2017: 174),

> Because of the political differences between the various forces that made up the government in the interim phase, this structure did not even work within the scope of the [Ministry of Social and Agrarian Development]. On May 27, 2016, Decree 8,780 transferred the entire old structure of the [Ministry of Agrarian Development] to the Civil House, a ministerial structure that ended up concentrating all of the responsibility for agrarian reform, the promotion of sustainable development of rural areas made up of family farmers, and the delimitation of the lands of the remaining quilombo communities and determination of their demarcations.

To this effect, the former duties of the Ministry of Agrarian Development were left in the hands of the Special Secretariat for Family Agriculture and Agrarian Development, under an agency directly connected to the president.

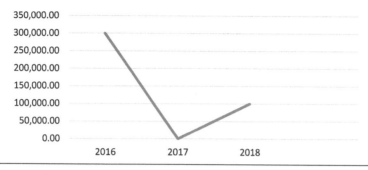

Figure 1. Humanitarian cooperation for food security (US$), 2016–2018 (data from http:// www.abc.gov.br/api/publicacaoarquivo/109).

Also in July 2016, before officially taking over as president but already acting as interim president, Michel Temer, through Decree 8,817 of July 21, 2016, eliminated the CGFome, removing from office the diplomat who had headed the agency because of his forceful opposition to the administration that was taking power in the country. According to a study conducted by the Instituto de Pesquisa Econômica Aplicada (Institute of Applied Economic Research) and the Agência Brasileira de Cooperação (Brazilian Cooperation Agency) (IPEA and ABC, 2018: 228), since the CGFome was eliminated some of its functions have been performed by the ABC, among them "coordination of emergency response actions having a humanitarian nature, including donations of food, medicine, and other essential items" and "monitoring of cooperation initiatives on humanitarian issues that were financed by Brazil alongside international organizations and other governmental and nongovernmental partners." However, there was a sharp decline in the amount devoted to humanitarian actions when the main reason for the donation was food security (Figure 1).

A caveat is required here: The budget earmarked for any action by the federal government, whether domestically or internationally, is always determined in the previous year. In other words, the allocation for international cooperation actions for 2016 was planned in 2015, when Dilma Rousseff was still president.

As is argued by Lima, Pereira, and Barbanti (2018: 398), we moved from a "diplomacy to combat hunger" during the Lula da Silva government to a foreign policy that benefited agribusiness in the Temer administration. Whereas the international initiatives under Lula da Silva opened up more opportunities for the representations of family and peasant agriculture and "Brazilian diplomacy has become one of the most important voices in international debates on how to fight hunger," foreign policy under Temer prioritized the opening of markets for Brazilian commodities in the hands of large agribusiness corporations. The prioritization of a political agenda that benefited big business bore fruit when, in October 2018, the candidate Jair Messias Bolsonaro was elected president through the intensive use of social media and massive propagation of fake news and conservative and misogynistic ideas.

THE COUP MATERIALIZES: THE DISMANTLING OF THE STRUCTURE TO FIGHT HUNGER IN BRAZIL AND POLITICAL INDIFFERENCE

"To say that people go hungry in Brazil is a big lie. Yes, there are people who are not doing well or not eating well; I can agree that happens. Starvation, however, is another matter." This utterance by Jair Bolsonaro at a press conference with the foreign media in Brasília on July 19, 2019, well represents the way in which the government has been dealing with this issue. The election of Bolsonaro in a runoff on October 28, 2018, followed a trend that some have called the "reactivation" (Singer, 2021) or "reorganization" (Fuks and Marques, 2020) of the right in Brazil. According to Singer (2021: 12), "right-leaning voters constituted a silent mass when there were no competitive conservative presidential candidates. The demonstrations of June 2013, Operation Car Wash in 2014, and the economic debacle that began in 2015 seem to have provided the missing opportunity. The impeachment in 2016 and Bolsonaro's campaign in 2018 sowed fertile ground." Fuks and Marques (2020: 417) have shown that ideology was a variable in voting in the 2018 elections: "Voters who, ideologically, identify with the right and who are more concerned with 'order,' tradition, and security voted according to such values."

Bolsonaro's main campaign promises related to privatization, social security reform, expansion of civilian carrying of weapons, and a controversial announcement of payment of a thirteenth installment of the Bolsa Família benefit (the only reference to a social program). The idea of the thirteenth installment served first to establish a belief among beneficiaries that this program would not be ended in a potential Bolsonaro administration and second to garner votes among the most vulnerable. This extra installment was paid in December 2019, but the provisional measure that would have made it permanent failed in the legislature in March 2020.

When he took power on January 1, 2019, Bolsonaro's first administrative act (Provisional Measure 870) eliminated the Special Secretariat for Family Agriculture and Agrarian Development, transferring its functions to the INCRA, and combined the Ministries of Social Development, Sports, and Culture to create the Ministry of the Citizenry—thus turning the decision-making process for each of these areas into a difficult task. In the area of food security, the CONSEA was eliminated on February 6, 2019. For the purposes of my analysis here, this is the decision that best represents the position of this type of agenda in Brazil's current administration. The CONSEA was internationally recognized for coordinating between key stakeholders at different levels and with varying interests, conducting research in the area, issuing reports and opinions, monitoring the implementation of policies, and representing Brazil in international forums (Menezes, 2010; Maluf, 2010; Burlandy, 2011; Sonnino, Torres, and Schneider, 2014; OBS, 2014; Mendonça, 2018). There were reactions to the order eliminating it from civil society, academia, scientific entities, medical and nutrition entities, and international organizations (Castro, 2019; FAO, 2019). One of the most emblematic arguments for the council's return was an article by former presidents of CONSEA (Recine et al., 2019) describing the

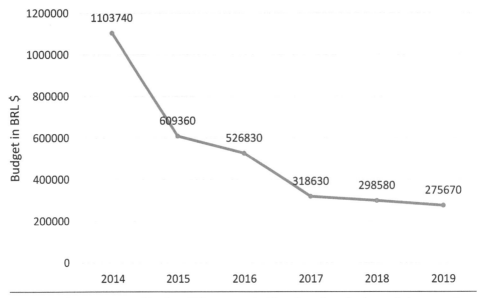

Figure 2. The PAA's annual budget (R$), 2014–2019 (data from http://mds.gov.br/assuntos/
seguranca-alimentar/programa-de-aquisicao-de-alimentos-paa).

trajectory of the council and its importance in the redemocratization of Brazil
and as an example in the area of food security. The article concluded by calling
the move a serious step backward in building an arena for debate on policy
relating to food and nutrition security.

After intense social pressure, the CONSEA was reinstated as part of the
Ministry of the Citizenry in the final text of the provisional measure approved
by Congress, but when the text was turned into Law 13,844/2019 Bolsonaro
vetoed the reinstatement. In April of the same year, an obstacle was raised to
social participation with the elimination of several councils and committees[13]
including the PNAE's consultative group and the PAA's consultative committee (Schottz, 2019: 93–94).

At the same time, there were disastrous further cuts to social programs. The
PAA's budget went from a little over R$1,100,000 in 2014 to about half that,
R$526,000, in 2016 and R$275,000 in 2019 (Figure 2).

With situations like this, the hollowing out of the food security agenda under
the Bolsonaro administration became crystal-clear. The social area had been
losing institutional structure in the ministries of successive administrations
since Michel Temer took power (see table in Cardoso Jr., 2019: 157). In addition
to the changes with regard to the Ministry of Agrarian Development discussed
earlier, the term "Fighting Hunger" disappeared from the Ministry of Social
Development under Temer in 2016, and "Social Development" itself ceased to
exist in the Bolsonaro administration, becoming an "area of action" within the
Ministry of the Citizenry.

In connection with this dismantling of policies to fight hunger and food insecurity, since 2017 the United Nations and its agencies have been warning of the
possibility that Brazil could reappear on the hunger map.[14] A report released on
September 11, 2018, stated that the fight against hunger in Brazil had stagnated

and that the numbers of people in a situation of food insecurity were the same as in previous years (UN, 2018).

Additionally, the Bolsonaro government has shown itself to be incapable of taking on the COVID-19 pandemic that launched a wave of infection in February 2020. Since the virus's first manifestations in the country, Brazil's president has been discrediting scientists and refusing to recognize the severity of the disease, disrespecting the health protocols and recommendations of the World Health Organization and the country's own health system. Several international agencies have warned about the perverse impact that the pandemic will have on the most vulnerable populations—increasing the number of people who will go hungry in the postpandemic world. The United Nations Food Program, for example, projects that the socioeconomic impact of the COVID-19 pandemic on Latin America and the Caribbean could leave an estimated 14 million people hungry this year (WFP, 2020). Scientific studies have also emerged to this effect. Sipioni et al. (2020: 16), for example, conclude their analysis by pointing out that "the weakening of food security policies has severe repercussions for the living conditions of the population, especially those most affected by the consequences of the pandemic. Policies and programs that already exist on the public agenda, although weakened, are fundamental for alleviating the tragedy of the hunger that is foreseen for the pandemic period and thereafter." Silva Filho and Gomes Júnior (2020: 2) warn of the loss of the role of the state as a guarantor of food and nutrition security in Brazil and mention that the pandemic has revealed the "perversity of state management in guaranteeing rights and basic human needs."

The most recent data from the household budget survey[15] carried out by the IBGE show that food insecurity in the country increased from 22.6 percent in 2013 to 36.4 percent in 2017–2018. Meanwhile, international newspapers and national and international NGOs[16] have warned about the risk of Brazil's returning to the hunger map with the increasing rates of people in a state of food insecurity and extreme poverty and the decline of the relative income of the population with the economic crisis and the pandemic. Upon assuming the presidency in January 2019, Jair Bolsonaro adopted a liberal agenda, reducing state investment in social programs, promoting an economic and privatization-centric agenda for everything public and internationally, and prioritizing agribusiness in commercial transactions. Despite his being only in the second year of his term, the decisions made so far have already had a negative impact on the nation's poorest and on Brazil's image internationally.

FINAL CONSIDERATIONS

Since the 1940s, the country has had a troubling history when it comes to hunger (as is reflected in Josué de Castro's classic *Geografia da fome*). The fight against hunger in Brazil reached its peak under the Lula da Silva administration, which created legislation and specialized agencies to deal with the issue and programs aimed at achieving the objective. Ever since Lula's successor, Dilma Rousseff, took office in 2011, fighting hunger has lost prominence because of the worsening effects of the international financial crisis on the nation's economy and the beginnings of a political crisis that would eventually lead to the removal of the president. Even so, in her first term, Rousseff managed to implement the Brasil sem Miséria plan. However, she was prevented from finishing her second term, and her replacement, Michel Temer, headed an administration with liberalizing tendencies and drastically reduced the state structure and the budgets for social programs. Jair Bolsonaro, elected president at the end of 2018, has further reduced the budgets for social programs in general, merged disparate areas into the same ministerial structures (shedding light on the fact that they are not priorities), and given minimal technical and financial attention to family farming, the largest supplier of healthy food, in favor of agribusiness. Consequently, hunger is being ignored, and it will probably worsen with the impacts of the pandemic and the inability of today's administration to deal with its socioeconomic effects.

Bolsonaro's decisions are already impacting the lives of the nation's poorest and Brazil's image internationally. The country is moving from a position in which it acted as a model of public policy in terms of food security and family farming that influenced other countries through soft power to that of an international pariah, alienating traditional allies including its neighboring countries, aligning itself unconditionally with the United States, and rejecting multilateral structures.

NOTES

1. Created via Provisional Measure 103 of January 1, 2003, which later became Law 10,683 of May 28, 2003.

2. The Ministry of Agrarian Development was created in the late 1990s, still under the government of Fernando Henrique Cardoso, to manage the issue of family farming and agrarian reform.

3. As regulated by Law 11,451 of July 7, 2007, the role of CGFOme was to "assist countries or populations in emergency situations, public calamities, social upheavals, natural or man-made disasters, armed conflicts, acute food insecurity, imminent or serious threat to life, health, guarantee of human or humanitarian rights, combining preventive, emergent, and structure-related actions."

4. http://www.fao.org/3/a-i4033e.pdf; http://www.fao.org/americas/noticias/ver/pt/c/260599/.

5. http://www.brasilalemanhanews.com.br/economia/alemanha-parabeniza-escolha-de-jose-graziano-para-a-fao/; https://www.gazetadopovo.com.br/mundo/fao-parabeniza-38-paises-por-avancos-na-luta-contra-a-fome-essjghiy6s9ixlcuddhjhhxzi/; https://www12.senado.leg.br/noticias/materias/2015/10/13/homenagem-aos-70-anos-da-fao-rende-aplausos-as-conquistas-do-brasil-no-combate-a-fome; https://exame.com/brasil/lula-apoio-africano-foi-fundamental-para-vitoria-na-omc/.

6. Rates calculated on the Central Bank of Brazil website: https://www.bcb.gov.br/conversao.

7. "A set of information on Brazilian families living in poverty and extreme poverty. This information is used by the Federal Government, as well as Brazil's states and municipalities, to implement public policies to aid in improving the lives of these families." http://www.caixa.gov.br/cadastros/cadastro-unico/Paginas/default.aspx.

8. https://www.camara.leg.br/internet/comissao/index/mista/orca/orcamento/OR2014/red_final/vol6/002_quadro_sintese_invest.PDF; https://www.camara.leg.br/internet/comissao/index/mista/orca/orcamento/OR2015/red_final/vol6/002_quadro_sintese_invest.PDF.

9. https://www.cnm.org.br/comunicacao/noticias/reportagem-com-dados-da-cnm-indica-em-dez-anos-merenda-por-aluno-cresceu-only-r-0-63.

10. A joint task force of several Brazilian agencies alongside the judiciary with the objective of fighting corruption. Legal, ethical, and political questions have been raised by specialists around the world as to the modus operandi of this task force. For an official version, see http://www.mpf.mp.br/grandes-casos/lava-jato/entenda-o-caso.

11. https://www1.folha.uol.com.br/poder/2016/05/1770780-leia-integra-do-discurso-de-posse-do-presidente-interino-michel-temer.shtml.

12. See also the final text of the investment budget at http://www.camara.gov.br/internet/comissao/index/mista/orca/orcamento/OR2017/red_final/Volume_VI.pdf.

13. Despite the fact that this decision continues to be questioned in court at higher levels of the Brazilian justice system, there is no longer any political or institutional space for these social councils to act, given that their funding and, above all, their mandate have been taken from them.

14. https://noticias.uol.com.br/politica/ultimas-noticias/2018/10/17/jose-graziano-fao-onu-mapa-da-fome-brasil-obesidade.htm.

15. https://biblioteca.ibge.gov.br/visualizacao/livros/liv101886.pdf.

16. https://www.nytimes.com/2021/04/23/world/americas/covid-brazil-hunger.html; https://www.economist.com/the-americas/2021/05/15/brazilians-are-increasingly-going-hungry; https://www.thenewhumanitarian.org/news-feature/2021/7/19/pandemic-puts-brazil-back-on-the-world-hunger-map; https://newint.org/features/2021/06/17/pandemic-has-worsened-brazil-hunger-crisis-fjf; https://www.worldhunger.org/brazil-danger-reinstated-uns-world-hunger-map/.

REFERENCES

Alves, Giovanni
2016 "A pulsão golpista da miséria política brasileira," pp. 146–157 in Carol Proner, Gisele Cittadino, Marcio Tenenbaum, and Wilson Ramos Filho (eds.), *A resistência ao golpe de 2016.* Bauru: Canal 6 (Projeto Editorial Praxis).
Burlandy, Luciene
2011 "A atuação da sociedade civil na construção do campo da alimentação e nutrição no Brasil: elementos para reflexão." *Ciência & Saúde Coletiva* 16 (1): 63–72.
Campello, Teresa, Tiago Falcão, and Patrícia Vieira da Costa (eds.)
2014 *O Brasil sem miséria.* Brasília: Ministério de Desenvolvimento Social e Combate à Fome.
Campello, Teresa and Janine Mello
2014 "O processo de formulação e os desafios do Plano Brasil sem miséria: por um país rico e com oportunidades para todos," pp. 33–65 in Teresa Campello, Tiago Falcão, and Patrícia Vieira da Costa (eds.), *O Brasil sem Miséria.* Brasília: Ministério de Desenvolvimento Social e Combate à Fome.
Cardoso Jr., José Celso
2019 "Desmonte do estado no governo Bolsonaro: menos república, menos democracia e menos desenvolvimento," pp. 151–169 in Fundação Perseu Abramo (ed.), *Brasil: Incertezas e submissão?* São Paulo: Fundação Perseu Abramo.
Cassel, Guilherme
2010 "Apresentação," pp. 7–10 in José Graziano da Silva, Mauro Eduardo Del Grossi, and Caio Galcão de França (eds.), *Fome Zero: A experiência brasileira.* Brasília: MDA.
Castro, Inês Rugani Ribeiro de
2019 *A extinção do Conselho Nacional de Segurança Alimentar e Nutricional e a agenda de alimentação e nutrição.* Cadernos de Saúde Pública 35 (2).
Cervo, Amado and Antônio Lessa
2014 "O declínio: inserção internacional do Brasil (2011–2014)." *Revista Brasileira de Política Internacional* 57 (2): 133–151.
Corsi, Francisco
2016 "A política econômica do governo Dilma: baixo crescimento e recessão." *Revista Novos Rumos* 53 (1): 153–165.

Costa, Breno
    2016 "Temer pede corte médio de 30% em programas sociais, mas verba para militares e agronegócio aumenta." *The Intercept.* https://theintercept.com/2016/09/02/temer-pede-corte-medio-de-30-em-programas-sociais-mas-verba-para-militares-e-agronegocio-aumenta/.
FAO (Food and Agriculture Organization)
    2019 "FAO participa de debate sobre a extinção do Consea, na Câmara dos Deputados." http://www.fao.org/brasil/noticias/detail-events/pt/c/1192253/.
Fillol, Adriana
    2014 "Estudio comparativo entre programas de protección social para la seguridad alimentaria: Brasil y Níger." Proyecto Investigación SARAO. resilienciaenafricaoeste.blogspot.com/2014/10/investigacion-sarao-estudio-comparativo.html.
Fuks, Mario and Pedro Henrique Marques
    2020 "Contexto e voto: o impacto da reorganização da direita sobre a consistência ideológica do voto nas eleições de 2018." *Opinião Pública* 26: 401-430.
Grabois, Cláudia and Meire Cavalcante
    2016 "Um golpe na inclusão social e no estado democrático de direito," pp. 74–79 in Carol Proner, Gisele Cittadino, Marcio Tenenbaum, and Wilson Ramos Filho (eds.), *A resistência ao golpe de 2016*. Bauru: Canal 6 (Projeto Editorial Praxis).
Graziano da Silva, José, Mauro Eduardo Del Grossi, and Caio Galvão de França (eds.)
    2010 *Fome zero: A experiência brasileira*. Brasília: MDA.
Grisa, Catia and Eric Sabourin (eds.)
    2018 *A difusão de políticas brasileiras para a agricultura familiar na América Latina e Caribe*. Santa Maria: Escritos Editora.
IBGE (Instituto Brasileiro de Geografia e Estatística)
    2015 "Apresentação: Contas nacionais 2015." https://agenciadenoticias.ibge.gov.br/media/com_mediaibge/arquivos/5b1e01e97aecb50cacc43bc6f140fac2.pdf.
IPEA (Instituto de Pesquisa Econômica Aplicada) and ABC (Agência Brasileira de Cooperação)
    2018 "A atuação internacional brasileira," pp. 21–266 in *Cooperação brasileira para o desenvolvimento internacional: 2014–2016*. Brasília: IPEA.
Jinkings, Ivana
    2016 "O golpe que tem vergonha de ser chamado de golpe," pp. 12–14 in Ivana Jinkings, Kim Doria, and Murilo Cleto (eds.), *Por que gritamos golpe? Para entender o impeachment e a crise política no Brasil*. São Paulo: Boitempo.
Lafer, Celso
    2001 *A identidade internacional do Brasil e a política externa*. São Paulo: Editora Perspectiva.
Lima, Maria Regina Soares de
    2005 "A política externa brasileira e os desafios da cooperação Sul-Sul." *Revista Brasileira de Política Internacional* 48 (1): 24–59.
Lima, Thiago, Iale Pereira, and Olympio Barbanti
    2018 "O agrogolpe e a política externa: desmantelo da diplomacia do combate à fome e fortalecimento do agronegócio." *Revista Okara: Geografia em Debate* 12: 396–421.
Löwy, Michael
    2016 "Da tragédia à farsa: o golpe de 2016 no Brasil," pp. 55–59 in Ivana Jinkings, Kim Doria, and Murilo Kim (eds.), *Por que gritamos golpe? Para entender o impeachment e a crise política no Brasil*. São Paulo: Boitempo.
Maffra, Lourrene and Sofia Boza Martinez
    2020 "Influencia de Brasil en la política alimentaria latinoamericana: el programa de compras públicas a la agricultura familiar de Chile." *Estudios Internacionales* 52 (195): 65–85.
Maluf, Renato
    2010 "O Consea na construção do sistema e da política nacional de segurança alimentar e nutricional," pp. 265–287 in José Graziano da Silva, Mauro Eduardo Del Grossi, and Caio Galvão de França (ed.), *Fome Zero: A experiência brasileira*. Brasília: MDA.
Martín López, Miguel Ángel
    2012 "The problem with the dependence on food imports in Africa and pathways to its solution." *African Journal of International and Comparative Law* 20 (1): 132–140.

Martuscelli, Danilo Enrico
    2020 "Polêmicas sobre a definição do impeachment de Dilma Rousseff como golpe de estado."
    Revista de Estudos e Pesquisas sobre as Américas 14 (2): 67–102.
Mattei, Lauro
    2017 "A política agrária e rural do governo Temer," pp. 169–178 in Renato Maluf and Georges
    Flexor (eds.), *Questões agrárias, agrícolas e rurais: Conjunturas e políticas públicas*. Rio de Janeiro:
    E-Papers.
Medeiros, Jenifer C. and Catia Grisa
    2020 "O Ministério do Desenvolvimento Agrário (MDA) e suas capacidades estatais na pro-
    moção do desenvolvimento rural." *Campo-Território: Revista de Geografia Agrária* 14 (34): 6–35.
Mendonça, Daniel Barbosa
    2018 "De dentro para fora: uma análise sobre a internacionalização da agenda do Consea entre
    2003 e 2010." Master's thesis, Instituto de Pesquisa Econômica.
Menezes, Francisco
    2010 "Participação social no Fome Zero: a experiência do CONSEA," pp. 247–264 in José
    Graziano da Silva, Mauro Eduardo Del Grossi, and Caio Galvão de França (eds.), *Fome Zero:
    A experiência brasileira*. Brasília: MDA.
Milhorance, Carolina
    2013 "A política de cooperação do Brasil com a África Subsaariana no setor rural: transferência
    e inovação na difusão de políticas públicas." *Revista Brasileira de Política Internacional* 56 (2):
    5–22.
OBS (Observatório Brasil e o Sul)
    2014 "O Brasil e a cooperação internacional para o desenvolvimento na CPLP: a segurança
    alimentar e nutricional em perspectiva." *Boletim Brasil e o Sul*, October.
Oliveira, Henrique Altemani de
    2005 *Política externa brasileira*. São Paulo: Saraiva.
Osorio, Cecilia
    2015 "Mecanismos de difusión de los programas de transferencia condicionada en América
    Latina: el caso chileno." *Íconos: Revista de Ciencias Sociales* 19 (31): 31-48.
Pinheiro, Letícia and Carlos R. S. Milani (ed.)
    2012 *Política externa brasileira: As práticas da política e a política das práticas*. Rio de Janeiro: Editora
    FGV.
Queiroz, Felipe
    2018 "Crise política no governo Dilma Rousseff: uma análise a partir do conflito de classes."
    CSOnline: Revista Eletrônica de Ciências Sociais, no. 27.
Ramos, Beatriz Vargas and Luiz Moreira
    2016 "Ingredientes de um golpe parlamentar," pp. 57–60 in Carol Proner, Gisele Cittadino,
    Marcio Tenenbaum, and Wilson Ramos Filho (eds.), *A resistência ao golpe de 2016*. Bauru: Canal
    6 (Projeto Editorial Praxis).
Recine, Elisabetta, Maria Emilia L. Pacheco, Renato S. Maluf, and Francisco Menezes
    2019 "Extinção do Consea: comida de verdade e cidadania golpeados." *Le Monde Diplomatique*,
    January 11.
Santos, Boaventura de Souza
    2016 "Os perigos da desordem jurídica no Brasil," in Carol Proner, Gisele Cittadino, Marcio
    Tenenbaum, and Wilson Ramos Filho (eds.), *A resistência ao golpe de 2016*. Bauru: Canal 6
    (Projeto Editorial Praxis).
Schottz, Vanessa
    2019 "A incorporação de princípios de segurança alimentar e nutricional ao programa nacional
    de alimentação escolar: trajetórias e perspectivas." *Raízes: Revista de Ciências Sociais e Econômicas*
    39 (1): 80–98.
Singer, André
    2018 *O lulismo em crise: Um quebra-cabeça do período Dilma (2011–2016)*. São Paulo: Companhia
    das Letras.
    2021 *A reativação da direita no Brasil*. Preprint version. https://doi.org/10.1590/
    SciELOPreprints.1664.

Sipioni, Marcelo, Manuella Riquieri, Jeanine Barbosa, Denise Biscotto, Thiago Sarti, and Maria Andrade
　2020 *Máscaras cobrem o rosto, a fome desmascara o resto: COVID-19 e o enfrentamento à fome no Brasil.* https://doi.org/10.1590/SciELOPreprints.660.
Sonnino, Roberta, Camilo Lozano Torres, and Sergio Schneider
　2014 "Reflexive governance for food security: the example of school feeding in Brazil." *Journal of Rural Studies* 36: 1–12.
Souza, Amaury
　2002 *A agenda internacional do Brasil: Um estudo sobre a comunidade brasileira de política externa.* Rio de Janeiro: CEBRI.
UN (United Nations)
　2018 "FAO: fome aumenta no mundo e afeta 821 milhões de pessoas." https://nacoesunidas.org/fao-fome-aumenta-no-mundo-e-afeta-821-milhoes-de-pessoas/.
Vaz, Dorian and Otavio Valentim Balsadi
　2004 *As propostas de inclusão social e de desenvolvimento local do Programa Fome Zero.* Brasília: Embrapa.
WFP (World Food Programme)
　2020 "COVID-19: Potential impact on the world's poorest people: a WFP analysis of the economic and food security implications of the pandemic." https://www.wfp.org/publications/covid-19-potential-impact-worlds-poorest-people.

Protests for Women's Rights and against the Bolsonaro Administration

by
Olivia Cristina Perez, Joana Tereza Vaz de Moura, and
Caroline Bandeira de Brito Melo

Translated by
Patricia Fierro

A review of the agendas of three recent Brazilian protests in defense of women's rights—#EleNão, International Women's Day, and the March of the Margaridas—and of the Bolsonaro government's actions regarding women's rights shows that confrontation is manifested on both sides. In a sense, the protests followed and encouraged the confrontation strategies used by the government.

Uma revisão das agendas de três recentes protestos brasileiros em defesa dos direitos das mulheres – #EleNão, Dia Internacional da Mulher e Marcha das Margaridas – e das ações do governo Bolsonaro em relação aos direitos das mulheres mostra que o confronto se manifesta em ambos os lados. De certa forma, os protestos acompanharam e estimularam as estratégias de enfrentamento utilizadas pelo governo.

Keywords: *Protests, Social movements, Feminist movements, Bolsonaro government, Political confrontation*

Brazil was led by presidents from the Partido dos Trabalhadores (Workers' Party—PT) for almost 14 years (from 2003 to 2010 with Luiz Inácio Lula da Silva and from 2011 to mid-2016 with Dilma Rousseff). In 2016, before completing her second term, Dilma Rousseff was removed from office after a controversial impeachment process. Michel Temer (of the Partido Movimento Democrático Brasileiro [Brazilian Democratic Movement Party—PMDB, later named the MDB, a party on the right end of the political spectrum), her vice president, replaced her and was president from 2016 to 2018. Before the 2018 elections, the candidate with the most votes, former President Lula, was arrested on charges of passive corruption and money laundering. In 2018, Jair Bolsonaro (who does not belong to any party) was elected president by the Partido Social Liberal (Social Liberal Party—PSL), marking the rise of a government that resisted the participation and the agendas of movements for social advance such as feminism.

Olivia Cristina Perez is an adjunct professor in the Master's program in political science and the doctoral program in public policy of the Universidade Federal de Piauí. Joana Tereza Vaz de Moura is an associate professor in the graduate program in urban and regional studies at the Universidade Federal de Rio Grande do Norte. Caroline Bandeira de Brito Melo is an assistant professor of law at the Facultade Differencial Integral Wyden. Patricia Fierro is an American Translators Association–certified translator living in Quito, Ecuador.

LATIN AMERICAN PERSPECTIVES, Issue 248, Vol. 50 No. 1, January 2023, 165–178
DOI: 10.1177/0094582X221150442

The rise of the political project led by Bolsonaro did not happen without resistance. Large protests, some of them led by activists and feminist social movements, among them the #EleNão (Not Him), were held in September 2018 in opposition to Bolsonaro's election. The protest of March 8, 2019, on International Women's Day, and the March of the Margaridas in August 2019 brought together thousands of working women in the federal capital. Despite the size and importance of these protests, since they were recent there is still no literature on them, but some knowledge about the cycles of the past decade has accumulated. The most emblematic ones were the June Days of 2013, when thousands of Brazilians protested with various agendas (Alonso and Mische, 2016; Purdy, 2017; Tatagiba and Galvão, 2019).

Several of these protests were marked by episodes of gender-based violence and by "attempts to focus on these violent practices at the very heart of the protests" (Sarmento, Reis, and Mendonça, 2017: 93). Although gender was not central to this cycle of protests, the defense of women's rights was a recurring issue, along with complaints addressed to the government and the political system and themes such as salary and working and living conditions (Tatagiba and Galvão, 2019). The Brazilian media called the strong defense of feminist agendas in major street protests or on social media the "Feminist Spring in Brazil" (Piscitelli, 2017). As is highlighted by Tatagiba and Galvão (2019), these protests produced changes in the political situation, generating new political opportunities that included a diverse set of actors and consolidating an environment of instability that contributed to Rousseff's impeachment. Promoted by this cycle, protests after the June Days began to support the political project led by the current president (Almeida, 2019).

Protests did not happen only in Brazil. In mid-2010 major protests took place in other parts of the world, such as the Tahir Square Days in Egypt, Occupy Wall Street in the United States, and the Indignados protest in Spain (Glasius and Pleyers, 2013). Feminist protests also occurred elsewhere. On the Internet, several women denounced episodes of harassment, including being harassed by celebrities, in a movement called #Yotambién in Argentina in reference to the North American #MeToo. In 2016 the #Miprimeroacoso (MyFirstHarassment) campaign, inspired by the Brazilian hashtag against harassment, was launched in Mexico (Agência Patrícia Galvão, 2018). In 2015, there was a protest in Argentina calling for an end to violence against women, Ni Una Menos (Not One Woman Less), that involved more than 200,000 people and had an impact on other Latin American countries such as Chile and Brazil (Lima-Lopes and Gabardo, 2019: 803).

To understand the recent protests of women in Brazil, we adopted the theory of political confrontation. According to McAdam, Tarrow, and Tilly (2009: 11), the exponents of this theory, "the political confrontation begins when, collectively, people make claims to other people whose interests would be affected if they were solved." They argue that the state and its leaders must be considered in these analyses, since they are targets of confrontations and create opportunities for them to occur. Social movements use shared repertoires that "are an expression of the historical and current interaction between them and their opponents" (24). In addition to acting according to those repertoires, they modify them, changing the opportunity structures "mainly by contributing to changes in the known ways of presenting claims, in the types of repression and facilitation by the authorities and established political identities" (27). Drawing on this framework of political confrontation, this paper answers the question "How have feminist movements and their agendas been changing in line with the political context?" by examining the positions of the Bolsonaro government in relation to women's rights and the agendas of protests in favor of these rights.

Our research is qualitative and descriptive. Data pertinent to the guidelines and position of the Bolsonaro government were collected from the main Brazilian press, especially *Folha de São Paulo*, from August to October 2019. To determine the agendas of the protests that responded to Bolsonaro's provocations, three protests in favor of women's rights organized in a political context of the current president's rise were chosen: #EleNão, on September 29, 2018, between the first and the second round of the presidential elections in Brazil; the protests on March 8, 2019, International Women's Day; and the March of the Margaridas in August 2019 in Brasília. The agendas of these protests were collected between August and October 2019 from documents and interviews produced by their organizers.[1]

The analysis of protest events generally produces a catalog commonly extracted from newspapers, although more recently other sources are being used (Tatagiba and Galvão, 2019). This analysis allows capturing the significance of recent phenomena in a comparative way, but it has its limitations. One is the selectivity of the sources consulted. In this work, for example, the protests' agendas were studied in terms of the information provided by the social movements and feminist activists themselves, but the speeches of activists are produced precisely to reproduce and provoke even more revolt against the government. At the same time, it is important to analyze the speeches that guide the protests, even if they are not sources of truth, because they reflect and constitute social practices.

In addition to interacting with the literature on social movements and protests, the work contributes to feminist studies. The writings of so-called black feminists such as Angela Davis and Kimberlé Crenshaw demonstrate the need for black women to have a voice, both to expose their difficulties and to propose actions to combat them. Davis (2016), for example, teaches about the legacies of colonization and the possibility of self-determination for black women. Latin American feminists (Bidaseca, 2011; Segato, 2013) have also drawn attention to the need for thought and action that go beyond the colonial legacy. From this perspective, gender inequalities are also related to the colonial past and the imposition of a type of feminism that is detached from the realities of Latin American and indigenous peoples. One of the aims of this work is to describe Brazilian feminist struggles in their own terms.

CHANGES IN GOVERNMENT GUIDELINES ON WOMEN'S RIGHTS

Under the Bolsonaro government, Brazil is facing a different political cycle from the previous one. Luís Inácio Lula da Silva of the PT was elected president in 2002 and reelected in 2006. The PT remained in power with the election of Dilma Rousseff in 2010, who was also reelected in 2014. The PT administrations brought social movements closer to the state in at least two ways. The first was the expansion of participatory bodies in which members of civil society developed public policy guidelines with the government. In the area of policies for women, these conferences legitimized demands for gender equity, especially in transforming into "government issues" topics that had traditionally been seen as intimate and private matters (Santos, Perez, and Szwako, 2017). The second was choosing leaders of social movements for central positions in the federal bureaucracy, a phenomenon called "state activism" (Cayres, 2017; Pires and Vaz, 2014) or, when it involved the appointment of feminists, "state feminism" (Bohn, 2010; Matos and Paradis, 2014). The increase in state activism was related to the fact that the PT had social movement activists on its staff in addition to providing for participation as one of its management guidelines. The interactions between social movements and the state in PT administrations resulted in important legislative advances for women's rights, such as the approval of the Maria da Penha Law against domestic gender violence and the Feminicide Law that made the murder of women a crime. Another result was the formulation of public policies more in tune with the demands of social movements (Santos, Perez, and Szwako, 2017).

The direction of the Brazilian government has changed substantially in recent years. Starting with the government of Michel Temer, a new right has emerged in Brazil whose administrative results have produced an "armored democracy." According to Goldstein (2019: 245), this involves

> the construction of a "leftist" enemy to justify the repression of activists and social movements, preserving a loyal base and manipulating anger if no economic gains are obtained; a political partisan role for judicial powers with strong interference from lobbying and military advisers; a weak democracy without political participation; the establishment of an order favorable to the market against the platform voted by the majority of Brazilians in the 2014 elections; right-wing advances in public discourse that have restructured culture and political analyses; and the accession of a far-right candidate to the Presidency for the first time since the re-democratization began in 1985.

This candidate, Jair Bolsonaro, was elected in 2018 and assumed "the guidelines of traditions . . . by pleasing the Christian forces of the National Congress" (Almeida, 2019: 200). Again according to Goldstein (2019: 257), this new right-wing order cannot be called a dictatorship, but it is a democracy whose potential has been mutilated.

Bolsonaro's administration is very different from those of the PT, especially with regard to women's rights. The National Secretariat for the Rights of Women, which in most PT governments had the status of a ministry with its own staff and budget, was transferred to the newly created Ministry of Women, Family, and Human Rights. The name given to the new ministry reveals the direction of Bolsonaro's government: women appear next to the family. The educator, lawyer, and evangelical pastor Damares Alves, appointed to lead the ministry, caused controversy by posting a video on the Internet shortly after Bolsonaro's victory claiming that "the new era has begun" and that from then on "boys would wear blue and girls pink" (Pains, 2019). The minister's statement went against the basic guidelines of feminist movements: equal rights for men and women.

Even before the election, Bolsonaro had argued that women should not receive the same salaries as men even if they performed the same function (Bragon, 2018). He also showed contempt for women when he said in 2017 that he had five children, "four boys, and for the fifth one I was weak and a girl was born" (*Folha de São Paulo*, April 6, 2017). In 2018, Bolsonaro's vice president, Hamilton Mourão, told *Folha de São Paulo* that families without "father and grandfather" and with "mother and grandmother" were "factories of misfits" who entered the drug trade, reaffirming an alleged advantage of having men in Brazilian homes (Gielow, 2018). These positions reveal that the governors of Brazil consider women inferior to men.

This agenda was central to Bolsonaro's candidacy. In particular, Alves was a pioneer in denouncing, in a sermon at the First Baptist Church in 2013, the supposed existence of textbooks "teaching homosexuality." Bolsonaro took the story to *Jornal Nacional* in 2018, accusing the PT of "promoting homosexuality" through booklets distributed in schools (Mesquita, 2019). The fight against so-called gender ideology has become one of the main concerns of the president and his supporters. For them, there is a movement orchestrated by teachers, universities, and schools dedicated especially to "teaching" and "encouraging" boys and girls to be homosexuals rather than playing their supposedly natural gender roles. Therefore, the discussion of gender must be prohibited in schools and other educational spaces. In this the Bolsonaro administration defends bills that follow the guidelines of the Escola Sem Partido (School Without Party) movement, which emerged as a reaction to a supposed instrumentalization of teaching for ideological, partisan, and electoral purposes. To end the expression of teachers' opinions in the classroom, Bolsonaro supporters advocated the supposed impartiality and neutrality of teachers and argued that if teachers could not express opinions on politics, they could not discuss gender and feminism.

Combating the discussion of gender issues is one of the central charges of the Ministry of Women, Family, and Human Rights. In this connection, it dissolved six committees in 2019, including those on gender and diversity and inclusion, which had acted to curb gender-based violence and promote sexual equality and diversity within the ministry. Decree 10.112 of November 12, 2019, on the Safe and Protected Woman program eliminated the word "gender" that occurred in previous regulations. Specifically, the section "gender mainstreaming in public policies" was changed to "mainstreaming women's rights in public policies." By failing to mention gender-based violence, the decree ended up restricting rights for cis women (women who identify with their biological gender). The decree also did not regulate the prevention policies that are fundamental in combating the various forms of violence against women.

Even in other areas of the government, censorship concerning gender has been taking place. For example, the Ministry of Foreign Affairs, whose minister is Ernesto Araújo, is guiding Brazilian diplomats to emphasize only the "traditional definition" of biological sex in multilateral international organizations (*Folha de São Paulo*, July 26, 2019). Law 13.931, of December 10, 2019, which provided for compulsory notification of the police by the health services in cases of suspected violence against women, was vetoed by the president as not in the public interest, but the veto was rejected by the Congress. Initiatives like this demonstrate the focus on combating physical violence against women, but, as Segato (2013) points out, violence plays a fundamental role in maintaining the gender order and is not a problem in a society that intends to remain sexist. Thus the focus of the Bolsonaro government on fighting gender-based violence loses significance because the government opposes the discussion on gender-related inequalities. As long as there are such inequalities, violence in its various forms will continue to exist.

Other Bolsonaro government decisions do not directly address gender issues but implicitly produce a loss of rights for women. One of the most important decisions was the 2019 pension reform, which required women to be at least 62 years old rather than only 60 to retire. The Bolsonaro government has also been fighting with the social movements on the issue of rights. Decree 9.759 of April 11, 2019, terminates the existence of all federal collegiate bodies (councils, committees, commissions, groups, boards, teams, tables, forums, halls) that are not regulated by law. It eliminates at least 34 councils, including the one for promoting LGBT rights.

The attempts of the Bolsonaro administration to limit women's rights and its costly discussions with feminist movements reveal the conservative reaction against advances in women's rights. According to Jacira Melo, the executive director of the Agência Patrícia Galvão (2015), the suppression of gender debate represents "a great risk that might bring about an immense setback. To face violence against women, it is necessary to work on a relationship of mutual respect and show that gender inequality is unfair." The fight against discussion of gender issues occurs in a context of increasing violence against women and indexes that place Brazil as one of the worst countries for women to live in, given the various forms of violence to which they are subjected. According to data from the 2015 violence map (Waiselfisz, 2015: 11), "between 1980 and 2013, at an increasing rate over time both in number and in rates, a total of 106,093 women died victims of homicide," and "only El Salvador, Colombia, Guatemala (three Latin American countries) and the Russian Federation show rates higher than those of Brazil" (27).

One of the emblematic recent cases of violence against women in Brazil was the murder of the Rio de Janeiro city councilwoman Marielle Franco in 2018. Franco was a sociologist affiliated with the Partido Socialismo e Liberdade (Socialism and Freedom Party—PSOL) and defended feminism and human rights. She also criticized the federal intervention in Rio de Janeiro and the military police and reported several cases of abuse of authority by the police against residents of poor communities. Two policemen were arrested on charges of having killed her in 2019, but it is not yet known who ordered her death. Her death was more than murder; it was an attempt to annihilate the ideals she espoused.

WOMEN'S PROTESTS AGAINST THE BOLSONARO GOVERNMENT

Civil society has reacted to the project led by Bolsonaro, especially in its relation to women's rights, in several ways. One of them is protests. The first of these is known for its hashtag on the social media, #EleNão (Not Him). It took place on September 29, 2018, and its main objective was to defeat Bolsonaro's candidacy for the presidency. Dozens of Brazilian cities held protests against Bolsonaro, bringing more than 100,000 women onto the streets. There were also events in cities such as New York, Lisbon, Paris, and London.

The protests were impressive in their number of participants. Céli Regina Jardim Pinto, a professor at the Universidade Federal do Rio Grande do Sul, told the BBC (Rossi, Carneiro, and Gragnani, 2018) that the #EleNão protest was the largest demonstration of women in the history of the country. The group of women that called for the protests published the manifesto Democracia Sim (Democracy Yes), a detailed list of the reasons Brazilian women resisted Bolsonaro. Among the main reasons were his support for labor reform, his defense of a security model that would encourage the extermination of black youth, his prejudice against LGBTs, his misogyny, and the fear of a return to military dictatorship.

The difference of these protests from others was in their form of organization; they arose from an initiative of digital media activists. The hashtag #EleNão was created by the publicist Ludimilla Teixeira after conversations with her friends about what could be done in the face of the increasing support for Bolsonaro. In an interview with *El País* (Oliveira, 2018) she said: "I noticed in my own networks many friends commenting and criticizing these positions [of Bolsonaro], so we decided to unite all these women and create a political event to show that a large part of the population was not in favor of this candidacy." With the increasing use of the hashtag #EleNão as a form of virtual protest, the activists created a group on Facebook called Mulheres Unidas Contra Bolsonaro (Women United Against Bolsonaro) that managed to bring together 3.8 million women (Cafardo, 2018). The planning of the protests against Bolsonaro's candidacy took place on its page. Another difference was the organizers' refusal to be linked to political parties. The group's creator herself declared that she had never participated actively in the feminist movement or joined any political party (Cafardo, 2018). The group's manifesto highlights its diversity: "We vote for different people and parties. We defend distinct causes, ideas, and projects." This rejection of political parties was expressed in the June Days (Tatagiba, 2014; Tatagiba and Galvão, 2019) and can be traced to the autonomous repertoire described by Alonso and Mische (2016).

The second set of protests took place on March 8, 2019, International Women's Day. Because they were organized locally, these demonstrations were varied. In addition to the protests, especially in big state capitals, there were public classes, ceremonies, and other forms of protest. A march with the slogan "Women against Bolsonaro! Cheers for Marielle, in Defense of Welfare, Democracy and Rights" brought together more than 80,000 people on the Avenida Paulista in São Paulo and 30,000 in Rio de Janeiro. Women also organized demonstrations in other parts of Brazil.

The protests' varied agendas were generally opposed to the "Social Security reform proposal, to the increase of militarization, to the criminalization of social movements, to the policy of 'surrendering' natural resources that affects national sovereignty, . . . sexism, gender violence, inequality, racism, and prejudice against LGBT people" (CUT, 2019). The death of Marielle Franco was remembered in several events, and the demonstrations also exposed the advance of the conservative wave, the attacks on democracy, and the escalation of violence against women (World March of Women, 2019a). The agendas of these protests include opposition to physical violence against women and point to the perception that violence and oppression are linked to social class, race/color/ethnicity, and sexual orientation—what is known as "intersectionality" (Rios, Perez, and Ricoldi, 2018). Considered by the World March of Women as responsible for opening "the calendar of mass protests against the reforms and the withdrawal of rights proposed by the government of Jair Bolsonaro," the protests held on dates close to March 8 included, in addition to the traditional defense of women's rights, criticisms of the current government.

Criticism of the new project in Brazil had been expressed in previous protests on International Women's Day. In 2017 they called for the forcing out of the interim president Michel Temer, but the central agenda was opposition to pension reform (World March of Women, 2017). In 2018, the March 8 protests were marked by demonstrations in favor of democracy and retirement (World March of Women, 2018), and in the protests of 2019 the criticism against Bolsonaro stood out. Sônia Coelho of the national leadership of the World March of Women declared that "the meaning of this March 8 [2019] was to show that women continue to resist Bolsonaro, against conservatism and fundamentally against the pension reform that will penalize poor black women more. In this sense, the protests fulfilled their objective, even bringing back the people who participated in #ElcNão" (World March of Women, 2019a). In other words, the protests of 2017 and 2018 were mainly against projects considered negative for the working class, especially women, but in 2019 the target was Bolsonaro and the entire political project that he represented.

Every year social movements participate in the organization of the March 8 protests in several cities in Brazil and elsewhere in the world, and some events are convened by feminist activists via the social media, as was the event created on Facebook in São Paulo called the Movimento 8 de Março (Eighth of March Movement). According to Morgans (2018), radical social movements face problems when they try to get involved in cyberspace, which is dominated by hegemonic actors, but this protest showed that the social media, despite their limitations, can strengthen protests organized by social movements in a synergy between virtual space and the movement's militancy.

A third protest was the March of the Margaridas in Brasília in August 2019, which involved more than 100,000 women from all over Brazil (World March of Women, 2019b). Its organization was carried out by the Confederação Nacional dos Trabalhadores na Agricultura (National Confederation of Workers in Agriculture—CONTAG) in partnership with feminist and working women's movements, unions, and international organizations such as the World March of Women, the Articulação de Mulheres Brasileiras (Brazilian Women's Network—AMB), and the União de Mulheres Brasileiras (Brazilian Women's Union—UBM). In 2019, the First March of Indigenous Women joined the March of the Margaridas, bringing together 3,000 women who camped in Brasília starting on August 9. The protest has taken place every four years since 2000 and is considered by its organizers the largest action by women in Latin America.

The March of the Margaridas first took place in August 2000 and had as its slogan "2,000 Reasons to March: Against Hunger, Poverty, and Sexist Violence." With Fernando Henrique Cardoso in the government, the march focused on the shortcomings of the country's rural development model and the impact of neo-liberalism on the lives of rural workers. This was the first time in history that the Brazilian government had spent time on the negotiation of a specific agenda for rural workers (Observatório Marcha das Margaridas, 2019). In August 2003, at the beginning of the first Lula administration, rural women workers conducted the second March of the Margaridas with a similar agenda ("2,003 Reasons to March against Hunger, Poverty, and Sexist Violence"). The march in 2007 maintained the sense of the slogan of the previous one but also, because of the close relationship between social movements and the PT, focused on rights and the reduction of social inequalities. In 2011 the slogan was "2,011 Reasons to March for Sustainable Development with Justice, Autonomy, Equality, and Freedom," and in 2015 it was "The Margaridas Are Still Marching for Sustainable Development with Democracy, Justice, Autonomy, Equality, and Freedom," the addition of "Democracy" being a clear response to the threat of the impeachment of Dilma Rousseff. In 2019, under the Bolsonaro government, the sixth March of the Margaridas was labeled "Margaridas in the Struggle for a Brazil with Popular Sovereignty, Democracy, Justice, Equality, and Freedom from Violence." The sovereignty of the people faced with a government resistant to conversation with the social movements that defend the expansion of rights became one of the motives of the protests.

Between 2000 and 2015, the march leadership had prepared guidelines addressed to the state with a view to their negotiation that included demands for access to land by women, credit, and social policies for the countryside such as health, education, and quality housing. In 2019 it chose not to draw up a political agenda for the state, understanding that the current government would not negotiate with it. As an alternative, it launched a political platform in which the March's agenda was presented. According to Mazé Morais of the CONTAG, "You cannot negotiate with a government that takes away rights. For this reason, this year we presented an agenda with the model of society defended by women" (Peres, 2019).

In 2019 the March "became a kind of exposure, a demarcation of positions, and, above all, a resistance" (Morais, 2019). In other words, in the PT governments before Bolsonaro, "the March presented a negotiating agenda that was able to contribute to the conquest of rights and public policies" (World March of Women, 2019b). In 2019, in its political platform, it denounced "the violence we are suffering, the increase in social inequalities, based on class, gender, and race relations, the deconstructions and violations of rights, the cut in the budget for social assistance, health, education, housing, and bonuses for food production . . . and the dismantling of the democratic rule of law." The agenda of the protest was also against Bolsonaro and some of his projects, such as pension reform (considered an attack on the rights of workers, especially women), flexibilization policies for pesticides, and the opening up for exploitation of the land of indigenous peoples and protected areas. More than the defense of women, the March of the Margaridas called for the return of rights for all workers. At the end of the event, Sônia Coelho declared: "That's what we're fighting for. Let's go back to every corner of this country, to each community, each union, each group of women, and say, 'We want you to leave, Bolsonaro, leave!'" (World March of Women, 2019b). The protest quickly turned into a criticism of the Bolsonaro government.

It is clear from the consideration of the protests' guidelines that various social movements and activists favoring women's rights chose their repertoires from among the possibilities for reconstructing public policies of a social nature and that confrontation was one of those repertoires. As explained by Tarrow (2012), repertoires are chosen according to the group's expectations based on a systematic analysis of possible paths and shared experiences. In this sense, they are part of a broader system of conflict and cooperation: while groups may cooperate with the state, they may also participate in conflictive processes in order to guide their demands in the political arena. In the case of the protests analyzed, the criticism of Bolsonaro's government for the reduction of women's rights made their guidelines different from those of the protests under PT governments. The difference reflects changes both in the political situation and in the confrontation engendered by social movements. In a government that now resists democratic ideals, protests began to defend the application of laws, including the right to speak out.

In short, the Brazilian political cycle and with it the repertoires and strategies of social movements and their manifestations have changed. The strategy of women's struggles is currently based on confrontation, just as confrontation is the strategy of the Bolsonaro government. For Tarrow (2009), the political confrontation emerges in a socio-historical context related to its opportunity structure. Thus repertoires are chosen as processes occur in the political, economic, cultural, and social fields. In the protests analyzed here, when governments become more vulnerable to social participation it is possible to present demands to the bureaucratic apparatus, either by the inclusion of militants in the government structure or via institutional channels of social participation. In the PT's governments, "social movements and state actors creatively experienced . . . historical patterns of state-society interaction and reinterpreted communication and negotiation processes in innovative ways" (Abers, Serafim, and Tatagiba, 2014: 326). Since 2016, however, feminist movements have no longer relied on closeness to the state, considerably reducing their chances of influencing public policies. They have had to recreate repertoires to because they have faced "disrespect with triggered gender biases" (Sarmento, Reis, and Mendonca, 2017: 109) in the institutional arena.

This study shows how social movements respond to and follow changes in the political cycle. This is not a novelty—the theory of political confrontation has already demonstrated the interactions between social movements and the state—but that theory has been used in Brazil mainly to explain the interactions between social movements and the state under the PT. Our work shows how these relations are being applied under the current government. In Bolsonaro's Brazil, the confrontation is both between social movements and within the government.

This study also shows the strength of feminist movements in large protests that oppose the conservative agenda of the Bolsonaro government. This is significant for understanding the role of women in contemporary societies. Even in different systems of domination (colonialism, sexism, racism, etc.), some of them have favored a democratic agenda, thus assuming feminist ideals such as that women should not have a subordinate role—that they should be key actors of historical change.

FINAL CONSIDERATIONS

After a certain advance (although with restrictions) in the feminist agenda of the PT's governments, there is now a conservative reaction. In response, one of the strategies of the feminist social movements has been street protests criticizing Bolsonaro and the elimination of rights due to his leadership. To reflect on this context, this study has analyzed the guidelines for protests in favor of women's rights and against the Bolsonaro administration. It has shown the emphasis of the confrontation in protests and in statements and guidelines of the Bolsonaro government in relation to feminist ideals. In this sense, the protests followed and encouraged the confrontation strategies used by the government, and therefore to understand the social movements and protests it is necessary to analyze the strategies of the state, because they are interrelated.

The study also describes how the agendas of protests have changed according to the political context, assuming, in addition to their confrontational nature, the very defense of democracy. What is at stake is no longer the expansion of rights but the preservation of a regime in which discussing rights is feasible. However, it is necessary to express some reservations. First, the protests existed even before Bolsonaro. Second, the stakes in the conflicts that are part of the agendas of the protest do not mean the abandonment of institutional channels. The strategies of social movements are multiple, and therefore researchers should focus on the forms that have become the most prominent, such as protests, without disregarding strategies such as participation and representation. It is by adopting a broader perspective that we will be able to understand and foster the different types of resistance of civil society.

NOTE

1. All information is available on Internet sites, mainly on webpage of the World March of Women (https://www.marchamundialdasmulheres.org.br), Transformatório das Margaridas (http://transformatoriomargaridas.org.br), and the Facebook page that organized the protest #Ele Não (https://www.facebook.com/movimentoelenao).

REFERENCES

Abers, Rebecca, Lizandra Serafim, and Luciana Tatagiba
    2014. "Repertórios de interação Estado-sociedade em um Estado heterogêneo: a experiência na Era Lula." *Dados* 57: 325–357.
Agência Patrícia Galvão
    2015 "Feministas criticam ameaça de extinção da SPM, SEPPIR e SDH." September 22. https://agenciapatriciagalvao.org.br/mulheres-de-olho/feministas-criticam-ameaca-de-extincao-da-spm-seppir-e-sdh/ (accessed October 17, 2019)

2018 "No Brasil, agenda feminista começou antes do #METOO." October 7. https://agencia-patriciagalvao.org.br/violencia/no-brasil-agenda-feminista-comecou-antes-do-metoo/ (accessed October 27, 2019).

Almeida, Ronaldo
2019 "Bolsonaro presidente: conservadorismo, evangelismo e a crise brasileira." *Novos Estudos CEBRAP* 38 (May): 185–213.

Alonso, Angela and Ann Mische
2016 "Changing repertoires and partisan ambivalence in the new Brazilian protests." *Bulletin of Latin American Research* 36 (April): 144–159.

Bidaseca, Karina
2011 "Mujeres blancas buscando salvar a mujeres color café: desigualdad, colonialismo jurídico y feminismo postcolonial." *Andamios: Revista de Investigación Social* 17: 61–89.

Bohn, Simone
2010 "Feminismo estatal sob a presidência Lula: o caso da Secretaria de Políticas para as Mulheres." *Revista Debates* 4 (2) : 81–106.

Bragon, Ranier
2018 "Bolsonaro se diz vítima de notícias falsas, mas recorre a 'fakes' sobre seu próprio passado." July 31. https://www1.folha.uol.com.br/poder/2018/07/bolsonaro-se-diz-vitima-de-noticias-falsas-mas-recorre-a-fakes-sobre-seu-proprio-passado.shtml (accessed August 21, 2019).

Cafardo, Renata
2018 "'Só acendi o fósforo no barril de pólvora,' diz criadora de grupo contra Bolsonaro." September 29. https://politica.estadao.com.br/noticias/eleicoes,so-acendi-o-fosforo-no-barril-de-polvora-diz-criadora-de-grupo,70002524582. (accessed August 21, 2019).

Cayres, Domitila
2017 "Ativismo institucional e interações Estado-movimentos sociais." *BIB* 82 (September): 81–104.

CUT (Central Única dos Trabalhadores)
2019 "Mulheres saem às ruas no 8 de Março contra os retrocessos do governo Bolsonaro." March 7. https://www.cut.org.br/noticias/8-de-marco-confira-lista-dos-atos-confirmados-em-todo-o-brasil-626e. (accessed August 21, 2019).

Davis, Angela
2016 *Mulheres, raça e classe*. São Paulo: Boitempo.

Gielow, Igor
2018 "Casa só com 'mãe e avó' é 'fábrica de desajustados' para tráfico, diz Mourão." September 17. https://www1.folha.uol.com.br/poder/2018/09/casa-so-com-mae-e-avo-e-fabrica-de-desajustados-para-trafico-diz-mourao.shtml (accessed August 21, 2019).

Glasius, Marlies and Geoffrey Pleyers
2013 "The global moment of 2011: democracy, social justice and dignity." *Development and Change* 44: 547–567.

Goldstein, Ariel
2019 "The new far-right in Brazil and the construction of a right-wing order." *Latin American Perspectives* 46 (1): 245–262.

Lima-Lopes, Rodrigo and Maristella Gabardo
2019 "Ni una menos: a luta pelos direitos das mulheres na Argentina e suas representações no Facebook." *Revista Brasileira de Linguística Aplicada* 19: 801–824.

Matos, Marlise and Clarisse Paradis
2014 "Desafios à despatriarcalização do Estado brasileiro." *Cadernos Pagu* 43 (July–December): 57–118.

McAdam, Douglas, Sidney Tarrow, and Charles Tilly
2009 "Para mapear o confronto político." *Lua Nova* 76: 11–48.

Mesquita, Sônia
2019 "Gênero e sexualidade (13): a bola está com Damares." January 25. http://editoramanifesto.com.br/site/2019/01/25/genero-e-sexualidade-13-a-bola-esta-com-damares/ (accessed November 17, 2019).

Morais, Karina
    2019 "Marcha das Margaridas: resposta coletiva ao ódio e ao retrocesso." August 19. https://marchamulheres.wordpress.com/2019/08/19/marcha-das-margaridas-resposta-coletiva-ao-odio-e-ao-retrocesso/ (accessed November 10, 2019).
Morgans, Catherine
    2018 "New media and the disillusion of Brazil's radical left." *Latin American Perspectives* 45 (1): 250–265.
Observatório Marcha das Margaridas
    2019 "Pautas das marchas." http://transformatoriomargaridas.org.br/?page_id=243l (accessed August 21, 2019).
Oliveira, Joana
    2018 "Um milhão de mulheres contra Bolsonaro: a rejeição toma forma nas redes." September 12. https://brasil.elpais.com/brasil/2018/09/12/actualidad/1536768048_321164.html (accessed November 15, 2019).
Pains, Clarissa
    2019 "'Menino veste azul e menina veste rosa', diz Damares Alves em vídeo." January 3. https://oglobo.globo.com/sociedade/menino-veste-azul-menina-veste-rosa-diz-damares-alves-em-video-23343024 (accessed April 3, 2019).
Peres, Christiane
    2019 "Mais 100 mil na Marcha das Margaridas por direitos e contra Bolsonaro." August 14. http://www.vermelho.org.br/noticia/322761-1 (accessed August 21, 2019).
Pires, Roberto and Alexandre Vaz
    2014 "Para além da participação: interfaces socioestatais no governo federal." *Lua Nova* 93: 61–91.
Piscitelli, Adriana
    2017 " '#queroviajarsozinhasemmedo': novos registros das articulações entre gênero, sexualidade e violência no Brasil." *Cadernos Pagu* 50 (July).
Purdy, Sean
    2017 "Brazil's June Days of 2013: mass protest, class, and the left." *Latin American Perspectives* 46 (2): 15–36.
Rios, Flávia, Olivia Perez, and Arlene Ricoldi
    2018 "Interseccionalidade nas mobilizações do Brasil contemporâneo." *Lutas Sociais* 22: 36–51.
Rossi, Amanda, Julia Carneiro, and Juliana Gragnani
    2018 "#EleNão: a manifestação histórica liderada por mulheres no Brasil vista por quatro ângulos." September 30. https://www.bbc.com/portuguese/brasil-45700013. (accessed November 13, 2019).
Santos, Gustavo, Olivia Cristina Perez, and José Szwako
    2017 "Gêneros da participação: refletindo sobre limites e possibilidades da participação social na promoção da equidade de gênero e da diversidade sexual em âmbito estatal." *Estudos de Sociologia (UFPE)* 23: 19–74.
Sarmento, Rayza, Stephanie Reis, and Ricardo Mendonça
    2017 "As jornadas de junho no Brasil e a questão de gênero: as idas e vindas da luta por justiça." *Revista Brasileira de Ciência Política* 22 (January–April): 93–128.
Segato, Rita Laura
    2013 *La escritura en el cuerpo de las mujeres asesinadas en Ciudad Juárez.* Buenos Aires: Tinta Limón.
Tarrow, Sidney
    2009 *O poder em movimento: Movimentos sociais e confronto político.* Petrópolis: Vozes.
    2012 *Strangers at the Gates: Movements and States in Contentious Politics.* Cambridge: Cambridge University Press.
Tatagiba, Luciana
    2014 "1984, 1992 e 2013: sobre ciclos de protestos e democracia no Brasil." *Política & Sociedade* 28 (September–December): 35–62.
Tatagiba, Luciana and Andrea Galvão
    2019 "Os protestos no Brasil em tempos de crise (2011–2016)." *Opinião Pública* 25 (1): 63–96.
Waiselfisz, Julio
    2015 *Mapa da violência 2015: Homicídio de mulheres no Brasil.* Brasília.

World March of Women

2017 "8 de março mobilizou milhares de mulheres contra a Reforma da Previdência em todo o país." March 9. http://www.marchamundialdasmulheres.org.br/8-de-marco-mobilizou-milhares-de-mulheres-contra-a-reforma-da-previdencia-em-todo-o-pais/(accessed August 21, 2019).

2018 "8 de março é marcado por manifestações, intervenções e ocupações por democracia e aposentadoria." March 20. https://www.marchamundialdasmulheres.org.br/8-de-marco-e-marcado-por-intervencoes-ocupacoes-e-atos-por-democracia-e-aposentadoria/ (accessed August 21, 2019).

2019a "8 de março inicia jornada de atos contra governo Bolsonaro." March 19. http://www.marchamundialdasmulheres.org.br/8-de-marco-inicia-jornada-de-atos-contra-governo-bolsonaro/ (accessed August 21, 2019).

2019b "Cem mil margaridas marcham em Brasília por terra, igualdade e democracia." August 15. http://www.marchamundialdasmulheres.org.br/cem-mil-margaridas-marcham-em-brasilia-por-terra-igualdade-e-democracia/ (accessed August 21, 2019).

Tongues of Fire

Silas Malafaia and the Historical Roots of Neo-Pentecostal Power in Bolsonaro's Brazil

by
Andre Pagliarini

Evangelical Christians and especially Neo-Pentecostals in Brazil have gone from accepting a position as junior partners in a broad governing coalition led by the Partido dos Trabalhadores (Workers' Party—PT) to asserting themselves as an indispensable pillar of the Jair Bolsonaro administration. A close examination of the career of the prominent Bolsonarist pastor Silas Malafaia suggests that if progressives want to improve their political relationship with evangelical voters they must first find discursive and material ways to neutralize or at least work around the most prominent and virulently conservative faith leaders.

Os cristãos evangélicos (em particular os neo-pentecostais) no Brasil passaram de aceitar uma posição de ser parceiros menores numa coligação governamental abrangente dirigida pelo Partido dos Trabalhadores (PT) para impor-se como pilar imprescindível do governo de Jair Bolsonaro. Uma análise exhaustiva da trajetória do renomado pastor bolsonarista Silas Malafaia constata que se os progessistas quiserem melhorar a sua relação política com eleitores evangélicos, eles devem por primeiro descobrir meios discursivos e materiais para neutralizar ou, no mínimo, evitar os líderes religiosos que são os mais preeminentes e fortemente conservadores nesses grupos sociais.

Keywords: *Jair Bolsonaro, Silas Malafaia, Luiz Inácio Lula da Silva, Pentecostalism, Workers' Party*

Two days after Christmas 1889, an American missionary with the Presbyterian Church in the United States (commonly called the Southern Presbyterian Church) arrived in Brazil.[1] Samuel Rhea Gammon was a 24-year-old bachelor representing a church closely associated with the values of the vanquished Confederate States of America. Indeed, *The Southern Presbyterian*, a newspaper in Columbia, South Carolina, had been the first religious newspaper in the South to call for secession (Daniel, 1967: 232). Thrust into a leadership position in Brazil, Gammon was committed to raising a "native church" that could be sustained by local leaders. While the Presbyterians were often well received, they faced occasional prejudice and suspicion. When they opened a school in the small town of Lavras, Minas Gerais, for example, the

Andre Pagliarini is an assistant professor of history at Hampden-Sydney College. He is currently preparing a book manuscript on the politics of nationalism in modern Brazil.

LATIN AMERICAN PERSPECTIVES, Issue 248, Vol. 50 No. 1, January 2023, 179–196
DOI: 10.1177/0094582X221147593

local Roman Catholic priest purportedly urged residents not to accept money from the Presbyterians because it would turn to coal in their hands. As David C. Etheridge (1994: 25–29) noted, "one reverend father, visiting from Rome, led a campaign to destroy the school physically." Twenty years after setting foot in Brazil, Gammon wrote a book urging other missionaries to commit to the country. In *The Evangelical Invasion of Brazil: Or, A Half Century of Evangelical Missions in the Land of the Southern Cross* (1910: 158–159), he described Brazil as fertile soil for the Protestant seed:

> Roman Catholicism does not form in the national life a basis for free institutions and such as is formed by Protestant Christianity. The Protestant missionary and the deep thinker among the Brazilians understand this, and some day the Brazilians and the Latin Americans generally will come to understand it. And when they do come to understand the real cause of their political and social troubles, there will be a tremendous drift away from Romanism and toward Evangelical Christianity. The history of Northern Europe in the 16th century may then be repeated in South America.

The "invasion" in the title of Gammon's tract was not meant pejoratively. It was a celebration of the sustained missionary work that sought to reverse the social symptoms of Catholic colonization, which steeped "the uneducated masses . . . in a system of superstitious idolatry that is much more closely akin to the ancient and modern paganism than to the religion of Christ Jesus" (Gammon, 1910: 70). Unsurprisingly, given his age and background, Gammon's view of Latin America was shaped by the Black Legend, the idea that Catholic Iberian colonization produced societies marred by backwardness and cruelty. Those inclined to accept the premises of the Black Legend called into question, as Luiz Aguiar Costa Pinto (quoted in Hanke, 1971: 126) put it, "the whole heritage of the archaic society—the economic, political, and intellectual heritage—its structures, its values, its prospects." Gammon called the Americas—referring to the entire continent, North and South—"the great battle-ground between pure and apostate Christianity," hence the importance of winning Brazil to "the Evangelical faith" (Gammon, 1910: 162).

It took longer than Gammon might have imagined, but evangelical Christianity is today a dominant force in Brazilian life. The country's politics make this clear. In 2018, Jair Bolsonaro, a far-right extremist, won 11 million votes more among self-declared evangelicals of different denominations than Fernando Haddad of the center-left Partido dos Trabalhadores (Workers' Party—PT), while Haddad prevailed among followers of Afro-Brazilian religions, atheists, and agnostics.[2] In a survey released days before Bolsonaro and Haddad faced off at the polls, 59 percent of evangelicals favored Bolsonaro against 26 percent for Haddad. Among Catholics, who still constitute the largest religious group in Brazil, they were practically tied.[3] Thus, Bolsonaro owed his victory to a decisive advantage among evangelicals. There are always uncertainties in politics, but one thing is for sure: one simply cannot understand the particularities of Bolsonaro's Brazil without grappling with the reach and influence of evangelicals. Doing so is an urgent task for anyone dissatisfied with the current state of Brazilian politics.

This article examines the political transformation of the evangelical movement in Brazil, especially its shifting relationship with the PT and the left in general. A key argument is that if progressives want to improve their political relationship with evangelical voters, they must find discursive and material ways to neutralize or at least establish a workable end run around the most prominent and virulently conservative faith leaders. Given that they can swing elections at the local, state, and national level, there is no more urgent question for Brazilian progressives today than how to arrest declining support among evangelical voters. This essay examines one aspect of why this will be so difficult: that the largest, best-organized, best-financed, and most influential evangelical churches in Brazil are under the control of a very small number of deeply reactionary pastors no longer inclined to compromise on what they consider articles of faith as their power base grows. I discuss the historical process by which Brazilian evangelicals—Pentecostals especially, given their preponderance among this segment of the population—went from accepting a position as junior partners in a broad governing coalition led by the PT to asserting themselves as an indispensable pillar of the present administration through a close examination of one especially prominent Bolsonarist pastor, Silas Malafaia. I focus on Malafaia, the religious leader closest to Bolsonaro, in order to understand Bolsonarism's claims to theological legitimacy among evangelicals.[4] Given the recency of the issues discussed here, I rely on journalistic accounts as much as on scholarship.

The association of evangelical Christianity with right-wing politics may seem natural. After all, this bond exists elsewhere, most notably in the United States and, increasingly, across Latin America. It was not, however, always a given in Brazil. Paul Freston (2008: 3–4) observed that, while "sometimes portrayed as a new religious right and even as given to undemocratic dreams of theocracy . . . in fact Latin American evangelicals have been extraordinarily diverse in their first two decades of public prominence since the early 1980s." Brazilian evangelicals did not abandon nominally progressive politicians en masse until relatively recently. Just over a decade ago, Alexandre Brasil Fonseca (2008: 164) wrote at length about the political prominence of evangelicals "on the left or center-left" rather than the right. On the eve of the 2006 presidential election, polls showed then-president Luiz Inácio Lula da Silva favored by 59 percent of self-declared evangelicals against 41 percent for São Paulo Governor Geraldo Alckmin of the center-right Partido da Social Democracia Brasileira (Party of Brazilian Social Democracy—PSDB). Four years later, the PT remained ahead among these voters, albeit by a smaller margin, with 51 percent for Dilma Rousseff and 49 percent for José Serra of the PSDB. The PT's first defeat among evangelicals came in the 2014 elections, with Senator Aécio Neves of Minas Gerais garnering 53 percent of evangelical voting intentions against 47 percent for Dilma (Balloussier, 2020a). This decline makes clear that the outcome for Haddad in 2018 was not an anomaly but the predictable conclusion of a slow-motion collapse in evangelical support for center-left candidates at the national level.

Evangelicals are the fastest-growing religious cohort in a country once defined by overwhelming Catholicism.[5] In 2000, according to Fonseca (2008), 15.5 percent of the population were Protestants. Today, that number is 31 percent

(Balloussier, 2020b). Between 1991 and 2010, the number of Catholics fell at a rate of 1 percent per year while the number of evangelicals increased by 0.7 percent. According to José Eustáquio Alves, a demographer at the Instituto Brasileiro de Geografia e Estatística (National Brazilian Institute of Geography and Statistics—IBGE), there are several indications that Catholics are now declining at a rate of 1.2 percent per year, with evangelicals rising annually by 0.8 percent. On the basis of these figures, Alves projects that by 2022, the bicentenary of Brazilian independence, the number of Catholics in the broader population will slip below 50 percent, shrinking to 38.6 percent of the population a decade later. Meanwhile, evangelicals are projected to make up 39.8 percent of the Brazilian population in 2032, outnumbering Catholics for the first time (Balloussier, 2020c). Evangelicals are likely to only increase their influence over Brazilian life going forward, shaping political discourse, social mores, and even patterns of criminality (see Phillips, 2022).

They are not, however, a monolith. Between 60 and 70 percent of Brazilian evangelicals are Pentecostals, making it the largest Protestant denomination. The two leading figures of this most far-reaching brand of evangelical Christianity are Silas Malafaia, linked to the World Assemblies of God Fellowship through his Victory in Christ ministry, and Edir Macedo of the Universal Church of the Kingdom of God. Both are linked to a tradition referred to as Neo-Pentecostalism. Pentecostalism generally refers to a type of Christian spiritual practice that prioritizes a direct relationship with the Holy Spirit in direct confrontation with the Devil. Neo-Pentecostalism sets itself apart through its reliance on what might be called spiritual showmanship. As Mookgo S. Kgatle (2017) has put it, "these churches idolize the miraculous, healing, deliverance and enactment of bizarre church performances often performed by charismatic and highly influential spiritual leaders." Malafaia in particular has been a steadfast Bolsonaro ally, consistently urging the faithful to support the president's authoritarian impulses.

Some on the left might find it distasteful to seek the support of evangelical voters. They worry about loosening legal protections for LGBTQ+ people, for example, and otherwise blurring the line between church and state. These are valid concerns that need to be handled carefully (Sesin, 2021), but any serious political project must have a specific strategy for appealing to evangelicals directly. The anthropologist Juliano Spyer (2020: 24) has criticized progressive academics in particular—including the runner-up in the 2018 election—for their ignorance of evangelical religious practice. This unwillingness to engage, he argues, has precluded the emergence of a popular progressive evangelical tradition in Brazil. If progressives are to sustain electoral success going forward, they must find ways to scale the walls separating most evangelicals from left-wing appeals that once sensitized religious people to pressing social issues like state violence, the need for land reform, and the crushingly high cost of living for the working class. The left needs to understand the faith of the faithful in order to compete for their support.

As the work of Emanuel de Kadt, John Burdick, Kenneth Serbin, and others has shown, Brazilian society in the second half of the last century was shaped as never before—or since—by an influential strain of progressive Catholicism (de Kadt, 1970; Burdick, 2004; Serbin, 2000). During that time, politically engaged clergymen helped rally pockets of dispossessed men and women, challenge military rule, and create lasting political organizations. The PT itself was founded with the explicit support of Catholic organizers and prominent Catholic clergymen (Barbosa, 2007). Whether progressives can effectively engage with evangelicals today as they did with Catholics then without sacrificing bedrock principles of social justice is an open question. As the number of evangelicals grows, so does the political clout of their spiritual leaders. It is therefore necessary to understand Malafaia so as to find ways around him. This article, tentative and necessarily schematic, takes a step in that direction. It begins with a brief overview of the history of Pentecostalism in Brazil before discussing Malafaia's trajectory and links to Bolsonarism. Next it considers the political implications of evangelical political activism in Brazil today in comparison with the United States and countries across Latin American undergoing similar religious transformations. Finally, it reflects on what the PT is doing and what it could still do to mitigate Bolsonaro's strong support among evangelical voters. An underlying concern of this article is to illustrate the extent to which political outcomes are shaped by the contingency of religious association. The past is beyond reach, but progressives may yet reassess, reorganize, and reengage evangelicals for the sake of the future. Amid the social ruins of Bolsonarism, it is clear that such a rapprochement stands to benefit the person of faith and the nonbeliever alike.

PENTECOSTALISM IN BRAZIL

Pentecostals use the Gospel of Luke and the book of Acts as a guide to the Pentecostal experience. Especially important is the account in Acts 2: 1–4 of the period after the resurrection of Jesus Christ and his ascent to Heaven 10 days later when the Holy Spirit visited Earth, an event the Bible refers to as "the day of Pentecost." On that day, the followers of Jesus gathered in Jerusalem: "And suddenly there came a sound from heaven as of a rushing mighty wind, and it filled all the house where they were sitting. And there appeared unto them cloven tongues like as of fire, and it sat upon each of them. And they were all filled with the Holy Ghost, and began to speak with other tongues, as the Spirit gave them utterance." These passages, and others such as Acts 10:10, give Pentecostals theological support for the doctrine of initial evidence that holds that glossolalia—speaking in tongues—is a sign of Spirit baptism. Pentecostals also believe in extraordinary spiritual gifts such as miracle cures, exorcism, and prophecies. Although these practices generally set Pentecostals apart, versions of them are sometimes found in older, more established strains of Christianity, as exemplified by the Catholic Charismatic Renewal movement (Lynch, 2012: 335). From its inception, Pentecostalism has preached an individual's intimate relationship with the gospel, but it has not always put much faith in the media to facilitate that connection. On this point, the Neo-Pentecostals would innovate.

When Pentecostalism arrived in Brazil in the first decade of the twentieth century, adherents preached "traditionalism in customs and moral rigidity," according to Jonas Christmann Koren (2016: 1). An Italian-American missionary named Louis Francescon was instrumental in establishing Pentecostalism in Brazil. Francescon grew up Catholic but converted to Presbyterianism before embracing Pentecostalism and the missionary life. He left Chicago for Brazil in 1910, the year Gammon published *The Evangelical Invasion of Brazil*. It is unclear whether he was aware of Gammon's writing, but it is entirely possible, since, like Gammon, he had been a Presbyterian connected to missionaries abroad. Upon his arrival, Francescon began preaching at the Presbyterian Church in the Brás neighborhood of São Paulo, where he eventually established the Congregação Cristã no Brasil (Christian Congregation in Brazil). The congregation grew quickly and is currently the second-largest Pentecostal church in Brazil, primarily concentrated in the state of São Paulo (Valente, 2015: 74).

In 1910, two Swedish-American Pentecostal missionaries also arrived in Brazil from Chicago, establishing the Assembly of God in the state of Pará and across the Amazon soon thereafter. They were joined in this effort by missionaries from Scandinavia. "Together they organized a flourishing Brazilian work on a completely indigenous basis, a rather unique approach for that time," notes John Thomas Nichol (1966: 53). Admiring this effort, the Pentecostal missionary and former president of Continental Bible College in Brussels, Belgium, Steve Durasoff (1972: 91) observed that "some of today's largest Pentecostal areas, such as Brazil, Indonesia, and Soviet Russia, were served by laymen or preachers who answered God's call through prophecy to be missionaries." This organic zeal led to the rapid expansion of the faith in Brazil.

At first, these Pentecostal pioneers shunned formal politics and rejected the media as a tool to increase their number of followers. Such activities, according to Koren (2016: 34), were considered "mundane or diabolical." This attitude shifted gradually, revealing differences between Francescon's Christian Congregation in Brazil and the Assemblies of God. According to a Pentecostal historian, Francescon sought to insulate his congregation in ways that "may be construed as parochial." He even chose not to use the term "Pentecostalism" in his ministry, an attempt to steer clear of internecine theological disputes rocking the Chicago area upon his departure. By contrast, Nichol observed in the 1960s, the Assemblies of God "broadcasts a program known throughout Brazil as 'Voz Evangelica das Assembléias de Deus,' publishes a biweekly religious periodical—*Mensageiro da Paz (Messenger of Peace)*—and sends missionaries to Portugal and among the Indians in Goyaz" (Nichol, 1966: 165).

A critical turning point for Brazilian Pentecostals was the return of democracy in the mid-1980s after two decades of military rule. The Assembly of God, by then the largest Pentecostal church in Brazil, immersed itself in politics, endeavoring to elect leaders from its ranks to the constituent assembly in 1986. The Christian Congregation in Brazil was eclipsed by the more assertive Assembly of God leaders. According to Rubia R. Valente, an assistant professor at the Austin W. Marxe School of Public and International Affairs at Baruch College and a longtime member of the Christian Congregation, its reluctance to engage in politics has led to its losing ground to other, more vocal evangelical strains to this day. In 1972, a bewildered Durasoff observed that, with more than half a million members, it "had no official organ to carry news of the Christian Congregations" (Durasoff, 1972: 101). Furthermore, according to Valente (2015: 78), members are "effectively banned from participating in politics and even in civil protests." This is a far cry from the pious multitude that took to the streets on September 7, 2021, at Malafaia's urging to support Bolsonaro's anti-institutional agenda (Balloussier, 2021). Whatever reluctance once existed among many Pentecostals regarding the use of the mass media dissipated as the Neo-Pentecostals took to the airwaves in the 1970s and 1980s. Religious groups must have the motivation, opportunity, and resources to engage in politics, writes Amy Erica Smith (2019: 164), noting that "all three . . . are necessary; absence of any one prevents a group from entering politics." Funded by the small-dollar donations of millions of followers and unabashed in their pursuit of political influence, Neo-Pentecostals would go on to build massive ministerial empires. Malafaia has been especially successful.

BOLSONARO'S FAVORITE PASTOR

Silas Lima Malafaia was born in Rio de Janeiro on January 20, 1958. His mother was a teacher, and his father served in the military and became a pastor after retiring. Both were members of the Assembly of God (Pinheiro, 2011). Malafaia is married to Elizete Malafaia, and they have a son and two daughters. In the early 1980s, Malafaia started one of the first evangelical programs on Brazilian television, today called *Vitória em Cristo*. In his official biography, Malafaia (2018) writes that, "to maintain the TV program and be able to support social projects, God [gave] him the strategy of founding the Associação Vitória em Cristo (Victory in Christ Association, AVEC), which currently serves more than 3,000 people daily through projects spread across Brazil and Africa." According to Malafaia, all AVEC projects are carried out by volunteers, reaching the faithful wherever they are through the sale of books, CDs, and DVDs. In 1999, Malafaia founded the Central Gospel publisher, now the country's second-largest producer of evangelical content.

The AVEC headquarters occupies an area of 40,000 square meters in the neighborhood of Jacarepaguá in the West Zone of Rio. According to Daniela Pinheiro (2011), the building's "modern and glassy construction contrasts with the surrounding poor commerce and empty abandoned lots. The Christian entity—deemed a nonprofit, which exempts it from paying taxes—finances the actions of Malafaia's religious ministry." Through countless projects, conferences, and meetings, AVEC reaches more than 100,000 people in public squares across Brazil, according to Pinheiro. In 2013 it brought in R$45 million, mostly through tithes and donations from the faithful. With these resources, Malafaia has personally become enormously wealthy and today travels Brazil and the world in a Gulfstream III jet purchased for US$4 million in the United States. Yet the pastor vehemently denies that religion is a source of opulence for him and his peers. A 2013 ranking by *Forbes* magazine named Malafaia the third-richest pastor in Brazil with a fortune of US$150 million (Antunes, 2013). "Enraged, Malafaia threatened to sue the publication" (Cardoso, 2013).

As a proponent of prosperity theology, Malafaia believes that individual financial blessings and physical well-being are always the result of God's will for the individual. The faithful must believe, think positively, and donate to religious causes in order to earn God's favor and, eventually, material wealth.

Malafaia has called pastors who disagree with this reading of scripture "idiots" (*Revista Igreja*, 2011). He is a prominent and highly influential leader but not immune to criticism from other believers. When accused of selling blessings he replied, "Anyone who thinks like that is stupid! You think I'm a child to sell blessings, young man! What I do, and it is biblical, is release a prophetic word" (Cardoso, 2013). But, as another critic pointed out, the exponents of prosperity theology do not encourage their faithful to give money to other people's charities or secular nongovernmental organizations. In short, "the 'blessing' is only valid if I sow in their field" (*Revista Igreja*, 2011).

In addition to enriching its best-known proponents, prosperity theology carries a broader political significance. According to the sociologist Gedeon Freire de Aguiar, prosperity theology makes sense only in a neoliberal context. "Prosperity theology and neoliberalism . . . are Siamese twins. One would not exist without the other." Aguiar asserts that, in the same way that neoliberalism could not have arisen in the 1920s, the economic and social conditions necessary for the growth of prosperity theology did not emerge in Brazil until after the 1970s (*Revista IHU*, 2010). Aguiar does not offer an explanation, but there must be something about the dissipation of progressive Catholic organizing that helped lead the charge against the military regime in collective, grassroots fashion. The consolidation of democracy and the stabilization of the economy may have eroded spiritual notions rooted in solidarity and inculcated instead the kind of individualism that prosperity theology not only sanctions but encourages. In any event, it is clear that the weakening of the state under neoliberal governments combined with growing individualism and consumerism fueled the rise of a cosmology centered around material abundance. The idea that the individual is responsible for the course of his life, and not the state, would find another form of expression in the approach to public safety articulated by Bolsonaro in the years leading to his election. This amounted to a recognition that the government was not up to the task of protecting "good citizens" and thus Brazilians should be permitted to own and carry firearms. This promise of individual agency appealed to many voters who felt legitimate fears about their safety and that of their families.

Malafaia, for his part, is intent on exerting political influence. In the past, he has offered many reasons evangelical Christians should not vote for leftist candidates. In a September 2016 YouTube video, he demanded emphatically that the faithful vote against Glauber Braga, then a candidate for mayor of Nova Friburgo, a city of almost 200,000 in the state of Rio de Janeiro. With theatrical disgust, he began with a warning that Braga was a member of the Partido Socialismo e Liberdade (Socialism and Liberty Party—PSOL): "Think about what is most radical against Christian thought," he raged. "These people support abortion, gay marriage, drug release, and gender ideology."[6] The latter, he insisted, was "one of the vilest things" because it "eroticizes children in school" and ignores the legal imperative that leaves the "moral education" of children up to the parents. Braga lost by 5,000 votes to Renato Bravo of the Partido Progressista (Progressive Party—PP). Malafaia recorded several videos against specific candidates in that year's elections, all with basically the same argument: progressive parties threaten the moral and economic values of evangelical voters. According to Malafaia's logic, a reactionary social and cultural agenda makes sense only when paired with neoliberal economics and vice versa. This is a distinctive feature of Malafaia's brand of evangelical Christianity.

Ahead of the 2018 campaign, Bolsonaro made a point of noting his closeness to Malafaia, whom the journalists Maiá Menezes and Thiago Prado (2018) referred to as "a kind of influencer." "I've established a friendship with Malafaia over the past 10 years. I think he's an exceptional guy," Bolsonaro said in 2017, adding that "the evangelical segment has its eye on the presidency in 2018 and I'm happy to be on their radar" (Alfano, 2017). This approximation made electoral sense for Bolsonaro, who had very little television time during the period reserved for political advertising. When Malafaia declared his support for Bolsonaro in March 2018, he predicted that the far-right candidate would win upwards of 80 percent of evangelical voters. "Bolsonaro is the only one who directly defends the ideology of the right," Malafaia declared, recognizing that the landscape would be different if former president Lula were in the race. It is worth noting, especially as the PT seeks to regain lost ground among evangelicals, that Malafaia specifically cited the conditional cash transfer program known as Bolsa Família—extinguished by Bolsonaro in 2021—as a reason for Lula's enduring appeal among evangelical voters (Menezes and Prado, 2018). Perhaps inadvertently, Malafaia raised a possible tension between the abstract conservative values he claimed that Bolsonaro embodied and the material plight of the rank-and-file faithful. In February 2020, Malafaia sat for a friendly conversation with Bolsonaro. Smiling and laughing, he praised the president for not negotiating with the venal political parties needed to form a governing base in Congress (a decision Bolsonaro has since reversed). According to Malafaia, such deal making had been one of the key drivers of corruption. Malafaia proceeded to argue in favor of the government's economic agenda, asking the president, "What is the point of guaranteeing so many benefits to the worker if it means he won't have a job?" Bolsonaro, who seeks to build on the market-friendly (or antiworker) agenda initiated with vigor under the administration of Michel Temer (2016–2018), replied, "It is better to have fewer [labor] rights and jobs than more rights and unemployment. That is the question of Brazil" (Malafaia, 2020).

More recently, Malafaia vocally backed Bolsonaro's calls for a major demonstration on September 7, 2021, Brazil's Independence Day. Intended as a political show of force against his opponents, the maneuver was viewed by many analysts as an attempt to undermine the separation of powers by intimidating individual members of the Supreme Court.[7] While the protests failed to meet the expectations of Bolsonaro and his allies, Malafaia solidified his standing as a reliable presidential ally. One journalist even noted some protesters in São Paulo clamoring for Malafaia to be Bolsonaro's running mate in the 2022 presidential election (Lima, 2021). This is exceedingly unlikely—Bolsonaro will have to satisfy evangelicals while not alienating the armed forces, represented most prominently in the administration in the figure of Vice President Hamilton Mourão—but is a testament to Malafaia's stature in Bolsonarist circles. With over 3 million followers on Instagram, 1.4 million on Twitter, 3.1 million on Facebook, and 1.45 million on YouTube, Malafaia retains the ability to communicate directly with vast numbers of evangelicals. This reach has clear political implications. As one of Brazil's most influential and savvy religious leaders,

Malafaia has burned whatever bridges he once maintained with parties and leaders left of center. He is all in on Bolsonaro, not least for pragmatic reasons such as shielding himself from long-running investigations into potential money laundering that go back to 2016.[8] Malafaia is a key player in the ongoing drama of Brazil's democratic erosion.

A COMPARATIVE PERSPECTIVE

To better understand how Brazilian evangelicals acquired their political strength and how their favor is being contested, it is helpful to look elsewhere across Latin America and to the United States, where this religious segment has played a pronounced role for decades. Ronald Reagan was the first modern politician on the American right to strategically mobilize the evangelical vote in a way comparable in Brazil to what Bolsonaro achieved in 2018. Since then, evangelicals have formed a central part of the conservative political base in the United States without which Reagan's party cannot win elections. In *The Power Worshippers: Inside the Dangerous Rise of Religious Nationalism*, Katherine Stewart, a journalist who has long covered the evangelical right in the United States, examines the strategies and key personalities of the movement that transformed religion into a tool of political domination. Her description of what draws ordinary people to right-wing evangelical activism is worth quoting at length (Stewart, 2020a: 6):

> The rank and file come to the movement with a variety of concerns, including questions about life's deeper meaning, a love and appreciation of God and Scripture, ethnic and family solidarity, the hope of community and friendship, and a desire to mark life's most significant passages or express feelings of joy and sorrow. They also come with a longing for certainty in an uncertain world. Against a backdrop of escalating economic inequality, deindustrialization, rapid technological change, and climate instability, many people, on all points of the economic spectrum, feel that the world has entered a state of disorder. The movement gives them confidence, an identity, and the feeling that their position in the world is safe.

This applies to Brazil, where violence, neoliberal reforms, and unemployment have hindered the emergence of secular solidarity networks in the past two decades or so. Indeed, Juliano Spyer (2020: 23) notes several ways in which the lives of poor evangelicals are materially made better by their association with a local church. "Yet," according to Stewart (2020a: 6),

> the price of certainty is often the surrendering of one's political will to those who claim to offer refuge from the tempest of modern life. The leaders of the movement have demonstrated real savvy in satisfying some of the emotional concerns of their followers, but they have little intention of giving them a voice in where the movement is going.

In Brazil, Neo-Pentecostal pastors like Malafaia draw a direct line between the election of extreme right candidates and the will of God. The political implications are clear: voting and organizing according to a defined political orientation is a prerequisite for belonging as well as a spiritual demand.

Bolsonaro, like Trump, received overwhelming support at the ballot box from evangelicals; in fact, Trump in 2016 received 80 percent of the white evangelical vote, the same number that Malafaia predicted Bolsonaro would garner in 2018 (see Gjelten, 2020). Although a few pastors refused to endorse Trump, citing his "racial, religious, and gender bigotry," the incumbent's support did not meaningfully decline in 2020 among white evangelicals. Bolsonaro too will undoubtedly enjoy widespread support from evangelicals in 2022, not least because he can point to the confirmation of André Mendonça, a Presbyterian pastor, to the Supreme Court as a 2018 promise kept. Even in the face of COVID-19, Malafaia has followed the president's lead, minimizing the devastating impact of the global pandemic. According to the anthropologist Joe Coyle (2020), Malafaia called quarantine a "farce" preventing churches from offering the "essential" services necessary for people's well-being. It is likely too soon to know whether the gradual erosion of Lulism as a political project over the past decade was the cause or the consequence of internal changes within evangelical Christianity in Brazil, but Malafaia is adroit at seizing political opportunities for himself and his constituency as they arise. He is a formidable ally for Bolsonaro and a wily opponent for the left.

Elections, however, are about margins. Barack Obama's presidential campaigns in 2008 and 2012 recognized this with clear eyes. In 2008, Obama's campaign launched the Joshua Generation Project, a direct attempt to appeal to court young evangelicals with house parties, concerts, and targeted events. Among other efforts, including the candidate's own carefully calibrated rhetoric on sensitive cultural issues and opposition to gay marriage, the Joshua Generation Project helped Obama improve upon John Kerry's numbers with evangelicals. Whereas John Kerry won 21 percent of that segment, Obama won 26 percent. Obama also bested Kerry by two percentage points specifically among white evangelicals (Pew Research Center, 2008). Obama's experience suggests that the combination of a deeply unpopular sitting president and a challenger that arouses the excitement of broad swathes of the electorate can in fact shake voters out of predictable patterns. Lula seemed poised to harness these same favorable winds heading into the 2022 presidential campaign.

When it comes to the rest of Latin America, Radha Sarkar (2021) is right to note the potential for "political innovations—and surprises—from the region's Evangelical communities as they gain in numbers and political acumen." Among other recent examples of left-of-center politicians' deliberately appealing to evangelical voters, she discusses Gustavo Petro's rhetorical invocations of saints, Jesus Christ, and the devil in his race for the presidency of Colombia. The issue with this tactical approach, however, aside from chipping away at the secular political vernacular that most modern left-wing parties favor, is that it risks backfiring. Will evangelical voters actually be moved to support progressive politicians who do not have a strong preexisting religious profile simply because they mention Jesus in their campaign speeches or publicly display a religious orientation? Perhaps, but it is more likely that voters will see through such electoral machinations. In 2018, Fernando Haddad, running for president against Bolsonaro, was ridiculed and verbally assaulted after attending mass by another churchgoer who called him an "abortionist" (Weterman, 2018). Whether Haddad or Petro are genuinely moved by deep religious conviction is less important than the fact that it had not been part of their public personas before they sought the presidency. Fairly or not, talking up their supposed religious convictions in the heat of a campaign comes off as self-serving and unseemly to voters for whom faith is central. Respect for political, social, and spiritual diversity should be at the center of progressive appeals across Latin America, linked in turn to materialist appeals. The left must constantly assert that religious and irreligious voters alike have a stake in fighting inequality and exclusion.

There is historical precedent for a progressive evangelical Christianity in Latin America. The Ecuadoran theologian, pastor, and activist René Padilla, who died in 2021, stands out in this regard. Pioneering what he called the *misión integral* (integral mission), he embraced a socially engaged role for evangelical Christians that eschewed the moralism of U.S. missionaries and their Latin American adherents. As David C. Kirkpatrick (2019: 11–12) observes, "prominent members of the American Evangelical Left have utilized this language [integral mission] as their theological framework for social Christianity," a vision that "synthesizes the pursuit of justice with the offer of salvation." Samuel Escobar (2012), a Peruvian-born Baptist minister who worked closely with Padilla, pointed out the frustration that the young evangelicals he interacted with in Brazil in the early 1960s felt about their lack of political influence: "Winning intellectual battles on campuses . . . was not enough. Evangelical students felt strongly challenged to deal seriously with issues of social justice and social change." Progressivism is clearly not the major chord in the refrain of Latin American evangelical Christianity today. However, the activism of Padilla and Escobar shows that there has historically been a theological basis—with deep regional links, no less—for a different kind of politics than that embraced by figures like Malafaia. Left-wing parties would do well to revisit this historical experience.

The experience of Hugo Chávez in Venezuela is also worth noting. Chávez always described himself as Catholic, but he took pains to empower evangelicals. During his first year in office, for example, he enforced a law passed by his predecessor that allowed evangelicals to teach religion courses as electives in public high schools, a role that had previously been carried out by Catholic lay clergymen (Smilde, 2012: 14). Indeed, as David Smilde has reported at length, Chávez performed surprisingly well among evangelicals in 1998, when he was first elected president. "A casual observer might reasonably expect a religious movement normally thought of as conservative, or at least politically cautious, to oppose a polemical candidate such as Hugo Chávez," Smilde wrote in 2004 (Smilde, 2004: 82). In fact, however, "evangelicals did not unify either for or against Chávez's candidacy and simply mirrored the tendencies of the larger population" ((Smilde, 2004: 83). Smilde argues that the Venezuelan case demonstrates that there is no single way to appeal to evangelicals. Those who would seek to understand and communicate with evangelical voters should note "the simultaneous coexistence of tendencies toward autonomy, individualism, and democracy, on the one hand; and patriarchy, corporatism, and authoritarianism, on the other" (Smilde, 2004: 75). Needless to say, it would have been a minor miracle for

Lula if evangelical voters in 2022 matched the voting habits of their peers in other social categories such as income, education, and gender. In the medium to long-term, however, it is by no means unthinkable.

OUTREACH AND ENGAGEMENT

Two separate but often overlapping paths present themselves for progressives hoping to make inroads among evangelicals in the 2022 presidential election in Brazil and thereafter. The first is to try to win over evangelicals by making theological or quasi-theological arguments, insisting that far-right values are not Christian values. The second is to deemphasize religious appeals in favor of broader material arguments. Rather than attempting to win over evangelicals *as evangelicals*, this strategy would treat evangelicals as individuals with unmet needs here and now. Again, these are not mutually exclusive rhetorical tactics. Lula himself is walking both paths at once, telling the rapper Mano Brown, "I don't believe Bolsonaro's God is the same as mine, who symbolizes love and brotherhood," and insisting on a secular, pluralistic state that works to improve the lives of every Brazilian. In interviews before and during the 2022 campaign, Lula implicitly acknowledged that the PT failed to halt the evangelical drift to the far right.

During his 580 days in prison in Curitiba, Lula, for whom television was one of the only distractions allowed, told the journalist Anna Virginia Balloussier that he used priests' and pastors' programs as an apprenticeship. He even joked that he wanted to "get into this" and that he has already developed "a kind of pastor style" (Balloussier, 2020a). Lula recognizes the country's shifting sociopolitical terrain and, in his own way, is signaling his intent to defuse the tensions that emerged between his party and the growing evangelical electorate that sees in Malafaia a great leader—tensions that revolve largely but not exclusively around the PT's support for the LGBTQ+ community. Despite Lula's stated aims, there are currently no pastors willing to publicly support progressive causes who come close to the stature of Malafaia or Edir Macedo on the other side.

But grassroots organizing against the titans of the conservative right has historically been a strength of the left. Pastor Daniel Elias, who leads a small Assembly of God church in Duque de Caxias, Rio de Janeiro, has embraced this project. His job, as he sees it, is to "arm believers with arguments" with which to push back against the notion that "a real Christian does not vote for the left." Elias stresses the importance of conducting this debate "from evangelical to evangelical," since "the fellow might not consider the outside world much. Pastors were the ones who said that Bolsonaro is sent by God. Those who countered that were not from inside [the Church]." Establishing that their interlocutor takes them and their faith seriously is a crucial first step in reaching evangelicals, Elias argues. He offers practical ways to refute conservative religious talking points. If an evangelical opposes same-sex marriage, he tells his followers to say, "Simple, then don't get married." Evangelicals apply this same logic to the consumption of alcoholic beverages, for example. Most evangelicals do not drink beer, but they don't advocate banning alcohol sales. Some evangelicals say they still feel a measure of prejudice from progressives. According to Nilza Valéria Zacarias, coordinator of the progressive Frente de Evangélicos pelo Estado de Direito (Evangelical Front for the Rule of Law), "It is very common to think that those who choose to embrace this faith do so because they have no alternative, that misery pushes people to that place. This perspective places the other in a place of suspicion, as if they had no autonomy." She also highlights problems in the left's attempt to create a religious counternarrative. When Lula says that he's developed "a kind of pastor style," it sounds good for those already likely to support him, but "anti-PT sentiment [antipetismo] makes this phrase sound disrespectful to many others" (Balloussier, 2020a).

Despite recent challenges, Lula has already shown that a progressive popular leader can win a significant portion of the evangelical vote, at least on occasion. At the risk of simplifying complicated political calculations, the PT would do well not to overthink its outreach strategy to evangelicals. It should not, for example, attempt to out-theologize individual pastors, coming up with Bible-based attack ads against figures like Bolsonaro. Such efforts could understandably be seen by many religious voters as self-serving and patronizing. The PT might also blunt at least some of the edge of Malafaia's criticism by noting his previous support for the party (this would also subtly draw attention to Malafaia's opportunism). After all, Malafaia admitted having voted twice for Lula, including in 1989, when, according to the journalist Balloussier (2020a), "he disagreed with his colleagues who saw [Lula] as a communist Beelzebub and supported him." During the Lula administration (2003–2011), the pastor boasted of his access to the corridors of power.[9]

Progressives should also avoid getting bogged down in substance-free debates about "the family" or "morals." Lula has contested this terrain, presenting himself as a committed family man in his personal life, but the abstract notion of family values should not be a pillar of a progressive agenda. Instead, going forward the PT should focus on aggressively posing the question of whether the average Brazilian family, which Bolsonaro claims to care about so much, benefited from the economic agenda implemented during his time in office. Progressives should constantly remind voters of the economic and social devastation that Bolsonaro and his allies produced. This is a strategy for both the short term and the long term. Even if the PT ultimately managed to peel few evangelical voters away from the political exhortations of figures like Malafaia in the 2022 presidential campaign, Lula's victory showed that progressives can win in a shifting religious landscape even in the face of open hostility from conservative mega-pastors. This outcome should bolster leftists across the continent anxious about whether long-held principles of social justice have to be sacrificed for the sake of evangelical support in future elections. There is obviously no guarantee of future success for political forces committed to such principles, but there is no empirical support for the defeatist notion that a rising evangelical tide will drown progressive priorities.

The earliest evangelical proselytizers in Brazil recognized the importance of grounding religious affiliation in material circumstances. Remarking on the potential for evangelical growth in Brazil over a century ago, Samuel Rhea Gammon wrote that when Brazilians "come to understand the real cause of their political and social troubles, there will be a tremendous drift away from Romanism and toward Evangelical Christianity." The same might be said today about a drift from Bolsonarism to a new progressive vision of a more just and equitable Brazil. In 2022 Brazilians went to the polls to elect not a pastor but a president, a politician responsive to their needs and demands in this life, here and now. The task for Brazilian progressives during the campaign and after is to make clear to evangelicals what the real cause of political and social troubles is—not their faith per se but the brand of politics represented most emblematically by Bolsonaro.

NOTES

1. The Southern Presbyterian Church was the product of a split within American Presbyterianism over several issues, the most important being slavery, in the years preceding the Civil War. Southern Presbyterians declared themselves "neither the friends nor the foes of slavery," an effective endorsement of human bondage (Johnson, 1911: 351).

2. I use the term "evangelicals" to refer broadly to Protestants because, as Fonseca (2008: 164) notes, Brazilians generally use these terms interchangeably. Specific denominations are cited when relevant.

3. The full results of the poll conducted by Datafolha can be found at http://media.folha.uol.com.br/datafolha/2018/10/26/3416374d208f7def05d1476d05ede73e.pdf (accessed August 22, 2020).

4. Ole Jakob Løland (2020), a postdoctoral researcher in theology at the University of Oslo, has helpfully identified "politically influential theologies" in Bolsonaro's Brazil—neoliberal supernaturalism, apocalyptic dualism, and neoconservative Catholicism.

5. For a deep look at the intertwined histories of conservative evangelical and Catholic politics in Brazil, see Cowan (2021).

6. For a very brief overview of the controversy surrounding gender ideology, see Butler (2019).

7. Fishman (2021), for example, argued that the September 7 demonstrations could be Brazil's January 6 (a reference to the storming of the U.S. Capitol by a Trump-supporting mob).

8. Federal police identified Malafaia as a beneficiary of a scheme to skim resources collected from mining contracts with various municipal governments. In his defense, Malafaia claimed to believe he had been receiving donations for his evangelizing work rather than illicit funds from an ongoing criminal enterprise.

9. Malafaia began distancing himself from the PT beginning in 2010 (Romero, 2011).

REFERENCES

Alfano, Bruno
    2017 "Bolsonaro revela que já conversa com pastor Silas Malafaia sobre apoio em 2018." *Extra*, January 3. https://extra.globo.com/noticias/brasil/bolsonaro-revela-que-ja-conversa-com-pastor-silas-malafaia-sobre-apoio-em-2018-20721954.html (accessed on September 22, 2021).

Antunes, Anderson
    2013 "The richest pastors in Brazil." *Forbes*, January 17. https://www.forbes.com/sites/andersonantunes/2013/01/17/the-richest-pastors-in-brazil/#3b5ad04d5b1e (accessed August 20, 2020).

Balloussier, Anna Virginia
    2020a "Com 'jeitão de pastor,' Lula quer PT perto de evangélicos, mas pastores veem deslizes." *Folha de São Paulo*, January 26. https://www1.folha.uol.com.br/poder/2020/01/com-jeitao-de-pastor-lula-quer-pt-perto-de-evangelicos-mas-pastores-veem-deslizes.shtml?origin=folhatw (accessed August 22, 2020).

2020b "Cara típica do evangélico brasileiro é feminina e negra, aponta Datafolha." *Folha de São Paulo*, January 13. https://www1.folha.uol.com.br/poder/2020/01/cara-tipica-do-evangelico-brasileiro-e-feminina-e-negra-aponta-datafolha.shtml (accessed August 23, 2020).

2020c "Evangélicos podem desbancar católicos no Brasil em pouco mais de uma década." *Folha de São Paulo*, January 14. https://www1.folha.uol.com.br/poder/2020/01/evangelicos-podem-desbancar-catolicos-no-brasil-em-pouco-mais-de-uma-decada.shtml (accessed August 23, 2020).

2021 "Liderados por Malafaia, pastores convocam evangélicos para apoiar Bolsonaro no 7 de Setembro." *Folha de São Paulo*, August 25. https://www1.folha.uol.com.br/poder/2021/08/liderados-por-malafaia-pastores-convocam-evangelicos-para-apoiar-bolsonaro-no-7-de-setembro.shtml (accessed September 15, 2021).

Barbosa, Imerson Alves
2007 "A esquerda católica na formação do PT." Master's thesis, Universidade Estadual Paulista, Campus de Marília. http://www.marilia.unesp.br/Home?Pos-Graduacao/CienciasSoiais/Dissertacoes/barbosa_ia_me_mar.pdf (accessed September 25, 2021).

Burdick, John
2004 *Legacies of Liberation: The Progressive Catholic Church in Brazil*. Aldershot: Ashgate Publishing Company.

Butler, Judith
2019 "The backlash against 'gender ideology' must stop." *New Statesman*. January 21. https://www.newstatesman.com/2019/01/judith-butler-backlash-against-gender-ideology-must-stop (accessed August 22, 2020).

Cardoso, Rodrigo
2013 'Interview with Silas Malafaia." *Istoé*, no.
2254, January 30. https://istoe.com.br/270456_JA+RECEBI+R+2+MILHOES+DE+UM+FIEL+/ (accessed August 23, 2020).

Cowan, Benjamin A.
2021 *Moral Majorities across the Americas: Brazil, the United States, and the Creation of the Religious Right*. Chapel Hill: University of North Carolina Press.

Coyle, Joe
2020 "COVID-19 and Evangelical Christianity in Bolsonaro's Brazil." Relatos: the CLACS Blog, University of Illinois Center for Latin American and Caribbean Studies. https://clacs.illinois.edu/news/2020-05-05/covid-19-and-evangelical-christianity-bolsonaros-brazil.

Daniel, W. Harrison
1967 "Southern Presbyterians in the Confederacy." *North Carolina Historical Review* 44 (3): 234.

de Kadt, Emanuel
1970 *Catholic Radicals in Brazil*. New York: Oxford University Press.

Durasoff, Steve
1972 *Bright Wind of the Spirit: Pentecostalism Today*. Englewood Cliffs, NJ: Prentice-Hall.

Escobar, Samuel
2012 "My pilgrimage in mission." *International Bulletin of Missionary Research* 36 (4): 206–211. http://www.internationalbulletin.org/issues/2012-04/2012-04-206-escobar.html (accessed January 23, 2022).

Etheridge, David C.
1994 "Educational ministry in Brazil: the potent agency of Samuel Rhea Gammon." *American Presbyterians* 72 (1): 23–32.

Fishman, Andrew
2021 "Jair Bolsonaro's pro-coup rally: September 7 is shaping up to be Brazil's January 6." *The Intercept*, September 5. https://theintercept.com/2021/09/05/bolsonaro-september-7-brazil-trump-january-6/ (accessed on January 26, 2022).

Fonseca, Alexandre Brasil
2008 "Religion and democracy in Brazil: a study of the leading evangelical politicians," pp.163–206 in Paul Freston (ed.), *Evangelical Christianity and Democracy in Latin America*. New York: Oxford University Press.

Freston, Paul
2008 "Introduction: The many faces of evangelical politics in Latin America," in Paul Freston (ed.), *Evangelical Christianity and Democracy in Latin America*. New York: Oxford University Press.

Gammon, Samuel R.
   1910 *The Evangelical Invasion of Brazil: or, A Half Century of Evangelical Missions in the Land of the Southern Cross*. Richmond: Presbyterian Committee of Publication.
Gjelten, Tom
   2020 "2020 faith vote reflects 2016 patterns." *NPR*, November 8. https://www.npr.org/2020/11/08/932263516/2020-faith-vote-reflects-2016-patterns.
Hanke, Lewis
   1971 "A modest proposal for a moratorium on grand generalizations: some thoughts on the Black Legend." *Hispanic American Historical Review* 51 (1): 112–127.
Johnson, Thomas C.
   1911 *History of the Southern Presbyterian Church*. New York: Charles Scribner's Son.
Kgatle, Mookgo S.
   2017 "The unusual practices within some Neo-Pentecostal churches in South Africa: reflections and recommendations," *Hervormde Theological Studies* 73 (3).
Kirkpatrick, David C.
   2019 *A Gospel for the Poor: Global Social Christianity and the Latin American Evangelical Left*. Philadelphia: University of Pennsylvania Press.
Koren, Jonas Christmann
   2016 "Ministério Silas Malafaia: evangelizando à direita (2000–2013)." Ph.D. diss., Universidade Estadual do Oeste do Paraná. http://tede.unioeste.br/bitstream/tede/3153/5/Jonas_Koren_2016 (accessed August 20, 2020).
Lima, Eudes
   2021 "A gangorra dos evangélicos." *Istoé*, no. 2696, September 17. https://istoe.com.br/a-gangorra-dos-evangelicos/ (accessed September 22, 2021).
Løland, Ole Jakob
   2020 "The political conditions and theological foundations of the new Christian right in Brazil." *Iberoamericana: Nordic Journal of Latin American and Caribbean Studies* 49 (1): 63–73.
Lynch, John
   2012 *New Worlds: A Religious History of Latin America*. New Haven: Yale University Press.
Malafaia, Silas
   2018 "Minha história." https://www.silasmalafaia.com/minha-historia/.
   2020 "Interview with Jair Bolsonaro." YouTube, February 3. https://www.youtube.com/watch?v=2lju58SIn_E (accessed August 24, 2020).
Menezes, Maiá and Thiago Prado
   2018 "Influenciador nas redes sociais, Silas Malafaia vai apoiar Bolsonaro com uso de canhão digital." *O Globo*, March 18. https://oglobo.globo.com/politica/influenciador-nas-redes-sociais-silas-malafaia-vai-apoiar-bolsonaro-com-uso-de-canhao-digital-22501478 (accessed September 22, 2021).
Nichol, John Thomas
   1966 *Pentecostalism*. New York: Harper and Row.
Pew Research Center
   2008 "How the faithful voted." November 10. https://www.pewforum.org/2008/11/05/how-the-faithful-voted/ (accessed September 22, 2021).
Phillips, Tom
   2022 "Christ and cocaine: Rio's gangs of God blend faith and violence." *The Guardian*, January 23. https://www/theguardian.com/world/2022/jan/23/christ-and-cocaine-rios-gangs-of-god-blend-faith-and-violence (accessed January 24, 2022).
Pinheiro, Daniela
   2011 "Vitória em Cristo." *Revista Piauí*, no. 60. https://piaui.folha.uol.com.br/materia/vitoria-em-cristo/ (accessed August 18, 2020).
Revista Igreja
   2011 "Interview with Silas Malafaia." January 9. https://noticias.gospelmais.com.br/silas-malafaia-pastores-teologia-prosperidade-idiotas-deveriam-perder-credencial.html.
Revista IHU
   2010 "Interview with Gedeon Freire de Alencar." May 15. http://www.ihu.unisinos.br/entrevistas/32457-a-teologia-da-prosperidade-e-o-neoliberalismo-sao-irmaos-siameses-entrevista-especial-com-gedeon-freire-de-alencar (accessed September 20, 2021).

Romero, Simon
    2011 "Evangelical leader rises in Brazil's culture wars." *New York Times*, November 25. https://www.nytimes.com/2011/11/26/world/americas/silas-malafaia-tv-evangelist-rises-in-brazils-culture-wars.html (accessed September 20, 2021).
Sarkar, Radha
    2021 "The alliances of leftists and evangelicals in Latin America." *North American Congress on Latin America*, October 12. https://nacla.org/alliances-leftists-and-evangelicals-latin-america?fbclid=IwAR2b5A8W0nzX3TRuCMDSwblsbItyUkSUqzLQXuowtDF8qGih5hRb15Ml3k4 (accessed January 25, 2022).
Serbin, Kenneth
    2000 *Secret Dialogues: Church-State Relations, Torture, and Social Justice in Authoritarian Brazil.* Pittsburgh: University of Pittsburgh Press.
Sesin, Carmen
    2021 "Why some of Latin America's leftist leaders are against abortion and gay rights." NBC News, November 1. https://www.nbcnews.com/news/latino/latin-americas-leftist-leaders-are-abortion-gay-rights-rcna3935.
Smilde, David
    2004 "Contradiction without paradox: evangelical political culture in the 1998 Venezuelan elections." *Latin American Politics and Society* 46 (1): 75–102.
    2012 "Religião e conflitos politicos na Venezuela: Católicos e evangélicos frente ao governo de Hugo Chávez." *Religião e Sociedade* 32 (2): 13–28.
Smith, Amy Erica
    2019 *Religion and Brazilian Democracy: Mobilizing the People of God.* Cambridge: Cambridge University Press.
Spyer, Juliano
    2020 *Povo de Deus: Quem são os evangélicos e por que eles importam.* São Paulo: Geração Editorial.
Stewart, Katherine
    2020 *The Power Worshippers: Inside the Dangerous Rise of Religious Nationalism.* New York: Bloomsbury Publishing.
Valente, Rubia R.
    2015 "Institutional explanations for the decline of the Congregação Cristã no Brasil." *PentecoStudies* 13 (1): 72–96.
Weterman, Daniel
    2018 "Haddad discute com mulher em igreja católica: 'Você deve ser ateia.'" *O Estado de São Paulo*, October 12. https://politica.estadao.com.br/noticias/geral,haddad-discute-com-mulher-em-igreja-catolica-voce-deve-ser-ateia,70002545004 (accessed January 25, 2022).

Brazil's Cultural Battleground

Public Universities and the New Right

by
Juliano Fiori and Pedro Fiori Arantes

After assuming the presidency in January 2019, Bolsonaro used the machinery of government to wage culture warfare. Public universities, sites of cultivation of a new moral radicalism of the left over recent decades, became primary cultural battlegrounds. With its attacks on public universities (demonization, unconstitutional government interference, budget cuts, and political persecution), Bolsonaro's government nurtured the reactionary imagination of Brazil's new right and challenged the cultural hegemony of the left and thus undermined a biopolitical pact that once tied public universities to the defense of a right to life.

Depois de assumir a presidência em Janeiro 2019, Bolsonaro utilizou a máquina do governo para fazer uma guerra cultural. As universidades públicas, viveiros pela formação de um novo radicalismo moral da esquerda durante as últimas décadas, se converteram em importantes campos de batalha culturais nessa guerra. Com sua ofensiva contra as universidades públicas (demonização, interferência do governo inconstitucional, cortes orçamentais e perseduções políticas), o governo Bolsonaro fomentou um imaginário reacionário na direita brasileira que desafiou a hegemonia cultural da esquerda e, por conseguinte, minou um pacto biopolítico que anteriormente vinculava as universidades públicas à defesa do direito à vida.

Keywords: Public universities, Culture war, Cultural Marxism, Left hegemony, New right

The explosion of discontent across Brazilian cities in June 2013 and the right's subsequent conquest of the streets demonstrated that the country's progressive neoliberal settlement was not as consolidated as its champions had supposed. But no one expected Bolsonaro. And yet, once the unexpected transpires, hindsight transforms it into the inevitable through vindication of a historical rationality. What else was to be expected? For many of Bolsonaro's detractors, his presidency was the result of elite betrayal of Brazilian democracy. For his devotees—those who call him Mito (Myth)—it represented the hope of salvation from ethical and cultural degeneracy. As political intrigue plowed fertile ground for counterrevolution, Bolsonaro's presidential election

Juliano Fiori is the director of Alameda, a new institute for research and social strategy. Pedro Fiori Arantes is an associate professor of art history, is one of the principal investigators at Sociedade, Universidade e Ciência Research Center (SoU_Ciência), and was vice provost of planning (2013–2021) at the Universidade Federal de São Paulo.

LATIN AMERICAN PERSPECTIVES, Issue 248, Vol. 50 No. 1, January 2023, 197–217
DOI: 10.1177/0094582X221147594

campaign of 2018 polarized these moral postures, presenting conflict between them as not just inevitable but essential.

With Bolsonaro in power, Brazil provided a dramatic example of the popular authoritarianism that has reshaped the ideological landscape of liberal democracies.[1] Bolsonaro nurtured the reactionary imagination of a new authoritarian right, according to which "cultural Marxism" appears as an imported threat to an essential, conservative Brazilian character. Identifying those at the forefront of progressive politics today—black, indigenous, and landless activists, feminists, members of the LGBTQI+ community, those engaged in historical struggles for rights—as internal enemies, he provided license for violence against them.

Over the past two decades, public universities have provided spaces for the cultivation of a new moral radicalism of the left, contributing to a progressive cultural politics that has stretched the moral contours of Brazil's conservative society (Arantes, 2021; 2022a; 2022b). Broadly celebrated by the Partido dos Trabalhadores (Workers' Party—PT) during its time in government, between 2003 and 2016, this cultural politics was integrated into a social pact that promised freedom to consume for the poor and freedom to accumulate for the rich— a biopolitical pact to the extent that consumption enabled by targeted state assistance (that is, without fundamental challenges to neoliberal hegemony) was imagined as guaranteeing a humanitarian minimum of survival.

But behind the picture of class conciliation presented by the PT government, old authoritarian tendencies of the Brazilian state persisted. Initially accelerating the deindustrialization begun in the 1980s, the PT entrenched a neoextractivist model of development. It expanded Brazil's "agricultural frontier," offering lucrative contracts to private energy and construction firms and colluding in the violent displacement of vulnerable populations in the Amazon and elsewhere. Meanwhile, the long genocide of poor black Brazilians in metropolitan peripheries continued unabated, as the militarized "pacification" of favelas caused thousands of civilian deaths. As Giorgio Agamben (1998: 71–72) has argued, the biopolitical rationality that affirms a right to life also makes life more vulnerable. The preservation of certain lives comes to depend on the disposability of others. In Brazil, race plays a particularly important role, alongside class, in determining this distinction. As a biopolitical pact was consolidated under PT rule, Brazil's black proletariat remained subject to a necropolitics that has now been generalized under Bolsonaro.

During the years of PT government, affirmative action and freedom of cultural expression, complements to assistentialism, became bound up in the defense of a right to life. The PT viewed public universities as important sites for their promotion. But as the new right grew between the presidential elections of 2014 and 2018, providing a political base for Bolsonarismo—the movement ideologically committed to supporting Bolsonaro—it singled out the public university as a symbol of the left's corruption of Brazilian society. For Bolsonaro, attacks on the public university would become functional to a rupture with Brazil's biopolitical pact.[2]

The new right has positioned itself in opposition to established knowledge and science, which it associates with the cultural hegemony of the left. All scientific research carried out by public universities thus becomes subject to sweeping epistemological contestation. And as the negation of science enables deforestation, the deregulation of toxic pesticides, and the promotion of unproven treatment for COVID-19 pandemic, it becomes convenient to the interests of economic elites on whom Bolsonaro's government is politically dependent.

BRAZIL'S CULTURE WAR

The notion that society is trapped in a culture war has become a commonplace of Brazilian political commentary over the past few years. Brazilian progressives have generally viewed cultural antagonism as reflecting a substantively new configuration of politics, which, taking form in the Anglosphere and then spreading across capitalist democracies, arrived belatedly in Brazil in the aftermath of the 2013 mass protests.[3] The impression, then, is that cultural warfare has been visited upon Brazil and promoted by capital to fracture the erstwhile consensus on consumerist inclusion. While a departure from Bolsonaro's Manicheism, this outlook nonetheless presupposes political polarization. But, in contemporary Brazil, as Rodrigo Nunes (2020a) has argued, polarization is asymmetric or, rather, polarization of cultural preferences does not map onto polarization of ideological propositions.[4] Radically opposite moral projects now emanate from the far right, on the one hand, and an inflated political center, on the other. The suggestion of polarization thus tends to obscure the relationship between the moderation of the left and the eruption of cultural war.

When the PT came to power, in 2003, under the leadership of Luiz Inácio Lula da Silva, it sought to expand economic and social opportunities for the historically marginalized. The cost of efforts to universalize the right to life was then suppression of political challenges to capital. His government consolidated social protection, raised the minimum wage, and broadened access to higher education, while attracting financial speculators with world-beating real interest rates and launching national agribusiness and mining companies into the global commodities festival. Bank profits increased eightfold under Lula's government (*Veja*, 2014); poverty was reduced by more than 50 percent (*O Globo*, May 3, 2011).

Cultural change within public institutions became important to the PT's project of inclusion. Although certain institutions remained beholden to a conservative oligarchy—most obviously, those of the judiciary—a progressive, neomanagerial ethos became hegemonic in those most directly involved in the reproduction of mores—those responsible for arts and culture, education, media, and human rights, for example. Universities, in particular, became vehicles for the expansion of a public sphere presumed to protect the right to life. Changes in the racial and class composition of university graduates—accelerated after Lula's successor, Dilma Rousseff, expanded affirmative action, in 2012—contributed to the growth of the professional class, albeit without commensurate upgrading in the labor market.

Gramscian ideas gained influence within the PT in the 1980s. At its Fifth National Assembly, in 1987, the party recognized the centrality of electoral politics in the pursuit of hegemony; it accepted the possibility of transforming civil society through legislative and institutional reform (Secco, 2003). Once in government, the PT was able to consummate the new cultural hegemony of the left, partly through its concessions to neoliberal political economy. After two terms, Lula's approval by 87 percent of Brazilians seemed to represent not only vindication for the moral ideal of inclusion but also near-realization of this ideal. But, as Francisco de Oliveira (2006: 22) argued, the PT had achieved "hegemony in reverse": the dominant had ostensibly accepted the morality of the dominated, on condition that the form of capitalist relations not be questioned.

After the 2013 uprisings, in the run-up to the 2014 presidential election, as the right, cheered on by the news media, took to the streets, a principal charge leveled against the PT government was that it had "rigged" the state in its favor: Public bureaucracies had been filled with left-wing ideologues, who had built up a clientelistic network around the party, profiting from corruption and preventing a democratic alternation of power. New reactionary groups, such as Movimento Brasil Livre (Free Brazil Movement) and Vem Pra Rua (Come to the Streets), then popularized the notion that the left's penetration of public institutions was part of a Gramscian strategy. Although there was an element of truth in this, the suggestion that the success of this strategy had taken Brazil to the brink of a communist takeover was indicative of a conspiratorialism that would be used to radicalize the right-wing protest movement. The primary intellectual influence on these groups was Olavo de Carvalho, who for a couple of decades had been penning diatribes against the propagation of left-wing ideas by figures from across the political establishment. In 1994, he wrote of Gramsci as "a prophet of imbecility" and "a character who has never been to Brazil, who died half a century ago, and who secretly directs events in this part of the world" (Carvalho, 2014: 55). Carvalho, who died in 2022, saw as a serious threat the infiltration of institutions by what he referred to as a "Gramscian mafia" (1999). The Gramscian cultural revolution, he asserted, was more subtle and more effective than Leninist vanguardism: "It infiltrates imperceptibly and leads to the psychological domination of the multitudes" (2014: 57).

In 1986, members of the armed forces initiated Project Orvil (*livro* [book] spelled backwards), a secretive endeavor aimed at countering critical accounts of the military regime. The book they produced—now accessible online in its 966-page entirety—organizes Brazil's political history since 1922 according to four phases of communist strategy. In the last of these, beginning after the suppression of armed struggle in 1974, communists infiltrate institutions to bring about a cultural transformation that will enable them to gain power without the need for violent revolution. As João Cezar de Castro Rocha (2020) points out, if communism is presented as an ideology alien and inimical to national culture, then it must be combated as a matter of national security. Any Brazilian deemed sympathetic to communist transformation then becomes an internal enemy.

Jair Bolsonaro explicitly subscribes to this logic, and so do many of the military figures who occupied key posts in his government—not least the retired generals who feel betrayed by the democratic concessions of the later military governments and slighted by the 2012 National Truth Commission. According to Rocha, the narrative of Orvil, the logic of national security, and their contemporary dissemination through the fanaticism of Olavo de Carvalho and his disciples configure Brazil's contemporary culture war.

The accusation that the left has used politics to impose a transgressive culture (feminism, antiracism, LGBTQI+ and indigenous rights) on Brazilian society became decisive during the 2018 election. Playing to political disaffection and creeping religious moralism, the PT's opponents had connected a decline in living standards to the corruption of what they had imagined to be essential Brazilian values. Bolsonaro's candidacy then emerged as a mimetic response to those who, without expectation of social transformation, sought affirmation of what it meant to be Brazilian—what it meant to be a "good citizen." The normalization of his nihilistic will to extreme violence seemed to confirm that Brazil and politics as such had parted ways. And yet, Bolsonaro's unequivocal threat to a right to life somehow represented a radicalization of the logic through which life had been progressively politicized. Bolsonaro secured the support of capital through an opportunistic neoliberal turn, but it was cultural warfare that won him the election. And he then relied on cultural warfare to consolidate his social base. Continuing to demonize the Gramscian left, his allies in Congress and online themselves would speak of the necessity of waging a "war of position."

"CULTURAL MARXISM": ARCHENEMY OF BOLSONARISMO

While Bolsonaristas regard "Gramscianism" as a method of political subversion, they regard "cultural Marxism" as the ideology being spread by the left. In a 1999 essay denouncing cultural Marxism, the retired U.S. Navy commander Gerald L. Atkinson argued that, although the Cold War had ended abroad, young middle-class students had "converted the economic theory of Marx to culture in American society," promoting radical feminism, "so-called civil rights," and other countercultural agendas. These "draft-dodging, pot-smoking hippies" had drawn inspiration from the Frankfurt School, as well as Gramsci. Notwithstanding Atkinson's garbled synthesis of this intellectual history, his essay is of note on account of its publication in a series of essays on cultural Marxism by military personnel—and on account of its connection of themes that would become central to the discourse of the alt-right. The pursuit of cultural hegemony through the infiltration of institutions, he argued, was a "quiet revolution" whose ultimate goal was the destruction of "American civilization"—"the most vital and precious descendant of Western civilization." Atkinson's immediate concern was the influence of cultural Marxists on education, specifically in military academies.

Atkinson did not coin the term "cultural Marxism," but he was among the first to deploy it as invective.[5] He followed the paleoconservative commentator William S. Lind (1997; 2004) in equating cultural Marxism with political correctness. Both picked up on the role of postwar counterculture and the new left in reshaping the moral contours of American society. But they failed to recognize that the postmodern demand for recognition of subjective experience had emerged from an immanent critique of orthodox Marxism. They instead imagined that the use of a new moral technology to silence conservatives had been determined by a coordinated revision of revolutionary strategy.[6]

The critique of cultural Marxism was popularized and radicalized through the Tea Party and, more recently, the alt-right. Conservative movements themselves have thus assumed an increasingly revolutionary character in relation to the stasis of progressives. Recognizing them as a viable electoral base, Trump pointed to cultural Marxism, in its putative international manifestation—"globalism"—as the cause of America's civilizational malaise.[7] And yet, to the extent that globalism can be considered to exist, it is surely a predominantly American invention. Indeed, as ethno-nationalists outside the United States have denounced globalism, they have replicated, *mutatis mutandis*, an American critique of American universalism.

Olavo de Carvalho, who took up residency in the United States in 2005 and accompanied the rise of these conservative movements, was most prolific in adapting the critique of cultural Marxism and globalism to the Brazilian context. But, as with many of Brazil's cultural imports from the United States, this critique has been adapted as burlesque. Its conspiratorialist character is performatively exaggerated in the manner of an outsider seeking authoritative recognition. Vulgar and obscure conspiracy theories from the past are revived to implicate cultural Marxists in the production of threats that are more pervasive, more imminent, and more dangerous. Carvalho claimed that Pepsi used aborted human fetuses to sweeten its cola and that Theodor Adorno composed songs for the Beatles.

Haunted by the specter of cultural Marxism in recent years, segments of Brazil's new right have often invoked a transcendental logic. The growth of fundamentalism across the country—most obviously in the form of socially conservative evangelicalism but also in the form of dogmatic commitment to neoliberal reason—has surely contributed to this. It is fitting that those who adhere to a closed belief system that can sustain the gratuitous contortion of facts should anoint as their leader someone they refer to as Mito.

Bolsonarismo is not exactly an anti-intellectual movement. Indeed, the performance of erudition has been crucial in building support for its historical revisionism—on the military dictatorship, on Nazism, etc. Rather, it has positioned itself in opposition to established knowledge, scientific expertise, and liberal truths as products of left-wing cultural hegemony. Its belief system is then imagined as producing authentic knowledge, accessible to outsiders to elite education and mainstream media. While Bolsonaro's opposition to scientific evidence, on COVID-19 or climate change, is a gesture to certain economic elites, it is primarily aimed at reinforcing the belief system of his movement. Since he relies politically on cultural warfare—on government by symbols—this opposition must be progressively radicalized.

It is unsurprising, then, that education has become the primary battleground in Brazil's culture war. Early critiques of cultural Marxism in the United States bemoaned indoctrination in universities, and, across the Western world, universities have become sites of dispute over free speech and the soul of liberalism. For Bolsonaro, dismantling public universities, considered long-standing strongholds of the left, was instrumental to the maintenance of political power and denial of the right to life.

THE ATTACK ON THE HUMANITIES AND PAULO FREIRE

From 2005 on, increase in the number of public universities and campuses expanded the academic job market and improved access to higher education in the frontier zones of Brazilian capitalism—in the semiarid hinterlands, in the Amazon region, on the periphery of major cities (Marques and Cêpeda, 2012; Vinhais, 2013). University campuses themselves became more plural environments, as affirmative action addressed the historical underrepresentation of black, low-income, indigenous, and disabled students (Passos, 2015; Fonaprace, 2019). New and redesigned humanities courses challenged existing research methods and agendas, focusing particularly on race, gender, sexual orientation, violence, and dispossession; engagement with decolonial, feminist, antiracist, and queer theories shifted attention to epistemology. At the same time, these courses drew on Brazil's Marxist tradition, rooted in the 1950s, to question the country's incorporation into the financialized world economy.

No longer the preserve of the white cosmopolitan middle class, humanities faculties became sites of cultivation of a new multiethnic intellectuality that would radicalize the cultural politics of the Brazilian left, breaking free of the well-behaved consensualism of the PT. Once again, they became targets of right-wing vitriol, with cultural warriors of the new right, as well as military hard-liners, singling them out as centers for the dissemination of cultural Marxism. Following Bolsonaro's election, the humanities became the focus of government attempts to undermine the financial stability and moral integrity of public universities. Cuts in government funding for research and postgraduate scholarships have disproportionately affected the humanities.[8]

Incorporated into the new right's moral critique of the humanities is a suggestion that they are not just unproductive but counterproductive to the expansion of business and entrepreneurial culture. Bolsonaro's government favors a model of financing for higher education that would withdraw all public funding from the humanities. During a protest against the Supreme Court in June 2020, Minister of Education Abraham Weintraub said, "As a Brazilian, I don't want more sociologists, I don't want more anthropologists, I don't want more philosophers" (*O Estado de São Paulo*, April 30, 2019; and see political cartoon at https://www.diariodocentrodomundo.com.br/ministerio-da-educacao-de-bolsonaro-por-clayton/). He had questioned the utility of the humanities since his inauguration as minister, in April 2019. "Rather than Northeastern universities doing sociology, doing philosophy in the hinterlands," he affirmed at that moment, "[they should] do agronomy" (quoted in Souza, 2019).

The Northeast is one of the most culturally diverse regions of Brazil. And, with the lowest human development index value, it is also one of the poorest, mainly on account of the oligarchic concentration of land and power, uneven development, and drought.[9] For the very reason that it exists on the margins of Brazil's fitful process of modernization, it has been a cradle of popular culture and critical thought. It has also historically voted for left-wing politicians, and it is the epicenter of political resistance to Bolsonarismo. In the second round of the 2018 presidential election, Bolsonaro lost in all the Northeastern states, and in 2022 he lost in all by an even greater margin.

It is no coincidence that the figure most hated by Brazil's new right is an educator and philosopher from the Northeast: Paulo Freire (1921–1997), perhaps Brazil's most influential intellectual export.[10] As it took form on the streets, the new right marched under banners demonizing Paulo Freire. One of the most common read: "Enough of Marxist indoctrination! Enough of Paulo Freire!" The founder of Escola Sem Partido (School without Political Party)—a campaign of the new right to call out "ideological bias" in the classroom—has argued that Freire's teachings are antithetical to the Brazilian constitution. Bolsonaro has called the educator an "energumen" and an "idol of the left" (Mazul, 2019). Weintraub tried to remove a bust of Freire from the main entrance of the Ministry of Education. A congresswoman allied with the government introduced a bill to depose Freire as patron of Brazilian education.

Freire was already identified as a threat during the dictatorship. On October 18, 1964, a few days after he was forced into exile, he was accused by a military inquiry of being "one of the people most responsible for subverting the less fortunate . . . a crypto-communist in the form of a literacy teacher."[11] For the new right, Paulo Freire has become symbolic of a three-tiered threat to Brazilian society: cultural Marxism, paving the way for an ascent of the masses and then for communism. His connection to liberation theology is taken as proof of his perversion of traditional morality. Eduardo Bolsonaro, a congressman and son of the president, has referred to him as the "Brazilian version of Antonio Gramsci."

But do humanities scholars, armed with the pedagogy of Paulo Freire, pose a sufficient threat to the political project of the new right to warrant their nomination as primary targets of cultural warfare? To be sure, their very existence challenges the new right's own designs on cultural hegemony and, by extension, the promotion of its political and economic reason. Despite a generalized commodification of expertise over recent decades, the humanities lend themselves less readily to the logic of market expansion. Indeed, predominantly progressive, humanities scholars in Brazil's public universities have tended to defend a conception of knowledge as a public good in itself, and therefore they have defended the autonomy of universities and freedom of thought. In the name of life and citizenship, they have often opposed the state and parastate violence, environmental depredation, precarization of labor, and religious intolerance promoted by Bolsonaro, and they have collaborated with the social movements, nongovernmental organizations, and multilateral institutions he seeks to criminalize. Most notably, perhaps, the humanities provide methods for critically engaging with the world—with historical processes, with human imagination, with facts. As humanities faculties produce teachers, artists, journalists, politicians, and activists, it is not only the spread of a particular progressive morality that threatens Brazil's new right but also the possibility of critique, which undermines authoritarian impositions and distortions.

BEDLAM! MORAL CONDEMNATION AND DECLINISM

Weintraub's predecessor, Ricardo Vélez Rodríguez, had been appointed as Bolsonaro's first minister of education on the recommendation of Olavo de Carvalho. A former professor at one of Brazil's main military academies and a long-standing opponent of progressive morality—in an interview in 2004 he criticized "the politically correct globalism that put forward the crazy proposal of 'gender education'" (Faermann, 2018)—he had taken office vowing to combat cultural Marxism.[12] But he had been dismissed three months later, purportedly because he lacked managerial experience.

Weintraub—a banking executive with limited academic credentials—would more clearly articulate the economic justification for culture warfare in the vernacular of neoliberal management. His first notable intervention following his inauguration was the announcement of budget cuts for federal universities causing "bedlam" (*balbúrdia*), "messing around, holding ridiculous events, with landless activists on campus, people naked on campus" (*O Estado de São Paulo*, April 30, 2019; and see screen capture from YouTube at https://www.youtube.com/watch?v=7C_qJnd5fT8). His criteria were questioned by the provosts and academic communities of the first three universities to face cuts. All three had exemplary performance indicators and had recently climbed the university rankings but had 20 percent of their discretionary budgets summarily blocked (Agostini, 2019). Over the following days, funding was suspended for all 68 federal universities. Universities would be granted full access to their budgets only after two major nationwide protests in defense of public education, in May and August 2019.

Among other unsubstantiated accusations against universities, Weintraub later suggested that they were cultivating "vast marijuana plantations" and using chemistry laboratories to produce "synthetic drugs and methamphetamines" (quoted in Bermúdez, 2019). In response, the União Nacional dos Estudantes (National Union of Students—UNE) filed a civil suit for defamation against the minister, who was ordered to pay R$50,000 to a federal fund. Weintraub was eventually forced out of the ministry after the publication of a recording of a ministerial meeting in which he recommended arresting members of the Supreme Court. He flew to the United States, apparently to escape investigation, and took up the post of regional director at the World Bank.

Over the coming days, two people were put forward to replace Weintraub and then discarded, one after being officially named minister. Neither was a cultural warrior, as Weintraub and Vélez Rodríguez had been, and the debacle exposed a struggle for control of the ministry between factions within the government. One of the two, Carlos Decotelli, a professor at the Naval Academy, had been put forward by senior military figures.[13] His nomination seemed indicative of the political ascendancy of the military. However, news networks were soon tipped off about inaccuracies in Decotelli's CV. It turned out that he had falsely claimed to have completed doctoral and postdoctoral studies. Two days after his nomination, he resigned, and the military lost an opportunity to capture the Ministry of Education.[14]

The installation as minister of Milton Ribeiro, a Protestant pastor, confirmed that, for now, education would remain a cultural battleground. During a sermon in 2018, Ribeiro had condemned public universities for encouraging "sexual practices totally without limits." "It doesn't matter," he had explained, "whether it is a man or a woman, this one or that one, old or young, what matters is the moment. . . . This is what they are teaching our children in universities" (UOL, 2020b). The new minister also attacked Freire: "I had the patience to read his most famous text, *The Pedagogy of the Oppressed*. I challenge a scholar to explain where he wants to go with his metaphors. He transplants values of Marxism and tries to instill them in teaching and pedagogy" (*Gazeta do Povo*, October 4, 2020).

In 2021, Ribeiro attempted to intervene in the national examination for access to superior education. Three years earlier Bolsonaro had criticized the inclusion of a question regarding homosexuality and transsexuality, and he had then continuously demanded that the exam reflect the moral values of his government. When Ribeiro eventually authorized the federal police to monitor the development of the exam, 37 senior members of the body responsible for administering the exam renounced their roles, claiming that they had been subject to harassment. One of them denounced the censorship of more than 20 questions by the body's president on behalf of the government. He noted that there had been particular interference with questions relating to Brazilian history over the past 50 years, covering the period of military dictatorship (SoU_Ciência, 2021).

During the ministerial meeting that led to Weintraub's demise, he had digressed toward another gripe of the new right. "I hate the term 'indigenous people,'" he railed; "I hate the 'gypsy people.' There is only one people in this country—the Brazilian people. . . . [Let's] end this affair of different peoples and their privileges" (Simon, 2020). Weintraub's aggressive opposition to multiculturalism is characteristic of a resurgent white nationalist discourse that attributes progress to the same rulers who upheld the legality of slavery longer than any country on earth. His last act before leaving the ministry was to suspend the postgraduate quota policy in federal universities.

Quotas for undergraduate courses, written into law in 2012, radically changed the profile of students at the most prestigious public universities. According to the Forúm Nacional de Pró-Reitores de Assuntos Comunitários e Estudantis (Brazilian National Forum of Vice Provosts for Community and Student Affairs), quotas increased the proportion of black and indigenous students in undergraduate cohorts from 36.2 percent in 2003 to 53.5 percent in 2018 (Fonaprace, 2019). They also notably improved access for students from low and lower-middle income families, who constituted 42.8 percent of the undergraduate student body in 2003 and 70.1 percent in 2018 (Arantes, 2021).

Cultural polarization cannot be neatly explained according to class distinctions, but class interests nonetheless underlie and shape the discursive struggles of the culture war. That, for the first time, affluent whites might be displaced from the intellectual vanguard of Brazilian society surely provokes their collective anxiety—if not resentment. Indeed, such sentiments are manifest in declinist narratives reproduced by the new right, according to which Brazil's public universities have fallen into decay. In fact, Brazil ranks twelfth in the world in terms of academic research and had the fifth-highest average research growth rate between 2008 and 2018.[15] According to the 2020 *Times Higher Education Ranking for Latin America*, 16 of the region's top 25 universities are Brazilian, and 14 of those are public. The ideology of declinists is exposed by their frequent assertion that Brazil's public universities have been overtaken by private universities. Bolsonaro himself has claimed that "few [Brazilian] universities have research, and, of those few, the majority are in the private sector" (Moura, 2019). But, according to the Brazilian Academy of Science, 95 percent of research in Brazil is produced by public universities (Moura, 2019), and of the country's top 20 universities in terms of research and quality of teaching 18 are public (*Times*, 2020).

THE ATTACK ON UNIVERSITY AUTONOMY

During the week before Bolsonaro was elected president, in October 2018, more than two dozen universities were targeted by police operations purportedly aimed at preventing the dissemination of electoral propaganda by public institutions. In a telling demonstration of the political allegiance of Brazil's military police and of the electoral judges who authorized the operations, manifestations in defense of democracy were deemed favorable to Bolsonaro's opponent, the PT's Fernando Haddad, who was minister of education under Lula. Evoking memories of censorship and political persecution during the military dictatorship, police tore down banners, interrupted classes, public debates, and protests, collected statements and personal information without warrants, and even detained students and teachers (Saldaña, 2018). Two days before the election, Supreme Court Justice Carmen Lúcia signed a precautionary measure preventing police interventions on university campuses. A few weeks later, the Supreme Court reiterated the constitutional principle of university autonomy and restricted the activity of state security forces in all public universities.

Faced with this obstacle to direct repression, Bolsonaro undermined the autonomy of public universities by interfering in their nomination of rectors[16] and in their democratic management procedures (established in accordance with Article 206 of the Brazilian constitution). Although Brazilian law grants the president the right to appoint rectors, it is conventional for the president to accept the nominations of university councils based on consultation with their academic communities. During his first two years in power, Bolsonaro appointed 14 rectors not nominated by universities, opting for candidates aligned with the ideology of his government. He also placed five universities under temporary external management in cases in which nomination processes were questioned.

In the hope of overriding the protocol for nominating rectors, Bolsonaro enacted two "provisional measures" (emergency measures that do not require congressional approval). The first remained in force for the maximum period of four months, allowing the government to nominate rectors without regard for the lists presented by university councils, and was rejected by Congress at the end of this period. A few weeks later, the government passed another, granting the Ministry of Education the power to name temporary rectors where the standard nomination process had been interrupted by the COVID-19 pandemic. After only 48 hours, Davi Alcolumbre, president of the Senate at the time and occasional ally of Bolsonaro, took the unusual step of suspending the measure, arguing that it represented an attack on the autonomy and democratic management of universities (UOL, 2020a). In October 2020, the Supreme Court began an inquiry into the legality of Bolsonaro's disregard for the nomination of rectors by university communities.

Under Bolsonaro, the federal government also notably increased surveillance of public sector workers, from police officials to academics. The Secretariat for Integrated Police Operations, established ostensibly to coordinate national police investigations, focused on monitoring members of "antifascist movements" (Valente, 2020). The government held dossiers on the political activity of more than 1,000 public sector workers, which it shared with military intelligence agencies. There were already loopholes in Brazilian antiterror law that could be used to justify political repression as a preventive measure. University teachers were victims of political persecution, outsourced to new-right activist groups, or dressed up as investigators of criminal misconduct.

University managers were subject to legal investigations that adopt the methods of Operation Car Wash—a highly politicized investigation into corruption involving the national oil company, Petrobras, and politicians from Brazil's largest parties. The aggressive condemnation-by-media characteristic of Operation Car Wash was used to undermine university management in the tragic and emblematic case against Luiz Carlos Cancellier, the rector of the Universidade Federal de Santa Catarina. Cancellier was arrested in 2017, accused of involvement in the illegal diversion of university funds. He was placed in preventive detention, despite there being no evidence that he was attempting to impede investigations. Freed a few days later, he was then prohibited from entering the university without police escort. Humiliated and demoralized, he committed suicide. "My death was decreed when I was banned from the university," he wrote in his suicide note (Charleaux, 2018).

Despite the shock caused by Cancellier's death and despite the absence of incriminating evidence against him, those involved in the investigation against the university showed no sign of remorse.[17] Erika Marena, the police chief leading the investigation and a former member of the Operation Car Wash prosecuting task force, was subsequently promoted to a role advising Bolsonaro's justice minister, Sérgio Moro (who had been the leading judge in Operation Car Wash and had controversially sentenced Lula to prison, preventing him from running for president in 2018). Staff at Cancellier's university who questioned the conduct of investigators were threatened with defamation charges. A few months after Cancellier's death, the federal police broke with due process once again, this time targeting the Universidade Federal de Minas Gerais, the country's highest-ranking federal university. University vice provosts and a former rector were preventively detained without any indication that there was proof against them (Rodrigues, 2017).

In the first month of the Bolsonaro government, Sérgio Moro and Ricardo Vélez Rodríguez, then minister of education, signed an order for an inquest into institutions of higher education. Bolsonaro referred to it as the "Car Wash for Education." However, it was later discreetly abandoned, and it disappeared from the news media. It had been intended as an investigation not only into public universities but also into public subsidies for private universities— "undue favors, embezzlement, the illegal granting of scholarships" (Gomes, 2019). The day after the investigation was announced, shares in private education dropped 7 percent, provoking a dip on the Brazilian stock exchange. Weintraub later claimed that announcement of the investigation would have "alerted education companies and their managers, who could have rushed to destroy any evidence" (Formenti, 2019).

The private education lobby had been responsible for the stillbirth of the Car Wash for Education. Elizabeth Guedes, president of the Associação Brasileira de Mantenedoras de Ensino Superior (Brazilian Association for Private Universities) and sister of Bolsonaro's powerful minister of the economy, Paulo Guedes, had acted against it. Guedes is himself an investor in private distance learning, and he has been the central figure in determining cuts to federal university budgets that create opportunities for the expansion of private higher education (Console, 2019). He is also being investigated by the Public Prosecutor's Office and the federal police on the charge that he defrauded state pension funds to favor his own companies, among them the investment fund BR Educacional (*Forúm*, 2020).

Although the inquest into higher education was scrapped, public universities remained subject to monitoring by the Federal Court of Accounts (Tribunal de Contas da União). Heightened scrutiny of university management in 2022 produced no evidence of the misuse of public funding. However, in March Ribeiro was revealed to have authorized a kickback scheme involving evangelical pastors, who were granted privileged access to negotiations of the allocation of funds through municipal governments (BBC Brasil, 2022; and see political cartoon at https://acasadevidro.com/bolsofascistas-no-poder/). The scandal forced Bolsonaro to exonerate Ribeiro, who was subsequently imprisoned.

CUTTING THE PUBLIC UNIVERSITY

In 2016, Dilma Rousseff's political opponents used accounting irregularities as a dubious but viable pretext to impeach her. Soon afterwards, the government of Michel Temer passed a constitutional amendment that placed a 20-year freeze on public spending except for inflation adjustments. Investment in education and health had steadily increased during Lula's two terms in office and Dilma's first. But it had stagnated in 2014, as the Brazilian economy entered an economic recession from which it has not since recovered—partly on account of the constitutional restriction on the use of government spending to stimulate aggregate demand.

Between 2014 and 2021, government funding for the maintenance of all 68 federal universities (excluding staff salaries) decreased by 73 percent, from R$10.2 billion to R$3.7 billion (according to the SoU_Ciência HE Public Budget Data Board; see Figure 1). The provision of basic services on campus, such as cleaning and security, has decreased, and low-paid service workers on precarious contracts have been dismissed. The investment budget of universities fell from R$3.16 billion to R$35 million. University buildings have fallen into disrepair and planned construction work has been suspended. Over the same period, there was a 59 percent drop in government expenditure on research and postgraduate programs, grants, and scholarships. The Conselho Nacional de Desenvolvimento Científico e Tecnológico (National Council for Scientific and Technological Development—CNPq) and the Coordenação de Aperfeiçoamento

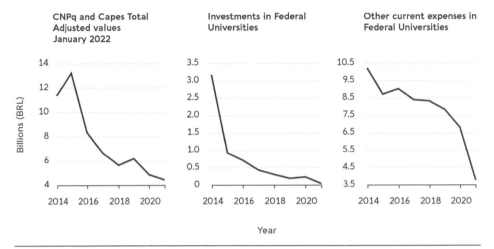

Figure 1. The decline in research funds and graduate scholarships by CNPq and CAPES *(left)*, **in investment (buildings, equipment and libraries)** *(middle)*, **and in the maintenance budgets of federal public universities** *(right)*, **in billions of reais, adjusted annually according to the IPCA, 2014–2021 (data from the National Treasury treated by Sou_Ciência Research Center).**

de Pessoal de Nível Superior (Coordination for the Improvement of Higher Education—CAPES) have had 61 percent of their funding cut since 2014.

Previously presented as an unfortunate necessity of economic management, cuts to public universities were presented by the Bolsonaro government with Panglossian enthusiasm. For Guedes, a protégé of Chile's "Chicago Boys," minimization of state expenditure is an ideological preference. While promoting reductions in university budgets and personnel, he called for the introduction of tuition fees, private financing of university programs, and competitive bidding for the provision of all nonacademic services within universities.[18] This is in keeping with World Bank recommendations set out in *A Fair Adjustment* (2017), according to which universities should follow the model of private financing in place in the United States since the late 1970s.

In May 2019, Weintraub announced a 30 percent cut in the discretionary budgets of federal universities. In the following days, the shares of Brazil's six largest private higher education companies registered an increase, while the Bovespa (São Paulo's stock market) was in decline. A week later demonstrations against the Bolsonaro governments in several cities drew more than 1 million. In July, Weintraub launched Future-se, a program that promised to "strengthen the financial autonomy of universities." "Financial autonomy," here, entailed a responsibility to raise funds independently, which implied a significant reduction in the academic autonomy of public universities. The program would have transformed them into sites of entrepreneurial activity and business consultancy, where research would be produced to meet the demands of the private sector. Universities would be free to treat campuses as real estate and issue securities in financial markets. The program would create barriers to tenure for university teachers, who would preferably be hired by private foundations and companies, through short-term contracts (Leher et al., 2020).

Bolsonaro's government also promoted distance learning as a means of cutting costs and expanding the profits of the private sector. Private higher education institutions had already been transitioning to a business model that prioritized virtual education—a process accelerated by the COVID-19 pandemic. Distance learning reduces expenditure on infrastructure and personnel; it encourages the organization of teaching into distinct products, accessible to students at their own convenience; lessons and learning materials can therefore be competitively bid, and permanent teaching staff become disposable (Sousa, 2019). In December 2019, Bolsonaro's government raised the limit for online components in on-campus courses from 20 percent to 40 percent.

That same month, federal universities and institutes, student unions, and social movements in São Paulo launched a manifesto entitled "Toward Another Future," challenging the government's plans for public education (Sudré, 2019). Those who blazed a trail into public universities for historically excluded groups have been called upon to defend the space they have come to occupy. Unions, scientific research associations, professional colleges, and civic movements also have an important role to play in mobilizing society in defense of public education, highlighting its relevance to the development of a more just and democratic society.

CONCLUSION: DEFENDING PUBLIC UNIVERSITIES, RESISTING ANNIHILATION

The COVID-19 pandemic exposed the frailty of the biopolitical pact through which liberal-democratic states have restricted political subjectivities with the promise of life. In Brazil, where the reproduction of "unpolitical" populations extends the legacies of slavery and colonial expropriation, the state has always treated a great many lives as disposable, even when this injustice is drowned out by celebration of the social diffusion of consumer power. Under the PT, public universities became spaces of social and cultural innovation that challenged the historical discrimination through which such injustice is rationalized (Arantes, 2021).

Sustained by a paroxysmal politics of annihilation, Bolsonaro found in the COVID-19 pandemic an opportunity to contest epistemological order and hasten a rupture with Brazil's fragile biopolitical pact. This rupture implies a disappearance of universities from the public sphere—the transformation of higher education into a private consumer good and its disconnection from social and civic goods that might protect a right to life. But that this was in the interests of certain segments of capital was of concern to Bolsonaro only because maintenance of their support was politically expedient.

Political power (along with the material benefits and legal protection this provides him and his family) was Bolsonaro's primary concern when inciting cultural warfare. And he responded to political challenges by intensifying his assault on public universities. In August 2020, as Brazil's official death toll from COVID-19 surpassed 100,000, the government informed rectors of federal universities that, in 2021, there would be a further cut of 18.2 percent in their unrestricted budgets, which are used to cover operating costs (Amaral, 2020). In October 2022, as Bolsonaro trailed Lula in the presidential race, he once again blocked university maintenance budgets, even withdrawing funds from federal university accounts, but the public universities' decisive response to the prospect of their collapse has demonstrated a capacity to resist.

Rather than readily accepting a transition from face-to-face undergraduate education to distance learning, public universities have increased the provision of open and extracurricular courses. They have reached beyond the academic community, organizing online debates and establishing solidarity networks that provide health care, including psychological support. Thus the continuation of many university activities, even at the height of the pandemic, contributed to the development of an open university model.

Public universities played an important role in disseminating scientifically grounded information on the epidemiology of COVID-19. Within three months of the virus's reaching Brazil, federal universities launched 1,200 research projects focused on prevention, diagnosis, and treatment, on hospital management, and on the implications for education, work, and income. They were also involved in the development of vaccines, many in partnership with scientific communities abroad.[19] Public university laboratories have been adapted to increase the production of ventilators, personal protective equipment, and basic medication. And, for the first time, all of the country's university hospitals have come together to establish a collective procurement system.

After Bolsonaro's defeat by Lula in the presidential election of October 2022, there exists an opportunity for government to reinforce the resistance of public universities to the predation of capital. But Lula, for whom conciliation is an ideal rather than a tactic, faces numerous challenges to changing the course of government policy. He will seek to satisfy the diverse demands of the very broad political coalition that accompanied him on his path to electoral victory. He will need to manage the expectations of a divided society, vulnerable to the manipulations of Bolsonaro's base, which refuses to accept defeat and will continue to petition for a military coup. And he will need to redress the devastation of state institutions—in particular those responsible for education, science and technology, health, the environment and the demarcated indigenous territories, culture, and human rights—by reversing recent laws that limit government spending.

If Lula is to reconstruct the state, he will need to reidentify the priorities of government while uniting and empowering his social base. To be sure, this is not an agenda of transformation. Nonetheless, it is one that can put the brakes on the social disintegration accelerated by Bolsonaro, reaffirming the essential, if minimum, value of human life. Its fortune may well be indicative of the possibilities of resisting and even overcoming contemporary necropolitical regimes elsewhere in the world. Brazil has been a laboratory for the spoliation practiced amidst modernity's collapse. Might it yet, then, show a more hopeful future to all those who, facing an impasse, nonetheless struggle to construct new pathways—new *alamedas*[20]—to a better society?

NOTES

1. Following Adam Przeworski, André Singer (2020) uses the phrase "furtive authoritarianism" to describe a process through which liberal democracies are being eroded from within, by stealth. This plays down the overt and cathartic celebration of antidemocratic violence through which new authoritarian movements have established a popular base, even if only in the critical moment of electoral disputes.

2. Rodrigo Nunes (2020b) argues that, through their fatally negligent response to COVID-19, the administrations of Bolsonaro in Brazil and Donald Trump in the United States, in particular, are experimenting with a mode of government that breaks from a putative biopolitical pact.

3. In one of the first articles to discuss Brazil's culture war, published in 2014, Pablo Ortellado made a case for its novelty. James Davison Hunter's *Culture Wars: The Struggle to Define America* (1991) is often cited as providing the terms of opposition between progressive and "orthodox" cultural positions.

4. Nunes draws on an interview with Paulo Arantes (Lucena, 2014) in his discussion of this asymmetric polarization. According to Arantes, "The official left in Brazil is moderate. The other side is not moderate."

5. The editor of *Telos*, Trent Schoyer, seems to have been the first to write of "cultural Marxism," in reference to the critical theory of the Frankfurt School (1973). Martin Jay (2011) suggests that the "opening salvo" in the attack on cultural Marxism came from a follower of the conspiratorialist Lyndon Larouche, Michael Minnicino, who in 1992 published an essay associating the Frankfurt School with political correctness. Iná Camargo Costa (2020) roots the critique of cultural Marxism in Hitler's attack on "cultural Bolshevism," which he imagined as a Jewish conspiracy. Samuel Moyn (2018) also argues that "the wider discourse around cultural Marxism today resembles nothing so much as a version of the Judeobolshevik myth updated for a new age."

6. Atkinson relies on a superficial reading of Herbert Marcuse to validate his argument on the unity of the new revolutionary struggle. Marcuse had written that "the traditional idea of revolution and the traditional strategy of revolution has [*sic*] ended" (2005: 124). Marcuse has become a favorite target of contemporary critics of cultural Marxism. He is also referenced in Project Orvil.

7. "The future does not belong to globalists," he said, during his speech to the United Nations General Assembly in September 2019.

8. This is demonstrated by figures published by the Associação Nacional de Pós-Graduados (National Association of Graduate Students—ANPG). http://www.anpg.org.br/16/07/2020/sem-cota-emprestimo-portaria-34-cortaria-bolsas-em-todas-as-areas-do-conhecimento/.

9. The so-called Northeastern Question is one of the classic themes of the social sciences and development studies in Brazil, addressed by Celso Furtado, Inácio Rangel, Francisco de Oliveira, and Victor Nunes Leal, among others.

10. Freire's *Pedagogy of the Oppressed* (1970) has been published in more than 20 languages. According to a 2016 study by Elliott Green of the London School of Economics, it is the third-most-cited work in the humanities worldwide, ahead of works by Michel Foucault and Karl Marx. https://blogs.lse.ac.uk/impactofsocialsciences/2016/05/12/what-are-the-most-cited-publications-in-the-social-sciences-according-to-google-scholar/.

11. The inquiry was led by Lieutenant Colonel Hélio Ibiapina Lima, who was later named by the National Truth Commission as having committed human rights violations during the years of military rule (Haddad, 2019).

12. Vélez Rodríguez (see 2006) had been protesting the influence of left-wing ideology on education for many years.

13. More than 6,000 members of the armed forces occupy positions in government, and Bolsonaro has appeared increasingly politically dependent on the senior generals who surround him.

14. Decotelli's resignation triggered a public debate about structural racism in Brazil. He would have been the country's first black minister of education and the only black minister in Bolsonaro's government. At least four of Bolsonaro's other ministers have lied in their CVs without being subjected to the same scrutiny. As Decotelli pointed out, "There are many white people with imperfections in their curriculums working without disturbing anyone" (Bermúdez, 2020).

15. This ranking is produced by the National Center for Science and Engineering Statistics of the National Science Foundation and is based on publication in peer-reviewed science and engineering journals, books, and conference proceedings. https://www.nsf.gov/statistics/2019/nsf19317/overview.htm.

16. We use the term "rector" to refer to the most senior official in university administration, known in Brazil as the *reitor*. This official is equivalent to the president in most U.S. universities and the vice chancellor in most UK universities.

17. No evidence was presented against Cancellier in either the 6,000-page inquiry or the 800-page final report of the investigation.

18. After the Bolsonaro government's pension reform was approved by the lower house of Congress, Guedes endorsed a proposal by Weintraub to reduce the budget of public universities, introduce tuition fees, and promote private financing (*Forúm*, 2019). This proposal gave rise to the Future-se project.

19. A data board entitled "Federal Universities in Defense of Life" produced by SoU_Ciência Research Center in partnership with Associação Nacional dos Dirigentes das Instituções Federais de Ensino Superior (National Association of Directors of Federal Higher Education Institutions—ANDIFES) summarizes the activities of Brazil's federal universities in response to the COVID-19 pandemic. https://souciencia.unifesp.br/paineis/universidadesemdefesadavida/.

20. This is a reference to the final speech of Salvador Allende, given shortly before his death, in September 1973: "Go forward knowing that, sooner rather than later, the great avenues [*las grandes alamedas*] through which the free man will walk to build a better society will open again."

REFERENCES

ADUSP (Associação Docente da Universidade de São Paulo)
    2020 "Demissões em massa nas universidades particulares atestam conversão acelerada para modalidade EaD e sinalizam desemprego estrutural dos docentes." July 14. https://www.adusp.org.br/index.php/defesa-do-ensino-publico/3744-demissoes-em-massa-nas-univ-ersidades-particulares-atestam-conversao-acelerada-para-modalidade-ead-e-sinalizam-des-emprego-estrutural-dos-docentes.
Agamben, Giorgio
    1998 *Homo Sacer: Sovereign Power and Bare Life*. Stanford, CA: Stanford University Press
Agostini, Renata
    2019 "Universidades acusadas de balbúrdia tiveram melhora de avaliação em ranking inter-nacional." *O Estado de São Paulo*, April 30. https://educacao.estadao.com.br/noticias/geral,universidades-acusadas-de-balburdia-tiveram-melhora-de-avaliacao-em-ranking-inter-nacional,70002810148.
Amaral, Luciana
    2020 "MEC deve cortar R$1,4bi de verba de universidades e institutos em 2021." UOL, August 10. https://educacao.uol.com.br/noticias/2020/08/07/mec-deve-cortar-18-do-orcamento-de-universidades-e-institutos-em-2021.htm.
Arantes, Pedro
    2021 "Higher education in dark times: from the democratic renewal of Brazilian universities to its current wreck." *Policy Reviews in Higher Education* 5: 1–27. doi: https://doi.org/10.1080/23322969.2021.1872412.
    2022a "Brazilian universities under attack: from the biopolitical pact to the necropopulist moment." *Critical Times* 5 (1): 97–108. doi: https://doi.org/10.1215/26410478-9536500.
    2022b "From Red São Paulo to Brazilian neofascism: urban, political and cultural heritage in the making of a public university," pp. 269–295 in Clare Melhuish et al. (eds.), *Co-curating the City: Universities and Urban Heritage Past and Future*. London: UCL Press.
Atkinson, Gerald
    1999 "What is the Frankfurt School (and its effect on America)?" in *"Cultural Marxism" at the U.S. Naval Academy*. http://wethepeopleradiorecords.com/20170903/WhatistheFrankfurtSchoolDr.GeraldAtkinson1999.pdf.
BBC Brasil
    2022 "Milton Ribeiro é preso pela PF: entenda o escândalo no MEC envolvendo ex-ministro e pastores." June. https://www.bbc.com/portuguese/brasil-61900067.
Bermúdez, Ana Carla
    2019 "Sem provas, Weintraub diz que federais têm plantações extensivas de maconha." UOL, November 22. https://educacao.uol.com.br/noticias/2019/11/22/weintraub-ha-plantacoes-extensivas-de-maconha-em-universidades-federais.htm.
    2020 "Decotelli: Brancos trabalham com imperfeições em curriculo sem incomodar." UOL, July 1. https://educacao.uol.com.br/noticias/2020/07/01/decotelli-brancos-trabalham-com-imperfeicoes-em-curriculo-sem-incomodar.htm.

Costa, Iná Camargo
2020 *Dialética do Marxismo cultural*. São Paulo: Expressão Popular.
Carvalho, Olavo de
1999 "Máfia Gramsciana." *Jornal da Tarde*, November 25. https://olavodecarvalho.org/mafia-gramsciana/.
2014 *A nova era e a revolução cultural: Fritjof Capra e Antonio Gramsci*. São Paulo: Vide Editorial.
Charleaux, João Paulo
2018 "Quais os questionamentos à Polícia Federal no caso Cancellier." *Nexo*, August 6. https://www.nexojornal.com.br/expresso/2018/08/06/Quais-os-questionamentos-%C3%A0-Pol%C3%ADcia-Federal-no-caso-Cancellier.
Console, Luciana
2019 "Como a associação liderada pela irmã de Paulo Guedes se beneficia de cortes no ensino." *Brasil de Fato*, May 9. https://www.brasildefato.com.br/2019/05/09/como-a-associacao-liderada-pela-irma-de-paulo-guedes-se-beneficia-de-cortes-no-ensino.
Faermann, Patricia
2018 "O novo Ministro da Educação contra os moinhos de Marx e Gramsci." *GGN*, November 24. https://jornalggn.com.br/artigos/o-novo-ministro-da-educacao-contra-os-moinhos-de-marx-e-gramsci/.
Fonaprace (Forúm Nacional de Pró-Reitores se Assuntos Comunitários e Estudantis)
2019 "5ª pesquisa do perfil socioeconômico e cultural dos estudantes de graduação." http://www.andifes.org.br/wp-content/uploads/2019/05/V-Pesquisa-do-Perfil-Socioecon%C3%B4mico-dos-Estudantes-de-Gradua%C3%A7%C3%A3o-das-Universidades-Federais-1.pdf.
Formenti, Ligia
2019 "Governo abandona ideia de 'Lava Jato da Educação.'" *Estadão*, November 5. https://politica.estadao.com.br/noticias/geral,governo-abandona-ideia-de-lava-jato-da-educacao,70003076114.
Forúm
2019 "Após reforma da Previdência, Bolsonaro deve anunciar projeto que inicia privatização das universidades públicas." July 11. https://revistaforum.com.br/politica/apos-reforma-da-previdencia-bolsonaro-deve-anunciar-projeto-que-inicia-privatizacao-das-universidades-publicas/.
2020 "Polícia Federal mira Paulo Guedes em investigação por crime de fraude bilionária em fundos de pensão estatais." July 5. https://revistaforum.com.br/politica/bolsonaro/policia-federal-mira-paulo-guedes-em-investigacao-por-crime-de-fraude-bilionaria-em-fundos-de-pensao-estatais/.
Freire, Paulo
1970 *Pedagogy of the Oppressed*. New York: Continuum.
Gomes, Wagner
2019 "Lava-Jato da Educação derruba ações de empresas no setor." *Estadão*, February 15. https://economia.estadao.com.br/noticias/mercados,lava-jato-da-educacao-derruba-acoes-de-empresas-do-setor,70002723340.
Haddad, Sérgio
2019 "Por que o Brasil de Olavo e Bolsonaro vê em Paulo Freire um inimigo." *Folha de São Paulo*, April 14. https://www1.folha.uol.com.br/ilustrissima/2019/04/por-que-o-brasil-de-olavo-e-bolsonaro-ve-em-paulo-freire-um-inimigo.shtml.
Hunter, James Davison
1991 *Culture Wars: The Struggle to Define America*. New York: Basic Books.
Jay, Martin
2011 "Dialectic of counter-Enlightenment: the Frankfurt School as scapegoat of the lunatic fringe." *Salmagundi* 168-9: 30–40.
Leher, Roberto et al.
2020 *Future-se: Ataque à autonomia das instituições federais de educação superior e sua sujeição ao mercado*. São Carlos: Diagrama.
Lind, William
1997 "What is 'political correctness'?" *Essays on Our Times* 43 (March).
2004 *"Political Correctness": A Short History of an Ideology*. Washington, DC: Free Congress Foundation.

Lucena, Eleonora de
2014 "Nova direita surgiu após junho, diz filósofo." *Folha de São Paulo*, October 31.
Marcuse, Herbert
2005 "On the new left," pp. 122–127 in Douglas Kellner (ed.), *The New Left and the 1960s: Collected Papers of Herbert Marcuse*. Vol.3. London: Routledge.
Marques, Antonio Carlos and Vera Alves Cêpeda
2012 "Um perfil sobre a expansão do ensino superior recente no Brasil: aspectos democráticos e inclusivos." *Perspectivas* 42: 161–192.
Mazul, Guilherme
2019 "Bolsonaro chama Paulo Freire de 'energúmeno' e diz que TV Escola 'deseduca.'" UOL, December 16. https://g1.globo.com/politica/noticia/2019/12/16/bolsonaro-chama-paulo-freire-de-energumeno-e-diz-que-tv-escola-deseduca.ghtml.
Minnicino, Michael
1992 "The New Dark Age: the Frankfurt School and 'political correctness.'" *Fidelio* 1 (1). Reprint. https://www.schillerinstitute.com/fid_91-96/921_frankfurt.html.
Moura, Mariluce
2019 "Universidades públicas respondem por mais de 95% da produção científica do Brasil." *Ciência na Rua*, April 11. https://ciencianarua.net/universidades-publicas-respondem-por-mais-de-95-da-producao-cientifica-do-brasil/.
Moyn, Samuel
2018 "The alt-right's favorite meme is 100 years old." *New York Times*, November 13. https://www.nytimes.com/2018/11/13/opinion/cultural-marxism-anti-semitism.html.
Nunes, Rodrigo
2020a "Todo lado tem dois lados." *Revista Serrote*, March. https://www.revistaserrote.com.br/2020/06/todo-lado-tem-dois-lados-por-rodrigo-nunes/.
2020b "Necropolítica de Bolsonaro aponta para um futuro distópico." *Folha de São Paulo*, June 18. https://www1.folha.uol.com.br/ilustrissima/2020/06/vidas-de-negros-e-pobres-se-tornam-descartaveis-na-pandemia-afirma-professor.shtml.
Oliveira, Francisco de
2006 "Lula in the labyrinth." *New Left Review* 42: 5–22.
Ortellado, Pablo
2014 "Guerras culturais no Brasil." *Le Monde Diplomatique* (Brazilian edition), December 1. http://diplomatique.org.br/guerras-culturais-no-brasil/.
Passos, Joana Célia dos
2015 "Relações raciais, cultura acadêmica e tensionamentos após ações afirmativas." *Educação em Revista* 31 (2): 155–182.
Rocha, João Cezar de Castro
2020 "Quanto maior o colapso do governo, maior a virulência da guerra cultural, diz pesquisador da UERJ." *Agência Pública*, May 28. https://apublica.org/2020/05/quanto-maior-o-colapso-do-governo-maior-a-virulencia-da-guerra-cultural-diz-pesquisador-da-uerj/.
Rodrigues, Léo
2017 "Professores protestam contra condução coercitiva de reitor da UFMG." *AgênciaBrasil*, December 6. https://agenciabrasil.ebc.com.br/geral/noticia/2017-12/professores-protestam-contra-conducao-coercitiva-de-reitor-da-ufmg.
Saldaña, Paulo
2018 "Universidades de todo o país são alvo de ações policiais e da Justiça Eleitoral." *Folha de São Paulo*, October 26. https://www1.folha.uol.com.br/cotidiano/2018/10/universidades-de-todo-o-pais-sao-alvo-de-acoes-policiais-e-da-justica-eleitoral.shtml.
Schroyer, Trent
1973 *The Critique of Domination: The Origins and Development of Critical Theory*. New York: George Braziller.
Secco, Lincoln
2003 "PT: passado e presente." *Gramsci e o Brasil (blog)*. https://www.acessa.com/gramsci/?id=240&page=visualizar.
Simon, Allan
2020 "Weintraub: Odeio o termo 'povos indígenas': Quer, quer. Não quer, sai de ré." UOL, May 22. https://noticias.uol.com.br/politica/ultimas-noticias/2020/05/22/weintraub-odeio-o-termo-povos-indigenas-quer-quer-nao-quer-sai-de-re.htm.

Singer, André
  2020 "Autoritarismo furtivo." *A Terra É Redonda*, June 13. https://aterraeredonda.com.br/autoritarismo-furtivo/?utm_source=rss&utm_medium=rss&utm_campaign=autoritarismo-furtivo&utm_term=2020-06-14.
SoU_Ciência
  2021 "Guerra ideológica chega ao ENEM." November. https://souciencia.unifesp.br/destaques/universidade-em-pauta/guerra-ideologica-chega-ao-enem.
Sousa, Andréa Harada
  2019 "Mercantilização e automação do ensino superior privado." *FEPESP*, November 22. http://fepesp.org.br/artigo/7078/.
Souza, Josias de
  2019 "Universidade nordestina não deve ensinar filosofia, diz novo titular do MEC." UOL, April 7. https://josiasdesouza.blogosfera.uol.com.br/2019/04/08/universidade-nordestina-nao-deve-ensinar-filosofia-diz-novo-titular-do-mec/.
Sudré, Lu
  2019 "Universidades federais de SP apresentam proposta alternativa ao projeto 'Future-se.'" *Brasil de Fato*, December 4. https://www.brasildefato.com.br/2019/12/04/universidades-federais-de-sp-apresentam-proposta-alternativa-ao-projeto-future-se.
Times
  2020 "Latin American university ranking." https://www.timeshighereducation.com/world-university-rankings/2020/latin-america-university-rankings#!/page/0/length/25/sort_by/rank/sort_order/asc/cols/undefined.
UOL
  2020a "Alcolumbre devolve MP que dava poder a Weintraub para nomear reitores." https://noticias.uol.com.br/politica/ultimas-noticias/2020/06/12/alcolumbre-vai-devolver-ao-planalto-mp-que-alterava-escolha-de-reitores.htm.
  2020b "Novas universidades ensinan 'sexo sem limite', disse ministro da educação em 2018." https://noticias.uol.com.br/ultimas-noticias/agencia-estado/2020/07/12/novas-universi-dades-ensinam-sexo-sem-limite-disse-ministro-da-educacao-em-2018.htm.
Valente, Rubens
  2020 "Ação sigilosa do governo mira professores e policiais antifascistas." UOL, July 24. https://noticias.uol.com.br/colunas/rubens-valente/2020/07/24/ministerio-justica-governo-bolsonaro-antifascistas.htm.
Veja
  2014 "Bancos lucraram 8 vezes mais no governo de Lula do que not de FHC." September 12. https://veja.abril.com.br/economia/bancos-lucraram-8-vezes-mais-no-governo-de-lula-do-que-no-de-fhc/.
Vélez Rodríguez, Ricardo
  2006 "O marxismo gramsciano, pano de fundo ideológico da reforma educacional petista." *Ibérica: Revista Interdisciplinar de Estudos Ibéricos e Ibero-Americanos* 1 (1).
Vinhais, Henrique
  2013 "Estudo sobre o impacto da expansão das universidades Federais no Brasil," Ph.D. diss., Universidade de São Paulo.
World Bank
  2017 "A fair adjustment: efficiency and equity of public spending in Brazil." https://www.worldbank.org/en/country/brazil/publication/brazil-expenditure-review-report.

Blowtorching Freirean Thought Out of Bolsonaro's Brazil

Alagoas's Escola Livre Law

by
Thiago Pezzuto

The state of Alagoas's Escola Livre law prohibited teachers from sharing with their students opinions that are political, partisan, religious, or philosophical in nature. Application to the analysis of its passage of the punctuated-equilibrium concepts of policy image and policy venue suggests that mutual reinforcement of (1) the return of the right in Latin America, (2) the rise of evangelicals, and (3) the advent of the School Without Party movement in the larger context of Dilma Rousseff's impeachment process created a unique window of opportunity that the law's author perceived and seized upon.

A Lei Escola Livre do estado de Alagoas proibiu que professores compartilhassem com seus alunos opiniões de natureza política, partidária, religiosa ou filosófica. A aplicação dos conceitos de equilíbrio pontuado de policy image e policy venue à análise de sua promulgação sugere que o fortalecimento mútuo entre (1) o retorno da direita na América Latina, (2) a ascensão de evangélicos, e (3) o advento do movimento Escola Sem Partido no contexto mais amplo do processo de impeachment de Dilma Rousseff criou uma janela de oportunidade única que o autor da lei autor identificou e explorou.

Keywords: Education, Education policy, Punctuated equilibrium, Latin America, Brazil

In November 2015, the Legislative Assembly of the state of Alagoas in Northeast Brazil, by a stunning unanimous vote, passed the law establishing the so-called Escola Livre (Free School) program (ultimately Law 7,800 of May 5, 2016). Contrary to what its title might suggest, instead of fostering meaning making, dialogue, and reflection, the Escola Livre law severely compromised teachers' ability to teach and, in turn, students' ability to learn by imposing a series of bans built on indefinable terms, the most (in)famous of them being "indoctrination": "The practice of political and ideological indoctrination and any other actions by teachers or school administrators that impose or induce political, partisan, religious, or philosophical opinions in students are hereby forbidden in classrooms in the state of Alagoas" (Article 2).

Thiago Pezzuto is a Ph.D. candidate in international education policy at the University of Maryland, College Park. His doctoral research draws on scientometric and visualization techniques to map the field of comparative and international education. His research interests also include the political economy of education and the role of ideology in education policy making. Previous works have appeared in such publications as *PS: Political Science & Politics* and Routledge's Studies in Global and Transnational Politics series. He thanks the peer reviewers from *Latin American Perspectives*, whose insights helped shape this article.

LATIN AMERICAN PERSPECTIVES, Issue 248, Vol. 50 No. 1, January 2023, 218–236
DOI: 10.1177/0094582X221147894
© 2023 Latin American Perspectives

The vagueness that permeates the text of the law is not the result of poor drafting but deliberate and systematic.[1] It is, at its most basic level, an attempt at creating a system riddled with impenetrable jargon that, through the dissemination of uncertainty and fear, undermines the use of certain pedagogical approaches, particularly those premised on critical inquiry. The practice of "indoctrination," for example, is not specified in law, nor is it a matter of consensus (see Snook, 1972); there are simply no clear criteria for determining whether a given instructional episode constitutes indoctrination. Accordingly, without clear legislative standards against which to test claims against teachers, virtually any action can reasonably be framed as "indoctrination."[2] Exploitation of vague language went beyond the spectrum of teachers' actions to cover the subjects not to be addressed in the classroom. Albeit limited (opening the way for the disingenuous argument that the ban merely applies to "certain" ideas), the specific areas indicated by the Escola Livre law are so broad that they could arguably be defined by what they *did not* cover, perhaps the best example being "philosophical opinions."

Failure to abide by the new rules could result in sanctions and penalties that ranged from warning to dismissal, and posters listing "teachers' duties" were to be displayed in classrooms. Combined with the inability to predict whether one's actions in the classroom could or would be arbitrarily construed as "indoctrination," "propaganda," or any practice otherwise deemed detrimental to students, such sanctions all but removed any incentive for inquiry, pedagogical experimentation, and collaborative learning. In practice, the program created and indeed required what Freire (2005: 71–72) calls the "banking" model of education:

> The teacher talks about reality as if it were motionless, static, compartmentalized, and predictable. Or else he expounds on a topic completely alien to the existential experience of the students. . . . Instead of *communicating* [emphasis added], the teacher issues communiqués and makes deposits which the students patiently receive, memorize, and repeat. This is the "banking" concept of education, in which the scope of action allowed to the students extends only as far as receiving, filing, and storing the deposits.

Vetoed by Governor Renan Calheiros Filho in January 2016, the law came back into force in the following April after that decision was overridden by a comfortable 10-vote margin. Predictably, its constitutionality was challenged before the country's Supreme Court by multiple petitioners, including the National Confederation of Teaching Establishment Workers, the National Confederation of Education Workers, and the Partido Democrático Trabalhista (Democratic Labor Party—PDT).[3]

In October 2016 Attorney General Rodrigo Janot issued the opinion that the law was unconstitutional in that it imposed a "disproportionate sacrifice" on freedom of expression and was "excessive and unnecessary" in that state law already had mechanisms to protect the students' freedom of conscience. In the same vein, in March 2017 Supreme Court Justice Luís Roberto Barroso provisionally suspended the law on the grounds that it was "so vague and generic" that it might achieve the opposite of what was intended—"ideological imposition and persecution of those who disagree with it." A conference was finally scheduled in August 2020, and the justices ruled 9–1 that it was unconstitutional. Notably, Justice Barroso's opinion quoted Elie Wiesel's ominous admonition that "silence encourages the tormentor, never the tormented."

Given the unreasonableness of what it tried to accomplish, one could assume that the program was just a hiccup in an otherwise functional, albeit flawed, educational system. There are, however, two major factors that warrant more detailed study. First, the Escola Livre law is but one manifestation of a countrywide movement called Escola Sem Partido (School Without Party—ESP). Created in 2003 by Miguel Nagib, a São Paulo State attorney, the ESP "aims to inhibit the practice of political and ideological indoctrination in the classroom and the usurpation of the parents' right over the moral education of their offspring" (Escola Sem Partido, n.d.).[4] The movement's most important initiative is a federal bill[5] whose proposal has been followed by a wave of similar bills at the state and local levels (in most cases simply mirroring the wording of the original document).

Second, the election of the long-serving right-wing legislator and retired military officer Jair Bolsonaro as president marked a major political victory and turning point for the ESP. Bolsonaro, who during the campaign vowed to "blowtorch" Paulo Freire's thought out of the Ministry of Education (Borges and Amin, 2019), is personally involved with the movement and, arguably, has become its face, and his sons Flávio and Carlos have introduced ESP-inspired bills in the Legislative Assembly of Rio de Janeiro and the Municipal Chamber of Rio de Janeiro, respectively.

Although it is limited to the educational system of Alagoas, the ruling has set a precedent for the way the courts will respond to future cases involving ESP-inspired programs. Given that Bolsonaro's job interview with Ricardo Vélez Rodríguez, the first (of four so far) minister of education of his administration, started with the question (referring to the appointee's new duties at the ministry) "Do you have a knife between your teeth to face this war?" (Guerra, 2018), it is likely that Brazilians should expect even more stringent if not more sophisticated versions of the Escola Livre law.

The purpose of this paper is to analyze the process by which a decades-long period of stability in education policy has been followed by a sudden, dramatic reversal. First, it explores the interaction of the basic punctuated-equilibrium concepts of policy image and policy venue and explains why they have been chosen for this examination of the passage of the Free School law. It goes on to describe the data sources used and then to analyze how the return of the right in Latin America, the rise of evangelicals, and the School Without Party movement changed the image of education policy in the country and how the impeachment of Dilma Rousseff offered a more favorable venue for consideration of the Escola Livre law.

THE THEORETICAL FRAMEWORK

Ever since the promulgation of the 1988 Constitution, which framed education as a "social right," most major legal milestones that directly or indirectly affected the teaching and learning environment enshrined two fundamental principles: "appreciation of education professionals" and "freedom to learn, teach, research and express thoughts, art, and knowledge." At all levels of state government, policy changes concerning teachers' rights and duties have strictly adhered to these principles. For the most part, they were incremental in nature and revolved around issues such as working conditions, training, and compensation, with the subject of freedom to teach receiving little to no attention. Given the overall stability that marked nearly three decades of policy making in the area, one could argue that analyses of most of those changes would have found a suitable approach in incrementalism (see Lindblom, 1959; Wildavsky, 1979). This, however, does not hold true for the Escola Livre law, which can only be properly understood in terms of a theoretical framework that foregrounds sudden and drastic departures from the status quo.

PUNCTUATED-EQUILIBRIUM THEORY

Therefore, this article draws on Baumgartner and Jones's (1991; 2009; see also 2002; Jones and Baumgartner, 2005; Baumgartner, Jones, and Mortensen, 2014; and Goertz, 2003) punctuated-equilibrium model of policy change, according to which a single process can explain both periods of extreme stability and short bursts of rapid change: the interaction between "beliefs and values concerning a particular policy," which they call "policy image," and "the existing set of political institutions," which they refer to as "institutional venues" (1991: 1044–1045).

The point of departure of Baumgartner and Jones's (2009: xxiii) theory is the assumption that policy-making processes are shaped by bounded rationality. Because "political systems, like people, can focus intensely only on a limited number of public policies," policy making ends up taking place in policy subsystems, each of which favors specific actors who are uniquely positioned to create and maintain policy monopolies. Although policy monopolies tend to be conducive to path dependencies, stability, and ultimately incremental change, "there remain other institutional venues that can serve as avenues of appeal for the disaffected" (Baumgartner and Jones, 1991: 1044)—avenues through which emerging agendas challenge prevailing ones, punctuations are initiated, and monopolies collapse. Doing so is not a simple undertaking, however, and requires a dual strategy: "On the one hand, [political actors] try to control the prevailing image of the policy problem through the use of rhetoric, symbols and policy analysis. On the other hand, they try to alter the roster of participants who are involved in the issue by seeking out the most favorable venue for the consideration of their issues" (1991: 1045).

POLICY IMAGES

Public policies can be associated with multiple images, which do change over time. At times a constituency or interest group's understanding of a policy issue is rooted in ideology or some other intangible goal, and at others it is informed by evidence and experience. Significantly, Baumgartner and Jones (2009: 7) distinguish between "positive" and "negative" policy images, the former being a precondition for the creation of monopolies. In fact, they go so far as to suggest that monopolies require images "so positive that they evoke only support or indifference by those not involved (thereby insuring their continued noninvolvement)." The creation of policy images may be influenced by a range of factors. One such factor is a given policy's level of complexity, especially the way in which such complexity is communicated. When discussed in terms of scientific minutiae, for example, policy-making processes are likely to be dominated by experts; conversely, discussions centered on "ethical, social, or political implications" are likely to include a larger roster of participants (1991: 1047). Closely related is whether one emphasizes the "empirical" component of a policy or its "evaluative" component, also referred to as its "tone" (2009: 26).

POLICY VENUES

Policy venues are "the institutional locations where authoritative decisions are made concerning a given issue" (Baumgartner and Jones, 2009: 32). Simple though it is, the definition comes with important caveats that call for consideration. First, it is assumed that, rules and regulations notwithstanding, one cannot determine with certainty which policy venue should enjoy policy-making authority over a specific policy issue (and such authority may in fact be shared among several policy venues). Second, Baumgartner and Jones have a rather broad understanding of the term "institution," which here extends far beyond formal, "hard" organizations such as legislatures or political parties: a policy issue "may be assigned to an agency of the federal government, to private market mechanisms, to state or local authorities, to the family, or to any of a number of institutions" (1991: 1047). Combined, these factors are referred to as "the venue problem."

POSITIVE FEEDBACKS AND PUNCTUATIONS

Drawing on the scholarship of Schattschneider (1960), Cobb and Elder (1972), and others, Baumgartner and Jones (2009: 36) approach the key interaction between policy image and policy venue through the concept of conflict expansion. The thrust of their argument is that political actors who find themselves unable to win certain political battles "have the incentive to look for allies elsewhere." Pluralistic societies offer a wide range of policy venues, each of which is made up of a specific set of actors with its own agendas and strategies. Some of them, the argument goes, may be reasonably expected to see a given policy issue in a more favorable light than key actors involved in the original debate surrounding it, thereby allowing participants "to change their losing position into the winning one, as more and more people become involved in the debate on their side" (1991: 1047).[6] Such a change in venue thus both creates and requires a change in the prevailing image surrounding a policy issue, and the interplay between new image and new venue generates the positive feedback that allows for sudden and drastic reversals, regardless of the strength of previously established policy monopolies (2009: 37):

> With each change in venue comes an increased attention to a new image, leading to further changes in venue, as more and more groups within the political

system become aware of the question. Thus a slight change in either can build on itself, amplifying over time and leading eventually to important changes in policy outcomes. The interactions of image and venue may produce a self-reinforcing system characterized by positive feedback.

Here it must be stressed that the somewhat misleading term "positive" is not to be construed as the quality of possessing inherently good attributes and characteristics. By "positive feedbacks" the authors mean processes that enhance a given change or effect and by "negative feedbacks" processes that reduce that change or effect.

FROM THEORY TO APPLICATION

Since the redemocratization of the 1980s, the image associated with education policy in Brazil (and, by extension, with teachers) had been a fundamentally positive one. In 1988 the country adopted a constitution whose language, doubtless influenced by Freirean thought, explicitly prevents the educational enterprise from being exclusively grounded in economic achievement (Article 205): "Education, which is the right of all and duty of the State and of the family, shall be promoted and fostered with the cooperation of society, with a view to the full development of the person, *his preparation for the exercise of citizenship* [emphasis added], and his qualification for work." Insofar as freedom to teach is concerned, for nearly three decades education policy underwent a stasis that not even the dramatic political changes ushered in by the electoral cycles of 1994 and 2002 could disrupt. Throughout this period, Brazil would flirt with populism, fully embrace the neoliberal experiment, and then strongly repudiate the latter in favor of a leftist agenda, but freedoms in general and freedom to teach in particular remained at all times insulated from ideological contagion. Public and technocratic understandings of the issue seemed to coincide, and strong monopolies at the Ministry of Education and state legislatures were formed as a result. The educational subsystem, remarkably, remained subject to a negative feedback process that kept the few pressures that emerged at bay, despite the inherent susceptibility to manipulation of education policy's image.[7]

The subsystem would be governed by negative feedbacks until the interaction of three phenomena—the return of the right in Latin America, the rise of the evangelicals, and the advent of the School Without Party movement—that fundamentally changed the way many Brazilians perceived the educational endeavor, especially the use of pedagogical approaches premised on critical inquiry. Teachers had come to be seen as a detriment to students, and the conditions were in place for a takeover of education policy. Nevertheless, as Baumgartner and Jones (2009: 27) point out, such conditions "do not automatically generate policy actions," for "arguments must be made and accepted that a given problem can be solved by government action." In Alagoas, those arguments would be provided by state deputy Ricardo Nezinho, the Escola Livre law's author. Nezinho's conflict expansion strategy centered on the fertile ground for policy change provided by the impeachment of Dilma Rousseff, which offered a countrywide audience for the debate on freedom to teach. This audience proved open to policies predicated on political neutrality, skills development, and parental rights. More than that, it proved inflexibly resolved on change in classroom practice.

The new venue provided by Rousseff's impeachment both facilitated and solidified the new rhetoric on education. As attention to the issue increased, so did the number of new groups driving the debate. "Indoctrination" became a flagship issue for Bolsonaro, who had already announced his desire to run and whose meteoric ascent to the national stage can only be matched by the sudden downfall of the Partido dos Trabalhadores (Workers' Party—PT). The political pendulum had swung to the opposite extreme, and criticism of leftist ideas had become so virulent that no coalition could be formed to defeat Nezinho's bill. The interaction between a new, unopposed image and a new venue that encompassed virtually the entirety of the electorate thus ignited a positive feedback process that culminated in the enactment of the Escola Livre law.

DATA SOURCES

For this article, I have used two main means of data collection. First, I have content-analyzed a number of documents obtained from official websites: all versions of the Escola Livre law; the bill's justification; reports of Alagoas's Constitution and Justice and Education Commissions; the Brazilian Constitution; the State of Alagoas Constitution; the governor's veto; direct actions of unconstitutionality 5,537/AL, 5,580/AL, and 6,038/AL; and both the Attorney General of the Republic's opinion and Justice Barroso's ruling on those actions. Second, I have examined editorials and articles retrieved from national, state, and local newspapers.

DISCUSSION

THE RETURN OF THE RIGHT IN LATIN AMERICA

The first phenomenon that contributed to a change in the way education policy is discussed in Brazil is what can be loosely called "the return of the right" in Latin America, a process that is relevant to the extent that it fundamentally challenges the notion of education as an empowering, liberating human right. After decades of dictatorship, 1998 marked a watershed year in Latin American politics with the election of Hugo Chávez in Venezuela. The victory of Chávez, however, was only the beginning of a trend that would shortly take over the region, including Brazil (Salvador Peralta and Pezzuto Pacheco, 2014). The "Pink Tide," as the movement has become known, was, however, short-lived. The 2000s commodities boom, which had allowed leftist administrations to implement wildly popular and successful antipoverty programs—the population living in poverty in the region fell from 45 to 25 percent between 2000 and 2014 (Levy, 2016)—has come to an end, and the reduced demand for Latin American goods has pushed leaders in the region such as Brazil's President Rousseff to turn to crippling austerity measures.

This has created a scenario of economic turmoil and general discontent that has proved open to the solutions offered by right-wing groups.[8] A common feature of those agendas is a heavy reliance on skills as a panacea for increasing employment and economic growth and, ultimately, reducing inequalities. Accordingly, much of Brazil's attention has turned to issues such as the country's educational apparatus, curriculum reform, and pedagogical practices. Because the right-wing alternative is one that changes education from a tool for social and cultural change to a tool for labor productivity improvement, ESP-inspired bills emerged as one of the leading political responses to Brazil's economic challenges despite their lack of economy-related provisions. In a sense, this approach to the educational experience became the tacit economic component of the Escola Livre law, a piece of legislation that, at first glance, seems to be primarily a product of social conservatism. By emphasizing the importance of skills development and job placement, the right-wing agenda filled a gap in the program, which was limited to outlining what teachers are *not* allowed to do in the classroom.

Nothing encapsulates the articulation and mutual reinforcement between the social character of ESP-inspired bills such as the Escola Livre law and the economic focus of the new right-wing regimes better than Bolsonaro's historic stance on education reform. His Government Plan, for example, provides that "teaching must be changed, both in content and method. More mathematics, science, and Portuguese, NO INDOCTRINATION AND EARLY SEXUALIZATION. In addition, initial priority must be given to basic, secondary, and technical education" (Bolsonaro, 2018: slide 41). Interestingly, not only does Bolsonaro consistently allude to the opposition between skills-based educational systems and indoctrination-based educational systems (as the only possibilities of a binary system) but also he tends to equate the promotion of critical thinking with indoctrination: "Go and ask a 15-year-old Chinese, Japanese, Israeli boy; he knows how to balance chemical equations, he can recite Isaac Newton's physics book by heart, he already knows derivatives and integrals. Our boys only have critical thinking; to know whether they are becoming men or women, that is their lives' big decision" (Bolsonaro, quoted in Bresciani, 2018). Therefore, whereas ESP-inspired bills focused on what teachers should not be doing, the revived right-wing movement strengthened their message by saying what teachers should be doing instead: teaching skills and skills only.

THE RISE OF THE EVANGELICALS

The second major phenomenon that contributed to a change in the way education policy is perceived can be described as a shift among Christians that pushed the country farther to the right on the political spectrum. This shift is relevant to the extent that it contributed to the increase in the proportion of the population that is likely to support bills predicated on parental rights and prerogatives. Brazil has the world's largest Catholic population, 123.3 million. This fact in itself should indicate that the country is, at least in principle, open to and supportive of bills that speak of "parents' right to have their minor children receive a moral education free of political, religious, or ideological indoctrination"

(Article 1 of the Escola Livre law). Recent demographic shifts, however, have refocused interest and debate on key social issues, and, as a result, Brazil is quickly becoming an even more conservative society.

Between 2000 and 2010, whereas the number of Brazilians who identified as Catholic dropped from 125 million (73.6 percent of the population) to 123.3 million (64.6 percent), the number of evangelicals soared from 26.2 million (15.4 percent) to 42.3 million (22.2 percent). For an idea of how unprecedented the 9-point decrease in the Catholic population is it is sufficient to recall that it took virtually a century, from the country's first census in 1872 to the 1970 survey, for the proportion of that population to shrink 7.9 points (from 99.7 to 91.8 percent). Evangelicals, in turn, amounted to a mere 5.2 percent of the Brazilian population in 1970 (IBGE, 2012).

In Brazil, Catholics and evangelicals practice their faith in markedly different ways. For example, the percentage of evangelicals who say they pray daily, attend services weekly, and consider religion very important in their lives far exceeds that of Catholics (60 percent vs. 23 percent). The same applies to the proportion of evangelicals who say they pray at least once a day outside of religious services (78 percent vs. 59 percent) and those who say they read or listen to Scripture at least weekly outside of religious services (62 percent vs. 17 percent). Remarkably, 83 percent of evangelicals, compared with 67 percent of Catholics, believe that the Bible is the word of God and should be taken literally (Pew Research Center, 2014: 19, 44, 48, 54). Evangelicals also are distinguished in that they seem to be particularly motivated to pursue an active and involved religious life. Whereas only 13 percent of Catholic churchgoers are members of church councils, lead small groups or ministries, or teach Sunday school, 36 percent of evangelicals show that level of involvement with congregational life (Pew Research Center, 2014: 47). Similar patterns of commitment hold true with respect to their political attitudes and behavior, and, unsurprisingly, evangelicals have become one of the most powerful caucuses in Congress, with 84 deputies and 7 senators (Damé, 2018).

Oddly, they have found in President Bolsonaro the fiercest champion of their social agenda. Bolsonaro, who is Catholic (since the 1980s, when he first ran for City Council, his campaign motto has been "Brazil above everything, God above everyone"), has always shown a shrewd understanding of the importance and potential of a growing evangelical community in Brazilian politics. In 2013, for example, his wedding with Michele Firmo, who has an evangelical background, was performed by Pastor Silas Malafaia, the leader of the evangelical Pentecostal church Assembly of God Victory in Christ and one of the most influential conservative religious leaders in the country. In May 2016, at the exact same time that the Senate was voting to hold the Dilma Rousseff impeachment trial, Bolsonaro was in Israel leaning back into the River Jordan in a white robe to be baptized in the arms of Pastor Everaldo, the president of the Evangelical Social Christian Party, who had himself run for president in 2014 (*Extra*, 2016).

Few issues have been more strategically targeted by the alliance than those of homosexuality and gender identity, with attacks insidiously cloaked in discourses based on more palatable jargons of "moral conduct" and "sexual morals." The spread of evangelical morality, Bolsonaro quickly learned, resulted in higher levels of intolerance toward the gay community. For example, an astounding 83 percent of Evangelicals believe that homosexual behavior is morally wrong (compared with 57 percent of Catholics), and only 25 percent of that population favor same-sex marriage (Pew Research Center, 2014: 21, 75).

This partly explains the convoluted nature of Bolsonaro's pronouncements and Government Plan with respect to education reform in general and ESP-inspired bills in particular. Although some of the ideas he tries to convey, such as the connection between mathematics education and job placement, are self-explanatory, elaborating on notions such as "indoctrination" is a much harder task. By reducing dialogical experiences in the classroom to the sexual indoctrination of children, however, not only does he add some concreteness to the core component of those bills but he does so by exploiting one of the notions evangelicals hold most dear: the "traditional family." Since he announced his candidacy in 2014, he has capitalized on the connection between indoctrination and early sexualization, and so have the authors of the first ESP-inspired bills. By 2015, the discourse had gained such a broad base of support that the new bills, in essence, equated "indoctrination" with "sexual indoctrination." One of the clearest examples of this phenomenon is the opening paragraph of the Escola Livre law's legal justification:

> It is a notorious fact that teachers and textbook authors have been using their classes and works in order to try to obtain the adherence of students and certain political and ideological currents; and to have them adopt judgment and moral conduct patterns—especially sexual morals—incompatible with those taught to them by their parents or legal guardians.

Powerful though they may have been, a general inclination toward a renewed emphasis on productivity improvement and demographic shifts within the Christian population were not enough to allow for a successful manipulation of the image of education policy in general and the issue of teachers' duties in particular. Here enters the ESP, a nationwide movement that for over a decade had been gathering support, followers, and attention and educating policy makers about the promotion of parental rights.

THE ESCOLA SEM PARTIDO MOVEMENT

The third contributing factor to the creation of a new image of educational services and the catalyst for action against freedom to teach in tangible and practical steps is the advent of the ESP. Rooted in the belief that "an organized army of militants acting as teachers" takes advantage of "classroom secrecy" to impose its worldviews upon students (Nagib, n.d.), the ESP has two main fronts. The first, which has inspired the Escola Livre law and a plethora of similar bills across the country, consists of efforts to promote laws against the perceived abuse of freedom to teach at the federal, state, and local levels. The second, equally important in that it provides an indispensable support for these bills, consists of the construction of an ever-growing informal association of parents and students confronting the "insurmountable refusal" of educators and entrepreneurs in the education sector "to admit the very existence of the problem" of indoctrination (Nagib, n.d.). Miguel Nagib, who launched the movement, has clearly drawn inspiration from the U.S. experience in developing the movement's overall strategy. For example, he cites the now-defunct NoIndoctrination.org in the United States, self-described as "an organization of parents who are disturbed that sociopolitical agendas have been allowed to permeate college courses and orientation programs" (Wright, n.d.), as the experience to be emulated (Nagib, n.d.). That initiative, in a nutshell, logged accounts of alleged bias in the classroom. The logic is that, by "giving voice to the voiceless," it informs the public about "the frequent lack of balance" in the classroom (NoIndoctrination.org, n.d.).

In the early years of the ESP, most of its high-profile cases revolved around perceived abuses by leftist administrations and were political in nature. One of them involved the 2009 National Assessment of Student Achievement exam for students of communication. Administered during former President Luiz Inácio Lula da Silva's second term, the exam became the subject of severe criticism for allegedly forcing students to take a positive stance toward him. For example, one item (INEP, 2009: 13) was:

> When President Luiz Inácio da Silva said that the global financial crisis was a tsunami abroad but, in Brazil, it would be a ripple, several media outlets criticized the presidential statement. Now it is the international press that remembers and confirms Lula's prediction. Considering the current reality of the economy, abroad and in Brazil, it is correct to say that critics have shown: (a) biased attitude; (b) irresponsibility; (c) free exercise of criticism; (d) media political manipulation; or (e) prejudice.

The notion that leftist administrations have sought to produce hegemony through apparatuses such as the Ministry of Education has been popularized by Olavo de Carvalho, a philosopher who, by all accounts, is the most influential conservative thinker in the country. De Carvalho (1997: 288) posits that in the wake of the 1964 military coup d'état that ushered in two decades of dictatorship in Brazil, leftist forces split into two major blocks: one that organized traditional Marxist guerrilla groups and was ultimately defeated by the regime and another that "took refuge in the cultural and academic ghetto, and there imposed a hegemony similar to that exercised by the right in the territory surrounding it." The success of the latter group, his argument goes, is attributable to a textbook application of Antonio Gramsci's neo-Marxist theory of cultural hegemony, at the heart of which lies the concept of the "organic intellectual." In contrast to guerrillas, who often attempt to change traditional power structures through violence, organic intellectuals pursue the elimination of opposing forces through the occupation of key cultural and educational apparatuses and the gradual creation of broad consensus. During the dictatorship years, de Carvalho (2013: 262) argues, this process was facilitated by the fact that the military government was so obsessed with fighting guerrillas that it ignored the peaceful, "apparently harmless" advances made by educators and school administrators focusing on legitimation.

De Carvalho, thus, provides the construct under which the alleged instances of bias and indoctrination disseminated by Nagib's ESP are subsumed. Interestingly, however, even though de Carvalho seems to be in full agreement with Nagib with respect to the origins of what they believe to be a structural problem plaguing the Brazilian educational system, the two could not be farther apart with respect to the appropriate response to it. A vehement critic of ESP-inspired bills, de Carvalho (2018) released a video titled "Warning to School Without Party" arguing that this was a battle to be fought in the intellectual arena, not the legal one (which would require extensive, quantitative documentation of the detrimental effects of leftist thought in schools and universities). In addition, he warned that any eventual victories of Nagib's strategy would have been achieved by force, not persuasion, and would as a result generate nothing but hate and resentment toward conservatism.

Even though the two biggest names associated with the ESP do not necessarily speak in unison, the fact of the matter is that the narrative of systematic indoctrination connected with a hegemony project that goes back to the dictatorship years had become so deeply embedded in education policy discourse in Brazil that no state or local ESP-inspired bill could possibly be discussed in light of its own merits. Accordingly, the Escola Livre law debate never got down to the specifics of alleged instances of bias and indoctrination in Alagoas. In practice, it became just another thread of a broader, nationwide discussion around a monolithic image of education carefully crafted by the ESP within a context of economic upheaval and demographic change.

THE IMPEACHMENT OF DILMA ROUSSEFF

We must now turn to the question of how the Escola Livre law's author, Ricardo Nezinho, who was and remains relatively obscure on the Brazilian political scene, managed to steer a debate that would have otherwise been limited to the Alagoas Legislative Assembly into a novel, immense institutional arena that proved exceedingly receptive to his image of education policy: the impeachment of Dilma Rousseff.[9]

Hailing from Arapiraca, Alagoas's second-largest municipality, Nezinho is a seasoned politician. After serving four consecutive terms as a city council member in Arapiraca (elections of 1992, 1996, 2000, and 2004), he was elected state deputy in the cycles of 2006, 2010, 2014, and 2018. In the legislature he has held highly prestigious positions throughout the years, including the chairs of both the Constitution and Justice Committee and the Budget Committee. He is affiliated with the Movimento Democrático Brasileiro (Brazilian Democratic Movement—MDB).

The Escola Livre law's tone has clearly been a primary concern of Nezinho's and a point of departure for his strategy of conflict expansion. As evidenced by the bill's justification, by relying on provisions such as Articles 5, VI ("freedom of conscience and of belief"), and 206, II ("freedom to learn"), of the Federal Constitution and Article 53 of the Child and Adolescent Statute ("right to be respected by educators") and Article 12 of the American Convention on Human Rights ("parents . . . have the right to provide for the religious and moral education of their children . . . that is in accord with their own convictions"), he aimed at introducing the law as a *protective* statute, not a *restrictive* one.

Significantly, although inspired by ESP templates, the Escola Livre law is lighter in tone, as evidenced by the treatment given to the issue of sexuality.

Whereas the templates provided for in the movement's website dedicate a specific article to the issue ("The Administration will neither interfere in the process of sexual maturation of students nor allow any form of dogmatism or proselytism in the approach to gender issues"), Nezinho did not include any such provision in the bill (although, as we have seen earlier, the subject figured prominently in the opening paragraph of the bill's justification).

While Nezinho and the ESP were on slightly divergent courses on the sexuality front, the same cannot be said about the wording, length, and clarity of the bill, which were subject to a rather unusual treatment as Brazilian law-making processes go. Similarly to most if not all of its ESP counterparts, it was short and focused on principles, refraining from governing every single possible scenario as is customary in the country (Nezinho, quoted in *Imprensa RNZ*, 2016):

> I reaffirm with conviction that the intention is not to "gag" anyone. I would never do anything that would harm such an important class. My wife is a teacher, I have relatives and friends who are also, and I am fully aware of what I did. I suggest that you have the curiosity to read the project, which is short, has only two pages, to understand that it is not rocket science.

Nezinho thus managed to craft a short, straightforward bill that deliberately omitted any reference to skills development, sexuality, or any of the hot-button issues that usually swirl around ESP-inspired legislation but one that would nonetheless carry the movement's imprimatur. Its ultimate success, however, would be determined neither by form nor content but by timing. Baumgartner and Jones (2009: 32) maintain that "how an issue gets assigned to a particular arena of policymaking is just as much a puzzle as how an issue comes to be associated with one set of images rather than another." To unravel the parts of the Escola Livre law puzzle, one needs to reconstruct the timeline of Rousseff's impeachment, a seemingly unrelated crisis in the ambit of the federal executive branch that would itself become the arena in which many a debate would take place, including the one on education. Such a focus is of great importance, since the success of his strategy of conflict expansion is less a product of bargaining, compromise, and coalition building[10] than one of shrewd reading of shifts in public opinion and masterful use of windows of opportunity.

Rousseff's impeachment, the second in the country within a quarter-century period, was tightly linked to two major corruption scandals. The first, called the Mensalão (Big Monthly Stipend), took the country by storm in 2005 and consisted of monthly payments to members of political parties in exchange for support of the PT minority government. The vote-for-cash scandal ultimately resulted in the arrest, in 2012, of José Dirceu, Lula's chief of staff, and José Genoíno, president of the PT, among others. The second, labeled the Petrolão (Big Oily), consisted of the diversion of Petrobras (the state-owned oil company) funds to the PT and its allies. In sum, it has been found that the Petrolão financed the Mensalão. Having been unveiled in 2014, the scandal has consumed billions of dollars and decisively contributed to the retraction of Brazil's GDP by 3.8 percent in 2015 and 3.6 percent in 2016.

By the end of the first quarter of 2015, Rousseff, who had been narrowly reelected in the previous October, already found herself in hot water when

protesters started what would become a year-long cycle of uninterrupted demonstrations. The first major such demonstration, which gathered nearly 2 million protesters nationwide, took place on March 15, sending shock waves
through the political community. The furor was such that Bolsonaro, a mere
month later, announced that he would be leaving the Progessistas to pursue his
"presidency dream" under a different banner (Passarinho, 2015).

Nezinho had big dreams himself. Although a formal announcement of his
intention to join the 2016 Arapiraca mayoral race would be put on hold for over
a year, his campaign, for all intents and purposes, began in March when he was
designated MDB party leader in the Legislative Assembly. A considerably more
momentous step came shortly after with the filing of the Escola Livre bill on
June 16, which established him as a champion of parents' rights and would
later become the centerpiece of his campaign.

During that period, opposition to anyone or anything that could possibly be
PT-related offered the clearest path to power. After more than 10 excruciating
years of continuous corruption-related revelations, the PT image had gradually
become extremely toxic in most of the country. For an idea of how intense the
sentiment had become, consider that, by April 2016, 72 PT mayors in 16 states
had broken with the party to run for reelection under other parties' banners
(Roxo, 2016).[11]

However, the effects of Rousseff's impeachment go far beyond reputational
damage to the PT, its leaders, and its candidates. Even though Brazil's infa-
mous electoral system features more than 30 political parties, the PT is, in effect,
the primary representative of liberal and progressive thought in the country.
Having secured a minimum of 30 percent of the valid vote in every single presidential election since 1998, the party had established itself as the hegemonic
force on the left. Because its agenda had become synonymous with the left's
agenda, as rejection rates for PT candidates increased so did the repudiation of
liberal and progressive ideals. In this context, opposition to ESP-inspired bills
was construed not as an attempt to preserve dialogue, openness, and tolerance
in the classroom but as support for a criminal organization that had driven the
country to financial ruin.

By the time the Escola Livre law was proposed, Rousseff's approval rating
had sunk to a dismal 10 percent and her impeachment was a foregone conclusion. Nezinho, who understood that, at that juncture of Brazilian history, just
as important as the ideas one stood for were the ideas one stood against,
pounced on it. The Escola Livre law had made clear that he was against pedagogical approaches premised on critical inquiry and, by extension, the PT,
Rousseff, and Freirean thought. The inference is no exaggeration.

Ever since the birth of the storied friendship between Lula and Freire, which
regrettably must be bypassed here, *petistas* (as PT members and supporters are
called) have seen themselves as upholders of Freirean thought, both in symbol
and in substance. In 2012, for example, Rousseff signed into law the declaration of Freire as "Patron of Brazilian Education" (Law 12,612 of April 13, 2012).
In the following year, her administration launched the so-called National
Policy of Popular Education in Health (Ordinance 2,761 of November 19,
2013). Expressly governed by the principles of "dialogue," "kindness," "prob-
lematization," "shared construction of knowledge," "emancipation," and

"commitment to the construction of the popular democratic project," the policy was arguably one of the purest applications of Freirean theory in the real world of policy. Significantly, kindness (*amorosidade*) is there defined as "the expansion of dialogue in care relationships and educational action through the incorporation of emotional exchanges and sensitivity, allowing for dialogue that goes beyond knowledge and logically organized arguments."

The Escola Livre law was therefore ipso facto the opposite of the PT's educational platform—in a context in which a big enough chunk of the electorate wanted to extirpate the party root and branch. Surely and not slowly, protests turned into political action and the drama reached a climax on October 21, when the opposition filed impeachment proceedings against Rousseff. If ever there was a perfect moment for change, this was surely it. Within less than a month the bill would be put up for a vote and unanimously passed (on November 17).

Remarkably, the research has not identified any major pronouncements (let alone signs of organized action) against the bill during the June-to-November window; those would be made only in the wake of the vote. Still, they were few and far between and came from stakeholders as involved with and affected by the new policy as Alagoas's Teachers' Union, which in January 2016 characterized it as a "disservice to the state" and urged Governor Renan Filho to veto it (Sindicato dos Professores de Alagoas, 2016). These were, naturally, expected developments but ones that would not hinder Nezinho's strategy. Time was on his side, and, if anything, the bill's chances would improve, and substantially. On January 25 Renan Filho, who is also affiliated with the MDB, heeded the Union's calls and vetoed the bill. By then, however, the Chamber of Deputies had already initiated impeachment proceedings, and the impeachment evolved from a broad public discussion to a formal process before the two congressional houses.

The governor's veto would not be reviewed immediately. The PT's downfall, which has already been explained by argument and events, continued into the next three months until the now historic session of April 16, 2016, when the Chamber of Deputies voted to approve the impeachment of Rousseff.[12] Two days later, with the PT at its lowest ebb of legitimacy, Nezinho finally announced his candidacy for mayor of Arapiraca, at the center of which lay his commitment to political neutrality.[13] In the following week the veto was put to a vote and overridden, clearing the path for the bill's passage on May 9.

CONCLUDING REMARKS

The most astonishing aspect of this process is not how much but how little its protagonist had to accomplish to bring the Escola Livre law into existence. Three external factors had interacted to change the way education was perceived in the country: a regional economic trend, a countrywide demographic change, and a movement that grew and expanded without any significant presence in Alagoas. As far as Nezinho was concerned, the crux of the matter was therefore simply whether a venue receptive to this new image of education could be found. This is not to suggest that the task was simple or to underestimate its achievement. By strategically drafting a bill that made no reference to sexuality (the other states' bills had at least the merit of candor), he created a message that fundamentally differed from that conveyed by most of its counterparts, however inconsequential the omission may appear at first glance. From a legislative standpoint, the Escola Livre law marked a significant step forward, for it became, at least in theory, the first passable ESP-inspired bill.

Not even that ostensibly lighter version of the ESP could succeed in typical institutional arenas, however, and Nezinho had to move the issue into a different venue—which he did on the grandest scale and at the most opportune time. Interestingly, his strategy of conflict expansion was not based on bargaining, compromise, and coalition building, as is evidenced by the lack of coordinated action with the ESP. In fact, he did not even have the full backing of his own party (as was apparent from the governor's veto), which at the very least suggests that "political neutrality" in the classroom was not at the center of the MDB's platform. Nezinho's involvement with the issue seems to have stemmed from a purely reactive and opportunistic response to an unlikely chain of national events, not an ideological one. Further speculation about his motivations, however, is idle, since our focus is on the results and not the roots of his actions.

The case of the Escola Livre law shows—if not conclusively, fairly convincingly—that punctuated-equilibrium analysis may be an invaluable tool for education scholars and practitioners, including those focusing on infant democracies. The interactions between policy images and policy venues, alongside a broader understanding of the very notion of "institution," can allow for the identification of key dynamics that might otherwise have remained obscure. The Escola Livre law may have been declared unconstitutional, but the processes that resulted in the unanimous vote of November 2015 provide invaluable lessons for analysts of education policy in general and Brazil's ESP movement in particular. So far, the ESP has proven both resilient and adaptable, and further attempts to undermine the use of pedagogical approaches premised on critical inquiry, legislative or other, are sure to follow. In this context, the Escola Livre law process is but a chapter in the ongoing ESP experiment.

The war that Bolsonaro pitched to Vélez Rodríguez back in 2018 was to be fought not only over several years but also across multiple fronts, and so it has been. In March 2021, for example, the president's fourth minister of education, Milton Ribeiro, appointed Sandra Ramos, a known collaborator of Nagib and the ESP, general coordinator for teaching materials. In this sense, as the president himself puts it, the ESP is, for all intents and purposes, an ongoing operation, the lack of new federal or state legislation notwithstanding (Costa, 2019).

NOTES

1. The law's general reliance on ill-defined and wide-reaching language is further exemplified by the prohibitions on "tak[ing] advantage of the inexperience, the lack of knowledge, or the immaturity of the students" (Article 3, I) and on "religious, ideological, or political-party propaganda" (Article 3, III), among other things.

2. Brazilian readers who are old enough to have endured the country's dictatorship (1964–1985) might find a striking similarity between this approach and the way in which the military

regime bastardized the then-ubiquitous term "subversive," under which any behavior perceived to constitute a threat to the regime was subsumed.

3. Direct actions of unconstitutionality 5,537/AL, 5,580/AL, and 6,038/AL, later consolidated under 5,537/AL.

4. For more information, see http://www.escolasempartido.org.

5. See PL 7180/2014; as of July 2021, 23 other bills on the subject had been attached to it.

6. To be sure, although the term "expansion" may be suggestive of a focus on ever-growing rosters of participants in political debates, "conflict expanders" may often find it more advantageous to adopt strategies around a single, specific target. More than a game of numbers, this is to be understood as a game of *change*.

7. In contrast to debates on intrinsically technical issues such as, say, energy policy, debates on education policy are not, in general, dominated by specialists (although they certainly can be and have been). Because debates in this particular subsystem are more likely to revolve around ethical, social, or political implications, they tend to attract a much broader roster of participants.

8. With the elections of Mauricio Macri in Argentina in 2015, Sebastián Piñera in Chile in 2017, and Jair Bolsonaro in Brazil in 2018, for the first time in decades the three largest economies in South America were in the hands of right-wing administrations.

9. By "impeachment" I mean the public discussions on the potential removal of President Rousseff from office.

10. The research has not identified any significant instances of collaboration between Nezinho and the leadership of the ESP movement, such as official pronouncements.

11. Their fears, the October elections showed, proved justified. The number of cities under PT control shrank from 638 to 254.

12. On August 31 the Senate would remove President Rousseff from office by a 61–20 vote.

13. He would ultimately lose a hard-fought and close race by only 259 votes (or 0.24 percent).

REFERENCES

Baumgartner, Frank R. and Bryan D. Jones
1991 "Agenda dynamics and policy subsystems." *Journal of Politics* 53: 1044–1074.
2002 "Positive and negative feedback in politics," pp. 3–28 in Frank R. Baumgartner and Bryan D. Jones (eds.), *Policy Dynamics*. Chicago: University of Chicago Press.
2009 *Agendas and Instability in American Politics*. Chicago: University of Chicago Press.
Baumgartner, Frank R., Bryan D. Jones, and Peter B. Mortensen
2014 "Punctuated-equilibrium theory: explaining stability and change in public policymaking," pp. 59–103 in Paul A. Sabatier and Christopher M. Weible (eds.), *Theories of the Policy Process*. Boulder: Westview Press.
Bolsonaro, Jair
2018 "O caminho da prosperidade: proposta de plano de governo." https://divulgacandcontas.tse.jus.br/candidaturas/oficial/2018/BR/BR/2022802018/280000614517/proposta_1534284632231.pdf (accessed December 6, 2021).
Borges, Helena and Júlia Amin
2019 "Entenda quem foi Paulo Freire e as críticas feitas a ele pelo governo Bolsonaro." *O Globo*, April 17. https://oglobo.globo.com/sociedade/entenda-quem-foi-paulo-freire-as-criticas-feitas-ele-pelo-governo-bolsonaro-23604772 (accessed December 6, 2021).
Bresciani, Eduardo
2018 "Bolsonaro defende educação a distância desde o ensino fundamental." *O Globo*, August 7. https://oglobo.globo.com/brasil/bolsonaro-defende-educacao-distancia-desde-ensino-fundamental-22957843 (accessed December 6, 2021).
Cobb, Roger W. and Charles D. Elder
1972 *Participation in American Politics: The Dynamics of Agenda-Building*. Boston: Allyn and Bacon.
Costa, Rodolfo
2019 "Bolsonaro defende Weintraub e diz que Escola sem Partido está em operação." *Correio Braziliense*, December 18. https://www.correiobraziliense.com.br/app/noticia/politica/2019/12/18/interna_politica,815051/bolsonaro-defende-weintraub-e-que-escola-sem-partido-esta-em-operacao.shtml (accessed December 6, 2021).

Damé, Luiza
    2018 "Em crescimento, bancada evangélica terá 91 parlamentares no Congresso." *Agência Brasil*, October 18. http://agenciabrasil.ebc.com.br/politica/noticia/2018-10/em-crescimento-bancada-evangelica-tera-91-parlamentares-no-congresso (accessed December 6, 2021).
de Carvalho, Olavo
    1997 *O imbecil coletivo: Atualidades inculturais brasileiras*. Rio de Janeiro: Faculdade da Cidade Editora.
    2013 *O mínimo que você precisa saber para não ser um idiota*. Rio de Janeiro: Record.
    2018 "Aviso ao Escola Sem Partido." YouTube, November 14. https://www.youtube.com/watch?v=qySuenfRkDk (accessed December 6, 2021).
Escola Sem Partido
    n.d. "Perguntas frequentes." http://www.escolasempartido.org/programa-escola-sem-partido/ (accessed December 6, 2021).
Extra
    2016 "Enquanto votação do impeachment acontecia, Bolsonaro era batizado em Israel." May 12. https://extra.globo.com/noticias/brasil/enquanto-votacao-do-impeachment-acontecia-bolsonaro-era-batizado-em-israel-19287802.html (accessed December 6, 2021).
Freire, Paulo
    2005 *Pedagogy of the Oppressed*. New York: Continuum.
Goertz, Gary
    2003 *International Norms and Decision Making: A Punctuated Equilibrium Model*. Lanham, MD: Rowman and Littlefield.
Guerra, Rayanderson
    2018 "'Tem faca nos dentes para enfrentar essa guerra?', perguntou Bolsonaro ao futuro ministro da Educação." *O Globo*, December 3. https://oglobo.globo.com/sociedade/educacao/tem-faca-nos-dentes-para-enfrentar-essa-guerra-perguntou-bolsonaro-ao-futuro-ministro-da-educacao-23277301 (accessed December 6, 2021).
IBGE (Instituto Brasileiro de Geografia e Estatística)
    2012 "Censo demográfico 2010: características gerais da população, religião e pessoas com deficiência." https://biblioteca.ibge.gov.br/visualizacao/periodicos/94/cd_2010_religiao_deficiencia.pdf (accessed December 6, 2021).
Imprensa RNZ
    2016 "'Se algum professor for preso ou demitido, eu renuncio ao mandato,' diz deputado Nezinho." May 3. http://ricardonezinho.com.br/se-algum-professor-for-preso-ou-demitido-eu-renuncio-ao-mandato-diz-deputado-nezinho/ (accessed December 6, 2021).
INEP (Instituto Nacional de Estudos e Pesquisas Educacionais Anísio Teixeira)
    2009 "Prova de comunicação social." http://public.inep.gov.br/enade2009/COMUNICACAO_SOCIAL.pdf (accessed December 6, 2021).
Jones, Bryan D. and Frank R. Baumgartner
    2005 *The Politics of Attention: How Government Prioritizes Problems*. Chicago: University of Chicago Press.
Levy, Santiago
    2016 "Poverty in Latin America: where do we come from, where are we going?" *Brookings*, May 10. https://www.brookings.edu/opinions/poverty-in-latin-america-where-do-we-come-from-where-are-we-going/ (accessed December 6, 2021).
Lindblom, Charles E.
    1959 "The science of 'muddling through.'" *Public Administration Review* 19 (2): 79–88.
Nagib, Miguel
    n.d. "Sobre nós." http://escolasempartido.org/quem-somos/ (accessed December 6, 2021).
NoIndoctrination.org
    n.d. "Mission statement." https://web.archive.org/web/20090719080635/http://www.noindoctrination.org/mission.shtml (accessed December 6, 2021).
Passarinho, Nathalia
    2015 "Bolsonaro pede desfiliação do PP para seguir 'sonho' da presidência." *Globo.com*, April 14. http://g1.globo.com/politica/noticia/2015/04/bolsonaro-pede-desfiliacao-do-pp-para-seguir-sonho-da-presidencia.html (accessed December 6, 2021).

Pew Research Center

2014 "Religion in Latin America: widespread change in a historically Catholic region." http://www.pewresearch.org/wp-content/uploads/sites/7/2014/11/Religion-in-Latin-America-11-12-PM-full-PDF.pdf (accessed December 6, 2021).

Roxo, Sérgio

2016 "Crise no PT afasta prefeitos, que deixam sigla para disputar reeleição." *O Globo*, April 10. https://oglobo.globo.com/brasil/crise-no-pt-afasta-prefeitos-que-deixam-sigla-para-disputar-reeleicao-19054014 (accessed December 6, 2021).

Salvador Peralta, Jesus and Thiago Pezzuto Pacheco

2014 "Resisting 'progress': the new left and higher education in Latin America." *PS: Political Science & Politics* 47: 620–23.

Schattschneider, Elmer E.

1960 *The Semisovereign People: A Realist's View of Democracy in America*. New York: Holt, Rinehart and Winston.

Sindicato dos Professores de Alagoas

2016 "Nota de repúdio." *Sinpro Alagoas*, January 7. http://sinpro-al.com.br/v2/?p=1936 (accessed December 6, 2021).

Snook, Ivan

1972 *Indoctrination and Education*. London: Routledge and Kegan Paul.

Wildavsky, Aaron B.

1979 *The Politics of the Budgetary Process*. 3d edition. Boston: Little, Brown.

Wright, Luann

n.d. "About us." NoIndoctrination.org. https://web.archive.org/web/20090719061642/http://www.noindoctrination.org/aboutus.shtml (accessed December 6, 2021).

The Movimento Brasil Livre and the New Brazilian Right in the Election of Jair Bolsonaro

by
Marcelo Burgos Pimentel dos Santos, Claudio Luis de Camargo Penteado,
and Rafael de Paula Aguiar Araújo
Translated by
Nick Ortiz

The Movimento Brasil Livre (Free Brazil Movement) has been one of the main propo-nents of the new Brazilian right since its emergence after the June Days of 2013. Through the strategic use of social networks, it has promoted a conservative agenda similar to those seen in other parts of the world. An examination of its mobilization strategies focused on its communicative power, its capacity to produce engagement, and its network mobiliza-tion shows how the use of information and communication technologies influenced the emergence of new political actors on the Brazilian right.

O Movimento Brasil Livre tem sido um dos expoentes principais da nova direita brasileira que é um movimento que surgiu após as Jornadas de Junho de 2013. Através do uso estratégico das redes sociais, ajudou a expandir uma pauta conservadora em con-sonância ao que ocurre em diferentes partes do mundo. A presente pesquisa avalia as estratégias de mobilização do movimento com enfâse no seu poder comunicativo, capacid-ade de produção de engajamento e poder de mobilização de rede para indicar como os usos das tecnologias de informação e comunicação influenciam a emergência de novos atores políticos no campo da direita brasileira.

Keywords: Information and communication technologies, Movimento Brasil Livre, New Brazilian right, Jair Bolsonaro, Social networks

Information and communication technologies produce social and political change in contemporary societies. They also establish new dynamics in inter-personal relationships and between citizens and political institutions. As a result, organized civil society has created new practices that, in turn, have gen-erated new political and social processes focused on civic participation (Castells, 2008; 2013; Subirats, 2011). The digital space provided by the Internet has become important for organizing events and for the mobilization and dissemi-nation of information produced by civil society movements. There are many

Marcelo Burgos Pimentel dos Santos is a professor of social sciences at the Universidade Federal de Paraíba and a former visiting fellow at Goldsmiths, University of London. Claudio Luis de Camargo Penteado is a professor at the Universidade Federal do ABC and in its graduate program in human and social sciences. Rafael de Paula Aguiar Araújo is a professor of social sciences at the Pontifícia Universidade Católica de São Paulo. Nick Ortiz is a writer, researcher, linguist, and translator with experience in translation relating to Latin American history and politics.

LATIN AMERICAN PERSPECTIVES, Issue 248, Vol. 50 No. 1, January 2023, 237–253
DOI: 10.1177/0094582X221146767
© 2023 Latin American Perspectives

examples of political movements that are organized, planned, and dissemi-nated through various Internet channels, among them the Arab Spring, the Indignados in Spain, the various Occupies around the world (Castells, 2013), the 2013 June Days in Brazil, and the movements behind the impeachment of Dilma Rousseff.

This article analyzes the political performance of the Movimento Brasil Livre (Free Brazil Movement—MBL) through its activities in cyberspace. More spe-cifically, it evaluates the strategies of network political mobilization used by a proponent of the new Brazilian right that, through the use of information and communication technologies, organized several mobilizations in a campaign that led to the impeachment of Dilma Rousseff. We examine three dimensions of the movement: its communicative power (Castells, 2009), its capacity to produce engagement (Coleman and Gøtze, 2001), and its network mobilization power (Ugarte, 2008). We adopt the definitions of "right" and "left" proposed by Heywood (2015), who considers the left as more likely to accept interventionism and collective projects and the right as favoring the individual and the market. From this perspective, the left is associated with fraternity, equality, protection of rights, social progress, internationalism, etc., while the right champions author-ity, hierarchy, order, tradition, nationalism, and other conservative ideas.

Although the reemergence of the Brazilian right in recent years expanded democratic spaces by introducing more voices and discourses into public space, this did not lead to an improvement in the quality of democracy (Diamond and Morlino, 2005). According to data from the *Economist* Intelligence Unit's (2015–2020) Democracy Index, democratic values have shifted in much of the world since the 2008 economic crisis, leading to the emergence of various protest movements. In the case of Brazil, this study identifies dissatisfaction with dem-ocratic institutions. In the period analyzed, Brazil was classified as a failed democracy, dropping from forty-fourth to fifty-second place in the overall ranking. It lost points in three areas, the functioning of government, political culture, and civil liberties, revealing a loss of confidence in democracy in the country. Political participation was the only area that saw an increase, apparent in the greater involvement of social minorities in political processes and the emergence in recent years of right-wing groups such as the MBL. However, the increase in participation relating to the right did not reflect a respect for democ-racy. The discourse in this field was often critical of democracy and endorsed authoritarian and autocratic practices (Levitsky and Ziblatt, 2018). Contrary to what many optimists argued at the beginning, the Internet has not lived up to its liberating potential, partly because of the inequality of Internet access and the differences in the cultural hubs used by different groups. This article shows that there are worldviews that support values, interests, and beliefs that con-tradict the initial optimism (Curran, Fenton, and Freedman, 2016).

NEW POLITICAL AND SOCIAL DYNAMICS

The Internet made possible the creation of a new associative and civic arrangement supported by virtual communities. This led to the creation of "new identities, new spaces, and new public spheres that increase political deliberation and reinforce new definitions of social autonomy" (Subirats, 2011: 45). There was a reconfiguration of social and political dynamics influenced by a communicative process that assumed a central role in the most diverse fields of human activity. New civic spaces emerged, allowing people to interact freely, share their interests, and exercise their right to expression and assembly (Dahlgren, 2016). This, in turn, expanded boundaries and made democracy more tangible.

This new form of activism connected the online and offline worlds. Defined by the plurality and ingenuity of its strategies, it changed the face of political activism by allowing a new type of opposition and pressure to be exerted on federal organizations (Araújo, Penteado, and Santos, 2015). Castells (2013) argues that the laterality in the network interaction of different groups is one of the factors that change power relations in contemporary society. The Internet has facilitated a horizontal communication that enables civil society groups to be more assertive in pursuit of their interests. It also generates a reorganization between government officials and those they govern. Communication networks are fundamental sources for building power and influence (Castells, 1999). Studies in Brazil and around the world corroborate the use of the Internet by civil society groups as a tool for defending their causes and attest to the fact that it increases participation and public debate outside traditional political institutions.

In this rearrangement of social and political relations mediated by the digital media, the use of the Internet makes traditional models of participation and representation in civil society more flexible and horizontal. It also produces a new sense of belonging and identity (Egler, 2010) and allows for new appropriations of common space (Subirats, 2011). Electronic devices (such as computers, iPhones, etc.) enhance the ability of isolated individuals to connect to different communication channels that generate unique forms of articulation and mobilization around specific causes. This technology enables direct and collective action and eliminates the need for intermediation from traditional forms of political representation and organization (Egler, 2010; Castells, 2013), establishing a new model for connective action (Bennett and Sergeberg, 2013). Political representation, in turn, has come to depend on a large audience or, rather, on an "audience democracy" (Manin, 1997) as the new technologies have hollowed out the traditional political institutions and amplified the mass media. This new audience is connected through a worldwide web that allows direct interaction without the mediation of the traditional media.

This new structure of digital communication can be seen as contradictory to formal politics (Rasmussen, 2013), providing the technical conditions for greater participation in public debate. However, the construction of a dominant normative discourse or consensus has proved more difficult. While the communicative ecosystem has become more open and democratic, the traditional political system has become unstable and subject to tensions and questions about its legitimacy. Since 2014 the MBL and other right-wing groups (Vem Pra Rua, Revoltados Online, et al.) have positioned themselves as new actors in this new type of politics. In 2018, Bolsonaro used this tension to question the traditional political system and position himself as an antiestablishment candidate. Changes in the communication structure enhance the ability of new actors to question the role of traditional institutions in politics (Rasmussen, 2013), and this allows for the transformation of political strategies. In Brazil, the process behind Dilma Rousseff's impeachment can be attributed to the difficulty of governing within traditional political institutions (such as political parties and Congress) and to the media coverage of Operation Car Wash. In addition to these factors, the mobilization of conservative sectors of social networks (within which the MBL was an important factor) contributed to a marked increase in social dissatisfaction and encouraged the estrangement of these sectors from traditional political institutions.

According to Ugarte (2008), the Internet is a tool for political action in that it represents a new sphere of social relationships that are constantly changing within information networks. The Internet's model for the dissemination of information is not a single transmission center but several. In this model, every member (network node) has the ability to communicate as a sender, distributor, receiver, or multiplier in a system that has no gatekeepers. This is a phenomenon that Castells (2013) calls "mass self-communication." According to Castells, starting in 2008 there were protests triggered by crises related to economic structural causes and political legitimacy in which autonomous individuals and organized civil society intervened in politics through the appropriation of digital communication devices. In the case of Brazil, these actions did not always result in progressive movements. Since the 2013 June Days, the most conservative sectors have continued to profit the most from the appropriation of digital tools (Silveira, 2015). The use of information and communication technologies can be a detriment to social and political causes and can undermine democratic values. Two examples of this phenomenon include the use of fake news in the U.S. presidential elections in 2016 and in the Brazilian presidential elections in 2018 (Ituassu et al., 2019).

SOME CHARACTERISTICS OF INTERNET ACTIVISM

The onset of a globalized world marked by neoliberal hegemony and the intensive use of the Internet produced what Castells (1999) has called a "network society," a social and political structure that is flexible and adaptable to rapid change. The dynamics of this model of network organization depend on the communicative capacity of its nodes (members or users), its capacity to absorb and disseminate information, and its ability to process this information efficiently. As a result, communication skills are essential to the dynamics of these networks. In a network society, new forms of domination rest on two basic factors: the ability to develop, program, and reprogram networks and the ability to connect and ensure the strategic cooperation of different networks by sharing goals and pooling resources (Castells, 2009). These mechanisms are operated by "programmers" and "switchers," respectively.

Programmers are social actors (individuals, collectives, or institutions) who identify the objectives of the networks they operate and modify them according to the networks' needs. Their performance is linked to communicative efficiency, the ability to create and expand the discourses that guide and direct the actions of network participants. From this perspective, the MBL's discourses influence the configuration of a "public mind" that guides individual and collective behavior. The programming of communication on the network is essential to achieving predetermined objectives. Switchers are social actors of different backgrounds that "monitor the points of connection between various networks" (Castells, 2009: 46), thus allowing for the expansion of the network's scope of action. The MBL's switchers generate alliances, partnerships, and cooperation with other groups that increase the group's ability to promote action and mobilization.

Another important component of contemporary society is the capacity for engagement on the part of the actors involved. For Putnam (2008), social capital allows one to avoid the dilemma of collective action. Coleman and Gøtze (2001) note that the expansion of citizen participation and the emergence of the connected citizen help social actors to overcome the current legitimacy crisis of representative democracy. For participation to be effective, more connections and community actions must be created to foster the capacity to build social capital and develop mechanisms of mutual trust based on shared relationships. For these writers, the use of information and communication technologies produces new social and political relationships. The production of social and political values in virtual communities guides collective action and produces the necessary engagement for participation in public life. At the time Coleman and Gøtze's study was published, blogs played this kind of unifying role. Unification continues to take place today on virtual community platforms such as Facebook, Twitter, Instagram, and YouTube, which have become fundamental to interaction in contemporary society.

In the decentralized communication model proposed by Ugarte (2008), whose new political configuration is called "pluriarchy," there are no binary decisions. Decisions depend on people's sympathy for proposals brought forward by network participants. Pluriarchy works in a configuration that contains an abundance of information in which specialized groups act to guarantee the fluidity of network flows. This stands in contrast to a traditional democracy, which operates in a system where information is scarcer and where the communicative process is vertical. In pluriarchy, netocrats, despite lacking the power to make decisions in the traditional political field, influence the trajectory of the networks and the goals that drive the actions of network participants. In addition to their communicative capacity, netocrats stand out from their peers in their prestige, their social capital, and the way they represent the network's values. Although the network has no gatekeepers, some actors play a major role in the production of discourses and meanings that influence it. What is published influences many citizens in hegemonic disputes over narratives and the interpretation of reality.

According to Ugarte (2008), the power of networks is inseparable from the ability of netocrats (specialized users who have the role of guiding the actions of groups on online environments) to create and deconstruct narratives to generate new interpretations that guide the actions of participants. Internet networks create collective entities and a spirit of solidarity that are influenced by these leaders. This does not necessarily mean a commitment to factual reality, as is apparent in the fake-news phenomenon of the 2016 U.S. and 2018 Brazilian presidential elections and during the COVID-19 pandemic, in which Bolsonaro's false posts were and continue to be challenged by Facebook, Twitter, and Instagram.[1]

It is in this context of informational capitalism that cyberactivism emerges. This new activism goes far beyond the simple use of technological tools by old activists and is characterized by the emergence of new actors and practices. Cyberactivism is political action that uses the Internet to disseminate a narrative and, in contrast to traditional media institutions, provides tools that allow people to mobilize on behalf of causes. It operates by distributing social and political values that, in turn, produce collective identities. Humorous and creative uses of information and communication technologies increase the scope of group actions and the visibility of causes by helping to spread their ideas. Cyberactivism is a strategy that tries to change the public agenda by including new themes or views that cyberactivists believe should be the order of the day (Ugarte, 2008).

The MBL came into being through the efficient use of digital communication channels. In addition to being on the front line in the mobilizations against Dilma Rousseff, it succeeded in electing its members to important positions, including Senators Marcos Rogério and Eduardo Girão and Deputies Kim Kataguiri, Zé Mario, Jerônimo Goergen, and Sóstenes Cavalcante, state deputies in various regions, and city council members. This article seeks to examine the MBL's network performance and the strategies it utilized to promote online and offline actions such as street demonstrations and its production of discourses that created new values and forms of subjectivity among social actors.

THE RIGHT IN BRAZIL

The resurgence of the right in Brazil in recent years reflects its historical significance. Right-wing sectors have always had a voice in Brazilian politics, whether it be during the nineteenth century during the imperial period, the period between the Proclamation and the end of the Old Republic, the Estado Novo (1937–1945), or the military dictatorship (1964–1985). In the nineteenth century there was a clash between liberals and conservatives. With the advent of the Republic, there was a rapprochement with the international fascist right (represented by the Integralists [Ação Integralista Brasileira, led by Plinio Salgado]), whose inspiration was Mussolini's government in Italy. During the Estado Novo, the Integralists formed the Partido de Representação (Popular Representation Party), which had considerable influence in the Italian and German colonies of southern Brazil (Kaysel, 2015).

During the democratic period of 1945–1964, the right sought to discourage any attempt at a progressive government that would try to implement policies against social inequality. One of the most recognizable names during this period was that of Carlos Lacerda, who was directly involved in several political watershed moments and was critical of any progressive vision. During the military dictatorship, the policies adopted were conservative, reactionary, and characterized by arrests, torture, assassinations, and disappearances of leftist leaders and their supporters. After the country's redemocratization, conservative political forces stayed relevant as subsequent governments (those of Sarney, Collor, Itamar, and Cardoso) implemented a neoliberal agenda and maintained Brazil's existing political structure and institutions.

Change (albeit not radical) would come with the governments ruled by the Partido dos Trabalhadores (Workers' Party—PT).

Lula's first term (2003–2006), despite some advances in social welfare, was marked by a corruption scandal known as the Mensalão in 2005. Nevertheless, he was reelected because of his inclusive policies and the degree of economic growth that occurred during his presidency. Lula ended his second term (2007–2010) as the most highly rated president in Brazilian history (with an 87 percent approval rating)[2] and ensured the election of Rousseff, one of his former ministers, in the 2010 elections. Dilma Rousseff was the first woman to be elected president of the Republic and was reelected in 2014 in a close election against the former governor of Minas Gerais and former senator Aécio Neves, who represented sectors of the center-right. Her second term would be interrupted by an impeachment trial in 2016.

During the PT period right-wing groups opposed the government's distributive policies (albeit not intensely or provocatively). Casimiro (2018) contends that even before the PT governments conservative sectors were seeking to increase their political representation and spread their ideas through foundations and business institutions (some of which are similar to think tanks). At the same time, however, a more extreme right wing, Integralist fascism, was trying to preserve its political ideas and actions in the Brazilian right (Gonçalves and Neto, 2020). One example was Cansei (Civic Movement for the Rights of Brazilians), which began after a plane crash in São Paulo in 2007.[3] One of its founders was an entertainment entrepreneur, João Dória Júnior, who is now the governor of São Paulo. Despite being from the center-right Partido da Social Democracia Brasileira (Brazilian Social Democracy Party—PSDB), which had selected Geraldo Alckmin as its candidate, Dória informally articulated a joint platform with Jair Bolsonaro.[4] Analyzing the protests of 2007–2015, Tatagiba, Trindade, and Teixeira (2015) identified posters such as "Fora Lula," "Basta," and "Cansei." Although there were no major conservative protests in between 2007 and 2013, they argue that, despite the popularity of the Lula government, there was continuity with regard to the ongoing clash between the left and the right.

In June 2013 demonstrations broke out in several cities across the country. The initial protest, organized by a group aligned with the left, was called to oppose the increase in ticket prices for urban transport, but soon after the demands of the protesters expanded to include slogans against traditional political parties (antipartisanship), corruption, the Dilma Rousseff government, and the holding of the 2014 World Cup and the 2016 Olympics in Rio de Janeiro. Similar to what was happening in other parts of the world, the demands of the protesters reached the traditional political system and signaled a crisis of representation that revealed the importance of social networks as a space for political mobilization and the expression of discontent (Castells, 2013). The agenda of a movement demanding a reduction of public transport fares ended up being hijacked and altered by right-wing movements. These protests became known as the June Days, and they mobilized millions of Brazilians across every region and in several cities across the country. The main targets of their hostility were the Dilma Rousseff government and the PT, "demonstrating a strong association between antipartisanship and anti-PT sentiment" (Tatagiba, Trindade, and Teixeira, 2015). The protests continued unabated through the World Cup contest and even during Rousseff's reelection campaign in 2014. In this electoral campaign, right-wing groups became stronger and more visible as they formed an anti-PT network that reached a wide audience through social media platforms.

Chaia and Brugnago (2014) note that the 2014 elections were the center of broad political discussions on the Internet. The ideas and values championed by the 2013 demonstrations and the reappearance of a conservative, militant right wing were the backdrop for these discussions and the basis of an anti-PT network. This network began to use social networks as a tool to mobilize and express its values and ideology. Silveira (2014) points to the clashes within social networks during the 2014 elections. The use of information and communication technologies by the Brazilian right has been a recurring theme since 2006. One example is the website Mídia sem Máscara (Media Unmasked), which criticized the press and the media in general by arguing that their newsrooms had been taken over by "communists." Since then, participation in these sites has continued to expand (Rocha, 2018), and right-wing groups continue to emerge offline. Vem pra Rua (To the Streets) and Endireita Brasil (Give Brazil Its Rights), among others, were supported by organizations such as the Instituto Liberal do Rio de Janeiro (Liberal Institute of Rio de Janeiro), Renovação Liberal (Liberal Renewal), and the U.S. Atlas Network.

Although Dilma Rousseff was reelected, this did not stop the conservative wave or the increase in visibility of right-wing forces, whose members occupied a large number of seats in Congress and would become fundamental in the 2016 impeachment trial. While the PT won the presidency, the right won the legislature. Immediately after the 2014 election, a demonstration in São Paulo was already demanding that the reelected president to be barred from taking office (Tatagiba, Trindade, and Teixeira, 2015; Rocha, 2018). The demonstrations against Dilma Rousseff intensified in 2015–2016. At the same time, the actions of Operation Car Wash, a program created to fight corruption and persecute members of the left, especially former president Lula, helped conservatives to develop their political ideas. As a result, many of these groups, including the MBL, ended up supporting Jair Bolsonaro's candidacy for the presidency.

The June Days in 2013 and the subsequent protests had several things in common, among them the use of the Internet (especially social networks) for organizing, mobilizing, and disseminating information (and counterinformation) to stimulate public debate (Silveira, 2014). Ruediger et al. (2014) contend that there is a new public sphere that is characterized not by consensus but by the intensification of conflict and polarization between new political actors that have privileged positions on the Internet. The engagement strategies of these new political actors allowed some groups to gain prominence in organizing protests and assume a central role in movements that supported the impeachment of Dilma Rousseff. They also have a right-wing agenda that combines the defense of neoliberal economic policies such as labor and social security reform with socially conservative values such as the opposition to abortion of movements such as Escola sem Partido (School without Party), which defends homeschooling in the belief that schools indoctrinate students into a leftist agenda. These conservative groups occupied spaces in the traditional media and expanded their influence in social networks (Tatagiba, Trindade, and Teixeira, 2015).

THE MBL

The MBL systematically uses social networks to advance its cause.[5] Its Facebook page[6] has more information than its official website, and "its goal is to mobilize [Brazilian] citizens in favor of a more free, just, and prosperous society."[7] It presents itself as a nonprofit organization that defends democracy, freedom of expression, the press, the Republic, the idea of a smaller state and bureaucracy, and the free market, and until 2015 it also portrayed itself as nonpartisan. On the eve of the 2016 municipal elections, the post that contained this information was removed because some of its main members, among them Fernando Holiday, had been elected to positions in various political parties. In 2018, Kim Kataguiri was elected a federal deputy and Arthur do Val a state deputy for São Paulo. All the MBL members elected were the candidates of center-right or right-wing parties. In addition to electing its own members, the MBL helped others who sought to use the movement's influence to support their own electoral campaigns such as Marcos Rogério and Eduardo Girão, who were elected senators.

The fact that it purposely concealed its nonpartisan orientation is important because it demonstrates the ability of the MBL to act as a programmer in forming the opinions of its followers. This antipartisan orientation had emerged during the 2013 June Days and produced new political actors that proved fundamental in gaining new followers. Because of the lawsuits that took place in Brazil between 2016 and 2018, the corruption and abuse committed by political parties was already well established in the social imaginary. This antipartisan discourse was incorporated by the traditional media that shape public opinion. The rejection of political parties and of politics itself was a factor in the protests and became an important element of the 2018 presidential election.

Another important factor was anti-PT discourse, which was also adopted by the traditional media. This discourse began with the Mensalão scandal in 2005 and led to the Cansei movement that gained ground during the protests associated with the 2013 June Days, the demonstrations against the holding of the World Cup in 2014, and the uproar over the handling of the Olympics in Rio de Janeiro in 2016 (an event that almost cost Dilma Rousseff her second term as president).[8] Anti-PT discourse, combined with antipartisan ideas, became entrenched with Operation Car Wash. Switchers assumed a major role in spreading this discourse, which was used by many political actors during the impeachment of Dilma Rousseff in 2015. This new discourse was embraced by the MBL, which knew how to take advantage of the situation in order to become a new political actor with nationwide appeal and importance.

These discourses against the traditional political system were supported by the traditional media and by programmers who reinforced the association between the PT government, the country's problems with corruption, and the economic crisis that erupted in 2014. The proposed solution (promoted both by the traditional media and by the social networks) was to impeach Rousseff. This element united the agendas of conservative and reactionary groups and gave them a united front with which to take to the streets in large numbers on various occasions. The fight against corruption, the PT, and the Lula and Dilma

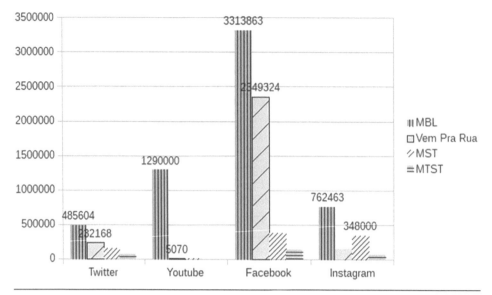

Figure 1. Presence of social movements in the social media.

governments was articulated by the MBL and helped mobilize a younger generation and audience into action.

The MBL adopted an efficient communication strategy that persuaded many constituents and increased its number of followers. This strategy consisted of using images, videos, and memes in a way that was critical of institutional politics and the corruption of the PT. The MBL also acted as a switcher in its ability to connect various smaller networks around a common goal defined by its conservative agenda. The group has its own YouTube channel with close to 1.2 million subscribers. In addition, some of its main leaders (such as Kim Kataguiri, Fernando Holiday, and Arthur do Val) found space in the traditional media with which to express their views.

The MBL put links on its pages to various articles and videos from traditional media sources such as Rede Globo, *Folha de São Paulo*, and *Veja*. It also directed people to the pages of intellectuals such as the historian Marco Antônio Villa and the journalist/celebrity Raquel Sheherazade. The social capital borrowed from conservative personalities and the traditional media helped maintain the large number of views on the MBL's webpage, which featured the group's agenda and functioned as the group's argument from authority. However, as time passed and the group became larger, the MBL began to reference more and more of its own leaders and members.

To illustrate the MBL's communicative power (Castells, 2009) and the reach of its publications, we have created two graphs (Figures 1 and 2). The first compares the number of the MBL's followers with those of Vem pra Rua (which also played a role in the protests surrounding the impeachment) and two other social movements traditionally associated with the Brazilian left, the Movimento Sem Terra (Landless Workers' Movement—MST) and the Movimento dos Trabalhadores Sem Teto (Homeless Workers' Movement—MTST). The second compares traditional political parties that were and continue to be influential

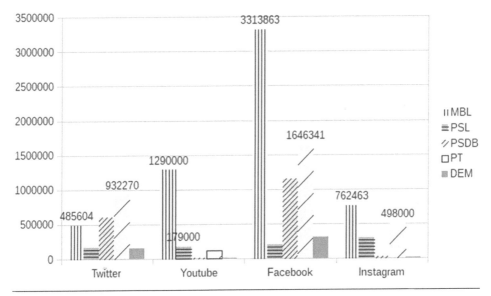

Figure 2. MBL and political parties in the social media.

in Brazil's political system (the Partido da Social Democracia Brasileira [PSDB], the PT, the Democratas [DEM]) and the party that helped elect Bolsonaro in 2018, the Partido da Social Liberal (PSL).

Figure 1 shows that the MBL performed the best on all the main social media platforms that were analyzed. Brazil has 140 million active users (66 percent of the population) and is ranked the second-highest in terms of time spent on social networks, with a daily average of 3 hours and 34 minutes on websites such as YouTube and Facebook, the two most popular forms of social media in Brazil).[9] It is apparent that the militants of the MST and the MTST are socially and digitally marginalized, with the Internet replicating existing social inequalities. It is also apparent that the MBL uses a logic of connective action described by Bennett and Segerberg (2013) as one in which one organizational mode is substituted for another—in this case an organization articulated through information and communication technologies.

Figure 2 shows that it was only on Twitter that the MBL had fewer followers than the major political parties that had played a historic role in governing the country in 1995–2002 (the PSDB) and 2003–2016 (PT). However, the MBL had more followers than the DEM (the party of the president of the Chamber of Deputies, Rodrigo Mara) and the PSL (the party that with the help of Bolsonaro elected the largest block in 2018). On the most popular platforms (Facebook and YouTube), the MBL had more followers and subscribers than any of the major political parties.

As did other groups that arose during this period, the MBL proved efficient at using digital communication to produce discourses that influenced public opinion. Much of this discourse was humorous and ironic, which increased the likelihood that this information would be shared. This allowed for the formation of networks that augmented the movement's symbolic capital. In general, the MBL reinforced existing stereotypes in Brazilian society, whose presence suggests that society had become increasingly indifferent to Brazil's traditional politicians. It made clever use of the economic crisis and the increasing discontent with traditional politics. It also knew how to choose its targets. This can be seen in its targeting of Dilma Rousseff and Lula. To advance its agenda, it attacked politicians (primarily from the PT) using irony and demonstrated its ability to produce social capital through its interaction with virtual communities and to generate a collective identity. This helped increase its power of engagement, and this in turn allowed it to play an important role in the impeachment of Dilma Rousseff and in the anti-PT discourse that propelled Jair Bolsonaro to the presidency.

The group's power of engagement (Coleman and Gøtze, 2001) was a factor in the propagation of shares and likes for the program it promoted on various Internet platforms. The same can be said for the emergence of street protests that were led by the MBL and contributed to the election of some of the MBL's leaders. The MBL worked alongside of the traditional media to promote its agenda. The coverage of these media (primarily those of the movements associated with the impeachment) contributed to its increasing visibility.

The production of engagement depends on constant communication that creates a collective identity. The criticism of traditional politics and political parties (mostly the PT) that was presented in traditional media settings gave groups like the MBL an opportunity to advance their goals. Initially, the MBL had simply reproduced information from traditional media sources. Later it produced its own content with MBLNews.[10] The daily sharing of MBL posts millions of times by millions of viewers is evidence of its engagement strategy.

The MBL also has marketing capability. It has a store that sells products related to its agenda such as mugs and T-shirts that reference Operation Pixuleco, which targeted Lula for corruption, or bear the image of the former judge Sérgio Moro. Another factor that contributes to engagement is the possibility of connecting through financial contributions. Currently, there are five monthly plans, ranging from R$30,000 to R$1,000,000, with ironic names that reinforce the MBL's right-wing profile: (1) CIA agent, (2) Koch Brothers, (3) Invisible Hand, (4) Pelego Exterminator, and (5) Steamroller.

The MBL is promoting proposals for public policies that were presented at a congress held in 2015—education, health, sustainability, political reform, economics, justice, transportation, and urbanization. These proposals provided the basis for the campaigns of their members in the 2016 and 2018 elections.[11] The MBL allied itself with parties from the right and center-right in order to give its members more autonomy in defending the movement's agenda even if it meant going against its own nonpartisan guidelines. This represents a new practice in Brazilian politics.

The creative strategies used by the MBL include the use of narratives and Internet resources. These constitute a new type of power that defines the role of the netocrat in contemporary politics. During the impeachment process, the MBL was able to observe the discursive disputes that were happening on the network and deconstruct arguments that contradicted its own. It used opinions and facts in a way helped it to rally Brazilians around the impeachment. Information was circulated in a way that made fun of government arguments and fomented a spirit of revolt and struggle against the corruption that, from

TABLE 1

Forms of Mobilization by the MBL during the Impeachment

Form of Mobilization	Frequency	%
Dissemination/announcement of protests	15	30
Dissemination of MBL content	8	16
Dissemination of information from traditional media	7	14
Dissemination of information from alternative media	1	2
Attacks/irony on the PT and its leaders	15	30
Attacks/irony on the left and its proponents	6	12
Others	3	6

Note: Here and elsewhere, a post may have more than one form of mobilization, and therefore the sum of percentages may be greater than 100.

TABLE 2

Mobilization Repertoire by the MBL during the Impeachment

Type of Attack	Frequency	%
Accusation	19	38
Irony	9	18
Protests	11	22
Online mobilization	1	2
Critical analysis of the government	5	10
Critical analysis of the left	1	2
Differentiation/antagonism	7	14
Others	1	2

TABLE 3

Interpretative Narratives Surrounding the Impeachment Used by the MBL

Narrative	Frequency	%
Blaming corruption and the PT	11	22
Fight against corruption	12	24
Criticism and irony of the left/communists	5	10
Criticism of Dilma	14	28
Defense of neoliberal policies	2	4
Lula as the main culprit	2	4
Others	13	26

its point of view, had invaded the country. The creation of memes with shocking images and catch phrases played a role in the construction of a narrative that was supported by the MBL and other social movements.

To illustrate the production capacity of its political discourses, we analyzed the 25 messages that received the most interaction (likes, comments, and shares) in 2015 and 2016 in the 50 publications with the greatest appeal for the MBL's followers (Tables 1–4).

MBL leaders also appeared in the videos that were analyzed. Thus the mobilization strategies of the netocrats support the idea that narrative construction and the mobilization of values fed on one another and were used to reinforce

TABLE 4
Values Utilized by the MBL during the Impeachment

Values	Frequency	%
Conservative	2	4
Punitive	2	4
Militarist	0	0
Liberal	3	6
Rejection of politics	3	6
Rejection/hatred of the PT	34	68
Others	7	14

existing anti-PT sentiment. The information circulated by the MBL resonated with the traditional media and reinforced agenda setting in an ecosystem of hybrid communication in which content constructed in social networks played an important and decisive role in public debate.[12]

CONCLUSION

The MBL acted as a broadcaster and creator of ideas for the Brazilian right through the efficient use of digital networks and the programming and connecting of various communities on online platforms. It organized a discourse around topics such as Dilma Rousseff's impeachment, anti-PT sentiment, and the fight against corruption and the traditional political system and used it to support the candidacies of some of its members and, in 2018, that of Jair Bolsonaro.[13] Led by young people who had not initially aligned themselves with any traditional political party, the MBL was able to gain a political role through its use of social networks to connect with people with a conservative profile who also despised the PT and its political leaders.

The MBL is a movement that has proved capable of penetrating social media platforms. Its engagement power is apparent in its amassing of social capital and the use of it to forge a collective identity and a new subjectivity. It has also used its capacity for network mobilization to influence Brazilian politics, employing a discourse that was supported by the traditional media and compatible with that of certain conservative sectors of the Brazilian population. Those in the MBL can be described as netocrats for their ability to produce large online mobilizations and their use of narratives to communicate. These abilities, in turn, have allowed it to assume a leadership position in the networks it operates.

The results of this study indicate that political action has a new modus operandi that is reconfiguring the dynamics of civil society. The use of the Internet consolidates new practices of political and social engagement, whether through communication, network mobilizations, or participation in new political and social movements. Right-wing groups are gaining a louder voice and assuming an important role in contemporary Brazilian politics. While the use of information and communication technologies for the purposes of mobilization, protests, and political resistance can be helpful in spreading democracy and creating a more plural communication system, this does not necessarily mean an improvement in the quality of democracy. These technologies are often used to promote autocratic practices that may corrupt and even destroy a democracy. Their use may also facilitate the rise of antiestablishment leaders who only deepen the crisis surrounding liberal democracy.

In 2020, after the first draft of this article was finished, a rearrangement of the conservative forces that helped elect Bolsonaro in 2018 took place. During the first two years of his term, Bolsonaro's speeches and policies had shifted toward the extreme right, with the persecution and arrest of journalists, scholars, and scientists, threats against the Supreme Court and against governors and mayors, meddling with the Federal Police, and treatment of the armed forces as if they were his personal bodyguards. This shift provoked a backlash and a distancing in relation to certain social sectors within the more moderate right, and the MBL distanced itself from Bolsonaro and even criticized him and his government. This distancing intensified after Sérgio Moro left Bolsonaro's government on April 24, 2019. The march of the extreme right led by Bolsonaro drove social and political sectors associated with the moderate right to try to create a broad front (or "third way") to oppose Lula's candidacy and compete in the 2022 elections. If they succeed, it will be unprecedented in Brazilian history and will signal a new configuration of political forces within the right.

NOTES

1. It is worth noting that Donald Trump was banned from Internet social networks such as Twitter in 2021. https://www.bbc.com/news/technology-57018148 (accessed May 29, 2021).

2. Based on data from the Instituto Brasileiro de Opinião Pública e Estatística survey of December 16, 2010. For more details, see http://g1.globo.com/politica/noticia/2010/12/popularidade-de-lula-bate-recorde-e-chega-87-diz-ibope.html (accessed November 8, 2022).

3. This was the biggest air accident in Brazil, and conservative social sectors blamed the PT government for what happened.

4. When he was a candidate, Dória articulated a campaign called "BolsoDória" (Bolsonaro for president and Dória for governor). Before his candidacy, he was already a well-known promoter of conservative values. A good example was the magazine he founded, *Caviar Lifestyle*.

5. For more details, see https://mbl.org.br (accessed May 20, 2021).

6. For more details, see https://www.facebook.com/mblivre/ (accessed May 20, 2021).

7. For more details, see https://www.facebook.com/pg/mblivre/about/?ref=page_internal (accessed May 20, 2021).

8. The official results from the Supreme Electoral Court showed that Dilma Rousseff obtained 51.65 percent of the votes in the election that led to her second term. In São Paulo, the epicenter of large protests, she received only 35.69 percent of the vote compared with 64.31 percent for her opponent, Aécio Neves.

9. For more details, see https://www.youtube.com/channel/UC8QAdpiEWAOg3AOCCF DCOYw (accessed May 25, 2021).

10. Data from the reports *Digital in 2019* and *We are Social*. https://wearesocial.com/global-digital-report-2019 (accessed May 19, 2020).

11. This can be seen with its Facebook page (111,939 followers), its profile on Twitter (23,581 followers), its Instagram (more than 35 million followers), and its channel on YouTube (more than 6,330 subscriptions) (data collected on May 19, 2020).

12. This process of institutionalization on the part of the MBL mirrors what other movements, such as Podemos in Spain, have accomplished across the world.

13. In Brazil, there are no independent candidates. Every candidate must be registered with a political party.

REFERENCES

Araújo, Rafael, Cláudio Penteado, and Marcelo Burgos Santos
    2015 "Democracia digital e experiências de e-participação: webativismo e políticas públicas."
    História, Ciência, Saúde: Manguinhos 22 suppl.: 1597–1619.
Bennett, W. Lance and Alexandra Segerberg
    2013 *The Logic of Connective Action: Digital Media and the Personalization of Contentious Politics.*
    Cambridge: Cambridge University Press.
Casimiro, Flávio Henrique
    2018 "As classes dominantes e a nova direita no Brasil contemporâneo," pp. 41–45 in Esther
    Solano Gallego (ed.), *O ódio como política: A reinvenção das direitas no Brasil.* São Paulo: Boitempo.
Castells, Manuel
    1999 *Sociedade em rede.* São Paulo: Paz e Terra.
    2008 "The new public sphere: global civil society, communication networks, and global gover-
    nance." *Annals of the American Academy of Political and Social Science* 616 (1): 78–93.
    2009 *Comunicación y poder.* Madrid: Alianza Editorial.
    2013 *Redes de indignação e esperança: Movimentos sociais na era da Internet.* Rio de Janeiro: Zahar.
Chaia, Vera and Fabricio Brugnago
    2014 "A nova polarização política nas eleições de 2014: radicalização ideológica da direita no
    mundo contemporâneo do Facebook." *Aurora: Revista de Arte, Mídia e Política* 7 (21): 99–129.
Coleman, Stephen and John Gøtze
    2001 *Bowling Together: Online Public Engagement in Policy Deliberation.* London: Hansard Society.
Curran, James, Natalie Fenton, and Des Freedman
    2016) *Misunderstanding the Internet.* 2d edition. London: Routledge.
Dahlgren, Peter
    2016 "The Internet as civic space," pp. 17–34 in Stephen Coleman and Deen Freelon (eds.),
    Handbook of Digital Politics. London: Edward Elgar.
Economist Intelligence Unit
    2020 "Democracy index (2015–2020)." https://www.eiu.com/topic/democracy-index.
Diamond, Larry and Leonardo Morlino
    2005 *Assessing the Quality of Democracy.* Baltimore: John Hopkins University Press.
Egler, Tamara Tania Cohen
    2010 "Redes tecnossociais e democratização das políticas públicas." *Revista Sociologias* 23:
    208–236.
Gonçalves, Leandro Pereira and Odilon Caldeira Neto
    2020 *O fascismo em camisas verdes: Do Integralismo ao Neointegralismo.* Rio de Janeiro: FGV
    Editora.
Heywood, Andrew
    2015 *Key Concepts in Politics and International Relations.* London: Palgrave Macmillan.
Ituassu, Arthur, Letícia Capone, Leonardo Firmino, Vivian Mannheimer, and Filipe Murta
    2019 "Comunicación política, eleciones y democracia: las campañas de Donald Trump y Jair
    Bolsonaro." *Perspectivas de la Comunicación* 12 (2): 11–37.
Kaysel, André
    2015 "Regressando ao regresso: elementos para uma genealogia das direitas Brasileiras," pp.
    49–74 in Sebastião Velasco e Cruz, André Kaysel, and Gustavo Codas (eds.), *Direita, volver! O
    retorno da direita e o ciclo político brasileiro.* São Paulo: Ed. Fundação Perseu Abramo.
Levitsky, Steven and Daniel Ziblatt
    2018 *How Democracies Die.* Harmondsworth: Penguin Books.
Manin, Bernard
    1997 *The Principles of Representative Government.* Cambridge: Cambridge University Press.
Putnam, Robert
    2008 *Bowling Alone: The Collapse and Revival of American Community.* New York: Simon and
    Schuster.
Rasmussen, Terje
    2013 "Internet-based media, Europe and the political public sphere." *Media, Culture & Society*
    35 (1): 97–104.

Rocha, Camila
    2018 "O boom das novas direitas: financiamento ou militância," pp. 47–52 in Esther Solano Gallego (ed.), *O ódio como política: A reinvenção das direitas no Brasil*. São Paulo: Boitempo.
Ruediger, Marco Aurélio, Rafael Martins, Margareth da Luz, and Amaro Grassi
    2014 "Ação coletiva e polarização na sociedade em rede: para uma teoria do conflito no Brasil contemporâneo." *Revista Brasileira de Sociologia* 2: 205–234.
Silveira, Sérgio Amadeu
    2014 "O embate nas redes." *Em Debate* 6 (7): 28–34.
    2015 "Direita nas redes sociais on line," pp. 213–230 in Sebastião Velasco e Cruz, André Kaysel, and Gustavo Codas (eds.), *Direita, volver! O retorno da direita e o ciclo político brasileiro*. São Paulo: Ed. Fundação Perseu Abramo.
Subirats, Joan
    2011 *¿Otra sociedad, otra política? De "no nos representan" a la democracia de lo común*. Barcelona: Icaria Editorial.
Tatagiba, Luciana, Thiago Trindade, and Ana Claudia Chaves Teixeira
    2015 "Protestos à direita no Brasil (2007–2015)," pp. 197–212 in Sebastião Velasco e Cruz, André Kaysel, and Gustavo Codas (eds.), *Direita, volver! O retorno da direita e o ciclo político brasileiro*. São Paulo: Ed. Fundação Perseu Abramo.
Ugarte, David
    2008 *O poder das redes*. Barcelona: El Cobre Ediciones.

Bolsonaro's Subservience to Trump, 2019 and 2020

A Demanding Agenda and Limited Reciprocity

by
Laís Forti Thomaz and Tullo Vigevani
Translated by
Heather Hayes

In the relationship between Brazil and the United States during the Bolsonaro and Trump administrations (2019 and 2020), Brazil advanced a demanding agenda that met with limited reciprocity. John Kingdon's concept of the policy window is useful for explaining that the two presidents, having similar worldviews, saw the possibility of moving forward with this agenda, but Brazil's subservient position ended up compromising its bargaining position. In the case of the commercial aspects of the Alcântara technological safeguards agreement, Brazil's unilateral concessions failed to generate concrete results before this window was closed and even set the country on the path toward becoming an international pariah.

O governo brasileiro promoveu uma agenda ambiciosa que facilitou pouca reciprocidade na relação entre o Brasil e os Estados Unidos durante os governos Bolsonaro e Trump (2019 e 2020). O conceito de John Kingdon do policy window é útil para explicar o fato que ambos os presidentes, além de partilhar visões semelhantes do mundo, viram a possibilidade de avançarem esta agenda. Contudo, a posição submissa do Brasil acabou em comprometer sua posição negocial. No caso dos aspectos comerciais do acordo das salvaguardas tecnológicas da Alcântara, o Brasil deixou passar essa oportunidade porque as concessões unilaterais do governo brasileiro falharam em produzir resultados concretos e, ademais, colocou o país no caminho de se tornar um paria internacional.

Keywords: Brazil–United States relations, Bolsonaro, Trump, Decision making, International negotiations

The goal of this paper is to analyze the relationship between Brazil and the United States in the Jair Bolsonaro and Donald Trump administrations (2019 and 2020). The hypothesis to be examined is that Brazil advanced a demanding agenda that met with limited reciprocity from its U.S. counterpart and failed to produce results in terms of foreign policy objectives. The Bolsonaro administration's demanding agenda was translated into the pursuit of agreements at any price, aiming to consolidate domestic power in a context of subservience.

Laís Forti Thomaz is an assistant professor at the Universidade Federal de Goiás and a researcher at the National Institute of Science and Technology for Studies on the United States. Tullo Vigevani is a full professor of political science at the Universidade Estadual de São Paulo and a researcher at the National Institute of Science and Technology for Studies on the United States. Thomaz thanks the Distrito Federal Foundation (SEI-GDF No. 798/2019-FAPDF/SUCTI/COOTEC) for financial support, and both authors thank Elisa Casc ão Ferreira for her contributions to this paper. Heather Hayes is a translator living in Quito, Ecuador.

LATIN AMERICAN PERSPECTIVES, Issue 248, Vol. 50 No. 1, January 2023, 254–271
DOI: 10.1177/0094582X231152903
© 2023 Latin American Perspectives

In his electoral campaign, Bolsonaro was seen as a sort of "Brazilian Trump," something that his supporters considered positive. His relationships, whether personal or through intermediaries, with the U.S. president and with Steve Bannon contributed to his legitimacy in the eyes of part of the U.S. right-wing elite. He benefited from the anti-Partido dos Trabalhadores (Workers' Party—PT) campaign that was first set off in 2005 and gained strength over the course of Operation Car Wash (P. Anderson, 2019; Hunter and Power, 2019; Singer, 2020). He openly favored bolstering the relationship with Trump's United States. According to Rodrigues (2019: 2), the "affinities between the two are not limited to their ideas, their neo-nationalist tendencies, propensity for post-truth politics (for example, denial of global warming and the military dictatorship in Brazil), and zest for governing via Twitter"; Brazil could well be considered a pivotal state for the far-right movement in Latin America. Shear and Haberman (2019) stress that the White House had the idea that Trump and Bolsonaro could work together to generate a closer connection in terms of trade and regional matters, including the Venezuelan crisis. This pro–United States stance triggered diplomatic incidents and attacks on China despite the fact that in the first two decades of the twenty-first century China had taken on great importance not only in the Brazilian economy but as a world superpower. Bolsonaro made four trips to the United States in his first two years in office—in March, May, and September 2019 and March 2020.

Our analysis focuses on whether success was achieved from the Bolsonaro administration's point of view during the Trump years. The main questions addressed are (1) Did the Bolsonaro administration generate an extreme change in foreign policy during Trump's term? (2) What gains were expected from this change? (3) Were the Brazilian expectations and demands of 2019 and 2020 met with reciprocity by the United States despite the asymmetry of power? We will address two objects that stood out on the bilateral agenda, trade negotiations and the Alcântara technological safeguards agreement, from the perspective of the decision-making assumptions of international negotiations. Our paper is divided into five parts, beginning with this introduction. The second section addresses the concepts and strategies in setting the 2019–2020 agenda and bargaining in international negotiations. The third reviews interpretations of the changes in relations between Brazil and the United States and their structural causes. The fourth provides two case studies, and the fifth provides an analytical assessment of the closure of the Bolsonaro-Trump policy window with the election of Joe Biden.

APPROACHES TO INTERNATIONAL NEGOTIATIONS: AGENDA AND BARGAINING POWER

Adapting Hudson's (2005) approach, our paper takes as the explanandum the relationship between Brazil and the United States in 2019 and 2020 and as the explanans aspects of the decision-making process and the influence of the actors involved. Of the degrees of change described by Hermann (1990)—(1) adjustment changes, (2) program changes, (3) problem/goal changes, and (4) international orientation—we highlight the last. Kingdon (1995) argues that

critical circumstances can generate policy windows for public policy by aligning the problem stream, the policy stream, and the political stream, which
together produce major changes in agenda priorities. Policy windows can be
expected when there are changes of government. The Bolsonaro administration's identification with the Trump administration's perceptions of political
problems and alternatives opened up a policy window that was radical compared with the traditional principles of Brazilian politics.

Pendergast (1990) argues that the agenda is one of the most important structural aspects of a negotiation, since it may determine power and influence in
the process and describes the tactics and strategies that should be considered
in a negotiation: (1) its scope, (2) the sequence and order of issues, (3) its framing, (4) whether proposals will be packaged or sequential, and (5) the nature of
the formula through which it is presented. Here, it is key to clarify what is
meant by a "demanding agenda." Bolsonaro was seeking agreements that were
in the interest of its partners and therefore susceptible to being used to increase
his domestic power. The official bilateral agenda detailed the issues that were
the focus of negotiations: "integration of value chains; improvement of the
business environment; promotion of investment; facilitation and reduction of
bureaucracy in trade; expansion of joint initiatives in science, technology, and
innovation and strengthening of cooperation in defense, security, energy, outer
space, education, and culture" (Ministério de Relações Exteriores, 2020). While
the scope of the agenda was not entirely trade-centered, the first four of these
topics were in fact related to trade.

Pendergast argues that packaging strategy can generate more efficient agreements both because the parties are called upon to engage in trade-offs and
because it is based on confidence of reciprocity. The packaging strategy can be
used to push forward major global agreements such as the Marrakesh Treaty of
1994, which created the World Trade Organization (WTO), and the environmental agreements that originated in the Rio de Janeiro Conference in 1992.
This strategy was also adopted for the Free Trade Area of the Americas (FTAA),
since it made it possible for the heads of state at the Summit of the Americas in
Mar del Plata in November 2005 to close out the negotiations when parts of
their states were opposed to its continuing.

Pendergast also identifies a hidden agenda that is part of bilateral negotiations—a set of issues that, while they do not formally originate in direct measures by states, do influence the nature of relationships. In this process, business
interest groups such as Amcham, CNI, and the Brazil–United States Business
Council exerted substantial influence. The demands of these groups had been
seen in previous periods, as in the Brazilian mission's agenda in Washington in
2014 (Flores, 2014), and had existed for decades. In the 2000s, beginning in the
Lula da Silva administration and particularly in the failed FTAA negotiations,
this agenda began losing influence in bilateral negotiations, but it came back
with force following Rousseff's impeachment in 2016, with signs of the opening
of a policy window that became a reality once the Trump and Bolsonaro administrations took power. One significant element was the similarity between the
two administrations on ideological and geopolitical aspects. The Bolsonaro
administration employed its discourse in such a way as to generate interpretations about its ability to produce outcomes and trade-offs, seeking to create

perceptions about relative gains and reciprocity in the negotiation process. An example of this was the unreciprocated visa waivers for U.S. citizens, which, despite criticism, members of the Brazilian government attempted to interpret as in the national interest.

In international negotiations, the parties involved often find themselves in differing positions of power, and when this occurs there are strategies whereby negotiators with less power can leverage their gains. When it comes to the negotiations between Brazil and the United States, this imbalance needs to be taken into account. The weaker party's capacity for negotiation can be strengthened through a simultaneous instead of sequential agenda (Balakrishna et al., 1993) and through comprehensive agreements that, for example, involve issues of investment in technology, security, and defense—in other words, agreements that encompass more than one agenda.

Another important strategy in international negotiations involves the use of alliances and coalitions—multilateral ways of increasing bargaining capacity in an asymmetric situation. Multilateralism like that adopted within the G-20 is one example. In the international negotiations during the Bolsonaro term, such as those focused on joining the Organization for Economic Co-operation and Development (OECD), the administration gave up on a coalition perspective that would have made it possible to find allies among the BRICS or the Mercosur countries.

INTERPRETATIONS OF CHANGES IN BRAZILIAN FOREIGN POLICY

In the multiple interpretations of Brazilian foreign policy, there are contrasting analyses of its position with regard to the United States in the course of history. Autonomy (Bandeira, 1973; Hirst, 2008; Chilcote, 2014; Ricupero, 2017) was significantly greater in the Goulart and Lula da Silva administrations (Amorim, 2015; Soares de Lima, 2018) and even in the military government of Geisel, albeit for different reasons (Spektor, 2009), while in the administrations of Dutra (Malan et al., 1980), Castello Branco (Loureiro, 2019), and Collor de Mello (Veiga, 1994) there was a closer alignment with the United States. This alignment was hardly unconditional. Even when there was an effective alliance, efforts were made to preserve the national interest, at least to a certain extent (McCann Jr., 1973; Skidmore, 1988). Alongside the binary analysis of alignment and autonomy, the development aspect addressed in dependency theory can bring important explanatory elements to the analytical framework. In the 1970s, Marini (2000) argued that the only way to confront and overcome the dependency experienced by Latin American countries, including Brazil, was through a socialist revolution.[1] From this perspective, underdeveloped countries were dependent because they reproduced a social system whose development was limited by national and international political and economic relations. For Marini (2000:109), dependency was to be understood as "a relationship of subordination between formally independent nations, within which the production relationships of subordinate nations are modified or recreated to ensure the expanded reproduction of dependency." The fundamental obstacle to any real development process was imperialism, which extracted practically all the surplus that underdeveloped countries produced (Marini, 1978).

From Escudé's (1995) perspective of peripheral realism, autonomy was an end in itself, as was the defense of multilateralism, rather than the goal of development. Under peripheral realism, achieving a greater degree of development was easier in association with developed capitalist countries, particularly the United States, which had a greater capacity for global projection. According to Escudé, this did not preclude the defense of specific and localized national interests.

According to Loureiro (2019), if one wanted to compare the Bolsonaro administration's direction with a previous experience one would have to choose the 1964 military coup. For him, the Castello Branco administration made a U-turn, abandoning the independent foreign policy of Jânio Quadros and João Goulart and resolutely moving closer to the United States, with radical changes in its position in the world—an international orientation as described by Hermann (1990).

Ever since the process that culminated in the PT's exiting the country's presidency in May 2016 following Dilma Rousseff's impeachment, vigorous arguments favoring alignment or convergence of values and interests with the United States have taken over. The use of lawfare methods contributed to this change, which began in the interim Michel Temer administration and became more accentuated in 2019. The weaknesses of the PT governments were detected to some extent by party leaders and intellectuals connected to a developmentalist-distributivist perspectives but above all by left-wing critics. Academic writings on the Lula da Silva and Rousseff administrations (Berringer, 2015) were clear on the difference between being in government and having effective command of the state. Even so, the destabilization that took place in 2016 had an element of surprise. The explanation for this will require research, but it most certainly will involve values, morality, rights, economics, and foreign policy. Above all, it is a matter of the connections between internal politics (the economy, social relations) and foreign policy.

On foreign policy, the interest lies in understanding the ideas put forth by Bolsonaro's minister of foreign affairs, Ernesto Araújo (2017: 354): "In Itamaraty, over the decades, we have learned to avoid at all costs any submission of Brazil to a bloc, in an effort to preserve our capacity to develop an autonomous foreign policy. . . . Brazil—even if it does not want to be—is part of the West, and that West is—even if it doesn't see it—stuck in a conflict of gigantic proportions for its very survival." Araújo argues for the need to forge a deep identification with the West, which for him is represented by Trump, and therefore Brazil's foreign policy needs both a foreign metapolitics and a theopolitics—a total repositioning. With regard to Bolsonaro's redirection of foreign policy, all of the former foreign ministers agreed that it was "distancing itself from the universalist vocation of Brazilian foreign policy and its capacity for dialogue and building bridges with a variety of countries, whether they be developed or developing, to benefit our interests" (Cardoso et al., 2020).

Trump's and Bolsonaro's *Weltanschauung* resembled conservative, traditionalist, and extreme economic liberal values—combating gender ideology, climate-change denial, defending the religious principles of the Judeo-Christian tradition, etc. (J. Anderson, 2019). For Casarões (2020: 87–88): "Bolsonaro's foreign policy displays an ultraconservative ideology that goes well beyond defending the Christian faith. . . . After all, he wanted to associate his own image with Donald Trump's, as the nation-loving underdog who ultimately spoke on behalf of the silent majority," According to Velasco e Cruz (2019), this approach to foreign policy made sense only if the instrumental perspective of private interests was adopted to strengthen Bolsonaro's supporters. Almeida (2019) analyzes the Bolsonaro administration's diplomacy as one of total alignment with and subservience to Trump, leading Brazil to completely break with its previous actions. Soares de Lima and Albuquerque (2019), along with Nobre (2019), point out that the overt use of ideology and even alignment with the United States are nothing new to Brazilian politics. The new elements here are the methods applied and the instrumental use of chaos—strategies that seek to undermine the credibility of traditional institutions to maintain the antisystem electoral base, especially through the social media.

The term "pariah" has been applied to the administration by several important specialists, including Rubens Ricupero (Leitão, 2020). Araújo (2020), in acknowledging the extent of the debate on the term, addressed the issue in a speech to the graduates of the Instituto Rio Branco: "It doesn't matter that Brazil seems a pariah in the world." Rather, he sought to oppose this idea, betting all his chips on the bilateral relationship with Trump. The Bolsonaro administration invested in continuing this relationship, which ended up being interrupted by Joe Biden's victory.

THE BILATERAL AGENDA: CASE STUDIES

TRADE NEGOTIATIONS

As we have seen, in the period analyzed, trade occupied four positions on Brazil's official agenda. In 2019, U.S. Secretary of Commerce Wilbur Ross emphasized the idea that the two countries should work together to reduce barriers and facilitate investment in various sectors from energy to agriculture and technology. He signaled the United States' economic, commercial, and political objectives related to Brazil as follows (Ross, 2019):

> President Trump is committed to a strong and dynamic relationship with Brazil, one that promotes democracy, commerce, and regional stability. One of President Bolsonaro's first acts as Brazil's new president was to declare a desire for the United States to become Brazil's number one trade and investment partner. Currently, Brazil is our thirteenth-largest trade partner globally and third in the Western Hemisphere after Canada and Mexico.

According to the Ministry of the Economy's ComexVis (Ministerio da Economia, 2019), the Brazilian export basket to the United States in 2019 was 82.7 percent manufactures, which partly explains the interest of business associations in advancing in bilateral relations. Since 2009 China has been Brazil's largest trading partner, receiving 0.7 percent of its exports in 1991, 2.0 percent in 2000, and 15.2 percent in 2010 before jumping to 28.1 percent in 2019. Meanwhile, the United States in those same years received 20.1 percent. 24.3 percent, 9.6 percent, and 13.2 percent of Brazilian exports (Comtrade, December

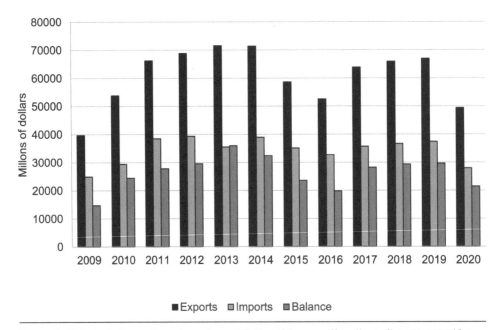

Figure 1. U.S. trade in goods and services with Brazil (seasonally adjusted), 2009–2020 (data from https://www.bea.gov/data/intl-trade-investment/international-trade-goods-and-services [accessed September 22, 2022]).

20, 2020), but these exports were of higher value added. China received mostly commodities. In the context in which this new commodity-based Brazilian economy was gaining ground, business groups that defended a closer relationship with the United States used this as their argument. While China's importance to Brazil and to the world as a whole is no small matter, Bolsonaro and his inner circle appear to deny this reality, generating an attitude that has caused diplomatic incidents in Sino-Brazilian relations.

The United States has a trade deficit with almost all its partners, Brazil being one of the few with which it has a surplus (Figure 1). This imbalance has existed since 2009. The greatest weight has been in services, where the positive balance in 2020 for the United States was US$10.2 billion for services and US$11.2 billion for goods (BEA, 2021). Following this trend, there is no prospect of improving Brazil's balance of trade.

The argument most used by the Americans in their foreign affairs—their interest in reducing the trade deficit (Drezner, 2006)—is not used by Brazil as a significant bargaining chip. It is not that we are ignoring the fact that economic theory exhaustively discusses the role of foreign affairs and that the balance of trade is not the only factor (Kindleberger, 1989; Cohen, 2014; Bresser Pereira, 2018). Others include investment, technology, quality of exchanges, insertion in production chains, exchange rate, educational level, technological development, allocation of resources, military power, cultural hegemony, transportation, etc.

Figure 2 provides data on the flow of direct investment, seasonally adjusted, from 2009 to 2019. In 2019 the volume was –US$990,350 million, and in 2020 it was –US$5,767 million.

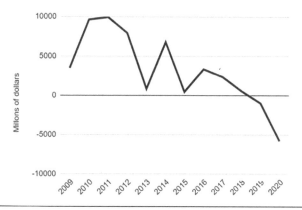

Figure 2. U.S. financial transactions without current-cost adjustment in Brazil, seasonally adjusted, 2009–2020 (data from https://www.bea.gov/international/di1usdbal September 22, 2022).

On the same occasion as Ross's visit to Brazil, Amcham Brasil (2019) presented 10 proposals considered by Brazilian business figures as priorities in the relationship between the two countries. Other meetings had similar agendas and sought to advance the bilateral agenda, including the trade dialogue meetings between Brazil and the United States held in 2019 and 2020 in an effort to advance a bilateral economic and trade partnership between the two countries (USTR, 2020a). Amcham Brasil, which represents more than 5,000 Brazilian and North American companies, developed proposals for a more ambitious bilateral partnership that, admittedly, would mean longer-term regulation. These proposals included a free-trade agreement between Brazil and the United States starting with negotiations on nontariff terms. Brazilian business people interested in a special relationship, taking advantage of this policy window, sought short-term measures. The entities representing entrepreneurs— Amcham, CNI, and the Brazil–United States Business Council—sent a letter systematizing the demands to the Office of the United States Trade Representative (USTR), the National Economic Council, and the ministries of the economy and foreign affairs (U.S. Chamber of Commerce et al., 2020). At no time did they take into consideration the opposition of the social movements, political parties, and nongovernmental organizations to the impact of these proposals.

The proposal of a free-trade agreement with Brazil was the subject of an agreement on trade and economic cooperation (USTR, 2020a). Whereas a broad agreement would have included investment, trade facilitation, competition rules, labor rights, intellectual property, environment, human rights, etc. (Lima-Campos and Gaviria, 2018), these associations pursued one of more limited scope, more of a short-term mini-deal that "would serve as a building-block for a potential FTA [free-trade agreement] in the longer term" (Neto et al., 2020). The protocol that was signed in October 2020 updated the agreement and dealt with customs administration and trade facilitation, good regulatory practices, and anticorruption measures (USTR, 2020b). These associations believed that by working sequentially they could achieve results using an incremental logic and that a possible free-trade agreement would evolve into a comprehensive agreement that was the final objective. The agenda for negotiations between Brazil and the United States proposed by the trade associations depended not only on tactics and negotiating styles or even on the declared common interests of the heads of state but on the influence of asymmetrical relations. Bargaining power depended on state action to achieve a balance and significant trade-offs and on institutional stability and reliability.

Schreiber (2020) writes that the strategy of a limited agreement also aimed at avoiding the need for bringing any agreement before Congress and bypassing any conflict with Mercosur rules. Despite excluding tariff issues, the October 2020 protocol ended up generating a worsening of relations with Brazil's Southern-trade-bloc partners. A specific trade agreement with the United States weakened the traditional Brazilian policy of privileging multilateralism and the South American continent. The negotiations were questioned by the U.S. Congress. In June 2020, Democratic representatives on the Ways and Means Committee addressed a letter to Ambassador Robert Lighthizer of the USTR stating their opposition to any economic agreement with Bolsonaro's Brazil (Neal, 2020):

> We write to share our strong objections to pursuing a trade agreement or expanded economic partnership with Brazil's President Jair Bolsonaro. . . . We consider it inappropriate for the Administration to engage in economic partnership discussions of any scope with a Brazilian leader who disregards the rule of law and is actively dismantling hard-fought progress on civil, human, environmental, and labor rights.

Brazilian credibility has been questioned since Rousseff's impeachment because of the ensuing instability. In the first two years of Bolsonaro's term, as a result of the Amazon rain forest fires, Democratic senators from the United States spoke out against the Brazilian president's stance (Schatz and Murphy, 2020), and then-candidate Joe Biden declared that he would be willing to apply sanctions if Bolsonaro did not adopt measures to protect the environment.

Despite its not being an issue raised in these negotiations, the idea of reducing tariff barriers and access to the U.S. consumer market has historically been a main point of the Brazilian agenda. What emerged as a novelty in 2019 was the government's belief in the priority of improving relations with the United States and the Trump administration at any cost. One example of this was the unilateral expansion and renewal of the U.S. ethanol import quota, which directly benefited U.S. producers and for which the United States failed to open up its market to Brazilian sugar despite sugar quotas' having been raised by the domestic dairy industry lobby to the benefit of several other countries. Another example was the creation of a quota for U.S. wheat, which was criticized by producers in Rio Grande do Sul and negatively affected Brazil's relations with Argentina. Even given Brazil's subservience, Trump and the USTR continued to employ defense mechanisms against Brazilian exports, in particular with regard to steel and aluminum. Alleging that Brazil was purposely devaluing its currency in October 2020, the U.S. government adopted an antidumping measure against it. Using other justifications, it also took measures against other aluminum-exporting countries (U.S. Department of Commerce, 2020).

The primary objective of the policy undertaken by the Bolsonaro cabinet was to improve relations with the United States in an attempt to maximize the possible policy window generated by two presidents sharing certain identity-related elements. This was accompanied by and supported by the trade associations. Trump, supported by his favorable asymmetric position, made no promises on tariff reduction or further market opening. Whether any of the objectives of the demanding Brazilian agenda were achieved would depend on the priority given to U.S. interests.

THE ALCÂNTARA SPACE CENTER

The second topic on the Foreign Ministry's agenda at the beginning of the Bolsonaro administration was related to science, technology, and defense and included the technological safeguards agreement that regulated the commercial use of the Alcântara Space Center. This was initially signed during the Cardoso administration in 2000 but was stopped in its tracks on the grounds that it put Brazilian sovereignty at risk. This argument penetrated the opinion of Congressman Waldir Pires (PT), who sits on the Committee on Foreign Relations and National Defense in the lower house of Congress (Morais, 2001), and prevailed during the PT governments. Michel Temer resumed negotiations on the matter. Alcântara, on the coast of Maranhão, was important for U.S. companies focused on ballistic missile launches and space research. Thanks to its location close to the Equator, it offered a significant reduction of launch costs and opened the way for more successful competition between the United States and the European countries that used bases in French Guiana (*Brazilian Report*, 2019). According to Candeas and Viana (2020), optical satellites are expected to be launched from the space center in 2021 and 2023 by the Brazilian space program.

The new stage of discussion of the agreement was formulated on the Brazilian side by the Ministries of Defense, Foreign Affairs, and Science and Technology, Innovation, and Communication. According to Minister Marcos Pontes, the agreement would authorize the United States to carry out rocket launches for peaceful purposes and would mark "the beginning of an era that will bring economic and social development to the region" by allowing Brazil to become a strong player in the launch segment of the global space market (MCTIC, 2019: 3, 7–8). The situation was compared to those of the communities neighboring the NASA Kennedy Space Center in Florida and Kourou in French Guiana.

In the congressional debate on the agreement, the Communist Party came out in favor of ratifying it. Congressman Márcio Jerry of Maranhão, deputy leader of the party in the House, defended approval of the agreement: "The [technological safeguards agreement] is not about national sovereignty, neither to harm it nor to protect it. It is a trade agreement that can boost the Brazilian aerospace program" (PCdoB, 2019). On the issue of a possible threat to national sovereignty, the ministry argued that the agreement "does not deal with the construction or operation of a U.S. base in Alcântara, delivery or control of the Center, military agreement, or even guarantee of exclusive use by the United States" (MCTIC, 2019: 12) and mentioned that jurisdiction over the area belonged to Brazil and that all North American activities would be monitored and assisted by the Brazilian authorities. In addition, there was the justification that 80 percent of the space equipment in the world had some U.S. component and therefore without the agreement the space center would not be able to launch any object that had U.S. content, leaving it practically out of the space launch market (MCTIC, 2019). The agreement entered into force in December 2019, after being passed by Congress, and was signed into law by the president in February 2020.

Oliveira et al. (2019) highlight the issues of geopolitics, technology, and trade involved in this agreement. One of these is consolidating the cadre of Brazilian scientists and technicians, and another is the connection with Brazilian cooperation in the same area of knowledge, especially with China. There are critics of the agreement, including PT's adviser to the Senate, Marcelo Zero (2019), especially with regard to Article 3, which "not permit significant quantitative or qualitative inputs of equipment, technology, manpower, or funds into the Alcantara Space Center from countries that are not Partners (members) of the Missile Technology Regime Control (MTCRl), except as otherwise agreed between the Parties" (MRE, 2020). (China is not part of the MTCR; since 1988 it has had an agreement with Brazil called the China-Brazil Earth Resources Satellite program [Oliveira et al., 2019]). The financial resources obtained from the activities of the space center are limited to the acquisition, development, production, testing, employment, or use of systems that cannot be used for MTCR Category I (systems with a range of more than 300 kilometers and load capacity of more than 500 kilograms). This category was part of the program's objectives to achieve higher loads in missile launch vehicles.This issue was widely discussed in 2000 by the United States and was flexibilized in 2019 (Candeas and Viana, 2020: 21)

The technological safeguards agreement also raised controversy about the protection of quilombola communities in the region (Serejo, 2019; Mitchell, 2020). The U.S. Congress discussed the issue and added an amendment to the National Defense Authorization Act for 2021 providing that "no federal funds may be obligated or expended to provide any United States assistance or security cooperation to defense, security, or police forces of the Government of Brazil to involuntarily relocate, including through coercion or the use of force, the indigenous and quilombola communities in Brazil" (U.S. Congress, 2020). Remarkably, a lawsuit filed by 800 families from traditional local communities in Maranhão without any dialogue with the Brazilian government had been defended by Representatives Deb Haaland, Joaquin Castro, and Hank Johnson and Senator Bernie Sanders in a letter to the House and Senate Armed Services Committees (Haaland et al., 2020). This position has been gaining strength as other lawsuits against the Bolsonaro government, especially those related to environmental issues, have gained notoriety.

Thus, while the economic and military areas of the Bolsonaro administration believed in the potential for strategic gains of a technological and military partnership with the United States, other segments of society—political elites, economists, scientists, the military, and social movements—evaluated these agreements in terms of autonomy, sovereignty, multilateralism, and the possibility of specific gains and social interests.

In the agreement that was negotiated, the transfer of technology was taken into consideration. The agreement was linked to the agreement on research, development, testing, and evaluation that was signed during Bolsonaro's March 2020 trip to Miami. According to the Ministry of Defense (Sardinha, 2020), it was to be a way for the two countries to "develop future joint projects aligned with the mutual interests of the parties, including the possibility of improving or providing new military capabilities." It would make Brazil a possible partner in the development of cutting-edge technologies on military issues and facilitate its access to sensitive technologies. The business sector that supports this kind of agreement is seeking to participate in a subordinate way in global production chains. Evans (1995) and Block and Keller (2011) have demonstrated that autonomous empowerment cannot be replaced by transfers in the field of science and technology. In other words, the purchase, association, or transfer of research and development does not create possibilities for independent, self-sustainable development and improving social conditions. On the contrary, it reproduces dependency, asymmetry, and a hierarchical and frozen international structure.

FINAL CONSIDERATIONS

In response to the questions set out in the introduction, our analysis suggests the following:

1.There are divergent opinions on the possibility of extreme changes in Brazilian foreign policy. There are even greater divergences with regard to the capacity for changes to produce results of national interest. According to Hermann (1990: 5), there has been considerable change in the international orientation of foreign policy made possible by a policy window such as is described by Kingdon (1995). This in itself provides evidence of its regulatory character. This extreme change may be identified either as necessary (Araújo, 2017), as a radical break with previous positions (Casarões, 2020; Almeida, 2019; Loureiro, 2019), or as an absence of policy (in that the new direction serves the interests of a particular group [Velasco e Cruz, 2020]) or a source of chaos (Soares de Lima and Albuquerque, 2019). A strong sign of radical change in Brazilian foreign policy seen with Bolsonaro (despite its actually having begun in 2016 under Temer), which generated a break with the negotiating capacity and autonomy demonstrated in other historical moments such as the independent foreign policy of the 1960s, the responsible pragmatism of the second half of the 1970s, and the *ativa e altiva* [active and prominent] diplomacy of the 2000s), was its abandonment of protagonism on the international stage. In several other historical moments, its negotiating capacity had been strengthened by various means, perhaps the main one being adherence to the principles of multilateralism. Meanwhile, the argument for an extreme change in international orientation is reinforced by the cases of the trade negotiations and the Alcântara Space Center. With Bolsonaro's inauguration there was a clear alignment of government agencies with the long-term demands of the trade associations, especially within the USTR, despite the opposition's being represented, in part, by Congress members and on other fronts.

2. What gains were expected from this change depended on the *Weltanschauung* from which one started. The Bolsonaro administration's argument in 2019 and 2020 was that closer ties with the United States were important because of their potential benefits. The objective was to position Brazil as a country that adhered to the rules of the developed countries and thereby attracted more investment, reinforcing its demands for greater incorporation into global value chains and membership in the OECD. To this end, the Bolsonaro administration promoted the trade associations' idea of a trade agreement. However, given Brazil's institutional instability and the instability produced by the Trump administration and then his defeat in the elections, this window was closed. With a fragile economy, Brazil lost more than it gained with this agenda (Jakobsen, 2020). In a bilateral relationship without the ability to compensate for asymmetry through tangible instruments, the expectation of gains was compromised.

3. Our initial hypothesis of low reciprocity has been confirmed. Although in relative terms U.S. hegemony is being called into question by China's growing power, an asymmetry of power has developed that is unfavorable to Brazil. By abdicating its diplomatic tradition, the Bolsonaro Administration produced subservience with nothing in return. By antagonizing China, it eliminated the possibility of increasing its bargaining power with the United States. A sequential negotiation with partial agreements such as bilateral trade can generate side effects that compromise the ability to maintain alliances and coalitions. The option of approaching the United States changed the concept traditionally used by the Foreign Ministry, which valued multilateralism as an instrument for leveraging interests and reducing asymmetries (Mercosur, the BRICS, IBAS, G-77, etc.)

Through its subservience, Brazil's demanding agenda in the 2019 and 2020 policy window compromised its bargaining power and resulted in direct losses. The case studies presented reflect the risks of a strategy that opts for unilateral concessions in a context where there are no real counterparts. U.S. investment in Brazil decreased significantly from 2016 on, signaling a development independent of the crisis that began in March 2020 with the COVID-19 pandemic. With Biden, the political relationship between the two countries changed significantly. Their positions in the international structure explain the extreme difficulty for Brazil and other dependent countries of changing their relationships when unilateral alignment is made a priority. In situations of underdevelopment, efforts to reproduce forms of social, productive, and technological organization, alongside the ideas of those who have the capacity for innovation and concentration of means, only increases the gap between states. The possibility of changing these structural relations is related to the capacity of elites in dependent countries to act under an agenda and to the international mobilization of civil society.

NOTE

1. Since that period, empirical experience has added new explanatory requirements. There is no such thing as absolute determinism in the historical process. China's continued development since the late 1970s demonstrates that even without structural changes (Waltz, 2000), the capacity of each player's agenda can be fundamental. Velasco e Cruz (2007) demonstrates how

this capacity determines the various international positions of countries, including in cases that do not disrupt the capitalist system. In Latin America, the revival of the Monroe Doctrine may mean greater obstacles for the region. The left-wing version of dependency theory or an update to the concept of uneven and combined development (Callinicos and Rosenberg, 2008) suggests that only social revolution has the power to change this structure. The possibilities of changing these relationships also depend on the capacity of the elites in dependent countries to create an agenda. Otherwise, it would be impossible to explain, as we have mentioned, the situation of China and other countries that did not break with capitalism but did manage to reach degrees of sustained autonomy.

REFERENCES

Almeida, Paulo Roberto
    2019 "O Senado e a diplomacia." *O Estado de São Paulo*. https://opiniao.estadao.com.br/noticias/espaco-aberto,o-senado-e-a-diplomacia,70002966504 (accessed October 21, 2020).
Amcham Brasil
    2019 "Amcham Brasil apresenta propostas para a relação comercial ao secretário de comércio dos EUA, Wilbur Ross." https://www.amcham.com.br/noticias/amcham-brasil/amcham-brasil-apresenta-propostas-para-a-relacao-comercial-ao-secretario-de-comercio-dos-eua-wilbur-ross (accessed October 21, 2020).
Amorim, Celso
    2015 *Teerã, Ramalá e Doha: Memorias de política atica e altiva*. São Paulo: Benvira.
Anderson, John L.
    2019 "Jair Bolsonaro's Southern strategy." *New Yorker*. https://www.newyorker.com/magazine/2019/04/01/jair-bolsonaros-southern-strategy (accessed October 21, 2020).
Anderson, Perry
    2019 "Bolsonaro's Brazil." *London Review of Books* 41 (3), February. lrb.co.uk/the-paper/v41/n03.
Araújo, Ernesto
    2017 "Trump e o Ocidente." *Cadernos de Política Exterior* 3: 323–357.
    2020 "Discurso do Ministro das Relações Exteriores, Ernesto Araújo, na formatura do Instituto Rio Branco." https://bit.ly/2Zhu6En (accessed January 26, 2021).
Bandeira, Moniz
    1973 *Presença dos Estados Unidos no Brasil: Dois séculos de história*. Rio de Janeiro: Civilização Brasileira.
BEA (Bureau of Economic Analysis)
    2021 "International trade in goods and services" and "U.S. direct investment abroad: balance of payments and direct investment position data." https://www.bea.gov/ (accessed August 2, 2021).
Berringer, Tatiana
    2015 *A burguesia brasileira e a política externa nos governos FHC e Lula*. Curitiba: Ed. Appris.
Block, Fred and Matthew R. Keller
    2011 *State of Innovation: The U.S. Government's Role in Technology Development*. Boulder: Paradigm Publishers.
Brazilian Report
    2019 "After decades, Brazil and the U.S. sign agreement on space station." https://brazilian.report/business/2019/03/11/brazil-usa-alcantara-space-station/ (accessed October 21, 2020).
Bresser Pereira, Luiz Carlos
    2018 "Nacionalismo econômico e desenvolvimentismo." *Economia e Sociedade* 27: 853–874.
Callinicos, Alex and Justin Rosenberg
    2008 "Uneven and combined development: the social-relational substratum of 'the international'? An exchange of letters." *Cambridge Review of International Affairs* 21 (1): 77–112.
Candeas, Alessandro and Benhur Peruch Viana
    2020 "O Acordo de Salvaguardas Tecnológicas Brasil-Estados Unidos e o Centro Espacial de Alcântara." *Cadernos de Política Exterior / Instituto de Pesquisa de Relações Internacionais* 6 (9):

5–27. http://funag.gov.br/biblioteca/download/cadernos_n9_21ago20D.pdf (accessed July 31, 2021). http://dx.doi.org/10.1590/1982-3533.2018v27n3art06 (accessed October 21, 2020).

Cardoso, Fernando H. et al.
2020 "Artigo: A reconstrução da política externa brasileira." *O Globo.* https://oglobo.globo.com/mundo/artigo-reconstrucao-da-politica-externa-brasileira-24416079 (accessed October 21, 2020).

Casarões, Guilherme
2020 "The first year of Bolsonaro's foreign policy," pp. 81–109 in Antonella Mori (ed.), *Latin America and the Global Order: Dangers and Opportunities in a Multipolar World*. Milan: Ledizioni Ledi Publishing.

Chilcote, Ronald H.
2014 "Intellectuals and political thought in twentieth-century Brazil," pp. 12–56 in *Intellectuals and the Search for National Identity in Twentieth-Century Brazil*. Cambridge: Cambridge University Press.

Cohen, Benjamin J.
2014 *A geografia do dinheiro*. São Paulo: Editora UNESP.

Drezner, Daniel W.
2006 "Free vs. fair: critical policy choices." *Council on Foreign Relations.* https://cdn.cfr.org/sites/default/files/pdf/2006/07/CPCTrade.pdf.

Escudé, Carlos
1995 *El realismo de los estados débiles*. Buenos Aires: GEL.

Evans, Peter
1995 *Embedded Autonomy: States and Industrial Transformation*. Princeton: Princeton University Press.

Flores, Mariana
2014 "CNI lidera reuniões do Conselho Empresarial Brasil-Estados Unidos, em Washington." *Agência de Notícias CNI.* https://noticias.portaldaindustria.com.br/noticias/internacional/cni-lidera-reunioes-do-conselho-empresarial-brasil-estados-unidos-em-washington/. (accessed October 21, 2020).

Haaland, Deb, Bernie Sanders, Joaquin Castro, and Ben Johnson
2020 "Call for protection of Afro-Brazilian communities." https://haaland.house.gov/media/press-releases/haaland-sanders-castro-johnson-call-protection-afro-brazilian-communities (accessed October 21, 2020).

Hermann, Charles F.
1990 "When governments choose to redirect foreign policy." *International Studies Quarterly* 34 (March): 3–21.

Hirst, Mônica
2008 *Brasil–Estados Unidos: Desencontros e afinidades*. São Paulo: Editora FGV.

Hudson, Valerie M.
2005 "Foreign policy analysis: actor-specific theory and the ground of international relations." *Foreign Policy Analysis* 1: 1–30.

Hunter, Wendy and Timothy J. Power
2019 "Bolsonaro and Brazil's illiberal backlash." *Journal of Democracy* 30 (January): 68–82.

Jakobsen, Kjeld
2020 "Avança acordo bilateral entre EUA e Brasil." *Fundação Perseu Abramo/Partido dos Trabalhadores.* https://fpabramo.org.br/2020/04/28/avanca-acordo-economico-e-comercial-bilateral-entre-eua-e-brasil/ (accessed October 21, 2020).

Kindleberger, Charles
1989 *Panics, Manias, and Crashes: A History of Financial Crisis*. New York: Basic Books.

Kingdon, John
1995 *Agendas, Alternatives, and Public Policies*. New York: Longman.

Leitão, Matheus
2020 "Bolsonaro faz o Brasil ser ameaça e virar país pária, diz Ricupero." https://veja.abril.com.br/blog/matheus-leitao/bolsonaro-faz-o-brasil-ser-ameaca-e-virar-um-pais-paria-diz-ricupero/ (accessed January 31, 2021).

Lima-Campos, Aluísio and Juan A. Gaviria
2018 *Introduction to Trade Policy*. Oxford and New York: Abingdon/Routledge.

Loureiro, Felipe
2019 "Relação de Bolsonaro com os EUA tenta repetir Castelo Branco, diz professor." *Folha de São Paulo.* https://www1.folha.uol.com.br/ilustrissima/2019/01/relacao-de-bolsonaro-com-eua-tenta-repetir-castelo-branco-diz-professor.shtml. (accessed October 21, 2020).

Malan, Pedro Sampaio et al.
1980 *Política econômica externa e industrialização no Brasil (1939/52).* Rio de Janeiro: IPEA/INPES.

Marini, Ruy Mauro
1978 "Las razones del neodesarrollismo (respuesta a F. H. Cardoso y J. Serra)." *Revista Mexicana de Sociologia* 40: 57–106.
2000 *Dialética da dependência: Uma antologia da obra de Ruy Mauro Marini.* Edited by Emir Sader. Petrópolis and Rio de Janeiro: Editora Vozes.

McCann Jr., Frank D.
1973 *The Brazilian-American Alliance.* Princeton: Princeton University Press.

MCTIC (Ministério da Ciência e Tecnologia, Inovações e Comunicações)
2019 "Conhecendo o acordo de salvaguardas tecnológicas Brasil Estados Unidos." http://www.aeb.gov.br/wp-content/uploads/2019/04/folder_AST-minist%C3%A9rios.pdf (accessed October 21, 2020).

ME (Ministério da Economia)
2019 "Visão geral dos produtos exportados para China e Estados Unidos." http://comexstat.mdic.gov.br/pt/comex-vis (accessed October 21, 2020).

Mitchell, Sean T.
2020 "Alcântara: Bolsonaro's illegal plan to expropriate Afro-Brazilian land for Trump deal." Brasil Wire, June 18. https://www.brasilwire.com/bolsonaros-illegal-plan-to-expropri-ate-afro-brazilian-land-in-alcantara-for-a-deal-with-trump/ (accessed March 20, 2021).

Morais, Christian
2001 "Comissão aprova acordo sobre base de Alcântara." Câmara dos Deputados. https://www.camara.leg.br/noticias/12015-comissao-aprova-acordo-sobre-base-de-alcantara/ (accessed October 21, 2020).

MRE (Ministério das Relações Exteriores)
2020 "Estados Unidos da América." http://www.itamaraty.gov.br/pt-BR/ficha-pais/5120-estados-unidos-da-america (accessed October 21, 2020).

Neal, Richard E.
2020 "Letter to Ambassador Lighthizer." June 3. https://waysandmeans.house.gov/sites/democrats.waysandmeans.house.gov/files/documents/20200603_WM%20Dem%20Ltr%20to%20Amb%20Lighthizer%20re%20Brazil.pdf (accessed October 21, 2020).

Neto, Abrão et al.
2020 "US-Brazil trade and FDI: enhancing the bilateral economic relationship." *ApexBrasil and Atlantic Council.* March 2020. https://atlanticcouncil.org/wp-content/uploads/2020/03/AC_US-Brazil-Trade-and-FDI_Final_March-5.pdf (accessed October 21, 2020).

Nobre, Marcos
2019 "O caos como método." *Piauí.* https://piaui.folha.uol.com.br/materia/o-caos-como-metodo/ (accessed October 21, 2020).

Oliveira, Flávio et al.
2019 "Base de Alcântara: entenda os pontos polêmicos do acordo com os EUA." *Carta Capital.* https://www.cartacapital.com.br/blogs/observamundo/base-de-alcantara-entenda-os-pon-tos-polemicos-do-acordo-com-os-eua/ (accessed October 21, 2020).

PCdoB (Partido Comunista do Brasil).
2019 "PCdoB reafirma apoio ao Acordo para uso da Base de Alcântara." https://pcdob.org.br/noticias/pcdob-reafirma-apoio-ao-acordo-para-uso-da-base-de-alcantara/ (accessed October 21, 2020).

Pendergast, William R.
1990 "Managing the negotiation agenda." *Negotiation Journal* 6: 134–145.

Ricupero, Rubens
2017 *A diplomacia na construção do Brasil 1750–2016.* Rio de Janeiro: Versal Editores.

Rodrigues, Gilberto
2019 "Trump dos trópicos? Política externa de ultradireita no Brasil." *Análisis Carolina* 6 (April): 1–11.

Ross, Wilbur
2019 "Remarks by Commerce Secretary Wilbur L. Ross at Amcham Centennial." https://br. usembassy.gov/remarks-by-commerce-secretary-wilbur-l-ross-at-amcham-centennial/ (accessed October 21, 2020).

Sardinha, Pedro
2020 *Brasil e EUA estreitam relações de defesa*. Ministério da Defesa, Assessoria de Comunicação Social, Brasília. https://www.defesa.gov.br/noticias/66640-brasil-e-eua-estreitam-relacoes-de-defesa (accessed October 21, 2020).

Schatz, Brian and Chris Murphy
2020 "The Amazon's rainforests are still on fire. If Trump won't act, Congress will." NBC News. https://www.nbcnews.com/think/opinion/amazon-rainforests-are-still-fire-if-trump-won-t-act-ncna1049556 (accessed October 21, 2020).

Schreiber, Mariana
2020 "Preocupados com ambiente político, empresários apressam Brasil e EUA a assinar acordo comercial." *Época Negócios*. https://epocanegocios.globo.com/Economia/noticia/2020/05/preocupados-com-ambiente-politico-empresarios-apressam-brasil-e-eua-assinar-acordo-comercial.html (accessed October 21, 2020).

Serejo, Danilo
2019 "Bolsonaro vai dar nossa terra aos americanos: concessão da base de Alcântara aos EUA ameaça Quilombolas." *The Intercept*. https://theintercept.com/2019/11/15/bolsonaro-entrega-alcantara-eua-ameaca-quilombolas/ (accessed October 21, 2020).

Shear, Michael D. and Maggie Haberman
2019 "For Trump, Brazil's president is like looking in the mirror." *New York Times*. https://www.nytimes.com/2019/03/19/us/politics/bolsonaro-trump.html (accessed October 21, 2020).

Singer, André
2020 "The failure of Dilma Rousseff's developmentalist experiment: a class analysis." *Latin American Perspectives* 47 (1): 152–168.

Skidmore, Thomas
1988 *Brasil: De Castelo a Tancredo 1964–1985*. São Paulo: Paz e Terra.

Soares de Lima, Maria Regina
2018 "A agência da política externa brasileira: uma análise preliminar," pp. 39–57 in Sergio Abreu et al. (eds.), *Política externa brasileira em debate: Dimensões e estratégias de inserção internacional no pós-crise de 2008*. Brasília: IPEA/FUNAG.

Soares de Lima, Maria Regina and Marianna Albuquerque
2019 "O estilo Bolsonaro de governar e a política externa." *Boletim OPSA* 1 (January/March). https://www.horizontesaosul.com/single-post/2019/07/26/O-ESTILO-BOLSONARO-DE-GOVERNAR-E-A-POL%C3%8DTICA-EXTERNA. (accessed October 21, 2020).

Spektor, Matias
2009 *Kissinger e o Brasil*. São Paulo: Coleção Nova Biblioteca de Ciências Sociais.

U.S. Chamber of Commerce et al.
2020 "Letter to Ambassador Lighthizer, Director Kudlow, Ministers Guedes and Araújo." https://www.brazilcouncil.org/wp-content/uploads/2020/04/U.S.-Brazil-Trade-Coalition-Letter.pdf (accessed October 21, 2020).

U.S. Department of Commerce
2020 "U.S. Department of Commerce issues affirmative preliminary antidumping duty determinations on common alloy aluminum sheet from 18 countries." https://www.commerce.gov/news/press-releases/2020/10/us-department-commerce-issues-affirmative-preliminary-antidumping-duty.

U.S. Congress
2020 "H.R.6395–William M. (Mac) Thornberry National Defense Authorization Act for Fiscal Year 2021." https://www.congress.gov/bill/116th-congress/house-bill/6395/text#toc-H5B13838D4AE141CBBDFE9BA2E96A1BBF (accessed October 21, 2020).

USTR (United States Trade Representative)
2020a "Brazil-U.S. joint statement on enhancement of bilateral economic and trade partnership." https://ustr.gov/about-us/policy-offices/press-office/press-releases/2020/april/brazil-us-joint-statement-enhancement-bilateral-economic-and-trade-partnership (accessed October 21, 2020).

2020b "United States and Brazil update agreement on Trade and Economic Cooperation with new protocol on trade rules and procedures." https://ustr.gov/about-us/policy-offices/press-office/press-releases/2020/october/united-states-and-brazil-update-agreement-trade-and-economic-cooperation-new-protocol-trade-rules (accessed on October 21, 2020).

Veiga, João Paulo C.
1994 "Os limites à formulação da política para a dívida externa brasileira." Master's thesis, Universidade de São Paulo.

Velasco e Cruz, Sebastião
2007 *Trajetórias: Capitalismo neoliberal e reformas econômicas nos países da periferia.* São Paulo: Editora UNESP.
2019 "O interesse nacional e a privatização da política externa." *Nexo.* https://www.nexojornal.com.br/ensaio/2019/O-interesse-nacional-e-a-privatiza%C3%A7%C3%A3o-da-pol%C3%ADtica-externa (accessed October 21, 2020).

Waltz, Kenneth
2000 "Structural realism after the Cold War." *International Security* 25 (Summer): 5–41. http://www.columbia.edu/itc/sipa/U6800/readings-sm/Waltz_Structural%20Realism.pdf.

Zero, Marcelo
2019 "O cavalo de Tróia espacial." PT no Senado. https://ptnosenado.org.br/61785-2/ (accessed October 21, 2020).

Conspiracy Theories and Foreign Policy Narratives

Globalism in Jair Bolsonaro's Foreign Policy

by
Feliciano de Sá Guimarães, Davi Cordeiro Moreira, Irma Dutra de Oliveira e Silva, and Anna Carolina Raposo de Mello

An analysis of more than 2,000 speeches and social media posts on foreign policy issues from four members of Jair Bolsonaro's government from January 2019 to December 2020 suggests that a conspiracy theory called "globalism," which explains current events using a series of intrigues and stratagems carried out by fictitious enemies to undermine the national order, has not only taken root in Brazil's foreign policy narrative but consistently been used over time by the cabinet members responsible for that policy. It also indicates that the use of "globalism" is not just a political strategy to persuade voters but a world-view embedded in Bolsonaro's far-right cabinet.

Uma análise de mais de 2.000 discursos e posts provenientes de redes sociais sobre questões da política externa do Brasil por quatro membros do gabinete do governo de Jair Bolsonaro de janeiro de 2019 a dezembro de 2020 indica que a teoria de conspiração denominada "globalismo," que explica atualidades em termos de uma série de intrigas e estratégias implementadas por inimigos fictícios para minar a ordem nacional, não se arreigou apenas na narrativa exibida na política exterior brasileira mas também se utilizou há anos pelos mesmos membros do gabinete que são responsáveis por sua elaboração. Isso significa que o uso do "globalismo" não é só uma estratégia política para convencer eleitores mas é também uma visão do mundo que é enraizada no gabinete de Bolsonaro cuja origem reside na extreme direita.

Keywords: *Conspiracy theories, Populism, Jair Bolsonaro, Globalism, Brazil*

In a world where fake news has become the new normal (Lazer et al., 2018), conspiracy theories are too serious to be seen as simply a hoax or a lunatic's dreams. Political leaders such as Donald Trump in the United States, Viktor Orbán in Hungary, and Jair Bolsonaro in Brazil have used conspiracy theories in their foreign policy narratives, and these ideas have had a real impact on people's lives. Indeed, political margins have become ubiquitous, and conspiracy theories have invaded foreign affairs from the hinterlands. Now the world must respond to the fact that such ideas have captured the popular consciousness and political power.

Feliciano de Sá Guimarães is an associate professor at the Institute of International Relations of the Universidade de São Paulo. Irma Dutra de Oliveira is a Ph.D. candidate at the institute, and Anna Carolina Raposo de Mello is Ph.D. candidate there and at King's College London. Davi Cordeiro Moreira is an assistant professor of political science at Universidade Federal de Pernambuco.

LATIN AMERICAN PERSPECTIVES, Issue 248, Vol. 50 No. 1, January 2023, 272–289
DOI: 10.1177/0094582X221147504
© 2023 Latin American Perspectives

The growing body of research on conspiracy theories in Europe and the United States shows that people's beliefs in conspiracies are associated with many political concepts, among them populism, ideology, identity, and even violence (Oliver and Wood, 2014; Silva, Vegetti, and Littvay, 2017; Vegetti and Littvay, 2022; Mancosu, Vassallo, and Vezzoni, 2017; Kruglanski et al., 2014). Scholars are becoming aware of the concrete influence of conspiracy theories on everyday politics and are no longer looking at them as simple intellectual frauds. There is a growing international-relations literature exploring the international implications of populist rhetoric tackling conspiracy theories marginally (Stengel, MacDonald, and Nabers, 2019; Boucher and Thies, 2019; Özdamar and Ceydilek, 2019; Wajner, 2021; Verbeek and Zaslove, 2015; 2017; Casullo, 2019; Moffitt, 2017; De Cleen, 2017; Plagemann and Destradi, 2018; Guimarães and Silva, 2020), along with a handful of studies analyzing conspiracy theories directly. These studies seek to assess whether and how conspiracy theories influence international politics, reconstructing the diffusion of the conspiracy narratives in foreign policy with anecdotal evidence (Sakwa, 2012; Aistrope, 2016; Yablokov, 2015; Hellinger, 2019; Roniger and Senkman, 2019; Wojczewski, 2021).

In this article we take a step farther by systematically analyzing whether and how populist leaders use conspiracy theories in their foreign policy narratives. Adopting a mixed-methods approach, we use text-as-data methods and qualitative content analysis to provide a systematic account of the way populist governments use conspiracy theories to create foreign policy narratives and in what circumstances conspiracies are used. Thus we aim to answer the following question: How does a populist government use conspiracy theories to structure a foreign policy narrative?

We take Jair Bolsonaro's administration in Brazil as an illustrative case of a pathological political ethos that has changed a traditionally stable and highly professional foreign policy into a series of conspiracy tales. We show that the officials responsible for Brazil's foreign policy making reproduce a set of ideas called "globalism" as justification for their acts and discourses in foreign policy. For them, "globalism" is a set of plots carried out by international agencies and China to impose "cultural Marxism" through the use of international law against the will of the "true people," seen as inherently nationalist, anticommunist, and Christian.

To understand whether Bolsonaro's government has employed conspiracy theories in the Brazilian foreign policy narrative, we analyzed 2,041 official speeches, interviews, and YouTube videos of four public officials—Jair Bolsonaro, Eduardo Bolsonaro (former president of the House Committee on International Affairs), Ernesto Araújo (foreign minister), and Filipe Martins (special foreign affairs adviser to the president)—from January 2019 to December 2020. We used human-coding textual analysis to select foreign policy speeches and social media posts and consider what we present here the largest classification to date of foreign policy documents about the Bolsonaro administration.

We have divided the article into four parts. First, we review the literature on conspiracy theories and populism to understand the relationship between conspiracy theories and populist foreign policy narratives. Second, we characterize

Bolsonaro's government conspiracy-related worldview and map the conspiracy-theories scenario among officials. Next, we report the results, and finally we discuss the implications of our findings for the literature.

CONSPIRACY THEORIES, POPULISM, AND FOREIGN POLICY

When academics or commentators identify conspiracy theories in foreign policy discourse, they regularly locate them not just on the political fringes of liberal democracies but also on the periphery of global power (Aistrope, 2016: 16). Yet conspiracy theories do not belong to the ordinary operation of international politics, where rational diplomacy should be the predominant type of narrative. However, some populist presidents seem to have moved conspiracy theories from the fringes to the center of their official foreign policy narratives. Sakwa (2012: 581–590) has argued that conspiracy theories are becoming a "distinctive mode of engagement" in foreign affairs, carrying a specific and Manichean view of how international politics work.

We do not know, however, precisely what the distinctive type of foreign policy inspired by conspiracy theories is. Almost no studies seek to understand whether conspiracy theories affect foreign policy narratives and, if so, how. Except for studies that discuss the international factors that give shape to conspiracy theories, such as international Judeo-liberal alliances and international communist infiltration (Aistrope, 2016; Yablokov, 2015; Hellinger, 2019; Gray, 2010), the literature on conspiracy theories has not yet properly addressed whether they systematically affect foreign policy. Roniger and Senkman's (2019) and Sakwa's (2012) studies are among the few to have done so.

However, while the analysis of conspiracy theories' influence in the international-relations literature is still incipient, there is growing evidence that they are associated with ideology, identity, discourse, and resentment of the elite. For instance, Oliver and Wood (2014: 952) have shown that half of the American public "consistently endorses at least one conspiracy theory and that the likelihood of supporting conspiracy theories is strongly predicted by a willingness to believe in unseen intentional forces and an attraction to Manichean narratives." Mancosu, Vassallo, and Vezzoni (2017: 1) find that belief in conspiracy theories in Italy is not only widespread but also negatively associated with education and positively with religiosity. Vegetti and Littvay (2021: 2) have shown consistent evidence that conspiracy theories provide narratives that may help people "channel their feelings of resentment toward political targets, fueling radical attitudes and even violence." There is also some evidence that belief in conspiracy theories is associated with factors signaling a lack of personal significance (Kruglanski et al., 2014). Finally, Silva, Vegetti, and Littvay (2017) have shown that it is associated with multiple subdimensions of populist attitudes such as antielitism and a good-versus-evil view of politics.

In our view, there are two reasons for this deficiency of the international-relations as contrasted with the domestic-politics literature. First, any academic foreign policy analysis has to focus either on a supposed rational diplomatic discourse or on the influence of essential concepts such as religion, ideology, or economic interests. Hence, the conspiracy-theories concept has been seen as too narrow and rare to be taken seriously. Second, the social phenomenon of the far-right rise is too recent for the literature to have responded appropriately. Only recently has it become clear that many far-right politicians use conspiracy theories to push their foreign policy agendas (Plagemann and Destradi, 2018; Guimarães and Silva, 2021; Wojczewski, 2021).

While there is in fact a growing literature on the international implications of populism (Özdamar and Ceydilek, 2019; Verbeek and Zaslove, 2015; 2017; Casullo, 2019; Moffitt, 2017; De Cleen, 2017; Plagemann and Destradi, 2018; Guimarães and Silva, 2021), these studies are focused on populism as a baseline conceptualization rather than on understanding how populist foreign policies operate. The exception is Wojczewski (2021), who analyzes conspiracy theories' relationship with populism and foreign policy to understand how it mobilizes "the people" in international relations, using the right-wing populist party Alternative for Germany as a case study. Indeed, the concept of populism does elaborate international politics in many terms other than conspiracy theories, but it seems that combining studies on populism and conspiracy theories into a single approach, as Wojczewski (2021) has done, would improve the analytical quality of the scholarly debate.

The conspiracy theory is not a neutral concept used merely to describe a particular political ideology or narrative but an evaluative term with significant pejorative connotations among academics. For Coady (2006: 5), "to allude to an account as a conspiracy theory is to make a judgment about its epistemic status; it is a way of branding an explanation untrue or insinuating that it is based on insufficient evidence, superstition, or prejudice." For Byford (2011: 22), the effectiveness of a conspiracy theory "as a strategy of exclusion and the means of 'cutting out' rival interpretations rests on the existence of the widespread intellectual presumption among academics against, or even hostility towards, conspiracy theories." As Jeffrey Bale (2007: 47) has put it, "very few notions nowadays generate as much intellectual resistance, hostility and derision within academic circles as a belief in the historical importance or efficacy of political conspiracies."

Nevertheless, conspiracy theories are more than just a hoax. Given the increasing evidence that they have political consequences, they cannot be automatically dismissed. Even skeptics agree that they can have political consequences when empowered by professional politicians (Hofstadter 1996 [1965]; Keeley, 1999; Pigden, 1995; Coady, 2006; 2012). In fact, Coady (2006: 4–5) argues that it is not so much that conspiracy theories have an exaggerated view of the prevalence of conspiratorial behavior as that they have an exaggerated view of how successful this behavior tends to be. The imaginaries of conspiracy theories are characterized by a "racialized understanding of agency—hyper agency—wherein elite individuals are constituted as causally driving and controlling history" (Millar and Costa Lopez, 2021: 3). Furthermore, once a professional politician exercising power uses them to impose his counternarrative, conspiracy ideas become the state's official narrative and, thus, the reality, as the example of Donald Trump has shown (Muirhead and Rosenblum, 2019).

Moreover, Fenster (2008: 84–90) has suggested that conspiracy theories can become a strategy for reallocating power among different political actors, "helping to unite the audience as 'the people' against the imagined 'Other,' represented as a secretive 'power bloc.'" As Karl Popper (1962: 123) once argued, a conspiracy theory has "very little truth in it. Only when conspiracy theoreticians come into power does it become like a theory which accounts for things that happen."

Despite their capacity to mobilize political actors, conspiracy theories are frequently wrong about how political events occur. For Fenster (2008: 11), they frequently "lack substantive proof, rely on leaps of logic, and oversimplify the political, economic, and social structures of power searching for an enemy." Conspiracy theories function as oversimplified realities demanding hyperactivity on the part of the beholder. More important, they very frequently express virulent hostility toward minorities and political adversaries, who tend to be seen as enemies that deserve elimination. For Dentith (2018), a conspiracy theory has three essential features: conspirators, secrecy, and objectives secretly desired by its main agents such as the elimination or sidelining of specific enemies.

The dominant explanation for conspiracy theories in the literature is the pathological model. According to Gray (2010: 4–10), this approach is centered on a public paranoia dependent on fallacies that lead to the distortion of analysis. Hofstadter (1996: 4) describes conspiracy theories as an expression of the "paranoid style"—"an alternative element in politics, one that operates at the margins but occasionally threatens the mainstream, consensus-driven operations of politics. Moreover, conspiracy theories rely on political entrepreneurs with a proper paranoid style to be effectively advertised." Paranoid political leaders tend to promote counterconspiracy theories to oppose the ones prevailing among their supporters. However, the "paranoid-style" hypothesis has its limitations. For example, Gray (2010: 22) argues that Hofstadter's analysis does not look into the dynamics between in-groups and out-groups that sustain conspiratorial narratives and therefore does not properly address the political impacts of paranoia in everyday politics. Our analysis seeks to fill this gap in foreign policy by looking into whether and how the belief in conspiracy theories affects foreign policy making.

Populist leaders are prone to use conspiracy theories. For Saull et al. (2015: 5–25), along with its historical forebears the contemporary far-right articulates politics as a conspiracy. The conspirators' identification and location have changed, but the theme of conspiracies associated with elites directed by "foreign" or "cosmopolitan" forces remains the same. The locus of the purported conspiracy is elites that are disengaged from the "true indigenous people." Implicit in this worldview is a demand for the reconfiguration of political society—a need to "cleanse" the political body of alien and corrupting influences.

Mudde (2000: 41–45) shows that extreme right parties in Europe exhibited not only a simplified version of nationalism in which the political power belonged to the "true people" but also a set of anti-Semitic and anticommunist conspiracy theories that motivated their behavior. More recently, in their analysis of the far-right in the United States, Mudde and Kaltwasser (2018) have shown that Islamophobic and global-warming conspiracy theories have also gained acceptance on the far-right.

Populists also use conspiracy and counterconspiracy theories to target (or create) their political adversaries. As Plagemann and Destradi (2018: 4) have argued, populist leaders tend to mock or disdain political competitors, arguing that they "might not be part of the proper people to begin with." In such an imaginary, "majorities act like mistreated minorities" and enemy images are kept alive so that "governing [is] a permanent campaign against the people's imaginary enemies" (Müller, 2016: 42). Conspiracy theories are also used to target not only domestic enemies but foreign ones, using foreigners as scapegoats for political purposes. The set of powerful foreign enemies ranges from international Jewish conspiracies to communist infiltration and liberal international institutions. For these populists the problem is that "instead of responding to the 'true' people, the government has been captured by those nefarious foreign forces" (Ostiguy, 2017: 108).

In this context, it should not be a surprise that populist leaders often use conspiracy theories to justify their protection of the "true people." For them, there is always a secret plot led by the elite to control the people's will under way (Norris and Inglehart, 2019; Mudde, 2016), and they respond to it with extravagant counterconspiracy theories that aim to secure their position in power and their place in the collective imaginary as the only representatives of the genuine people capable of protecting them. In this connection, Wojczewski (2021) argues that populist leaders appeal to their bases through a narrative that blames conspirators for the people's problems and identifies the leaders themselves as the only political force capable of reversing the plot against them.

As Oliver and Wood (2014: 953) have argued, conspiracy theories are motivated by specific political messages and individual predispositions. They function as a critical strategic element of the populist message. They ignite the predispositions of individuals who tend to see the world in black-and-white and are prone to mobilize. Van Prooijen, Krouwel, and Pollet (2015) have shown that people at political extremes endorse conspiracy theories more strongly than those at the political center. The extremes of the political spectrum tend to see each other as inherently evil and dangerous (Brandt et al., 2014; Swami et al., 2018).

It seems clear that conspiracy theories and the recent populist attacks on democracies are closely intertwined. The rise of populism in recent decades represents the increasing tensions within liberal democracies. More than ever, constituencies are governed by elected officials and powerful bureaucrats who continue to gain power in an ever-growing technification of life (Mouffe, 2018; Mudde, 2016). The same can be said in international politics, where the growing influence of international organizations is under attack by populists (Copelovitch and Pevehouse, 2019). Just as in domestic politics, in international relations conspiracy theories provide believers with a unified narrative against external enemies that serves domestic interests. Thus, both in domestic and in international scenarios where elites can easily be seen as paper tigers, the use of conspiracy theories by Manichean populists is rampant. At the same time, Giry and Tika (2020) argue that the discipline has provided very little empirical qualitative research on specific organized groups of conspiracy theorists, especially in Latin America. There are a few studies on conspiracy theories in Latin America (Hopper, 2020; Roniger and Senkman, 2019), but no study has systematically addressed their role.

MAPPING BOLSONARO'S FOREIGN POLICY

In 2019, a national survey carried out by the opinion institute Datafolha showed that more than 11 million people in Brazil (at least 7 percent of the population) believed that the earth was flat, with poorer and religious respondents being more prone to do so (*Folha de São Paulo*, July 19, 2019). Another survey conducted in 2021 (UOL, May 7, 2021) showed that 22 percent of Brazilians believed that the earth was flat, and 50.7 percent believed that the coronavirus was made in a Chinese laboratory. Bolsonaro has profited tremendously in this environment. After analyzing more than 5,000 speeches of Brazilian presidents since the return to democracy in 1985, Ricci, Izumi, and Moreira (2021) found that Bolsonaro most often uses the duality elite-vs.-people (in 12.5 percent of his speeches). Kalil et al. (2021) have shown that he is constantly mobilizing fear, connecting an alleged "communist conspiracy" to the coronavirus pandemic by creating the terms "Chinese virus" and "Chinese vaccine."

Without any doubt, in 2018 Brazil turned to the extreme right. For the election specialist Jairo Nicolau (2020: 14),

> Bolsonaro's victory is the most impressive accomplishment in the history of Brazilian elections. He ran with a micro party, spent virtually no campaign money, had the shortest TV time for a competitive candidate in any presidential race. He also ran a campaign rejecting what manuals always recommend: moderate speech to convince the centrist voter. And still, Bolsonaro won in most of Brazil's metropolitan areas, gaining the support of men and evangelicals as no candidate before him had.

The impressive combination of political factions that elected Bolsonaro eventually found a place in his cabinet. In interview-based research, Kalil et al. (2018) identified 16 types of Bolsonaro supporters according to social class, race/ethnicity, gender, religion, and beliefs, ranging from radical evangelical zealots to moderate antileft voters. In our view, these different types of voters found political expression in five political factions that emerged victorious in the 2018 campaign: the ideological, the evangelical, the agribusiness, the military, and the neoliberal.

The first group, made up of hard-core antiglobalists such as the former Foreign Minister Ernesto Araújo, the international affairs adviser Filipe Martins, Environment Minister Ricardo Salles, and Deputy Eduardo Bolsonaro (one of the president's sons), was greatly influenced by the late controversial self-proclaimed philosopher Olavo de Carvalho. Rooted in the United States and a friend of Steve Bannon's, he defended ultraconservative foreign affairs ideas (Teitelbaum, 2020; Guimarães and Silva, 2021).

The evangelical group was led by Human Rights and Family Minister Damares Alves, the informal representative of the highly influential evangelical congressional caucus. For this group, the close relationship with Israel established by Bolsonaro was the most critical foreign policy issue, and they have shown steady support for Bolsonaro's international agenda (Guimarães et al., 2022; Almeida, 2019; Smith, 2019).

The third faction, strongly supported by the agribusiness causus in Congress, was led by Agriculture Minister Tereza Cristina. For this group, environmental policies need to be relaxed and the government must secure stable international trade, especially with China, Brazil's most important trade partner. When Bolsonaro's administration was at odds with Beijing in 2019–2021, the agribusiness sector pushed for the removal of Araújo, who was seen as anti-China and antiglobalist (Mello, 2019; Camarotti, 2021).

The fourth group included many former and active military personnel. The Bolsonaro administration relied extensively on the military to run the state, since its political party had almost no government expertise. This group tends to be very nationalistic and sovereignty-oriented, primarily with regard to the protection of the Amazon. Its leaders are the vice president and retired general Hamilton Mourão, the retired general Augusto Heleno (the president's security chief), and Secretary for Strategic Affairs Admiral Flávio Rocha (Hunter and Vega, 2022; Guimarães and Silva, 2021).

Finally, the neoliberal faction includes the powerful Minister of the Economy Paulo Guedes, an ultraliberal "Chicago Boy" who had been Bolsonaro's primary adviser for economic and financial issues during the campaign. For this group, Brazil must join the Organization for Economic Co-operation and Development (OECD) and undertake deep market-oriented reforms. Although highly ineffective in terms of legislation and reform, the neoliberal group has partially succeeded in convincing the rest of the administration of the importance of Brazil's fully joining the OECD (Mello, 2020).

In our view, however, the struggle to control the foreign policy narrative among these groups has been reduced to only two factions—the antiglobalists and the military—with the former apparently dominant. Bolsonaro's inner circle slowly isolated the military, and many, especially those closest to the president, were fired or demoted.[1] Nevertheless, some military personnel retained relevant ministries and secretaries over the years, such as the Ministry of Defense and the Special Secretary for Strategic Affairs.[2] In international affairs, however, the military has not been able to create an alternative narrative to the dominant antiglobalism. Mourão tried to counter Bolsonaro's position toward China but eventually had to backtrack under Bolsonaro's antiglobalist pressure.[3]

Many academics and pundits see the antiglobalist foreign policy of Jair Bolsonaro as the most controversial in history (Spektor, 2019; Spektor and Fasolin, 2018; Chagas-Bastos and Franzoni, 2019; Casarões and Flemes, 2019, Guimarães and Silva, 2021). Former diplomats have criticized Bolsonaro's personality, suggesting that his foreign policy expresses his worst traits. Former Foreign Affairs Minister Celso Lafer has argued that "Bolsonaro's confrontational personality . . . operates from the distinction between them and us. His foreign policy is an expression of that strategy. The current foreign policy has nothing to do with reality. . . . Instead of asserting the Brazilian presence internationally, we are fighting imaginary enemies" (quoted in Duchiade, 2020). However, Bolsonaro's foreign policy is more than just an expression of the president's pathologies. It is supported by a vast network of public officials, entrepreneurs, digital influencers, and religious and social groups that resonates with his positions on multiple foreign affairs issues. Moreover, studies have revealed an organic and self-sufficient network of extreme-right supporters across all social classes and religions and in tandem with the administration's internal factions that supports Bolsonaro's electoral victory and his administration (Kalil et al., 2018; Gallego, Ortellado, and Moretto, 2017; Rocha and Solano, 2019; Smith, 2019).

The investigation of the conspiracy theories in Bolsonaro's foreign policy begins with a look at its three elements—the conspirators, the secrecy, and the plan. The most common conspiracy theory found among his officials is globalism and involves plots carried out by international agencies and leftist governments to impose "cultural Marxism" through the use of international law against the will of the "true people," seen as nationalist and having pro-Christian values (Busbridge, Moffitt, and Thorburn, 2020), and the alignment of contemporary communist regimes such as China and Cuba with these international bureaucrats to make "cultural Marxism" the standard moral background for international law. In Bolsonaro's worldview, globalism is an ideology that germinates in every sphere of life from foreign policy to basic education. For him, "the globalist agenda is aimed at class division. Divided and valueless people are easily manipulated. Changing the educational guidelines implemented over the decades [in Brazilian schools] is one of our goals to prevent the manufacturing of political activists" (Facebook, March 3, 2019). Eduardo Bolsonaro (Facebook, January 24, 2020) has summarized what "globalism" means as follows:

> The uber capitalist George Soros, who has a project to destroy the millenary Western civilization by attacking its fundamental Judeo-Christian values, does in the United States what Viktor Orbán did not allow him to do in Hungary: an anti-Western university. Like any good globalist, in the best New Left style, he will deny this intention. . . . Anyone who celebrates Soros's attitude has the same worldview and agrees with him or is a naïve pawn in this political chess game.

For Olavo de Carvalho (Carvalho and Dugin, 2012: 38), Bolsonaro's intellectual guru, being a globalist is an excuse to be bullied by the traditional media: "I have written pages without end in the Brazilian media, to the point of being accused, for this reason, of being 'a conspiracy theorist,' the standard defamatory label that the globalist elite uses most frequently to intimidate those who dare to challenge it." And, finally, Araújo (2019) puts all the elements of globalism together in a synthetic paragraph in the U.S. conservative journal *The New Criterion*:

> In foreign policy, the system played the globalist tune without a flaw. It helped the transfer of power from the United States and the Western alliance to China; it favored Iran; it worked tirelessly to raise a new socialist iron curtain over Latin America by fostering left-wing governments. . . . Brazil was indeed a wonderful showcase for globalism. Starting with a traditional crony capitalism . . . the country went through fake economic liberalism in the 1990s, until it got to globalism under the Workers' Party: cultural Marxism directed from within a seemingly liberal and democratic system, achieved through corruption, intimidation, and thought control.

In sum, for the antiglobalist faction, antiglobalism is a worldview that gives meaning to political action. For Olavo de Carvalho, the real America and the

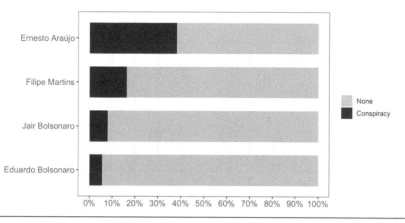

Figure 1. The proportion of documents referring to conspiracy-theory terms per official.

real Brazil were not the center of globalism but its primary target. Conservatives worldwide had to join forces to fight globalism in all its manifestations (Teitelbaum, 2020: 318). Everything that was not included in a narrow and fraudulent version of "Western Civilization" built on Christian values had to be fought to guarantee a supposed order that had historically guided Western societies. One of his most prolific students, Alexandre Costa (2015: 147–149), argued,

> The New World Order will be, first and foremost, anti-Christian. The repressive spiral that leads us to this suffocating reality advances without facing resistance and uses mechanisms such as political correctness, fashion, and fear. It is made up of increasing embarrassment and isolation that will undoubtedly lead to persecution and condemnation of all who defend the words and examples of Our Lord Jesus Christ.

To understand whether globalism was embedded in Bolsonaro's government narrative, we analyzed 2,041 speeches, Facebook posts, interviews, and videos from four officials who were key to the development and implementation of Bolsonaro's foreign policy between January 2019 and December 2020. Of these items, 353 were considered official speeches and were collected from websites such as the Foreign Ministry and the Presidency, and the remaining 1,683 were collected from Facebook and YouTube. In this encompassing database—which probably includes the vast majority of speeches on foreign policy ever uttered by these four officials—there were 1,009 from Eduardo Bolsonaro, 848 from Jair Bolsonaro, 141 from Ernesto Araújo, and 43 from Filipe Martins. The proportion of documents referring to globalism per official varied (Figure 1), with Araújo employing it the most.

The frequency of references to globalism in the narratives of all four officials (Figure 2) indicates that the use of this element has been consistent over time.

The distribution of official versus non-official documents per individual (Figure 3) shows that for Eduardo Bolsonaro and Filipe Martins virtually all their speeches were non-official.

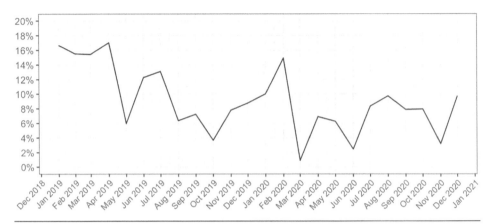

Figure 2. The use of conspiracy-theory terms over time by the four officials.

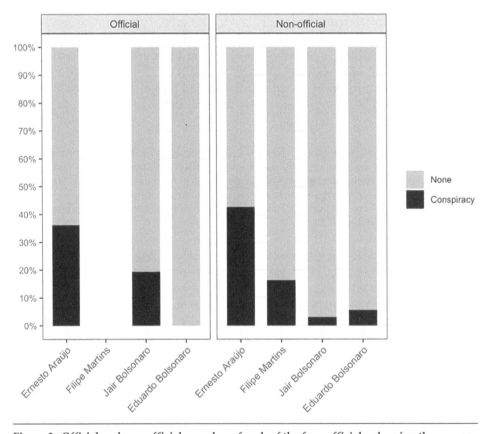

Figure 3. Official and non-official speeches of each of the four officials, showing the proportions of conspiracy-theory terms in each category.

The associations between "globalism" and other terms, some of them conspiracy-theory terms, in official and non-official documents (Figures 4 and 5) show a general similarity in their use across these categories.

These results may be summarized as follows: Antiglobalism has become the official narrative of Brazil's foreign policy. Anecdotal evidence had already

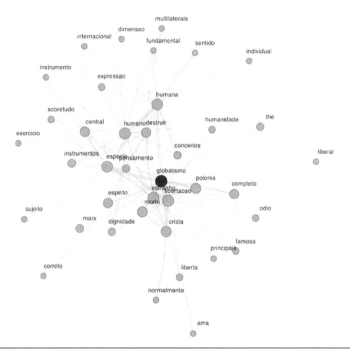

Figure 4. Association of various terms with "globalism" in official documents.

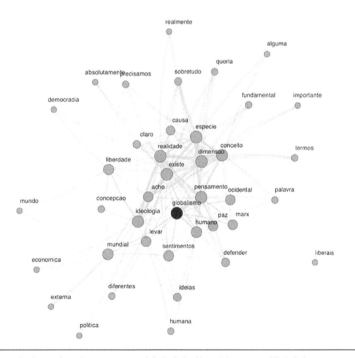

Figure 5. Association of various terms with "globalism" in non-official documents.

shown that "antiglobalist rhetoric was one of Bolsonaro's main foreign policy identities" (Guimarães and Silva, 2021). Here we have shown that "globalism" was present to various degrees in the speeches of all the cabinet members responsible for Brazil's foreign policy making: the president used it in his official narrative, while Araújo used it in 40 percent of his official speeches and Martins in around 20 percent of his unofficial ones. Two of the central figures in designing Brazil's foreign policy have argued that imaginary enemies are trying to turn Brazil into Cuba or Venezuela.

The term "globalism" was pervasive in the speeches of all four officials and was consistent over time, indicating that it was not just a strategic tool for capturing radical followers but an ideology embedded in the cabinet's worldview. These officials appeared to use conspiracy theories indiscriminately regardless of the arena. While the use of "globalism" was slightly more frequent in official documents, this may have been an artifact of sample size. The "globalism" narrative seemed to be cohesive in both official and non-official documents. There was apparently not much difference between what the president said officially and what he said non-officially. The concept was related to "freedom," "ideology," and "Marx" in both arenas. There was no official narrative for the elite as contrasted with an unofficial narrative for the people.

CONCLUSIONS

This study has four implications for the academic debate on the use of conspiracy theories.

1. It shows how a far-right cabinet can systematically use conspiracy theories to enact foreign policy narratives. The literature had yet to show empirically how conspiratorial ideas that originated in the ideological fringes could be introduced by populist leaders into an official state discourse and become the cornerstone of a foreign policy narrative. Most of the studies either tackled the relationship between conspiracy theories and foreign policy laterally or analyzed it with anecdotal evidence. Here we have provided a more systematic account that corroborates the assertion in the literature that populist foreign policies use conspiracy theories to justify their actions or convince political supporters.

2. While the concept of populism has much more to say about foreign policy than conspiracy theories do, the systematic analysis of conspiracy theories sheds light on a relatively obscure aspect of the way populist leaders act and behave. Moreover, the way populist leaders use conspiracy theories to develop foreign policy narratives elucidates the more refined daily operation of populist ideas in foreign policy. The concept of globalism is the concretization of the elite-vs.-people opposition in foreign policy making.

3. For a long time the literature on conspiracy theories focused on the characterization of what they meant and how they worked in radical minds. More recently, the specialized literature in political science has shown growing evidence of its political consequences for violence, party politics, and elections. Our study contributes to this debate in providing a systematic account of the way conspiracy theories are used in foreign policy narratives.

4. Bolsonaro's foreign policy is under increasing academic scrutiny. Many studies are trying to grasp what it means for Brazilian foreign policy to have a far-right populist as its primary driver—something unparalleled in its foreign affairs. Also, many studies are analyzing the rise of populist foreign policies in Latin America. Our contribution to this growing literature is hard evidence of the way a populist foreign policy constructs its narrative and when the use of conspiracy theories occurs.

We have not attempted to describe the reasons for or even the consequences of adopting conspiracy theories in foreign policy narratives. Nevertheless, drawing on our findings, we have formulated some questions: What kinds of international alliances does a conspiracy-theories-based foreign policy create? How does it affect regional integration? What are themes in the agenda that become relevant for a country whose cornerstone is the fight against globalism? Do typically economic and commercial issues lose ground to moral and security considerations? We will answer these questions in future studies.

NOTES

1. Bolsonaro fired the moderate general and Secretary of Government Carlos Alberto de Santos Cruz when he said that he "did not know any of Olavo de Carvalho's books" and considered the writer "wacky." General Maynard Santa Rosa, who was in charge of the Secretariat for Strategic Affairs, left the government claiming that he quit because he "did not have the support of his superior" (*The Guardian*, June 13, 2019; see also *Folha de São Paulo*, November 4, 2019).

2. At the beginning of the administration, the military influenced some critical issues, such as Venezuela. However, internal disputes between the Olavists and the military have ended, mainly with the military's being fired or losing influence. Some examples of isolation of the military wing can be seen in the growing political distance between Bolsonaro and his vice president (*Defesanet*, July 8, 2019).

3. While Bolsonaro had condemned China on multiple occasions, Mourão had a more realistic view of the relationship. On May 19, 2019, he traveled to China, trying to create an amicable atmosphere after Bolsonaro had visited Taiwan during the campaign and thus created an uncomfortable situation with Beijing. His successful trip was pragmatic in its approach and mostly aimed at the neoliberal wing, but he was advised to cancel some of his interviews by the Presidency (*Defesanet*, July 8, 2019).

REFERENCES

Aistrope, Tim
2016 *Conspiracy Theory and American Foreign Policy*. Manchester: Manchester University Press.
Almeida, Ronaldo
2019 "Bolsonaro Presidente: conservadorismo, evangelismo e a crise brasileira." *Novos Estudos CEBRAP* 38 (1): 185–213.
Araújo, Ernesto
2019 "Now we do." *New Criterion*, January.
Bale, Jeffrey
2007 "Political paranoia v. political realism: On distinguishing between bogus conspiracy theories and genuine conspiratorial politics." *Patterns of Prejudice* 41 (1): 45–60.
Boucher, Jean Christophe and Cameron Thies
2019 "'I am a tariff man': the power of populist foreign policy rhetoric under President Trump." *Journal of Politics* 81 (2): 1–18.
Brandt, Mark, Christine Reyna, John Chambers, Jarret Crawford, and Geoffrey Wetherell
2014 "The ideological-conflict hypothesis: intolerance among both liberals and conservatives." *Current Directions in Psychological Science*, no. 23, 27–34.

Busbridge, Rachel, Benjamin Moffitt, and Joshua Thorburn
    2020 "Cultural Marxism: far-right conspiracy theory in Australia's culture wars." *Social Identities* 26: 722–738.
Byford, Jovan
    2011 *Conspiracy Theories: A Critical Introduction*. London: Palgrave Macmillan.
Camarotti, Gerson
    2021 "Reação de Ernesto Araújo à crise Brasil-China preocupa diplomatas e governo é alertado pelo agro." *Folha de São Paulo*, March 20.
Carvalho, Olavo de and Aleksandr Dugin
    2012 *The USA and the New World Order: A Debate between Olavo de Carvalho and Aleksandr Dugin*. Inter-American Institute for Philosophy, Government, and Social Thought. https://inter-american.org/the-usa-and-the-new-world-order-a-debate/.
Casarões, Guilherme and Daniel Flemes
    2019 "Brazil first, climate last: Bolsonaro's foreign policy." *GIGA Focus Lateinamerika*, no. 5, 1–12.
Casullo, Maria Esperanza
    2019 *¿Por qué funciona el populismo? El discurso que sabe construir explicaciones convincentes en un mundo en crisis*. Buenos Aires: Siglo Veintiuno Editores.
Chagos-Bastos, Fabrício and Marcela Franzoni
    2019 "The dumb giant: Brazilian foreign policy under Jair Bolsonaro." *E-International Relations*, October 16. e-ir.info/2019/10/16/the-dumb-giant-brazilian-foreign-policy-under-jair-bolsonaro.
Coady, David
    2006 "The pragmatic rejection of conspiracy theories," pp. 167–170 in David Coady (ed.), *Conspiracy Theories: The Philosophical Debate*. Hampshire: Ashgate.
    2012 *What to Believe Now: Applying Epistemology to Contemporary Issues*, Singapore: Wiley-Blackwell.
Copelovitch, Mark and Jon Pevehouse
    2019 "International organizations in a new era of populist nationalism." *Review of International Organizations*, no. 14, 169–186.
Costa, Alexandre
    2015 *Introdução à nova ordem mundial*. Campinas: Vide Editorial.
De Cleen, Benjamin
    2017 "Populism and nationalism," pp. 342–362 in Cristóbal Rovira Kaltwasser, Paul Taggart, Paulina Ochoa Espejo, and Pierre Ostiguy (eds.), *The Oxford Handbook of Populism*. Oxford: Oxford University Press.
Dentith, M. R. X.
    2018 "Expertise and conspiracy theories." *Social Epistemology* 32 (3): 196–208.
Duchiade, André
    2020 "Ex-chanceleres e ministros de toda a Nova República pré-Bolsonaro se eúnem para atacar 'diplomacia da vergonha.'" *O Globo*, April 28.
Fenster, Mark
    2008 *Conspiracy Theories: Secrecy and Power in American Culture*. Minneapolis: University of Minnesota Press.
Gallego, Esther Solano, Pablo Ortellado, and Márcio Moretto
    2017 "Guerras culturais e populismo antipetista nas manifestações por apoio à operação Lava Jato e contra a reforma de previdência." *Em Debate* 9 (2): 35–45.
Giry, Julien and Pranvera Tika
    2020 "Conspiracy theories in political science and political theory," pp. 108–121 in Michael Butter, and Peter Knight (eds.), *Routledge Handbook of Conspiracy Theories*. London: Routledge.
Gray, Matthew
    2010 *Conspiracy Theories in the Arab World: Sources and Politics*. London: Routledge.
Guimarães, Feliciano and Irma Dutra Silva
    2021 "Far-right populism and foreign policy identity: Jair Bolsonaro's ultra-conservatism and the new politics of alignment." *International Affairs* 97: 345–363.
Guimarães, Feliciano, Irma Silva, Karina Caladrin, and André Miquelasi
    2022 "The evangelical foreign policy paradigm: evangelicals and Jair Bolsonaro's foreign policy in Brazil." Paper presented to the International Sociological Association, Nashville, TN.

Hellinger, Daniel
2019 "The deep state, hegemony, and democracy," in Daniel Hellinger (ed.), *Conspiracies and Conspiracy Theories in the Age of Trump*. London: Palgrave Macmillan.

Hofstadter, Richard
1996 (1965) *The Paranoid Style in American Politics and Other Essays*. Cambridge: Harvard University Press.

Hopper, Rosanne
2020 "Populism and conspiracy theory in Latin America: a case study of Venezuela," pp. 660–673 in Michael Butter and Peter Knight (eds.), *Routledge Handbook of Conspiracy Theories*. London: Routledge.

Hunter, Wendy and Diego Vega
2022 "Populism and the military: symbiosis and tension in Bolsonaro's Brazil." *Democratization* 29: 337–359.

Kalil, Isabela, Álex Kalil, Felipe Paludetti, Gabriela Melo, Weslei Pinheiro, and Wiverson Azarias
2018 "Quem são e no que acreditam os eleitores de Jair Bolsonaro." Fundação Escola de Sociologia e Política de São Paulo, October. fespsp.org.br/upload/usersfiles/2018/Relatorio%20para%20Site%20FESPSP.pdf

Kalil, Isabela, Sofia Cherto Silveira, Weslei Pinheiro, Álex Kalil, João Vicente Pereira, Wiverson Azarias, and Ana Beatriz Amparo
2021 "Politics of fear in Brazil: far-right conspiracy theories on COVID-19." *Global Discourse* 11: 409–425.

Keeley, Brian
1999 "Of conspiracy theories." *Journal of Philosophy* 96 (3): 109–126.

Kruglanski, Arie et al.
2014 "The psychology of radicalization and deradicalization: how significance quest impacts violent extremism." *Advances in Political Psychology* 35: 69–93.

Lazer, David et al.
2018 "The science of fake news." *Science* 359 (6380): 1094–1096.

Mancosu, Moreno, Salvatore Vassallo, and Cristiano Vezzoni
2017 "Believing in conspiracy theories: evidence from an exploratory analysis of Italian survey data." *South European Society and Politics*, no. 22, 327–344.

Mello, Flávia
2020 "The OECD enlargement in Latin America and the Brazilian candidacy." *Revista Brasileira Política Internacional* 63 (2): 1–17.

Mello, Patricia Campos
2019 "Ruralistas reclamam de viés anti-China no governo Bolsonaro." *Folha de São Paulo,* March 15.

Millar, Katharine and Julia Costa Lopez
2021 "Conspiratorial medievalism: history and hyperagency in the far-right Knights Templar security imaginary." *Politics*, 1–17.

Moffitt, Benjamin
2017 "Liberal illiberalism? The reshaping of the contemporary populist radical right in Northern Europe." *Politics and Governance* 5 (4): 112–122.

Mouffe, Chantal
2018 *For a Left Populism*. London: Verso.

Mudde, Cas
2000 *The Ideology of the Extreme Right*. Manchester: Manchester University Press.
2016 *On Extremism and Democracy in Europe*. New York: Routledge.

Mudde, Cas and Cristóbal Kaltwasser
2018 "Studying populism in comparative perspective: reflections on the contemporary and future research agenda." *Comparative Political Studies*, no. 51, 1667–1693.

Muirhead, Russel and Nancy Rosenblum
2019 *A Lot of People Are Saying: The New Conspiracism and the Assault on Democracy*. Princeton: Princeton University Press.

Müller, Jan-Werner
2016 *What Is Populism?* Philadelphia: University of Pennsylvania Press.

Nicolau, Jairo
　　2020 *O Brasil dobrou à direita: Uma radiografia da eleição de Bolsonaro em 2018*. Rio de Janeiro: Zahar Editores.
Norris, Pipa and Ronald Inglehart
　　2019 *Cultural Backlash: Trump, Brexit, and Authoritarian Populism*. Cambridge: Cambridge University Press.
Oliver, J. Eric and Thomas Wood
　　2014 "Conspiracy theories and the paranoid style(s) of mass opinion." *American Journal of Political Science* 58: 952–966.
Ostiguy, Pierre
　　2017 "Populism: a socio-cultural approach," in Cristóbal Rovira Kaltwasser et al. (eds.), *The Oxford Handbook of Populism*. Oxford: Oxford University Press.
Özdamar, Özgür and Erdem Ceydilek
　　2019 "European populist radical right leaders' foreign policy beliefs: an operational code analysis." *European Journal of International Relations* 26 (1): 137–162.
Pigden, Charles
　　1995 "Popper revisited, or What is wrong with conspiracy theories?" *Philosophy of the Social Sciences* 25 (1): 3–34.
Plagemann, Johannes and Sandra Destradi
　　2018 "Populism and foreign policy: the case of India." *Foreign Policy Analysis* 15 (2): 283–301.
Popper, Karl
　　1962 *Conjectures and Refutations: The Growth of Scientific Knowledge*. New York: Basic Books Press.
Ricci, Paolo, Mauricio Izumi, and Davi Moreira
　　2021 "O populismo no Brasil (1985–2019): um velho conceito a partir de uma nova abordagem." *Revista Brasileira de Ciências Sociais* 36 (107): 1–22.
Rocha, Camila and Esther Solano (eds.)
　　2019 *As direitas nas redes e nas ruas*. São Paulo: Expressão Popular.
Roniger, Luis and Leonardo Senkman
　　2019 "Fuel for conspiracy: suspected imperialist plots and the Chaco War." *Journal of Politics in Latin America* 11 (1): 3–22.
Sakwa, Richard
　　2012 "Conspiracy narratives as a mode of engagement in international politics: the case of the 2008 Russo-Georgian War." *Russian Review* 71: 581–609.
Saull, Richard, Alexander Anievas, Neil Davidson, and Adam Fabry
　　2015 "The longue durée of the far-right: an introduction," pp. 1–20 in Richard Saull, Alexander Anievas, Neil Davidson, and Adam Fabry (eds.), *The Longue Durée of the Far-Right: An International Historical Sociology*. London: Routledge.
Silva, Bruno, Federico Vegetti, and Levente Littvay
　　2017 "The elite is up to something: exploring the relation between populism and belief in conspiracy theories." *Swiss Political Science Review* 23: 423–443.
Smith, Amy
　　2019 *Religion and Brazilian Democracy: Mobilizing the People of God*. Cambridge: Cambridge University Press.
Spektor, Matias
　　2019 "Diplomacia da ruptura," pp. 324–338 in *Democracia em risco: 22 ensaios sobre o Brasil hoje*. São Paulo: Companhia das Letras.
Spektor, Matias and Guilherme Fasolin
　　2018 *Bandwagoning for Survival: Political Leaders and International Alignments*. FGV Working Paper. https://ssrn.com/abstract=3265876.
Stengel, Frank, David B. MacDonald, and Dirk Nabers
　　2019 "Introduction: Analyzing the nexus between populism and international relations," in Frank A. Stengel, David B. MacDonald, and Dirk Nabers (eds.), *Populism and World Politics: Exploring Inter-and Transnational Dimensions*. Cham, Switzerland: Palgrave Macmillan.
Swami, Viren, David Barron, Laura Weis, and Andrew Furnham
　　2018 "To Brexit or not to Brexit: the roles of Islamophobia, conspiracist beliefs, and integrated threat in voting intentions for the United Kingdom European Union membership referendum." *British Journal of Psychology*, no. 109, 156–179.

Teitelbaum, Benjamin
  2020 *War for Eternity: Inside Bannon's Far-Right Circle of Global Power*. New York: Dey Street Books.
Van Prooijen, Jan-Willem, André Krouwel, and Thomas Pollet
  2015 "Political extremism predicts belief in conspiracy theories." *Social Psychology Personality Science* 6: 570–578.
Vegetti, Federico and Levente Littvay
  2022 "Belief in conspiracy theories and attitudes toward political violence." *Italian Political Science Review* 52: 18–32.
Verbeek, Bertjan and Andrej Zaslove
  2015 "The impact of populist radical right parties on foreign policy: the Northern League as a junior coalition partner in the Berlusconi governments." *European Political Science Review* 7: 525–546.
  2017 "Populism and foreign policy," pp. 384–405 in Cristóbal Rovira Kaltwasser, Paul Taggart, Paulina Ochoa Espejo, and Pierre Ostiguy (eds.), *The Oxford Handbook on Populism*. Oxford: Oxford University Press.
Wajner, Daniel
  2021 "Exploring the foreign policies of populist governments: (Latin) America First." *Journal of International Relations and Development*, preprint, 1–32.
Wojczewski, Thomas
  2021 "Conspiracy theories, right-wing populism and foreign policy: the case of the Alternative for Germany." *Journal of International Relations and Development*, preprint, 1–29.
Yablokov, Ilya
  2015 "Conspiracy theories as a Russian public diplomacy tool: the case of Russia Today (RT)." *Politics* 35: 301–315.

Book Review

A Generation of Conflict in Contemporary Brazil

by
Ronald H. Chilcote

Armando Boito *Reform and Political Crisis in Brazil: Class Conflicts in Workers' Party Governments and the Rise of Bolsonaro Neo-fascism.* Leiden and Boston: Brill, 2022.

Anyone desiring a comprehensive analysis of twenty-first-century Brazil and its political economy should turn to Armando Boito's *Reform and Political Crisis in Brazil*, a substantially revised and updated edition of his 2018 work in Portuguese published in Brazil. Boito is a participating editor of *Latin American Perspectives* and an editor in Brazil of the important journal *Crítica Marxista.* The book is divided into two parts, a useful explanatory preface, and an afterword. The preface identifies and distinguishes the five governments: 1995 to 2022, under Fernando Henrique Cardoso, with the abandonment of the "developmental state" and establishment of the neoliberal form by minimizing the state and pursuing a foreign policy in concert with the United States; 2003–2010, under Luís Inácio Lula de Silva, with neodevelopmentalism, involving state intervention to stimulate the economy and reduce poverty; 2011–2016, under Dilma Rousseff, with two governments in support of reforms for social movements; 2016–2018, under Michel Temer, after the orchestrated impeachment of Dilma, with privatizations of national enterprises and neoliberal reforms; and 2019–2022, under Jair Bolsonaro, with neoliberal reforms and a neofascist repression of democratic practice.

The first part of the book focuses on the Lula governments. Here Boito briefly identifies early significant Marxist studies on Brazil and adopts their emphasis on state and class to examine the Brazilian bourgeoisie, including bankers, industrialists, and large landowners as members of the capitalist class within a state that serves its interests and, using Nico Poulantzas's concept of the "bloc in power," to identify and analyze fractions of that ruling class. His attention to social classes in the PT governments and the power bloc leads initially to understanding the political rise of the industrial bourgeoisie but ultimately to an understanding of the hegemony of financial capital and the influence of neodevelopmentalism and its politics. His approach to the Lula years leads him to a Marxist conception of populism and a critique of Lulism as a type of Bonapartism. The analysis moves on to the influence of neodevelopmentalism on social classes and foreign policy under the PT governments and then to unionism and its decisive influence on Lula's reelection in 2006.

The second part begins with the contradictions in Dilma's neodevelopmentalist government and the rise of "new" neoliberal political forces challenging and seeking the overthrow of her government and moving toward the interests of international capital. The analysis explores the neoliberal offensive during the early years of the Dilma government, identifying the activity of the upper middle class and the role of the working class to show the growing instability of democracy and the government's retreat rather than political offensive. Boito looks at the bloc in power and class alliances and examines the political regime and the contradictions within the state bureaucracy and the role of the Brazilian Development Bank and the oil monopoly Petrobras for the big internal bourgeoisie. He also delves into Operation Car Wash, which brought down the

Ronald H. Chilcote is managing editor of *Latin American Perspectives*.

LATIN AMERICAN PERSPECTIVES, Issue 248, Vol. 50 No. 1, January 2023, 290–296
DOI: 10.1177/0094582X221138566
© 2022 Latin American Perspectives

Dilma government, asserting that those involved acted as "members and representatives of the upper fraction of the middle class, and also as state bureaucrats whose particular function was to maintain the capitalist order" (153). The final chapter focuses on the weakness of the government in the face of the 2016 coup, showing divisions within the "internal bourgeoisie," the passivity of workers in general, and the subordinate position of unionized workers within the Dilma government.

The afterword looks at neofascism under the Bolsonaro government and argues that gradually a conciliation evolved between the traditional right and the fascist right. Boito considers various forms of fascism, including those identified in the work of Marxist writers, and argues that while the Bolsonarist movement is fascist and occupies a dominant position in the current government, Brazil is not a fascist dictatorship but a "bourgeois democracy" in crisis. He asserts that while the big bourgeoisie is accepting of the fascist government it will not tolerate a fascist dictatorship.

Boito gives us a concise synthesis and overview of contemporary Brazil that is effectively drawn from past and current journal articles and focuses on a nuanced analysis of social classes and complex political and economic institutions. It is a serious study deserving of our attention.

Latin American Studies
The Multifaced History of a Rebellious Academic Field

by
Felipe Antunes de Oliveira

Ronald H. Chilcote *Latin American Studies and the Cold War*. London: Rowman and Littlefield, 2022.

DOI: 10.1177/0094582X221142329

"Latin America" is an unusual research object. Perhaps more than with other objects of social inquiry, it is impossible to separate scholarly knowledge about Latin America from the conditions of production of that knowledge. In fact, the very process of doing research in and about the region changes and challenges the researcher. Latin America is an object that talks back, sometimes asking uncomfortable questions about the researcher's motivations and her social and political positionality.

Latin American Studies and the Cold War was intended by its editor, Ronald Chilcote, as a "historical" and "pedagogical" collection of essays: "historical in providing background to the origins and evolution of Latin American studies and pedagogical as a foundation for those desiring to study Latin America" (15). The 10 contributions in this edited volume end up going far beyond the editor's intention. More than presenting the most complete global history of Latin American studies to date, they reveal the dialectical process of the constitution of a transdisciplinary and inherently critical field under the difficult conditions posed by the Cold War on both sides of the Iron Curtain. Recounting the origins and evolution of Latin American studies in the United States, the United Kingdom, the Netherlands, Germany, Czechoslovakia, the Soviet Union,

Felipe Antunes de Oliveira is a lecturer in global governance and international development at Queen Mary University of London.

China, and Cuba, this volume shows over and over again that narrow imperialist, colonial, or economically motivated scholarship has always been contested by newer generations of Latin Americanists committed to actually understanding Latin America in its complexity and contributing to its social and political emancipation rather than serving top-down imperialist, geopolitical, or commercial designs.

As is candidly recognized by Chilcote, U.S. Latin American studies has imperialist roots in the Monroe Doctrine of 1823 and the annexation of former Mexican and Spanish territories and the creation of different forms of declared and undeclared colonies and protectorates in Central America and the Caribbean. Since its inception, the field has never been far from U.S. state power. It is no surprise, therefore, that the consolidation of Latin American studies as an academic field in the 1950s and 1960s went hand in hand with strategic geopolitical calculations in the context of the Cold War. Important centers for Latin American studies such as Stanford trained military personnel and contributed directly and indirectly to the CIA. Whereas the Cold War led to the expansion of government investment and interest in the field, opening new research possibilities, it also imposed fundamental constraints on scholarship. In the early days of the Cold War, the field was thus largely shaped by what Chilcote aptly calls "the university-government-foundation nexus" (37). Although great pioneering Latin Americanists such as Ronald Hilton and Kalman Silvert managed to maintain a degree of independence (especially in the case of Hilton) and plant important seeds of critical scholarship, early Latin American studies complicity with U.S. imperialism is hard to miss.

Largely reflecting Latin America's own social and anti-imperialist struggles, dissidence and resistance from within the Latin American studies community soon started to emerge. Chilcote identifies the antidemocratic U.S. intervention in Guatemala in 1954 as "an awakening for Latin American studies" (38). Other important political landmarks include the failed invasion of the Bay of Pigs in 1961, the U.S.-supported coup d'état in Brazil in 1964, and the deposition of Salvador Allende in Chile in 1973, just to mention a few episodes of blatant imperialism. In the 1960s and 1970s, as a new generation of progressive Latin Americanists conducted fieldwork and started listening to Latin American anti-imperialist and anticapitalist voices, Latin American studies passed through major transformations. Chilcote illustrates the disputes in the field through a brief history of the Latin American Studies Association, which had been founded in 1966 by mainstream U.S. scholars largely excluding women and Latin Americans only to become a space of intense political and intellectual confrontation in the 1970s. In the process of disputing the mainstream and denouncing U.S. imperialism, critical scholars created outlets such as the North American Congress on Latin America and *Latin American Perspectives*, which played key roles in diffusing alternative readings of political events and promoting world-class critical scholarship from Latin America. In the course of the 1970s, Latin American studies thus went from an instrument of imperialism to one of the most progressive fields in U.S. academia.

A parallel if perhaps less contentious evolution of the field happened during the same years on the other side of the Atlantic. World War II marked the moment of the final ebbing of European imperialism in Latin America after centuries of direct colonial domination followed by a long period of neocolonial commercial and financial relations. An investigation of the remote roots of European knowledge production about Latin America would involve digging into this imperialist past, with particular attention to important centers of Iberic scholarship and elite training such as Coimbra and Salamanca and the instrumental economic knowledge produced by British, Dutch, and

French finance in the late nineteenth and early twentieth centuries. During the Cold War, however, as Latin America fell squarely within the U.S. zone of influence, European Latin American studies could evolve less constrained by direct geopolitical endeavors. Thus, according to Rory Miller, "Cold War concerns played little part in the institutional origins of Latin American studies in Britain" (77). Instead, the Parry Report, the fundamental document of the early 1960s that gave impetus to Latin American studies in the UK, arguably focused on the "intrinsic academic interest and economic potential" of the region (78). Michiel Baud makes a similar argument, remarking that Latin American studies initially began in the Netherlands as "an academic and quite apolitical specialization" (121). Hans-Jürgen Puhle argues that in West Germany (in contrast with East Germany), Latin America was not considered a geostrategic priority, and the field was therefore not as "politically contested" and "polarized" as in the United States (126), evolving largely at the margins of more established disciplines, in particular history, languages, literature, and, later, the social sciences.

The Western European experience demonstrates that there was nothing inevitable about the impact of the Cold War on Latin American studies scholarship. Reflecting different geopolitical constraints, Latin American studies became either politically central and contentious or politically irrelevant and marginalized, with several shades in between. What emerges from the juxtaposition of these cases is a clear sense that, since the late 1950s, dramatic events in Latin America itself and the emergence of distinctive Latin American intellectual and political perspectives such as dependency theory and liberation theology continued to shake the field, forcing different groups of Global North scholars to take a stand and react within their respective intellectual environments. For instance, Baud recounts the impact of the 1979 Sandinista revolution in the Netherlands, Puhle comments on the influence of dependency theory in Berlin, and Miller concludes that "the influence of political events and global and regional intellectuals led to an academic world that was rather more radical and critical of British and U.S. roles in Latin America than the professors of history who made up the majority of the Parry Committee would have expected" (99).

The most original contributions to this volume are the chapters by Josef Opatrný, Russell Bartley, and Mao Xianlin and Shi Huiye, who respectively map the evolution of Latin American studies in Czechoslovakia, the USSR, and China. These chapters offer the U.S. and Western European academic audiences a wealth of little-known references and sources, opening several possibilities for further research. Although the direction of Latin American studies in the former Eastern bloc and postrevolutionary China has been largely determined by top-down priorities imposed by centralized states and their foreign policy concerns, the special relationship cultivated over the years with the Latin American left, in particular Cuba, has created unique windows into Latin American culture and society. What is more, in all these cases it is possible to witness the silent work of scholars truly committed to hearing and understanding Latin American voices, thereby forcing the boundaries of and at times clashing with official scholarship.

Any intellectual history of a field as diverse as Latin American studies is bound to be incomplete. The most important gap in this book refers to the evolution of Latin American studies in Latin America itself. In fairness, Ronald Chilcote touches on the subject in his introduction and first chapter. Beyond mentioning the impact of some seminal Latin American scholars in the United States, Chilcote briefly reviews the contributions of important institutions such as the Centro de Estudios Socioeconomicos

(CESO) at the Universidad de Chile and the Centro de Estudios Latinoamericanos (CELA) of the Universidad Nacional Autónoma de México, as well as the work of FLACSO and CLACSO, with special attention to their fruitful collaboration with *Latin American Perspectives*. Luís Suárez Salazar also contributes to partially filling this gap with an institutional history of the Centro de Estudios sobre América (CEA), in Cuba. The varied output of the CEA before its "deactivation" in 2010 included tens of edited books and the organization of several seminars, resulting in an extensive network of researchers across Latin America and beyond. Still, future editions of the book would benefit from additional chapters on the evolution of Latin American studies in countries such as Argentina, Brazil, Chile, and Mexico, including more space for the institutional histories of the Universidade de Brasília, the CELA, the CESO, FLACSO, and CLACSO. It would also be fascinating to map the impact of Latin American studies across the former Third World outside of Latin America. The contribution of Latin American and Global South scholars at large would have helped to increase the diversity (of the 11 contributors, 7 are white male scholars based in the Global North) of the voices represented in this volume.

Taken together, the chapters in this volume form a mosaic of different styles and expressions of Latin American studies during the years of the Cold War. The book shines a light on the very different social, political, and institutional constraints on Latin American studies scholarship. Indeed, the field has served different purposes in different places, sometimes being more clearly determined by geopolitical factors, sometimes being an instrument of imperialism, and sometimes offering significant openings for critical scholarship. At each step of the way, however, the book traces how the agency of Latin Americans has challenged Latin Americanists and forced the constant transformation of the field in surprising new directions.

Popular Struggle and Resistance in Latin America

by
Ronald H. Chilcote

Carlos Fuentes *The Great Latin American Novel*. Victoria: Dailkjey Archive Press, 2016.

Juan Pablo Dabove *Bandit Narratives in Latin America: From Villa to Chávez*. Pittsburgh: University of Pittsburgh Press, 2017.

Sarah Sarzynski *Revolution in the Terra do Sol: The Cold War in Brazil*. Stanford, CA: Stanford University Press, 2018.

DOI: 10.1177/0094582X221140417

Three recent works deal with literature as a means to understanding how common people attempt to improve their way of life. In his sweeping synthesis *The Great Latin American Novel*, the renowned novelist Carlos Fuentes offers insights not only into the great writers who have shaped our understanding but also into the cultural landscape and political realities that motivated them. For Latin Americanists whose research and writing are driven by disciplinary training, it is important to become familiar with the

Ronald H. Chilcote is managing editor of *Latin American Perspectives*.

literature of the places we study, and Fuentes facilitates this task. He begins with Bernal Díaz del Castillo, Latin America's "first novelist," who wrote about a world that had disappeared decades after accompanying Hernán Cortés on his arrival in Mexico and who influenced Bartolomé de las Casas and his denunciation of the peaceful coexistence between "the devastated world of the indigenous peoples and the triumphalist attitude of the white man in the New World" (50) and the Leyenda Negra. He celebrates Machado de Assis and his *The Posthumous Memoirs of Brás Cubas* (1981), and he turns to the great Colombian novelist Gabriel García Márquez's novel *One Hundred Years of Solitude*, which has enchanted many of us. He reminds me how I discovered Cervantes in a Spanish-literature class: "There was one world before the publication of *Don Quixote* in 1605, afterwards, another one, forever different—the novel of La Mancha . . . is indispensable in order to speak about fiction, or the immediate past, of today, of tomorrow" (398).

The works of Juan Pablo Dabove, with its focus on "how men of letters articulate the bandit trope in order to reflect upon their own practice, their own place in society, or to carry out a particular literary or political project" (98) and Sarah Sarzynski, for whom themes of "cangaceiros, rural poor and Coroneis, slavery, and messianism formed the language of the political debates" (17) during the 1950s and 1960s in Northeast Brazil, are based on broad research but generally presented through case studies. Both are of particular interest to me because early in my career (see Chilcote, 1972) I organized a series of colloquia at UC Riverside and UCLA focused on movements and charismatic individuals that organized against the state and the ruling class in pursuit of a better life. Our research drew partly on case studies in the Brazilian Northeast that at the time had been romanticized in the literature. One of our cases, by Amaury de Sousa, focused on social banditry, and my early assessment attempted to advance an agenda for further, deeper research. Both Dabove and Sarzynski have contributed significantly to that objective.

Dabove organizes *Bandit Narratives in Latin America* around cases in Argentina, Peru, Brazil, Mexico, Peru, and Venezuela. The first part focuses on banditry, portraying Pancho Villa and Hugo Chávez as part of an insurgent tradition aimed against established authority. Both are viewed not as outlaws but as influenced by social banditry aimed at societal improvement, examining Villa through an autobiographical work and Chávez through reference to an "anti-imperialist" lineage dating to the sixteenth century. The second part looks at the role of banditry in twentieth-century nationalism as seen in the novels of Rómulo Gallegos, Antonio Uslar Pietri, Rafael Muñoz, and Enrique López Albújar. A third part of the book, devoted to left thinking, movements, and policy, discusses Latin American Marxist writers including José Carlos Mariátegui, Jorge Amado, and José Revueltas. A final part draws out the emphasis on social banditry in the writing of Jorge Luis Borges, João Guimarães Rosa, Mario Vargas Llosa, and Ricardo Piglia. The final chapter, which seeks to explain the meaning of "bandit," might well have been placed at the beginning, since the term has many meanings and implications. Dabove justifies its placement as follows: "This book is not about bandits per se. It is about how men of letters articulate the bandit trope in order to reflect upon their own place in society, or to carry out a particular literary or political project" (98). He suggests two ways of understanding banditry—the realist (implying robbery, perhaps for profit in the midst of wars and revolutions) and the nominalist (violent and perhaps revolutionary, criminal, or outlaw)—and explores this distinction in academic writings. Then he turns to Eric Hobsbawm, who said that social bandits were peasant outlaws considered criminals by the state but viewed in peasant society as "champions, avengers, fighters for justice" (269).

My own interest began long ago with Hobsbawm's highlighting social banditry and through many years of field research in the Brazilian Northeast, including in two rural communities of the sertão of Bahia and Pernambuco, where I studied family domination in the face of cultural manifestations and popular movements struggling to survive since the late nineteenth century. I immersed myself in the vast literature of the region, including the poetic writings of the cantadores or troubadours who roamed the backlands singing about social banditry.

Several years of research and teaching in urban Recife led me to a study of the communist parties from early in the twentieth century to the Cold War period of the 1950s and the military coup of 1964, around which Sarah Sarzynski frames her *Revolution in the Terra do Sol*. My recent *LAP* book on the Cold War and its impact on Latin American studies (Chilcote, 2022) has no essay on Brazil, but she could surely fill that gap from her impressive research. Indeed, she briefly explores this theme in her introduction by reference to the Yale historian Gilbert Joseph's "new history" of the Cold War in Latin America, which leads her to look closely at the grassroots level. She takes "a cultural approach . . . to uncover the significance of the political and cultural debates about Northeastern Brazil during the Cold War" (12). She also smartly contends with Durval Muniz de Albuquerque Júnior's depiction of the Northeast as an "invention" and instead delves into "a myriad of political and cultural actors—rural social movement leaders and participants, foreign and local politicians, intellectuals, journalists, large landowners, military officials, filmmakers, and popular poets" (243).

The Cold War is the backdrop to her study of the revolutionary fervor spreading throughout Latin America in the wake of the Cuban Revolution and the protests, strikes, and land invasions in Northeast Brazil. She refers to Euclides da Cunha's classic work on the Northeast, *Os Sertões: Rebellion in the Backlands* (1902), as a "national epic" descriptive of the desperation of the Northeasterner, which was profoundly influential on my own work. She turns to Glauber Rocha's "cinematic masterpiece" *Deus e o diabo*, released in 1964 in midst of the Northeast political and social turmoil and impending military intervention but depicting "historical struggles involving messianic cults, violent bandits, hired thugs, greedy large landowners and miserable, ignorant rural people" (1). What ensues is an interesting synthesis of Brazil and its Northeast cultural traditions and politics. A lengthy introductory chapter looks at revolution in Brazil in an effort to depict the major institutions (in particular the peasant leagues, the communist party, and rural workers), the radicalization of the Catholic Church, and party politics regionally. The ensuing chapters turn to documentary films, songs, and poetry of the *literatura de cordel*; the *cangaceiro* or bandit as depicted in history and film; the *coronel*, the rural political boss who controlled large stretches of land; slavery and the *quilombos*; and religion as a political and revolutionary means of improving life in the Northeast.

The book's theme of the Cold War and the Northeast is worthy of our consideration and deserving of more study. Through interviews, archival research, documentary film, and reviews of a massive literature, Sarzynski briefly looks at life of the lower class, the disadvantaged poor, the marginalized peasant farmer, the rural workers and small merchants, and the dominant landowning coroneis of the past. It is fascinating narrative, a foundation for future deep class analysis of traditional rural life in Northeast Brazil. Having lived in Brazil through most of the period under study, I found that this book refreshed my past experience and opened up new paths for understanding the complexity of culture and politics in Northeast Brazil.

REFERENCE

Chilcote, Ronald H. (ed.)
    1972 *Protest and Resistance in Angola and Brazil: Comparative Essays*. Berkeley and Los Angeles: University of California Press.
    2022 *Latin American Studies and the Cold War*. Lanham, MD: Rowman and Littlefield.

Winner of three International Latino Book Awards . . .

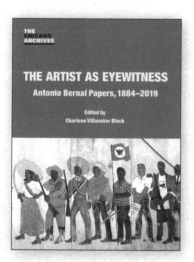

The Artist as Eyewitness: Antonio Bernal Papers, 1884–2019

Edited by Charlene Villaseñor Black
The Chicano Archives, volume 8

Gold Medal: Best Biography–English
Honorable Mention: Best Arts Book
Honorable Mention: Best Nonfiction–Multi Author Book

The Artist as Eyewitness: Antonio Bernal Papers, 1884–2019, edited by Charlene Villaseñor Black, is the first survey of the life and work of Antonio Bernal. Bernal is often identified as a muralist—his 1968 mural in Del Rey, California, has been cited as the first Chicano mural—yet his career has been wide-ranging. He has been a union organizer and an iconoclastic educator, an actor and author, and an artist of paintings and drawings as well as murals. All have been shaped by his unwavering political viewpoint and commitment to truth telling.

Each of these facets of Bernal's work is explored through assessments not only of his visual art but also his writings. A finding aid for the Antonio Bernal Papers, a special collection at the UCLA Chicano Studies Research Center, completes the volume.

The Artist as Eyewitness features more than sixty black-and-white and eleven color illustrations.

The Chicano Archives series is distributed for CSRC Press by the University of Washington Press.

UCLA Chicano Studies Research
Center Press
www.chicano.ucla.edu

UNIVERSITY OF WASHINGTON PRESS
Seattle uwapress.uw.edu

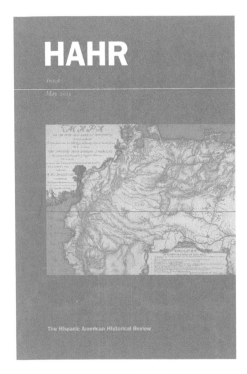

LATIN AMERICAN PERSPECTIVES IN THE CLASSROOM SERIES

Series Editor: Ronald H. Chilcote

NEW

Contemporary Latin American Revolutions
Second Edition
By Marc Becker

"This is a splendid introduction to Lain American revolutionary traditions with a much-needed focus on the role of women and Indigenous peoples."
—*Barry Carr, La Trobe University, Australia*

"Offers a geographically and chronologically diverse and theoretically rich array of primary sources, short biographies, and analysis of a spectrum of Latin American revolutionary movements and thought over the course of the twentieth century and into the twenty-first. The text will be an essential teaching tool to integrate Latin America into more general courses on revolutions, popular movements, and social change and to highlight the enduring significance of revolutions in Latin America's history."
—*Aviva Chomsky, Salem State University*

"Rigorous, thought-provoking, and highly readable. . . . This is the best overview of Latin American revolutions I have read. Scholars and students alike will learn a great deal from this timely and stimulating volume."
—*Carlos Aguirre, University of Oregon*

This clear text extends our understanding of revolutions with critical narrative analysis of key case studies. Becker analyzes revolutions through the lens of participants and explores the sociopolitical conditions that led to a revolutionary situation, the differing responses to those conditions, and the outcomes of the political changes.

2022 • 374 pages
978-1-5381-6373-3 • $34.00 / £26.00 • Paper
978-1-5381-6372-6 • $94.00 / £72.00 • Cloth
978-1-5381-6374-0 • $32.50 / £25.00 • eBook

Professors, a free examination copy is available in paperback or ebook format for course adoption consideration. Visit our website to order today!

ROWMAN & LITTLEFIELD

www.rowman.com | 800.462.6420

Reassessing Development: Past and Present Marxist Theories of Dependency and Periphery Debates

Issue 242 & 243 | Volume 49 | Number 1 & 2 | January and March 2022

Edited by Ronald H. Chilcote and Joana Salém Vasconcelos

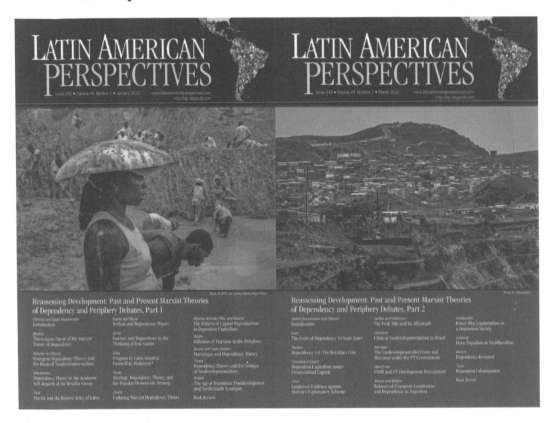

Latin American Perspectives was launched nearly a half century ago in the midst of a paradigmatic shift in thinking about development. Concerned with backwardness, underdevelopment, and dependency, the new thinking was led by Rodolfo Stavenhagen in Mexico, Agustín Cueva in Ecuador, Aníbal Quijano in Peru, and Vania Bambirra, Theotônio dos Santos, and Ruy Mauro Marini in Brazil—all founding editors of LAP. Four early LAP issues carried debate around essential questions and new theoretical direction. The January 2022 (Part 1) issue returns to this early historical thought and to contemporary Marxist debates of past and present theories of dependency and peripheral debates. The March 2022 issue (Part 2) looks at the relevance of this theory to contemporary Latin American case studies.

Read the issue here: https://journals.sagepub.com/toc/lapa/49/1

Listen to the Podcast for this special issue!

https://latinamericanperspectives.com/podcasts-2/

NEW

Latin American Extractivism
Dependency, Resource Nationalism, and Resistance in Broad Perspective
Edited by Steve Ellner

"A timely and invaluable study. . . . The collection of essays, beyond the specific focus on extractivism, provides an essential guide to making sense of Latin America's recent past and possible futures."
—*William I. Robinson, University of California at Santa Barbara; author of The Global Police State*

"This well-crafted volume offers fresh perspectives on increasingly dogmatic, closed debates over extractive development."
—*Eduardo Silva, Tulane University*

"The book is essential reading for anyone who seeks to understand how states have experimented with alternative models of economic development in Latin America, even within the constraints of global capitalism."
—*Kenneth M. Roberts, Cornell University*

This cutting-edge book presents a broad picture of global capitalism and extractivism in contemporary Latin America. Leading scholars examine the cultural patterns involving gender, ethnicity, and class that lie behind protests in opposition to extractivist projects and the contrast in responses from state actors to those movements.

Special Features:
- An essential guide to making sense of Latin America's recent past and possible futures through the lens of the mining industry and its opponents
- A critical case study of the dynamics of global capitalism
- Written by leading scholars

2021 • 304 pages
978-1-5381-4156-4 • $39.00 / £30.00 • Paper
978-1-5381-4155-7 • $94.00 / £72.00 • Cloth
978-1-5381-4157-1 • $37.00 / £28.00 • eBook

Professors, a free examination copy is available in paperback or ebook format for course adoption consideration. Visit our website to order today!

ROWMAN & LITTLEFIELD
www.rowman.com | 800.462.6420

LATIN AMERICAN PERSPECTIVES IN THE CLASSROOM SERIES
Series Editor: Ronald H. Chilcote

Latin American Social Movements and Progressive Governments
Creative Tensions between Resistance and Convergence
Edited by Steve Ellner, Ronaldo Munck, and Kyla Sankey

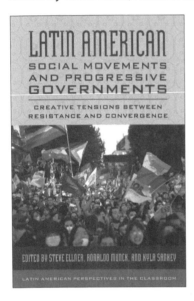

"Pragmatic and nuanced, Ellner, Munck, and Sankey's edited volume does an excellent job of grappling with Latin America's social movements' often contradictory dance between autonomy and engagement with the region's leftwing governments. Country study chapters substantiate the book's conclusions by teasing out these complexities."
—Linda Farthing, co-author of *Coup: A Story of Violence and Resistance in Bolivia*

"This collection deftly captures the many paradoxes that govern Latin American politics, including the mutually dependent relationship between the state and social movements. The editors—Steve Ellner, Ronaldo Munck, and Kyla Sankey—have provided a work of essential reading for anyone who wants to understand Latin America today." —**Greg Grandin, Yale University**

"Framed by conceptually engaging essays by some of the leading scholars in the field, this impressive volume offers a state-of-the-art primer on the dynamic relations between progressive states and new social movements in twenty-first-century Latin America. Broad enough to embrace the significantly different regimes that have been viewed as representatives of Latin America's embattled but resilient Pink Tide, this unique collaboration effectively dissects the 'creative tensions' that have imbricated states and social movements in Pink Tide and neoliberal politics. It makes clear that an earlier generation of scholarship that stressed the autonomy of social movements must be reassessed. Not least, the collection's ability to render complex political phenomena in very clear terms will make it indispensable for undergraduate courses on contemporary Latin America."
—Gilbert M. Joseph, co-author of *Mexico's Once and Future Revolution: Social Upheaval and the Challenge of Rule since the Late Nineteenth Century*

This book examines the tensions and convergences between social movements and twenty-first century progressive Latin American governments. Focusing on feminist, indigenous, environmental, rural, and labor movements, leading scholars present a well-rounded picture on a controversial topic and argue against the accepted view that robust Latin American social movements are independent of the state. This cutting-edge book will be an invaluable supplement for Latin American studies and beyond for courses on democracy, peace studies, labor studies, gender studies, and ethnic studies.

2022 • 336 pages
978-1-5381-6395-5 • $39.00 / £30.00 • Paper
978-1-5381-6394-8 • $94.00 / £72.00 • Cloth
978-1-5381-6396-2 • $37.00 / £28.00 • eBook

Professors, a free examination copy is available in paperback or ebook format for course adoption consideration. Visit our website to order today!

ROWMAN & LITTLEFIELD
www.rowman.com | 800.462.6420

Call for Manuscripts for a Thematic Issue of *Latin American Perspectives*

Revisiting the Brazilian Democratic Transition

This thematic issue reassesses the state of democracy in Brazil forty years after the election of the first civilian president in 1985, after 21 years of military dictatorship (1964-1985.) Despite vigorous mobilization by civil society, and amid grave political and economic crises, Brazil's generals exercised significant control over the process of democratization, although less than they envisioned for the planned political opening ('*abertura*') in the mid-1970s which was intended to create a restricted democracy with limited popular engagement and leadership by elites supportive of the dictatorship. In the pivotal year of 1985 the military regime's political candidate lost the indirect presidential elections and a Constituent Assembly was approved by the Brazilian Congress, setting the stage for the enactment of the most democratic constitution (1988) in the country's history but retaining authoritarian legacies that guaranteed that no institutions of transitional justice would come to fruition in the near term.

Forty years later, in what seems to be a "forever democratic transition," Brazil is experiencing what has been called a process of "de-democratization", begun after the contested 2014 presidential elections and accelerated by the 2016 impeachment of President Dilma Rousseff and the election of Jair Bolsonaro in 2018.The purposeful mischaracterization and misremembering of the dictatorship and post-1985 democratic transition has exacerbated this trend. For instance, not only was Brazil the last country in the Southern Cone to hold a truth commission in 2012-14, but no military officer has ever been punished in criminal courts for human rights violations. Nonetheless, Brazilian far right groups, led by Bolsonaro, still regard the period around 1985 as the key moment in the construction of an imagined "leftist hegemony" in Brazil. The recent presidential contest between Bolsonaro and Luiz Inácio 'Lula' da Silva highlighted the urgency of putting past and present into dialogue.

Older scholarship on the legacies of dictatorship and the transition largely consolidated along two major axes - emphasizing either continuities between the authoritarian period and the present or moments of democratic rupture and the resurgence of civil society. Contemporary scholarship includes actors previously excluded from accounts of democratization and expands our understanding beyond the usual focus on electoral politics.

This issue seeks to deepen and focus scholarly understanding of the democratic transition through both case studies and theoretical works, including comparative perspectives that examine Brazil's experience relative to other transitions. It aims to not only produce a new synthesis of contemporary work, but to critically examine the very notion of a "democratic transition." We invite submissions on all relevant topics, but especially encourage works that situate the transition period within historical processes and/or in relation to contemporary phenomena. Articles can be submitted in English, Portuguese, and Spanish that address but are not limited to the following:

- The democratic transition as a "pacted" process, civil-military relations, and transitional justice
- Social movements, citizenship, democracy and changes in social mobilization including labor, Afro-Brazilians, Indigenous people, women, LGBTQ+, landless, unhoused, and other marginalized groups
- The democratic transition and the multicultural turn; race and identity in relation to democratization
- The restoration of constitutional rule, especially social mobilizations related to the Constituent Assembly
- Socioeconomic inequality and social welfare policy
- Politics, democracy and media, including social media
- Democracy and the business community, state-business relations, including the debates over privatization
- Foreign relations and national development including "responsible pragmatism" and South-South relations
- The far right and conservative forces including the continued consolidation of the religious right
- Environment, climate change, democracy and Indigenous rights in relation to environmental issues

For full details about this and other calls for manuscripts and submission information, see:

http://latinamericanperspectives.com/current-calls-for-manuscripts/

Call for Manuscripts for a Thematic Issue of *Latin American Perspectives*

Participatory Democracy in Chile

This thematic issue seeks to open debates on replacing classic and post-dictatorial institutional democracy, as those forms developed under precarious social, political and cultural conditions, especially the historical level of inequality which began with the dictatorship and deepened with increasing levels of impoverishment and social precariousness even after the return to elected government. We seek to open broad discussions, from Marxist and Postmarxist perspectives to Fung and Olin Wright (2003, 2010); from feminist critiques of the social contract (Carol Pateman, Nancy Fraser, et al.) to intersectional gender perspectives (K. Oyarzún, 2021); as well as Latin American debates about new constitutions and plurinationality (Fernando Pairican and Salvador Millaleo, among others). Ruiz Encina (2021), Vergara (2020), and others, highlight experiences of participatory governments with decision-making power, based on massive social movements, in order to go beyond both traditional electoral participation and merely consultative plebiscites. This issue will examine the unfolding contradictions between Chile´s advanced stage of neoliberalism and the country´s present potential as a key laboratory of "Popular Democracy" in the context of mass popular protest, the election of Gabriel Boric as president and the ongoing effort to democratically create and adopt a new constitution,.

Popular, participatory democracy strengthens deliberation, gender equality, and intercultural dimensions as an alternative to neoliberal democracy and techno-bureaucratic and authoritarian tendencies. The October 2019 popular revolt was further fueled by militarized repression and massively spread throughout most of the country. No social coalition or political party could be identified in a leadership position as the movement displayed a unity unseen since the Popular Unity years (although not tension-free.) Sectors included, the Social Coordinator (Mesa Social), the CUT (Central Workers Confederation), dock workers, teachers and miners, and Coordinadora 8M, a massive feminist coalition, among key, decentralized movements.

Popular rebellions have opened possibilities for structural post-dictatorial transformations. There are clear signs of new, popular, grassroots, decentralized imaginaries and political actors. This issue specifically aims to encourage debate on interdisciplinary aspects of Chilean popular democracy not always understood outside Chile such as how student, feminist, and massive, general protest movements explain and respond to the specific nature of advanced late capitalist transformations in Chile and whether such movements point to short or long term neoliberal cycles.

Articles can be submitted in English, Spanish and Portuguese that address but are not limited to the following topics:
- Democratic theories in the context of Chile´s current social and political crisis of representation; new Latin American constitutional movements, and participatory, communal democracies.
- Participatory democratic theory and practice in decentralized Chilean social and political movements
- Neoliberalism, inequality, dissatisfaction with key institutions and demands for participatory democracy
- Current debates on the nature of the State: the actual neoliberal state and alternatives :
- Participatory democracy and indigenous peoples; conceptions of the plurinational state
- Role of classic trade unions and other workers in the rebellions and protest
- Democracy and the new Constitution in Chile.
- Limits and new challenges of gender politics
- Role of the armed forces and police in the current crisis and future constructions of democracy.
- Human rights violations under post-dictatorial democracy and future prospects
- Social Rights: public health, pension policies, public education and democratic alternatives
- Artistic interventions in Chilean social and political movements (students, women, etc.)
- Comparative perspectives on Chile and other experiences of constructing participatory democracy
- Participatory democracy at the local and national levels and within organizations

For full details about this and other calls for manuscripts and submission information, see:
http://latinamericanperspectives.com/current-calls-for-manuscripts/